GUIDE BOOK OF UNITED STATES CURRENCY

THIRD EDITION REVISED

LARGE SIZE • SMALL SIZE • FRACTIONAL

Compiled and Edited by
Kenneth Bressett

Valuations in up to seven grades
with Pricing Analysis by Philip Bressett

INCLUDES THE WORKS OF
William Donlon – A.M. Kagin – Don Kagin
Neil Shafer – Matt Rothert

Cover Design by Matthew W. Jeffirs

Whitman® Coin Products

Copyright © 2004 by
WHITMAN PUBLISHING, LLC
3101 Clairmont Road • Suite C
Atlanta, GA 30329

ISBN: 0-307-48003-8　　　　　　　　　　　　Printed in China

TABLE OF CONTENTS

FOREWORD

I have known Ken Bressett since the late 1960s and have always admired his great numismatic knowledge, accomplishments, and very personable nature. When I looked through the contents of the revised and updated *Guide Book of United States Currency*, I was encouraged by the very useful information contained within its pages. This impressive reference guide contains a comprehensive history of all issues of our U. S. Federal money from the War of 1812 to the current Federal Reserve Notes.

With a great selection of illustrations and information on most of the denominations issued, this book is a must for any numismatist's library. Other facts, figures and interesting information are also contained in the reference along with a "grades and terms" section. As a pricing guide, it is a very useful tool and gives prices for notes in grades from Fine to Choice CU.

After reviewing this updated third edition, I complimented Ken for bringing to our numismatic market place yet another authoritative and useful reference. It is a comprehensive book that will help me make sound decisions when purchasing or selling U. S. federal paper money.

Congratulations and thank you for an excellent reference!

John W. Wilson

American Numismatic Association Governor

American Numismatic President (2001 - 2003)

PREFACE

This price catalog is a compilation of three separate books that have served collectors for many years. It incorporates the work of several authors and many contributors who have given us the benefit of their research and experience in the field of paper money collecting. The trilogy of books used as the basis for this volume are:

United States Large Size Paper Money 1861 to 1923 by William P. Donlon, Revised by A.M. Kagin and Don Kagin. Sixth Edition 1979.

A Guide Book of United States Fractional Currency by Matt Rothert. 1963.

A Guide Book of Modern United States Currency by Neil Shafer. Eighth Edition 1979.

The list of contributors to these books reads like a history of those who have devoted their lives to the study of this fascinating hobby. Their participation is again acknowledged here for without such assistance the original books could not have been compiled. Among those who were most helpful to the original authors and in past editions are:

Thomas C. Bain • A.E. Bebee • Hy Brown • Amon G. Carter • H.K. Crofoot • Don Fisher
John J. Ford,Jr. • Dennis J. Fargue • Harry J. Forman • Arthur Friedberg • Jack Friedberg
Harry E. Jones • Paul S. Kagin • Theodore Kemm • Lyn F. Knight • Michael Kohlman, Jr. • A. Kosoff
Chester L. Krause • Robert H. Lloyd • John H. Morris, Jr. • Eric P. Newman • Dean Oakes
V.H. Oswald • M. Perlmutter • Arlie R. Slabaugh • L.S. Werner • Thomas J. Settle

The information and values presented in this catalog are based on current price trends reflected by various auctions and fixed price lists. They are not an offer to buy or sell any of these items. The editors and publisher do not conduct commercial numismatic transactions, and all such listings are shown only for informational purposes. Details about the various issues and known specimens of these notes is based on the latest data available to the editor.

Pricing Contributors to this Edition

Harry Jones • Judith Kagin • Robert J. Kravitz • David M. Sundman • John Wilson

CONDITION: Grades and Terms

Correctly speaking to merit the distinction of being "Uncirculated" a note would have to be extracted from a pack of unused notes and carefully placed in a protective holder. Present day acetate holders were not available in the last century, and very few notes enjoyed this careful state of preservation.

The term "Uncirculated" rather than "new" is used by most collectors. This description should only be used to describe a note which has all the appearance of having been carefully preserved as above stated. It must be clean, bright, sharp in every detail with no discoloration and no evidence of horizontal or vertical folds. Minor corner creases and very slight evidence of tellers' or collectors' careless handling may be present.

In the early issues, needle holes are often present. These small punctures, sometimes called "pinholes" were frequently caused by the sewing together a pack of notes to prevent theft. The most demanding perfectionist should not hesitate to accept early, rare issues because of a few needle holes. Holes of any type in later issues would lower their value.

CHOICE CRISP UNCIRCULATED (Ch. CU) — An almost perfect new note, of only slightly less than gem quality. Centering may be just a little off. It may show slight aging or light counting smudges or wrinkles.

CRISP UNCIRCULATED (CU) — No trace of circulation or folding. May not be perfectly centered, and can have a few defects such as pin holes, counting smudges, wrinkles, close margins or a corner tip fold that does not extend into the design.

ABOUT UNCIRCULATED (AU) — Only slightly less than the definition of Uncirculated. Close examination will show minor imperfections. Light folds may be noticeable but not sufficient to break the paper or impair the design. May have corner folds, but no fading or mutilation.

EXTREMELY FINE (Ex. Fine) — Note shows light circulation but still has most of its crispness and is bright and attractive. May have some folds and minor imperfections.

VERY FINE (VF) — Shows some evidence of circulation and handling; but is still bright, not badly soiled and without tears. May show several folds and will have lost some of its crispness and color. Notes that have been cleaned or pressed will grade no higher than Very Fine.

FINE — Shows considerable circulation but is still quite clean and has very little crispness left. Edges may be rough or torn, but no portions may be missing. Must not be badly stained or faded.

VERY GOOD (VG) — Will be fairly well soiled and may be significantly worn. Edges can be rough and corners rounded. Notes may be lightly stained or faded with little or no crispness.

GOOD — Only the rarest notes are collected in "Good" condition. These pieces are well worn, may have tears on margins, and even a stain or ink mark. They have generally lost all crispness and may be soiled, limp and somewhat unattractive.

NON-COLLECTIBLE

The term "non-collectible" when used in any listing signifies that if any specimens exist, they are owned by museums or institutions and will not likely be offered for sale.

FACE AND BACK, NOT OBVERSE AND REVERSE

"Face" and "Back" are the terms used by the Bureau of Engraving and Printing in referring to what is called "obverse" and "reverse" on coins. These terms do seem more descriptive and are used throughout the text.

VALUATIONS, DEMAND AND SUPPLY

Valuations given in the price section are based upon estimated SUPPLY of the various issues and the DEMAND for those issues. This information has been obtained from many well known suppliers and from actual public offerings during the past few years. Prices have risen considerably since the last edition of this catalog, but that does not necessarily mean that the trend will continue. Values are given as a guide to what the collector might expect to pay. They are not to be construed as an offer to buy or sell on the part of the author or publisher or the prices a collector might hope to obtain when a collection is sold to a dealer who must include a fair margin of profit.

SPECIALIZE!

A word of advice to the neophyte collector — SPECIALIZE!

The collector should specialize, not only because a limited budget might dictate this plan, but also to afford the opportunity to more thoroughly study and assimilate knowledge of the various types or series selected.

Collectors with a limited budget have erroneously believed that a collection of United States paper money is too costly. Facts prove that a prize-winning collection of the large size or small size issues may be assembled for less outlay and afford more pleasure and attract more attention if displayed with pertinent information, than a complete collection of uncirculated Lincoln cents. And it will find a more ready market when the time comes to sell.

United States paper money affords numerous ways to specialize, depending on the imagination and personal preference of the collector. To name just a few:

A Type Collection. A note of each major design of one or more denominations. Strange as it may seem, denominations of $5 or higher might be easier to acquire than $1 and $2.

A Signature Collection. All issues of one or more combination of signatures of Treasury Officials. This is a fascinating endeavor. A signature collection with a brief commentary on the officials whose signatures appear, makes a prize winning exhibit.

A Collection of Various Seals. There were many attractive seals used throughout the large size issues. Securing one of each type of each denomination will require some patience and effort, but the chase will be rewarding to the serious collector.

A Collection of Famous Persons. All issues which show a portrait of Washington, Lincoln, Hamilton, Jefferson or any other selected person. This makes a very interesting and attractive exhibit when displayed with a biographical sketch of the person and a description of the notes.

A National Bank Note Collection. National Bank Notes of the First, Second and/or Third Charters offer real opportunities to the collector with imagination. Most popular are the notes of all Charter periods issued by the banks of the collector's own state. Also popular are notes with odd names of banks or places, or industrial or commercial titles such as Traders National Bank, Mechanics National Bank, Brotherhood of Locomotive Engineers, etc. The National Banks of Pennsylvania afford many odd names of points of issue. A note from various State Capitols is always interesting.

Historic, Art and Other Special Features. Many notes depict famous paintings and scenes of historic interest. The Coat of Arms of the state are on the backs of most $5 First Charter Nationals and Second Charter Brown Backs. Also a varied collection of eagles is shown on several series.

Only a few suggestions have been given. Numerous other plans of collecting will suggest themselves and will afford the collector hours of pleasure, recognition if exhibited and often financial gain.

HOUSING THE COLLECTION

Collectors of earlier days resorted to the use of envelopes, composition books, scrapbooks and many other forms of housing for their paper money. These makeshifts at times resulted in damage to a prized note.

Demand by thousands of new followers of this fascinating and profitable hobby has developed many forms of protection. Acetate and mylar holders designed for a single note or for two notes back to back seems to be the favorite. These holders allow handling and exhibiting without damage to the notes.

VINYL PAGES which house 3 notes to each page are less expensive but notes should be placed in individual acetate holders before placing in vinyl. Experience has shown that notes will absorb oil when placed unprotected in vinyl. This will not occur if notes are first placed in individual holders.

INVENTORY

The serial numbers on U.S. paper money provide a positive means of identification. The inventory system may be a very elaborate card file or as simple as personal choice dictates. It should include catalog number, condition, serial number, date of purchase, from whom and cost.

The inventory should be kept in a secure place but not with the collection. Such a complete record will prove most helpful if all or part of the collection is lost or eventually sold.

HOW TO DETECT COUNTERFEITS

Counterfeiting has been practiced since coins and currency were first circulated and before the issuance of U.S. coins or currency. In early history it was punishable by death. At the time of the Civil War, counterfeiting was unusually prevalent, with the result that about one-third of the currency in circulation was counterfeit.

On July 5, 1865 the U.S. Secret Service was established to suppress this crime which had become very lucrative for the forgers, but also a potential danger to the nation's economy. This agency was instrumental in materially reducing the number of counterfeit notes in circulation and making attempts at counterfeiting unpopular.

Today, forgeries are again on the increase due to modern photographic, scientific and electronic equipment. The printing of paper money with no change in design has not proved to be the deterrent which was expected. Many have suggested that notes with more colorful designs, as used by other countries, would be more difficult to duplicate.

It is hoped that the illustrations and information will assist new and old collectors in determining whether a note is genuine or counterfeit.

By permission of the Treasury Department, United States Secret Service.

GENUINE

On a GENUINE NOTE the portrait is lifelike and stands out distinctly. Magnification will show hairlines to be sharp and distinct. Points on spiked seals are sharp and even. Scalloped seals and round seals have well defined outlines.

COUNTERFEIT

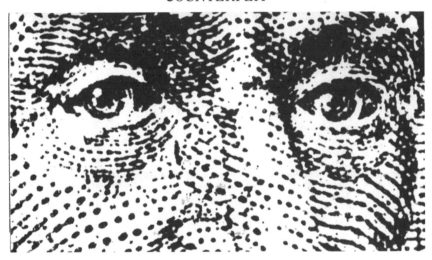

On a COUNTERFEIT NOTE the portrait is lifeless and background probably too dark. Criss-crossed fine lines are not clear or uniform. Points on spiked seals are uneven, blunt or broken. Scalloped seals and round seals usually have thick "sloppy" outlines. The paper has no colored threads, but some counterfeits have red and blue lines simulating threads.

Comparison of genuine and counterfeit. Note sharpness of
genuine note on right side of illustrations.

PORTRAITS ON U.S. PAPER MONEY

By law, no living person can be portrayed on U.S. currency or any other obligation of the United
States. The reason for this legislation goes back to Civil War days. At that time portraits of
President Lincoln and the Secretary of the Treasury Salmon P. Chase had appeared on U.S. cur-
rency while both were still living. No objection had apparently been made.

While Spencer M. Clark was still chief clerk of the National Currency Division of the U.S.
Treasury, his portrait appeared on a half million 5 cent fractional currency notes. This caused
Representative M. Russell Thayer of Pennsylvania to propose an amendment forbidding the practice of showing any living person on U.S. currency or other obligations. The bill passed and
became law, and has not been changed.

Third Issue 5¢ Fractional Currency showing the portrait of
Spencer M. Clark on the face.

TREASURY NOTES OF THE WAR OF 1812

It may come as a surprise to some that the first paper money circulated in the United States after the Constitution was issued in 1812 — preceding by 49 years the Demand Notes of 1861. Occasioned by the War of 1812 and the expiration of the charter of the First Bank of the United States, the federal government authorized five Treasury note issues between 1812 and 1815. These notes are considered among the rarest of all issues of American currency.

In total, over $36 million in denominations of $3 to $1000 were emitted. The last issue included small circulating notes in denominations of less than $100. Because of the shortage of adequate circulating medium and revenue to conduct the War of 1812, these notes proved to be extremely useful as they were transferable by delivery and receivable for duties, taxes, and public use at par plus accrued interest. They also served as interest-bearing reserves for banks since they were convertible into any kind of money and bore interest simultaneously.

The success of the Treasury notes was demonstrated by the fact that they were fully subscribed and accepted by the banks and merchants. In addition, the small Treasury note issues of 1815 indirectly served to increase the circulating medium of the country. They were used to buy goods and services by individuals, pay custom duties by merchants, and acted as cash reserves for banks, preventing bank notes from being discounted.

These Treasury Notes thus became the first circulating currency issued by the United States after ratification of the Constitution.

LISTING OF KNOWN TREASURY NOTES AND THEIR VALUES

Date	Denomination		Number Known	VF	CU
6/30/1812	$1000	Unsigned	2	$20,000	$30,000
	100	Unsigned	2	15,000	25,000
1/25/1813	$1000		0		
	100		0		
3/4/1814	$1000		0		
	100	Signed	3	20,000	30,000
	20		0		
12/26/1814	$100	Unsigned	2	15,000	25,000
	100	Signed	3	12,500	17,500
	20	Unsigned	1	7,500	10,000
	20	Signed	6	8,000	12,000
2/24/1815	$100	Unsigned	3	8,000	12,500
	100	Signed	0		
	50	Unsigned	0		
	50	Signed	9	6,000	9,000
	20	Unsigned	6	6,500	10,000
	20	Signed	2	3,000	4,500
	10	text at right Unsigned	0		
	10	text at right Signed	4	5,500	8,000
	10	no text at right Unsigned	2	6,000	9,000
	10	no text at right Signed	17	5,000	7,500
	5	Unsigned	11	5,000	7,500
	5	Signed	1	10,000	15,000
	3	Unsigned	10	5,500	11,000
	3	Signed	4	7,000	12,500

Unsigned notes may be Proofs

TREASURY NOTES OF THE WAR OF 1812

Examples of Treasury Notes of the War of 1812.

UNITED STATES LEGAL TENDER NOTES

The first Series of March 10, 1862, was printed in denominations of $5, $10, $20, $50, $100, $500 and $1000. The Second Series of August 1, 1862, was printed in denominations of $1 and $2. The face design on these notes indicates that a $3 denomination was also contemplated but never issued. A proof specimen of the $3 design of this series does exist.

The Third Series dated March 10, 1863, was almost identical with the First Series, excepting change in the back design, and was printed in the same denominations, $5 to $1000.

The Fourth Series had the greatest number of series, signature and seal changes, and comprised the series of 1869, 1874, 1875, 1878, 1880, 1907 and 1917. All bear the designation of "United States Note," excepting the series of 1869 which is designated on the face as "Treasury Note." As a deterrent to counterfeiting, paper with silk threads was used for the first time in all denominations of the 1869 series.

The Fourth Series was printed in the following denominations:

1869:	1,	2,	5,	10,	20,	50,	100,	500,	1000
1874:	1,	2,	X	X	X	50,	X	500,	X
1875:	1,	2,	5,	10,	20,	50,	100,	500,	X
1878:	1,	2,	5,	10,	20,	50,	100,	500,	1000

Also a $5000 and a $10,000 denomination in the 1878 series.

1880:	1,	2,	5,	10,	20,	50,	100,	500,	1000
1907:	X	X	5	X	X	X	X	X	X
1917:	1,	2,	X	X	X	X	X	X	X

FACE DESIGNS, First Series 1862 and Third Series 1863

$5   On the lower right, Alexander Hamilton, 18th century Statesman killed in a duel with Aaron Burr in 1804. On the left, the Washington Capitol statue of Columbia, previously shown on several bank notes.

$10   Portrait of Abraham Lincoln in upper right. On the left, allegorical female portrait representing Art.

$20   Vignette of Library with shield and sword in center.

$50   Alexander Hamilton. Different from that on the $5 note. Engraved by James D. Smillie.

$100   The first note to feature the American Eagle.

$500   Albert Gallatin, Secretary of the Treasury, 1801-1813.

$1000   Robert Morris, a signer of the Declaration of Independence and Superintendent of Finance, 1781 to 1784.

FACE DESIGNS, Second Series 1862

$1   Vignette of Salmon P. Chase, Secretary of the Treasury.

$2   The Capitol Building and Thomas Jefferson, third President of the United States. Portrait of Alexander Hamilton, Jas. D. Smillie engraver.

On all denominations of United States Legal Tender notes, the obligation or promise to pay appears on the FACE of the notes, not on the back as stated in some catalogs. The obligation reads "The United States will pay the Bearer…Dollars."

BACK DESIGNS, First, Second and Third Series 1862-1863

First Series 1862 and Third Series 1863, denominations $5 to $1000. Attractive lathe-work designs with two types of inscription.

Type One inscription reads: "This note is a Legal Tender for all debts public and private, except on duties on Imports and Interest on Public Debt, and is exchangeable for U.S. Six per cent Twenty Year Bonds, redeemable at the pleasure of the U. States after Five Years." Space in the design evidently prevented the word "United" from being spelled out.

Type Two inscription reads: "This note is a Legal Tender for all debts public and private, except duties on Imports and Interest on the Public Debt, and is receivable in payment for all Loans made to the United States."

Second Series, $1 and $2 notes, series 1862, carry the Type Two inscription in the center of the lathe-work design.

FACE DESIGNS, Fourth Series 1869-1907

The major portion of the face design remained the same throughout the entire Fourth Issue. The obligation on the face reads "United States will pay the Bearer...Dollars." The words "At the Treasury in New York" appearing on the first three issues have been removed with the single word "Washington" substituted on the 1869 series, and "Washington D.C." on later series.

The stars following the serial numbers on the 1869 series *do not* indicate replacement notes. Star numbers were not substituted for damaged notes until 1910.

$1	1869 to 1917. Head of Washington facing left and Columbus sighting land. Signature of engraver A. Sealey can be seen at lower edge of Washington portrait on many notes.
$2	1869 to 1917. Capitol Building vignette in center. Thos. Jefferson at left end.
$5	1869 to 1907. The well-known "Pioneer Family" and head of Andrew Jackson. Collectors of designs showing animals should observe that a dog appears prominently in this design.
$10	1869 to 1880. Daniel Webster, Secretary of State and the Presentation of the Indian Princess, representing introduction of Old World to the New. Best known as the "Jackass Note" so-called because when the note is inverted, the eagle on the face design appears to be a rather long-eared jackass.
$20	1875 to 1880. Alexander Hamilton and figure of Victory with shield and sword from original sketch by John W. Casilear.
$50	1869. Henry Clay, Secretary of State and female holding a statue of Mercury.
$100	1869 to 1880. Abraham Lincoln with allegorical figure of Architecture.
$50	1874 to 1880. Benjamin Franklin, engraved by Charles Burt after a Duplesis painting, with figure of Liberty.
$500	1869. John Quincy Adams, sixth president of the United States.
$500	1874 to 1880. Major General Joseph K. Mansfield, mortally wounded in the Civil War Battle of Antietam.
$1000	1869 to 1880. Dewitt Clinton, Governor New York State; Columbus seated at left.
$5000	1878. James Madison, fourth president of the United States.
$10,000	1878. Andrew Jackson, "Old Hickory," Seventh president.

BACK DESIGNS, Fourth Series 1869-1907

The words "and is receivable in payment for all Loans made to the United States" have been removed from the Type Two clause of the former issues.

Throughout the entire Fourth Series the backs of all notes carry the warning against counterfeiting which first appeared on the series of 1869. Counterfeiting had become very prevalent with the issue of paper money backed by the United States and is even more so today

FACE DESIGNS, Fifth Series 1901

$10	1901. Bison design with Lewis and Clark, famous explorers. There are nine signature combinations on this popular design.

The note was designed by Ostrander Smith from a sketch of the Bison by Charles Knight, noted animal artist, author and publisher. The design was engraved by Marcus N. Baldwin. The portraits of Lewis and Clark and the portraits beside them were engraved by G.G.C. Smillie after Walter Shirlaw.

BACK DESIGN, Fifth Series 1901

Columbia stands between two pillars and two scrolls which carry the modified inscription appearing on the Fourth Issue.

THE SIXTH SERIES 1923

The series of 1923 comprising only $1 and $10 notes has always been listed as part of the Fourth Series. To avoid confusion we are now describing this series as the Sixth Series, it having followed the designated Fifth Series of 1901.

The $1 and $10 notes are type designs issued with one set of signatures.
Face design $1–Washington facing right as on small size notes.
Back design $1–Very plain back design, unlike Fourth Series.
Face design $10–Andrew Jackson, seventh U.S. President.
Back design $10–Attractive lathe-work. No inscription.

The words "On Demand" have been added to the obligation to pay on face of notes.

TERMS OF TREASURY OFFICIALS

These signatures appear on United States large size paper money, with terms of office compiled from information obtained by the Treasury Department.

Register	Treasurer	Term Began	Term Ended
Chittenden	Spinner	April 17, 1861	Aug. 10, 1864
Colby	Spinner	Aug. 11, 1864	Sept. 21, 1867
Jeffries	Spinner	Oct. 5, 1867	March 15, 1869
Allison	Spinner	April 3, 1869	June 30, 1875
Allison	New	June 30, 1875	July 1, 1876
Allison	Wyman	July 1, 1876	June 30, 1877
Allison	Gilfillan	July 1, 1877	March 23, 1878
Scofield	Gilfillan	April 1, 1878	May 20, 1881
Bruce	Gilfillan	May 21, 1881	March 31, 1883
Bruce	Wyman	April 1, 1883	April 30, 1885
Bruce	Jordan	May 1, 1885	June 5, 1885
Rosecrans	Jordan	June 8, 1885	May 23, 1887
Rosecrans	Hyatt	May 24, 1887	May 10, 1889
Rosecrans	Huston	May 11, 1889	April 21, 1891
Rosecrans	Nebeker	April 25, 1891	May 31, 1893
Rosecrans	Morgan	June 1, 1893	June 19, 1893
Tillman	Morgan	July 1, 1893	June 30, 1897
Tillman	Roberts	July 1, 1897	Dec. 2, 1897
Bruce	Roberts	Dec. 3, 1897	Mar. 17, 1898
Lyons	Roberts	April 7, 1898	June 30, 1905
Lyons	Treat	July 1, 1905	April 1, 1906
Vernon	Treat	June 12, 1906	Oct. 30, 1909
Vernon	McClung	Nov. 1, 1909	March 14, 1911
Napier	McClung	March 15, 1911	Nov. 21, 1912
Napier	Thompson	Nov. 22, 1912	March 31, 1913

Register	Treasurer	Term Began	Term Ended
Napier	Burke	April 1, 1913	Oct. 23, 1913
Parker	Burke	Nov. 1, 1913	Dec., 31, 1914
Teehee	Burke	March 24, 1915	Nov. 20, 1919
Elliott	Burke	Nov. 21, 1919	Jan. 5, 1921
Elliott	White	May 2, 1921	Jan. 24, 1922
Speelman	White	Jan. 25, 1922	Sept. 30, 1927
Woods	White	Oct. 1, 1927	May 1, 1928
Woods	Tate	May 31, 1928	Jan. 17, 1929
Jones	Woods	Jan. 22, 1929	May 31, 1933

FEDERAL RESERVE NOTES, Large Size

Secretary	Treasurer	Term Began	Term Ended
McAdoo	Burke	April 1, 1913	Dec. 15, 1918
Glass	Burke	Dec. 16, 1918	Feb. 1, 1920
Houston	Burke	Feb. 2, 1920	Jan. 5, 1921
Mellon	White	May 2, 1921	May 1, 1928

UNITED STATES or LEGAL TENDER NOTES
ONE DOLLAR— FOUR TYPES

Face Design. See descriptions. Type 1, 2, 3 and 4.

Back Design

UNITED STATES NOTES-ONE DOLLAR

Series	Register	Treasurer	Seal at Left	Fine	VF	Ex. Fine	AU	CU	Ch. CU

Red serial numbers. Highlighted numeral in center denotes denomination.

| 1862 | Chittenden | Spinner | Sm. red | **Rare** | — | — | — | — | — |

National Bank Note Co. American Bank Note Co., lower border.
No Monogram. Scarcest of the four types.

| 1862 | Chittenden | Spinner | Sm. red | 250.00 | 475.00 | 625.00 | 800.00 | 1,100 | 1,900 |

As above, with monogram ABN Co. upper right.

| 1862 | Chittenden | Spinner | Sm. red | 250.00 | 450.00 | 600.00 | 750.00 | 1,000 | 1,800 |

National Bank Note Co., twice in lower border. No Monogram.

| 1862 | Chittenden | Spinner | Sm. red | 300.00 | 525.00 | 675.00 | 850.00 | 1,200 | 2,200 |

As above, with monogram ABN Co. upper right.

Face Design. Large Red Spiked Seal.

Back Design, with Counterfeit Warning
This Back design used only on Series 1869.

Series	Register	Treasurer	Seal at Left	Fine	VF	Ex. Fine	AU	CU	Ch. CU

Red serial numbers. First with counterfeit warning and blue end paper.

| 1869 | Allison | Spinner | Lge. red | 350.00 | 500.00 | 750.00 | 1,000 | 1,200 | 1,800 |

National Bank Note Co., lower portion back design.
Suffix star on 1869 series does not indicate a replacement note.

UNITED STATES NOTES-ONE DOLLAR

Robert H. Lloyd in a Numismatic Scrapbook article, Nov. 1964, states that there are two types of the $1 1869 notes. The noticeable difference being that Type One was not printed on the blue tint paper of Type Two. There are other minor variations on the face design. Type One is undoubtedly the scarcer but for the present is not given a separate valuation in this catalog.

Series 1874 to 1878 — Face Design. Red ornamentation at right.

Series 1874 to 1917 — Back Design. Variations are described.

UNITED STATES NOTES-ONE DOLLAR

Series	Register	Treasurer	Seal at Left	Fine	VF	Ex. Fine	AU	CU	Ch. CU
Red serial numbers. Red ornamentation at right, face design.									
1874	Allison	Spinner	Sm. red	100.00	225.00	400.00	500.00	650.00	800.00
Face, micro at right, "Engraved & Printed at the Bureau Engraving & Printing."									
Back, Columbian Bank Note., twice in lower portion.									
1875	Allison	New	Sm. red	100.00	200.00	375.00	500.00	700.00	850.00
Issued in five additional series, same design excepting Series Letter.									
1875 Series "A"				500.00	600.00	700.00	800.00	1,500	1,800
1875 Series "B"				550.00	650.00	800.00	1,000	1,750	2,000
1875 Series "C"				500.00	600.00	700.00	800.00	1,500	1,800
1875 Series "D"				600.00	800.00	950.00	1,200	1,900	2,200
1875 Series "E"				700.00	900.00	1,000	1,400	2,200	2,750
1875	Allison	Wyman	Sm. red	100.00	200.00	375.00	500.00	675.00	800.00
1878	Allison	Gilfillan	Sm. red	120.00	220.00	400.00	550.00	700.00	850.00
"Series 1878" top margin, back design.									
"Printed by Bureau of Engraving & Printing" lower margin, back design.									

Series 1880 — Face Design. Red ornamentation replaced by large seal.

Series	Register	Treasurer	Seal at Right	Fine	VF	Ex. Fine	AU	CU	Ch. CU
Red serial numbers. Ornamentation removed.									
1880	Scofield	Gilfillan	Lg. brown	125.00	175.00	265.00	400.00	475.00	700.00
1880	Bruce	Gilfillan	Lg. brown	110.00	160.00	240.00	375.00	450.00	650.00
1880	Bruce	Wyman	Lg. brown	110.00	160.00	240.00	375.00	450.00	650.00
Blue Serial numbers. Seal at right.									
1880	Rosecrans	Huston	Lg. red	525.00	800.00	1,200	1,750	2,000	2,750
1880	Rosecrans	Huston	Lg. brown	525.00	800.00	1,300	1,800	2,200	2,900
1880	Rosecrans	Nebeker	Lg. brown	525.00	800.00	1,300	1,850	2,400	3,000
Blue Serial numbers. Seal at left.									
1880	Rosecrans	Nebeker	Sm. red	100.00	150.00	225.00	275.00	325.00	650.00
1880	Tillman	Morgan	Sm. red	100.00	150.00	225.00	275.00	325.00	650.00

Series 1917 — Small scalloped red seal at left.

Series	Register	Treasurer	Seal at Left	Fine	VF	Ex. Fine	AU	CU	Ch. CU
1917	Teehee	Burke	Sm. red	65.00	75.00	85.00	125.00	175.00	220.00
1917	Elliott	Burke	Sm. red	65.00	75.00	85.00	125.00	175.00	220.00
1917	Burke	Elliott	Sm. red	150.00	300.00	400.00	500.00	725.00	950.00

Signatures transposed on Plate No. 1519 only.

Series	Register	Treasurer	Seal at Left	Fine	VF	Ex. Fine	AU	CU	Ch. CU
1917	Elliott	White	Sm. red	65.00	75.00	85.00	125.00	175.00	220.00
1917	Speelman	White	Sm. red	60.00	70.00	80.00	120.00	160.00	200.00

★ *Star replacement notes for series 1917 are valued approximately double these prices.*

Series 1923 — Face Design. Washington faces right.

UNITED STATES NOTES-ONE DOLLAR

Series 1923 — Back Design. Counterfeit Warning removed.

Series	Register	Treasurer	Seal at Left	Fine	VF	Ex. Fine	AU	CU	Ch. CU
1923	Speelman	White	Sm. red	65.00	100.00	135.00	225.00	265.00	400.00

★ *Star replacement notes for series 1923 are valued approximately double these prices.*

TWO DOLLARS

Face Design.

Back Design.

UNITED STATES NOTES-TWO DOLLARS

Series	Register	Treasurer	Seal at Right	Fine	VF	Ex. Fine	AU	CU	Ch. CU

Red serial numbers. Vertical numerals in center denote denomination.
Plate was engraved for $3 denomination but notes were never issued.

Series	Register	Treasurer	Seal at Right	Fine	VF	Ex. Fine	AU	CU	Ch. CU
1862	Chittenden	Spinner	Sm. red	400.00	975.00	1,500	2,000	2,350	2,750

American Bank Note Co., vertically at left, face design, National bottom.

Series	Register	Treasurer	Seal at Right	Fine	VF	Ex. Fine	AU	CU	Ch. CU
1862	Chittenden	Spinner	Sm. red	425.00	950.00	1,400	1,850	2,200	2,600

National Bank Note Co., vertically at left, face design & at bottom.

Patented April 23, 1860, National Bank Note Co. in lower border, on both types.
Both Types have Type Two inscription on back.
All uncirculated $2.00 large size notes are scarce.

Face Design. Large Red Spiked Seal.

Back Design, with Counterfeit Warning.
This design used only on series 1869.

Series	Register	Treasurer	Seal at Right	Fine	VF	Ex. Fine	AU	CU	Ch. CU

Red serial numbers.

Series	Register	Treasurer	Seal at Right	Fine	VF	Ex. Fine	AU	CU	Ch. CU
1869	Allison	Spinner	Lg. red	450.00	800.00	1,500	1,850	2,300	3,600

"Engraved and printed at the Treasury Department," vertically at left, face design.
American Bank Note Co. bottom left, face design and twice below back design.
The suffix star on all series of 1869 notes, does not indicate a replacement note.

UNITED STATES NOTES-TWO DOLLARS

Face Design. Minor changes.

Back Design. Minor variations.

Series	Register	Treasurer	Seal at Left	Fine	VF	Ex. Fine	AU	CU	Ch. CU
Red Serial numbers. Red ornamentation at right.									
1874	Allison	Spinner	Sm. red	360.00	550.00	925.00	1,200	1,350	1,800
Face engraved and printed at the Bureau of Engraving & Printing.									
Back, Columbian Bank Note Co., Washington, D.C.									
1875	Allison	New	Sm. red	360.00	525.00	675.00	850.00	1,100	1,500
Issued in two additional series, same design.									
1875 Series A. lower right of face design				425.00	600.00	775.00	1,000	1,350	1,850
1875 Series B, lower right of face design				400.00	550.00	725.00	900.00	1,200	1,750
1875	Allison	Wyman	Sm. red	360.00	525.00	675.00	850.00	1,100	1,500
1878	Allison	Gilfillan	Sm. red	360.00	475.00	650.00	775.00	950.00	1,350
1878	Scofield	Gilfillan	Sm. red	2,200	5,500	7,500	—	—	—

UNITED STATES NOTES-TWO DOLLARS

Face Design. Red ornamentation replaced by large seal.

Back Design.

Series	Register	Treasurer	Seal at Right	Fine	VF	Ex. Fine	AU	CU	Ch. CU
Red Serial numbers. Ornamentation removed.									
1880	Scofield	Gilfillan	Lg. brown	120.00	180.00	300.00	475.00	550.00	850.00
1880	Bruce	Gilfillan	Lg. brown	135.00	200.00	325.00	500.00	575.00	900.00
1880	Bruce	Wyman	Lg. brown	120.00	180.00	300.00	475.00	550.00	850.00
Blue Serial numbers. Large seal.									
1880	Rosecrans	Huston	Lg. red	725.00	1,200	2,400	3,000	3,600	6,000
1880	Rosecrans	Huston	Lg. brown	750.00	1,300	2,500	3,200	3,800	6,500
Blue Serial numbers. Small seal.									
1880	Rosecrans	Nebeker	Sm. red	100.00	160.00	235.00	365.00	425.00	800.00
1880	Tillman	Morgan	Sm. red	100.00	150.00	225.00	325.00	400.00	750.00

UNITED STATES NOTES-TWO DOLLARS

Face Design.

Back Design. Series date added.

Series	Register	Treasurer	Seal at Right	Fine	VF	Ex. Fine	AU	CU	Ch. CU
Red Serial numbers.									
1917	Teehee	Burke	Sm. red	65.00	80.00	110.00	140.00	190.00	325.00
1917	Elliott	Burke	Sm. red	65.00	80.00	120.00	150.00	220.00	350.00
1917	Elliott	White	Sm. red	65.00	80.00	120.00	150.00	220.00	350.00
1917	Speelman	White	Sm. red	60.00	75.00	100.00	135.00	180.00	300.00

★ *Star replacement notes for series 1917 are valued at over double these prices.*

Face Design. Type One.

Back Design. Type One Inscription.

Series	Register	Treasurer	Seal at Right	Fine	VF	Ex. Fine	AU	CU	Ch. CU
Type one inscription on back. Red Serial numbers.									
1862	Chittenden	Spinner	Sm. red	350.00	550.00	750.00	850.00	950.00	1,500
American Bank Note Co. in top border face design, Series and Patented.									
Type two inscription. Red serial numbers.									
1862	Chittenden	Spinner	Sm. red	365.00	575.00	800.00	900.00	1,100	1,750
American Bank Note Co.-National Bank Note Co. lower border face design.									
1863	Obverse of 1862 - Without "Series"						V. Rare		
American Bank Note Co. & National Bank Note Co.									
1863	Chittenden	Spinner	Sm. red	365.00	575.00	800.00	900.00	1,100	1,750
American Bank Note Co., twice in lower border face design. One serial number.									
1863	Chittenden	Spinner	Sm. red	350.00	550.00	750.00	850.00	950.00	1,500
American Bank Note Co., twice in lower border. Two serial numbers.									

UNITED STATES NOTES-FIVE DOLLARS

Back Design with Type 2 inscription.

Face Design. Large Red spiked Seal.

Back Design, used only on Series 1869.

UNITED STATES NOTES-FIVE DOLLARS

Series	Register	Treasurer	Seal at Right	Fine	VF	Ex. Fine	AU	CU	Ch. CU

Red Serial numbers.

| 1869 | Allison | Spinner | Lg. red | 350.00 | 460.00 | 775.00 | 925.00 | 1,100 | 1,500 |

Face: Bureau, Engraving & Printing, upper left face design.
Back: American Bank Note Co., upper and lower margin.

Face Design. Red ornamentation with "V".

Back Design. Variations as described.

Series	Register	Treasurer	Seal	Fine	VF	Ex. Fine	AU	CU	Ch. CU

Red Serial numbers. Large "V" in red ornamentation at right.

| 1875 | Allison | New | Sm. red, left | 160.00 | 235.00 | 375.00 | 500.00 | 600.00 | 950.00 |

Face printed at Bureau, back by Columbian Bank Note Co.

Issued in two additional series, same design.

1875 Series A in lower right of face design.				200.00	285.00	475.00	650.00	800.00	1,250
1875 Series B in lower right of face design.				190.00	260.00	425.00	600.00	750.00	1,150
1875	Allison	Wyman	Sm. red, left	160.00	235.00	375.00	500.00	600.00	950.00
1878	Allison	Gilfillan	Sm. red, left	220.00	325.00	435.00	485.00	575.00	1,000

Note: The Bureau assumed the complete printing of all notes October 1877.

UNITED STATES NOTES-FIVE DOLLARS

Face Design. Ornamentation replaced by large seal.

Series	Register	Treasurer	Seal at Right	Fine	VF	Ex. Fine	AU	CU	Ch. CU
Red Serial numbers.									
1880	Scofield	Gilfillan	Lg. brown	500.00	1,200	1,900	3,000	—	—
1880	Bruce	Gilfillan	Lg. brown	175.00	285.00	525.00	585.00	675.00	1,000
1880	Bruce	Wyman	Lg. brown	175.00	285.00	525.00	585.00	675.00	1,000
Blue Serial numbers.									
1880	Bruce	Wyman	Lg. red, plain	180.00	300.00	530.00	590.00	680.00	1,100
1880	Rosecrans	Jordan	Lg. red	185.00	320.00	550.00	650.00	750.00	1,200
1880	Rosecrans	Hyatt	Lg. red	225.00	340.00	600.00	750.00	950.00	1,600
1880	Rosecrans	Huston	Lg. red, spk.	250.00	385.00	650.00	800.00	1,000	1,850
Similar with large brown seal.									
1880	Rosecrans	Huston	Lg. brown	225.00	350.00	600.00	750.00	950.00	1,650
1880	Rosecrans	Nebeker	Lg. brown	300.00	475.00	700.00	850.00	1,200	2,000

Face Design. Small scalloped red seal.

Series	Register	Treasurer	Seal at Right	Fine	VF	Ex. Fine	AU	CU	Ch. CU
1880	Rosecrans	Nebeker	Sm. red	90.00	140.00	235.00	325.00	400.00	700.00
1880	Tillman	Morgan	Sm. red	90.00	140.00	235.00	325.00	400.00	700.00
1880	Bruce	Roberts	Sm. red	90.00	140.00	235.00	325.00	400.00	700.00
1880	Lyons	Roberts	Sm. red	90.00	150.00	250.00	340.00	435.00	765.00

UNITED STATES NOTES-FIVE DOLLARS

Face Design. Ornamental "V" added over "FIVE" at left.

Series	Register	Treasurer	Seal at Right	Fine	VF	Ex. Fine	AU	CU	Ch. CU
Red Serial numbers. Ornamental "V" at left.									
1907	Vernon	Treat	Sm. red	130.00	150.00	225.00	260.00	325.00	450.00
1907	Vernon	McClung	Same	120.00	145.00	220.00	250.00	300.00	400.00
1907	Napier	McClung	Same	120.00	145.00	220.00	250.00	300.00	400.00
1907	Napier	Thompson	Same	250.00	400.00	600.00	900.00	1,200	1,500
1907	Parker	Burke	Same	130.00	150.00	225.00	260.00	325.00	450.00
1907	Teehee	Burke	Same	130.00	150.00	225.00	260.00	325.00	450.00
1907	Elliott	Burke	Same	130.00	150.00	225.00	260.00	325.00	450.00
1907	Elliott	White	Same	130.00	150.00	225.00	260.00	325.00	450.00
1907	Speelman	White	Same	110.00	135.00	200.00	235.00	275.00	375.00
1907	Woods	White	Same	150.00	190.00	260.00	300.00	375.00	500.00

★ *Star replacement notes for series 1907 are valued at approximately three times these prices.*

Early issues of U.S. paper money were printed by Columbian, National or American Bank Note Cos., only the seals and serial numbering being added at the Treasury Dept. Later notes were partially printed at the Bureau which assumed more and more of the operation. On October 1, 1877, the Bureau took over the entire printing job.

The design below shows the elimination of the name of the private company, and the addition of "Bureau of Engraving and Printing" in the upper and lower border of the back design.

UNITED STATES NOTES-TEN DOLLARS

Face Design. Three types described.

Back Design. Type One inscription.

Series	Register	Treasurer	Seal at Right	Fine	VF	Ex. Fine	AU	CU	Ch. CU
Type One inscription on back. One red serial number.									
1862	Chittenden	Spinner	Sm. red	850.00	1,600	2,100	3,000	3,500	5,000
American Bank Note Co. upper border.									
Type Two inscription on back. One red serial number.									
1862	Chittenden	Spinner	Sm. red	775.00	1,400	1,925	2,750	3,200	4,750
American Bank Note Co. upper border.									
Type Two inscription on back. One red serial number.									
1863	Chittenden	Spinner	Sm. red	800.00	1,500	2,000	2,900	3,400	4,850
National Bank Note Co. lower border.									
1863	Chittenden	Spinner	Sm. red	775.00	1,400	1,925	2,750	3,200	4,750
American Bank Note Co. upper and lower borders.									
Type Two inscription on back. Two red serial numbers.									
1863	Chittenden	Spinner	Sm. red	750.00	1,350	1,850	2,500	3,000	4,500
American Bank Note Co. upper and lower borders.									

UNITED STATES NOTES-TEN DOLLARS

Back Design with Type 2 inscription.

Face Design. Large spiked red seal.

Back Design. Inscription and counterfeit warning.

UNITED STATES NOTES-TEN DOLLARS

Series	Register	Treasurer	Seal at Right	Fine	VF	Ex. Fine	AU	CU	Ch. CU
Red serial numbers.									
1869	Allison	Spinner	Lg. red	550.00	750.00	1,200	1,750	2,000	3,500

Face: Bureau of Engraving and Printing. Back: National Bank Note Co.

Face Design. "TEN" in red ornamentation.

Back Design, with minor variations.

Series	Register	Treasurer	Seal at Right	Fine	VF	Ex. Fine	AU	CU	Ch. CU
1875	Allison	New	Sm. red	460.00	625.00	1,100	1,600	2,200	4,500
Issued in one additional series, same design.									
1875 Series A in lower right of face design.				460.00	625.00	1,100	1,600	2,200	4,500
1878	Allison	Gilfillan	Sm. red	485.00	640.00	950.00	1,350	1,600	3,600
1878	Allison	Gilfillan	Similar with pink background	—	—	—	—

UNITED STATES NOTES-TEN DOLLARS

Face Design. Large "TEN" replaced by Seal.

Back Design by COLUMBIAN BANK NOTE CO.

Series	Register	Treasurer	Seal at Right	Fine	VF	Ex. Fine	AU	CU	Ch. CU
Red serial numbers.									
1880	Scofield	Gilfillan	Lg. brown	400.00	700.00	875.00	1,250	1,450	1,850
1880	Bruce	Gilfillan	Lg. brown	375.00	650.00	825.00	1,150	1,300	1,650
1880	Bruce	Wyman	Lg. brown	400.00	700.00	875.00	1,250	1,450	1,850
Blue Serial numbers									
1880	Bruce	Wyman	Lg. red	420.00	675.00	925.00	1,200	1,350	1,900
1880	Rosecrans	Jordan	Lg. red	460.00	750.00	975.00	1,175	1,475	1,950
1880	Rosecrans	Hyatt	Lg. red	460.00	750.00	975.00	1,175	1,475	1,950
1880	Rosecrans	Hyatt	Red spikes	420.00	700.00	950.00	1,150	1,400	1,850
1880	Rosecrans	Huston	Red spikes	600.00	800.00	1,000	1,200	1,500	2,200
1880	Rosecrans	Huston	Lg. brown	420.00	675.00	925.00	1,200	1,350	1,900
1880	Rosecrans	Nebeker	Lg. brown	——	——	——	Very Rare	——	——
1880	Rosecrans	Nebeker	Sm. red	350.00	500.00	675.00	850.00	1,000	1,500
1880	Tillman	Morgan	Sm. red	450.00	600.00	850.00	1,100	1,400	1,800
1880	Bruce	Roberts	Sm. red	350.00	500.00	675.00	850.00	1,000	1,500
1880	Lyons	Roberts	Sm. red	350.00	500.00	675.00	850.00	1,000	1,500

UNITED STATES NOTES-TEN DOLLARS

Face Design. The Bison note.

Back Design.

Series	Register	Treasurer	Seal at Right	Fine	VF	Ex. Fine	AU	CU	Ch. CU
Red serial numbers. Large "X" at left.									
1901	Lyons	Roberts	Sm. red	500.00	750.00	1,150	1,600	1,850	2,750
1901	Lyons	Treat	Same	500.00	750.00	1,150	1,600	1,850	2,750
1901	Vernon	Treat	Same	500.00	750.00	1,150	1,600	1,850	2,750
1901	Vernon	McClung	Same	500.00	750.00	1,150	1,600	1,850	2,750
1901	Napier	McClung	Same	500.00	750.00	1,150	1,600	1,850	2,750
1901	Parker	Burke	Same	500.00	750.00	1,150	1,600	1,850	2,750
1901	Teehee	Burke	Same	500.00	750.00	1,150	1,600	1,850	2,750
1901	Elliott	White	Same	500.00	750.00	1,150	1,600	1,850	2,750
1901	Speelman	White	Same	500.00	750.00	1,150	1,600	1,850	2,750

★ *Star replacement notes for series 1901 are valued at over double these prices.*

UNITED STATES NOTES-TEN DOLLARS

Face Design. Andrew Jackson. A Type Note.

Back Design. Issued in series 1923 only.

Series	Register	Treasurer	Seal at Left	Fine	VF	Ex. Fine	AU	CU	Ch. CU
Red serial numbers. Large "X" at right.									
1923	Speelman	White	Sm. red	**750.00**	**1,150**	**1,800**	**2,400**	**2,850**	**4,000**

★ *Star replacement notes for series 1923 are extremely rare.*

The series 1923 $10 United States note by reason of being of especially attractive design, as well as a type note, has always been popular with collectors. In recent years very few have been offered in strictly uncirculated condition. The above evaluation is believed to be conservative. Only 696,000 were issued. Many were converted by the public to the current small size issues.

UNITED STATES NOTES-TWENTY DOLLARS

Face Design. Three types described. Above Type One.

Back Design. Type One inscription.

Series	Register	Treasurer	Seal at Right	Fine	VF	Ex. Fine	AU	CU	Ch. CU
Type One inscription on back. One red serial number.									
1862	Chittenden	Spinner	Sm. red	1,900	2,500	4,000	4,500	5,200	8,200
American Bank Note Co. lower border.									
Reportedly less than ten known in uncirculated condition.									
Type Two inscription on back. One red serial number.									
1862	Chittenden	Spinner	Sm. red	2,000	2,750	4,250	4,750	5,500	8,500
National Bank Note Co. American Bank Note Co. at bottom.									
Type Two inscription on back. One red serial number.									
1863	Chittenden	Spinner	Sm. red	1,650	2,250	3,850	4,350	4,750	7,750
ABN at bottom.									
ABN and NBN above, at bottom.				1,900	2,500	4,000	4,500	5,200	8,200
Type Two inscription on back. Two red serial numbers.									
1863	Chittenden	Spinner	Sm. red	1,600	2,200	3,750	4,200	4,500	7,500

UNITED STATES NOTES-TWENTY DOLLARS

Back Design. Type 2 inscription.

Face Design. Large spiked red seal at left.

Back Design. Numeral "20" repeated 105 times.
"XX" repeated 103 times.

UNITED STATES NOTES-TWENTY DOLLARS

Series	Register	Treasurer	Seal at Left	Fine	VF	Ex. Fine	AU	CU	Ch. CU
Blue Serial numbers.									
1869	Allison	Spinner	Lg. red	**1,750**	**2,250**	**3,250**	**3,750**	**4,750**	**7,000**
Face printed by the Bureau. Back, American Bank Note Co.									

Face Design. "XX" twice. Red Seal.

Back Design. Variations described.

Series	Register	Treasurer	Seal at Right	Fine	VF	Ex. Fine	AU	CU	Ch. CU
Blue serial numbers. "XX" twice on face of note.									
1875	Allison	New	Sm. red	**850.00**	**1,200**	**1,750**	**2,300**	**2,750**	**3,500**
Face printed by the Bureau. Back, Columbian Bank Note Co.									
1878	Allison	Gilfillan	Sm. red	**650.00**	**900.00**	**1,200**	**1,750**	**1,900**	**3,000**
Printed by the Bureau of Engraving and Printing, as were all subsequent issues.									

UNITED STATES NOTES-TWENTY DOLLARS

Face Design. Twin "XX" removed.

Series	Register	Treasurer	Seal at Right	Fine	VF	Ex. Fine	AU	CU	Ch. CU
Blue Serial numbers. "XX" removed.									
1880	Scofield	Gilfillan	Lg. brown	525.00	725.00	1,250	1,650	1,900	2,350
1880	Bruce	Gilfillan	Lg. brown	525.00	725.00	1,250	1,650	1,900	2,350
1880	Bruce	Wyman	Lg. brown	575.00	800.00	1,350	1,800	2,100	2,750
1880	Bruce	Wyman	Lg. red	750.00	1,000	1,750	2,400	4,000	5,000
1880	Rosecrans	Jordan	Lg. red	575.00	800.00	1,350	1,800	2,100	2,750
1880	Rosecrans	Hyatt	Lg. red	625.00	850.00	1,400	2,000	2,250	3,000
1880	Rosecrans	Hyatt	Red Spikes	520.00	720.00	1,200	1,600	1,800	2,250
1880	Rosecrans	Huston	Red Spikes	525.00	725.00	1,250	1,650	1,900	2,350
1880	Rosecrans	Huston	Lg. brown	520.00	720.00	1,200	1,600	1,800	2,250
1880	Rosecrans	Nebeker	Lg. brown	575.00	800.00	1,300	1,750	2,000	2,650
1880	Rosecrans	Nebeker	Sm. red	300.00	525.00	775.00	1,000	1,150	1,750
1880	Tillman	Morgan	Sm. red	300.00	525.00	775.00	1,000	1,150	1,750
1880	Bruce	Roberts	Sm. red	300.00	525.00	775.00	1,000	1,150	1,750
1880	Lyons	Roberts	Sm. red	325.00	565.00	825.00	1,050	1,200	2.000
1880	Vernon	Treat	Sm. red	300.00	525.00	775.00	1,000	1,150	1,750
1880	Vernon	McClung	Sm. red	310.00	550.00	800.00	1,050	1,200	1,800
Red Serial numbers.									
1880	Teehee	Burke	Sm. red	265.00	500.00	750.00	825.00	900.00	1,250
1880	Elliott	White	Sm. red	265.00	500.00	750.00	825.00	900.00	1,250

UNITED STATES NOTES-FIFTY DOLLARS

Face Design. Three types described.

Back Design. Type 2 inscription.

Series	Register	Treasurer	Seal in Center	Fine	VF	Ex. Fine	AU
Type One inscription on back. Red Serial numbers.							
1862	Chittenden	Spinner	Sm. red	7,250	12,500	20,000	—
American Bank Note Co.							
Type Two inscription on back. Red Serial numbers.							
1863	Chittenden	Spinner	Sm. red	6,750	11,500	18,500	—
National Bank Note Co.							
Type Two inscription on back. Red Serial numbers.							
1863	Chittenden	Spinner	Sm. red	6,750	11,500	18,500	—

National Bank Note Co. and American Bank Note Co. at top.
Many counterfeits of the above series were made in the 19th century.

UNITED STATES NOTES-FIFTY DOLLARS

Face Design. Large red seal in center.

Back Design. Used only on series 1869.

Series	Register	Treasurer	Seal in Center	Fine	VF	Ex. Fine	AU
Blue Serial numbers.							
1869	Allison	Spinner	Lg. red	**12,500**	**25,000**	**35,000**	**50,000**

Face printed by the Bureau. Back, American Bank Note Co.

The above is a type note, design used on series 1869 only. It well qualifies for the description "rare." Counterfeits were made of the above shortly after release in the 1870's.

UNITED STATES NOTES-FIFTY DOLLARS

Position of signatures transposed.

Back Design by Columbian Bank Note Co.

Series	Signatures	Fine	VF	Ex. Fine	AU	CU	Ch. CU
Signatures transposed. Small red seal center.							
Blue serial numbers. Ornate "L" twice on face.							
1874	Spinner-Allison	4,250	6,000	7,500	10,000	17,500	—
Face engraved and printed by the Bureau of Engraving and Printing.							
Back, Columbian Bank Note Co.							
1875	Wyman-Allison	—	—	Very Rare	—	—	—
1878	Gilfillan-Allison	4,500	6,250	8,500	15,000	20,000	—
Printed at the Bureau as were all later issues.							

Transposed signatures are the rule not the exception as sometimes emphasized. This applies to all series 1874, 1875, 1878, and all series 1880 excepting Bruce-Roberts and Lyons-Roberts.

UNITED STATES NOTES-FIFTY DOLLARS

Face Design. Without ornate "L" left and right.

Back Design. Printed at the Bureau.

Series	Signatures		Seal at Right	Fine	VF	Ex. Fine	AU	CU	Ch. CU
Blue Serial numbers in center, unlike any other series.									
Signatures transposed until Tillman-Morgan.									
1880	Gilfillan	Bruce	Lg. brown	3,750	5,200	6,200	9,000	10,500	—
1880	Wyman	Bruce	Lg. brown	3,600	5,000	6,000	8,750	10,000	—
1880	Jordan	Rosecrans	Lg. red	4,500	5,750	8,500	12,000	17,500	—
1880	Hyatt	Rosecrans	Lg. red	Rare	—	—	—	—	—
1880	Hyatt	Rosecrans	Red Spikes	3,500	4,750	5,750	8,500	9,500	—
1880	Huston	Rosecrans	Red Spikes	3,600	5,000	6,000	8,750	10,000	—
1880	Huston	Rosecrans	Lg. brown	3,500	4,750	5,750	8,500	9,500	—
1880	Tillman	Morgan	Sm. red	2,500	3,750	5,000	6,250	6,750	—
1880	Bruce	Roberts	Sm. red	Very Rare	—	—	—	—	—
1880	Lyons	Roberts	Sm. red	2,500	3,750	5,000	6,250	6,750	—

UNITED STATES NOTES-ONE HUNDRED DOLLARS

Face Design. Three types described.

Back Design. Type 2 inscription.

Series	Register	Treasurer	Seal at Right	VG	Fine	VF	Ex. Fine	AU
Type one inscription on back. Red Serial numbers.								
1862	Chittenden	Spinner	Sm. red	7,500	13,500	20,000	28,000	—
American Bank Note Co. or National Bank Note Co.								
Type two inscription on back. Red Serial numbers.								
1863	Chittenden	Spinner	Sm. red	8,000	14,000	22,000	30,000	—
National Bank Note Co. and American Bank Note Co. at top.								
Type two inscription on back. Red Serial numbers.								
1863	Chittenden	Spinner	Sm. red	7,500	13,500	20,000	28,000	—
National Bank Note Co. at top.								

The above series were counterfeited soon after issue. Genuine notes show the small "100" design in the right reverse. Counterfeits show "001" instead of "100."

UNITED STATES NOTES-ONE HUNDRED DOLLARS

Face Design. Large red seal, right.

Back Design. Used only on series 1869.

Series	Register	Treasurer	VG	Fine	VF	Ex. Fine	AU
Blue Serial numbers. Large red seal at right.							
1869	Allison	Spinner	8,500	12,000	18,500	27,500	—
Face printed by the Bureau, Back by American Bank Note Co.							

The back design used on the series 1869 $100 United States Notes was changed on subsequent issues. The face design, with minor changes, remained the same throughout all later series of United States notes of this denomination.

Very rare and popular.

UNITED STATES NOTES-ONE HUNDRED DOLLARS

Face Design.

Back Design.

Series	Register	Treasurer	Seal at Right	VG	Fine	VF	Ex. Fine	AU
1875	Allison	New (Series A)	Sm. red	6,000	12,000	18,500	28,000	—
1875	Allison	Wyman	Sm. red	7,500	13,500	20,000	30,000	—
1878	Allison	Gilfillan	Sm. red	5,500	10,000	18,000	27,500	—

Printed by the Bureau, as were all subsequent issues.
All scarce. Series "A" 1875 rare.

UNITED STATES NOTES-ONE HUNDRED DOLLARS

Face Design. Various seals.

Back Design.

Series	Register	Treasurer	Seal at Right	VG	Fine	VF	Ex. Fine	AU	CU
1880	Bruce	Gilfillan	Lg. brown	3,500	4,500	8,800	17,000	27,500	37,500
1880	Bruce	Wyman	Lg. brown	3,500	4,500	8,800	17,000	27,500	37,500
1880	Rosecrans	Jordan	Lg. red	3,200	4,200	8,500	16,000	25,000	35,000
1880	Rosecrans	Hyatt	Lg. red	Very Rare	—	—	—	—	—
1880	Rosecrans	Hyatt	Red spikes	3,200	4,200	8,500	16,000	25,000	35,000
1880	Rosecrans	Huston	Red spikes	3,200	4,200	8,500	16,000	25,000	35,000
1880	Rosecrans	Huston	Lg. brown	3,200	4,200	8,500	16,000	25,000	35,000
1880	Tillman	Morgan	Sm. red	2,500	3,800	7,600	13,000	18,000	22,000
1880	Bruce	Roberts	Sm. red	2,750	4,000	7,800	13,500	19,000	27,500
1880	Lyons	Roberts	Sm. red	2,500	3,800	7,600	13,000	18,000	22,000

UNITED STATES NOTES-FIVE HUNDRED DOLLARS

Series	Register	Treasurer	Seal
		Type one inscription on back. Red Serial numbers.	
1862	Chittenden	Spinner	Sm. red, left
		Type two inscription on back.	
1862	Chittenden	Spinner	Sm. red, left
1863	Chittenden	Spinner	Sm. red, left
1869	Allison	Spinner	Lg. red, left
1874	Allison	Spinner	Sm. red, left
1875	Allison	New	Sm. red, left
1875	Allison	Wyman	Sm. red, left
1878	Allison	Gilfillan	Sm. red, left
1880	*		

*This series was issued with ten different signature combinations. Seals were small red, large red, and large brown. All are extremely rare.

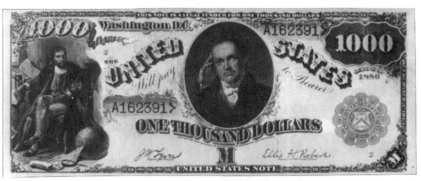

Face Design.

Back Design.

ONE THOUSAND DOLLARS

Issues of this denomination are extremely scarce. It would be presumptuous to evaluate these high denominations. No confirmed records are available as to number issued or known to exist.

FIVE THOUSAND AND TEN THOUSAND DOLLARS

Legal Tender notes of $5,000 and $10,000 were issued. All have been redeemed.

SILVER CERTIFICATES

Acts of Congress, February 28, 1878 and August 4, 1886.

Large size Silver Certificates of all issues are very popular with collectors, and afford a variety of designs, seals and signatures. There were five issues from series 1878 to series 1923.

FIRST ISSUE, 1878 and 1880

The First Issue, series 1878 and 1880, included denominations from $10 to $100. The face of the notes certifies: "There have been deposited with the Treasurer of the United States at Washington, D.C." (or the Assistant Treasurer at New York or San Francisco. See illustrations) "payable at his office to the bearer on demand (amount) Silver Dollars." The notes were inscribed "Certificate of Deposit."

FACE DESIGNS, Series 1878 and 1880

$10	Robert Morris, a signer of the Declaration of Independence and U.S. Senator 1789-1795.
$20	Stephen Decatur, Naval Commander, killed in a duel in 1820.
$50	Edward Everett, Governor of Massachusetts, United States Senator and Secretary of State under President Millard Fillmore.
$100	James Monroe, fifth president of the U.S. and founder of the "Monroe Doctrine."
$500	Charles Sumner, U.S. Senator. Leader in the abolishment of slavery.
$1000	William L. Marcy, N.Y. State Governor, Secretary of War under Pres. James K. Polk and Secretary of State under Pres. Franklin Pierce.

The Treasury Seal on the countersigned certificates of 1878, through error in designing, has the Key in Red Seal pointing to the right instead of the left. This error was corrected on the series of 1880.

BACK DESIGNS, Series 1878-1880

This is the only series of United States paper money with backs printed in black ink. The word SILVER in large letters stands out on the very striking black scroll work design. The inscription in the back design is "This Certificate is Receivable for Customs, Taxes, and all Public Dues and When so received May be Reissued."

SECOND ISSUE 1886, 1891 and 1908

The Second Issue of Silver Certificates comprises the series of 1886, 1891 and 1908. Series 1886 was issued in $1, $2, $5, $10 and $20 denominations. Series 1891 included these denominations and also $50, $100 and $1000 certificates. Series 1908 was issued in $10 denomination only, with three combinations of signatures and a blue seal in contrast to the red or brown seals of earlier series.

The certification on the face of series of the second issue reads: "This certifies that there have been deposited in the Treasury of the United States...Silver Dollars payable to the Bearer on Demand."

FACE DESIGNS, Series 1886, 1891 and 1908

$1	Series 1886 and 1891, Martha Washington.
$2	Series 1886, General Winfield Scott Hancock, died February, 1886.
$2	Series 1891, William Windom, Secretary of the Treasury 1881-1884 and again from 1889 until his death in 1891.

Both $2 certificates commemorate the passing of great Americans.

$5	Series 1886 and 1891, Ulysses S. Grant, Civil War General and 18th President.
$10	Series 1886 and 1908, Thomas A. Hendricks, Vice President with Grover Cleveland, serving only nine months until his death in November 1885. This design may also be said to commemorate the passing of an American Statesman.

SILVER CERTIFICATES

$20   Series 1886 and 1891, Daniel Manning, born in Albany, N.Y., 1831. Secretary of the Treasury, 1885-1887.

$50   Series 1891, Edward Everett, portrait to right as on Series 1878 and 1880, with modified design.

$100   Series 1891, James Monroe, design modified, with portrait as on Series 1878 and 1880.

$1000   Series 1891, William L. Marcy, same portrait as Series 1878 and 1880, but now at right in small oval.

BACK DESIGN, Series 1886

The attractive green over-all lathe-work designs used throughout the 1886 series should be examined with a glass to properly appreciate the intricacies of these designs and the skill of the designer and engraver. Large numerals denoting the denomination are featured, and the certification is the same as that of series 1878 and 1880.

The back design of the $5 certificate is unique. It features in actual size five facsimile silver dollars, the obverse of one showing the date "1886." Being a type design, this note is in great demand. The National Gold Bank Notes of California and this $5 certificate, are the only issues featuring designs of United States coins.

BACK DESIGNS, Series 1891 and 1908

On certificates of series 1891 and 1908, the lathe-work designs of series 1890 were changed to a more open design intended to prevent counterfeiting which prevailed on many early issues. Large numerals, and on some denominations, Roman numerals indicate the denomination. The certification remains the same as on previous series.

THIRD ISSUE, Series 1896

Thomas F. Morris, Designer, and Chief of the Engraving Division of the Bureau of Engraving and Printing, Nov. 1, 1893 to June 30, 1897, designed and/or re-designed the three denominations of this well known and popular "Educational Series." Thomas F. Morris II, artist and numismatist, is the son of the former Chief, and has contributed many factual articles to the various numismatic media.

Other designers of this series were: Will H. Low, $1; Edwin H. Blashfield, $2; and Walter Shirlaw, $5. Known engravers of the series were Charles Schlecht and Geo. F.C. Smillie.

Claude M. Johnson, Chief of the Bureau of Engraving and Printing, is credited with advocating the printing of more artistic and representative designs in currency. The original plan was to eventually have this type of artistic and educational design used on all denominations of silver certificates $1 to $1000.

The $1, $2 and $5 denominations were printed and released. The plates for a $10 note were engraved but notes were never issued. The higher denominations apparently were not designed. The three denominations released enjoyed a very short life, much to the regret of present day collectors.

FACE DESIGNS, Series 1896

Beautiful allegorical scenes are depicted in the face designs, as follows:

$1   History Instructing Youth. A background of the Washington Monument and Capitol. The Constitution of the United States is shown in an open book. Names of twenty-three great American statesmen are shown in an attractive border design.

$2   "Steam and Electricity," represented by two youthful figures, are presented to "Commerce and Manufacture," mature female figures, by "Science," also a mature female.

$5   This beautiful allegorical scene depicts "Electricity," represented by a winged female, as a powerful controlling factor in world history.

SILVER CERTIFICATES

The obligation to redeem in silver dollars is on the face of each of the three denominations. It reads: "This certifies that there have been deposited in the Treasury of the United States...Silver Dollars, payable to the Bearer on demand."

BACK DESIGNS, Series 1896

The green back designs of all three denominations are also eye-catching.

$1   Portraits of Martha and George Washington in center double ovals.

$2   Two great inventors, Samuel F.B. Morse and Robert Fulton.

$5   Generals Ulysses S. Grant and Phillip Henry Sheridan.

FOURTH ISSUE, Series 1899

The Fourth Issue of Silver Certificates comprising only one series, 1899, in three denominations, is notable for the number of signature combinations. Eleven combinations on $1, ten on $2, and eleven on $5 certificates. The scarcest signature combination in this series is that of James C. Napier and Carmi A. Thompson, in office only four and one-half months.

FACE DESIGNS, Series 1899

$1   The well known American Eagle design with portraits of Lincoln and Grant; all three engraved by G.F.C. Smillie.

$2   George Washington between figures representing Mechanics and Agriculture also engraved by G.F.C. Smillie. Two figures from sculptured group by D.C. French.

$5   "Running Antelope," a Sioux Indian, best known as "Chief Onepapa." The most popular of the many versions of how the Indian Chief design was created seems to be that the Chief of the Uncpapa or Hunkpapa Sioux tribe, wore a headdress with three feathers which projected too high to look well. A Pawnee warbonnet was procured, but as it belonged to a rival tribe, the Sioux Indian refused to pose with it. The bonnet was photographed on an employee of the Engraving Division, cut out and super-imposed on the photograph of the Sioux. The design was engraved by Geo. F. C. Smillie in November, 1899.

BACK DESIGNS, Series 1899

The green back designs were modified considerably from those of earlier issues. The denomination is indicated by large numerals. The Roman numeral "V" is featured in the center design of the $5 certificate. The inscription in the back design is the same as on earlier issues.

FIFTH ISSUE, Series 1923

The Fifth Issue of Silver Certificates consists of a single series, 1923, with only two denominations, $1 and $5. There were three signature combinations on the $1 series 1923 certificate, and only one signature combination on the $5 denomination. The latter is therefore a type note.

FACE DESIGNS, Series 1923

$1   George Washington, as on Series 1923, $1 Legal Tender note.

$5   Abraham Lincoln in center of circular design. Sometimes referred to as the "porthole" note.

The certification that silver dollars have been deposited with the Treasurer of the United States, and the obligation to pay in silver dollars on demand, is the same as on earlier issues. The inscription, formerly in the back design, is on the face at left with seal.

BACK DESIGNS, Series 1923

$1   Open design, "The United States of America, One Dollar" prominent in center.

$5   Attractive design features the front or obverse of "The Great Seal of the United States." There is no legend or inscription other than "The United States of America" and the denomination.

Face Design. Various small and large seals.

Back Design. Series 1886.

Back Design. Series 1891.

SILVER CERTIFICATES-ONE DOLLAR

Series	Register	Treasurer	Seal at Right	Fine	VF	Ex. Fine	AU	CU	Ch. CU
Blue serial numbers on all Silver Certificates, all denominations.									
1886	Rosecrans	Jordan	Sm. red	240.00	360.00	600.00	775.00	1,000	1,300
1886	Rosecrans	Hyatt	Sm. red	240.00	360.00	600.00	775.00	1,000	1,300
1886	Rosecrans	Hyatt	Lg. red	240.00	360.00	600.00	775.00	1,000	1,300
1886	Rosecrans	Huston	Lg. red	275.00	400.00	700.00	850.00	1,200	1,500
1886	Rosecrans	Huston	Lg. brown	240.00	360.00	600.00	775.00	1,000	1,300
1886	Rosecrans	Nebeker	Lg. brown	240.00	360.00	600.00	775.00	1,000	1,300
1886	Rosecrans	Nebeker	Sm. red	240.00	360.00	600.00	775.00	1,000	1,300
1891	Rosecrans	Nebeker	Sm. red	225.00	300.00	475.00	600.00	800.00	1,100
1891	Tillman	Morgan	Sm. red	225.00	300.00	475.00	600.00	800.00	1,100

Face Design. History Instructing Youth.

Back Design. Martha and George Washington.

Series	Register	Treasurer	Seal at Right	Fine	VF	Ex. Fine	AU	CU	Ch. CU
1896	Tillman	Morgan	Sm. red	300.00	375.00	575.00	750.00	900.00	1,500
1896	Bruce	Roberts	Sm. red	325.00	400.00	600.00	800.00	950.00	1,600

SILVER CERTIFICATES-ONE DOLLAR

Above shows series date below serial number.

Series date vertically at right.

Series	Register	Treasurer	Seal at Right	Fine	VF	Ex. Fine	AU	CU	Ch. CU
Series date above serial number.									
1899	Lyons	Roberts	Sm. blue	90.00	100.00	145.00	160.00	260.00	450.00
Series date below serial number.									
1899	Lyons	Roberts	Sm. blue	85.00	95.00	140.00	155.00	255.00	425.00
1899	Lyons	Treat	Sm. blue	85.00	95.00	140.00	155.00	255.00	425.00
1899	Vernon	Treat	Sm. blue	85.00	95.00	140.00	155.00	255.00	425.00
1899	Vernon	McClung	Sm. blue	85.00	95.00	140.00	155.00	255.00	425.00
Series date vertically at right.									
1899	Vernon	McClung	Sm. blue	100.00	120.00	160.00	175.00	275.00	500.00
1899	Napier	McClung	Sm. blue	82.00	92.00	138.00	152.00	252.00	410.00
1899	Napier	Thompson	Sm. blue	175.00	250.00	400.00	700.00	950.00	1,200
1899	Parker	Burke	Sm. blue	82.00	92.00	138.00	152.00	252.00	410.00
1899	Teehee	Burke	Sm. blue	82.00	92.00	138.00	152.00	252.00	410.00
1899	Elliott	Burke	Sm. blue	82.00	92.00	138.00	152.00	252.00	410.00
1899	Elliott	White	Sm. blue	82.00	92.00	138.00	152.00	252.00	410.00
1899	Speelman	White	Sm. blue	80.00	90.00	135.00	150.00	250.00	400.00

★ *Star replacement notes for series 1899 are valued at approximately double these prices.*

SILVER CERTIFICATES-ONE DOLLAR

Back Design. Modified design.

Face Design. Washington, as on small size notes.

Back Design.

Series	Register	Treasurer	Seal at Left	Fine	VF	Ex. Fine	AU	CU	Ch. CU
1923	Speelman	White	Sm. blue	30.00	35.00	45.00	50.00	65.00	80.00
1923	Woods	White	Sm. blue	35.00	40.00	50.00	55.00	70.00	85.00
1923	Woods	Tate	Sm. blue	60.00	70.00	90.00	125.00	350.00	450.00

★ *Star replacement notes for series 1923 are valued at approximately double these prices.*

SILVER CERTIFICATES-TWO DOLLARS

Face Design. Three types of seals.

Back Design. Unusual lathe work in green.

Series	Register	Treasurer	Seal at Right	Fine	VF	Ex. Fine	AU	CU	Ch. CU
1886	Rosecrans	Jordan	Sm. red	475.00	760.00	1,150	1,350	1,600	1,900
1886	Rosecrans	Hyatt	Sm. red	475.00	760.00	1,150	1,350	1,600	1,900
1886	Rosecrans	Hyatt	Lg. red	475.00	750.00	1,100	1,300	1,500	1,800
1886	Rosecrans	Huston	Lg. red	490.00	775.00	1,175	1,400	1,650	2,000
1886	Rosecrans	Huston	Lg. brown	500.00	800.00	1,200	1,450	1,750	2,200

The above is a type design used only on series 1886. It commemorates the passing of Winfield Scott Hancock in 1886 following his long career. He participated in the Mexican War and the Civil War in which he was shot but recovered. He was Democratic candidate for the U.S. presidency in 1880, but was defeated by James A. Garfield.

SILVER CERTIFICATES-TWO DOLLARS

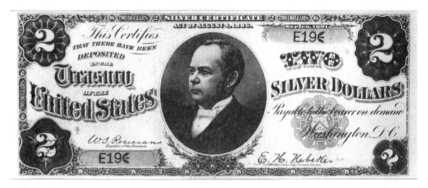

Face Design. Wm. Windom, Small Issue.

Back Design. This issue only.

Series	Register	Treasurer	Seal at Right	Fine	VF	Ex. Fine	AU	CU	Ch. CU
1891	Rosecrans	Nebeker	Sm. red	400.00	725.00	1,300	1,800	2,000	3,400
1891	Tillman	Morgan	Sm. red	375.00	700.00	1,250	1,750	1,900	3,200

The above design used only on series 1891 honors William Windom, American Financier and states-man who died in January 1891. He enjoyed a brilliant political career during which he served in the U.S. Congress and U.S. Senate. Windom was an early advocate of the gold standard.

SILVER CERTIFICATES-TWO DOLLARS

Face Design. Educational series.

Back Design. Inventors Morse and Fulton.

Series	Register	Treasurer	Seal at Right	Fine	VF	Ex. Fine	AU	CU	Ch. CU
1896	Tillman	Morgan	Sm. red	500.00	1,000	1,750	1,900	2,200	3,200
1896	Bruce	Roberts	Sm. red	500.00	1,000	1,750	1,900	2,200	3,200

Face Design. Washington, Mechanics, Agriculture.

SILVER CERTIFICATES-TWO DOLLARS

Back Design.

Series	Register	Treasurer	Seal at Right	Fine	VF	Ex. Fine	AU	CU	Ch. CU
1899	Lyons	Roberts	Sm. blue	200.00	240.00	360.00	460.00	500.00	750.00
1899	Lyons	Treat	Sm. blue	200.00	240.00	360.00	460.00	500.00	750.00
1899	Vernon	Treat	Sm. blue	200.00	240.00	360.00	460.00	500.00	750.00
1899	Vernon	McClung	Sm. blue	200.00	240.00	360.00	460.00	500.00	750.00
1899	Napier	McClung	Sm. blue	200.00	240.00	360.00	460.00	500.00	750.00
1899	Napier	Thompson	Sm. blue	250.00	325.00	475.00	725.00	1,000	1,500
1899	Parker	Burke	Sm. blue	200.00	240.00	360.00	460.00	500.00	750.00
1899	Teehee	Burke	Sm. blue	200.00	240.00	360.00	460.00	500.00	750.00
1899	Elliott	Burke	Sm. blue	200.00	240.00	360.00	460.00	500.00	750.00
1899	Speelman	White	Sm. blue	190.00	235.00	350.00	450.00	490.00	740.00

★ *Star replacement notes for series 1899 are valued at from two to three times prices shown here. None are known for the Napier-Thompson issue.*

Face Design. Ulysses S. Grant

SILVER CERTIFICATES-FIVE DOLLARS

Back Design. The "Silver Dollar" back.

Series	Register	Treasurer	Seal at Left	Fine	VF	Ex. Fine	AU	CU	Ch. CU
Blue Serial numbers.									
1886	Rosecrans	Jordan	Sm. red	650.00	1,400	2,200	2,750	2,900	4,200
1886	Rosecrans	Hyatt	Sm. red	650.00	1,400	2,200	2,750	2,900	4,200
1886	Rosecrans	Hyatt	Lg. red	650.00	1,400	2,200	2,750	2,900	4,200
1886	Rosecrans	Huston	Lg. red	650.00	1,400	2,200	2,750	2,900	4,200
1886	Rosecrans	Huston	Lg. brown	650.00	1,400	2,200	2,750	2,900	4,200
1886	Rosecrans	Nebeker	Lg. brown	650.00	1,400	2,200	2,750	2,900	4,200
1886	Rosecrans	Nebeker	Sm. red	675.00	1,500	2,350	3,000	3,750	5,000

All very scarce, especially in uncirculated.
A very popular series in all conditions.

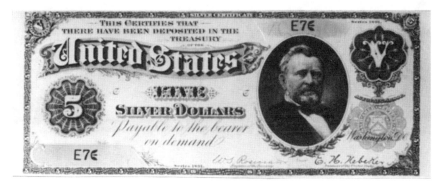

Face Design. Only two signature combinations. Red scalloped seals.

SILVER CERTIFICATES-FIVE DOLLARS

Back Design. Silver dollars eliminated.

Series	Register	Treasurer	Seal at Right	Fine	VF	Ex. Fine	AU	CU	Ch. CU
Blue Serial numbers.									
1891	Rosecrans	Nebeker	Sm. red	425.00	740.00	1,200	1,600	2.200	3,200
1891	Tillman	Morgan	Sm. red	425.00	740.00	1,200	1,600	2,200	3,200

First used on series 1886 $5 silver certificates, the above design honors the former Civil War General and our 18th president. Named "Hiram Simpson Grant" at birth in 1822, Grant's name was entered as "Ulysses Simpson Grant" when he entered West Point Military Academy in 1839. Grant continued to use this name until his death in July, 1885.

Face Design. Vignette depicts "Electricity" enlightening the world.

SILVER CERTIFICATES-FIVE DOLLARS

Back Design. Grant and Sheridan.

Series	Register	Treasurer	Seal at Right	Fine	VF	Ex. Fine	AU	CU	Ch. CU
			The Educational series.						
1896	Tillman	Morgan	Sm. red	**850.00**	**1,750**	**2,600**	**3,850**	**4,750**	**6,750**
1896	Bruce	Roberts	Sm. red	**850.00**	**1,750**	**2,600**	**3,850**	**4,750**	**6,750**
1896	Lyons	Roberts	Sm. red	**900.00**	**1,800**	**2,750**	**4,000**	**5,000**	**7,000**

Face Design. Sioux Indian. A composite design.

Through common usage the Chief of the Uncpapa or Hunkpapa Tribe of Sioux Indians is best known as "Onepapa."

SILVER CERTIFICATES-FIVE DOLLARS

Back Design. Featuring Roman "V."

Series	Register	Treasurer	Seal at Right	Fine	VF	Ex. Fine	AU	CU	Ch. CU
1899	Lyons	Roberts	Sm. blue	460.00	650.00	950.00	1,225	1,400	1,850
1899	Lyons	Treat	Sm. blue	460.00	650.00	950.00	1,225	1,400	1,850
1899	Vernon	Treat	Sm. blue	460.00	650.00	950.00	1,225	1,400	1,850
1899	Vernon	McClung	Sm. blue	460.00	650.00	950.00	1,225	1,400	1,850
1899	Napier	McClung	Sm. blue	460.00	650.00	950.00	1,225	1,400	1,850
1899	Napier	Thompson	Sm. blue	500.00	700.00	1,000	1,350	1,800	2,400
1899	Parker	Burke	Sm. blue	460.00	650.00	950.00	1,225	1,400	1,850
1899	Teehee	Burke	Sm. blue	460.00	650.00	950.00	1,225	1,400	1,850
1899	Elliott	Burke	Sm. blue	460.00	650.00	950.00	1,225	1,400	1,850
1899	Elliott	White	Sm. blue	460.00	650.00	950.00	1,225	1,400	1,850
1899	Speelman	White	Sm. blue	450.00	640.00	940.00	1,200	1,350	1,800

★ Star replacement notes for series 1899 are valued at from two to three times the prices shown here.

Face Design. A type note of small issue.

SILVER CERTIFICATES-FIVE DOLLARS

Back Design. Features Great Seal in attractive setting.

Series	Register	Treasurer	Seal at Left	Fine	VF	Ex. Fine	AU	CU	Ch. CU
Lincoln Design. A type note.									
1923	Speelman	White	Sm. blue	400.00	700.00	950.00	1,300	1,600	1,850

★ *Star replacement notes for series 1923 are valued at approximately double the prices shown here.*

Issued only in series 1923, the Lincoln "porthole" design is very popular with collectors. Its value has steadily increased. The Lincoln pose continued to be used on small size notes.

TEN DOLLARS

Face Design. Five Types in the $10 denomination.
Above Type 3, with three signatures.

A large suffix "X" with serial number appears only on the three signature notes. The key in the seal points RIGHT on the 1878 series. It was corrected on the 1880 series.

No series date appears on the 1878 series.

Back Design. Attractive black on white "Silver."

Series	Countersigned by	Good	V.G.	Fine	VF
Scofield-Gilfillan signatures. Blue serial numbers. Countersigned by Assistant Treasurers.					
1878	J.C. Hopper	4,500	6,500	17,500	—
1878	W. G. White	4,500	6,500	40,000	—
1878	A.U. Wyman	4,500	6,500	17,500	—
1878	T. Hillhouse	4,500	6,500	20,000	—
1880	T. Hillhouse	4,500	6,500	45,000	—

Types 1, 2 and 5, place of deposit: New York.
Type 3 place of deposit: Washington, D.C.
Series 1878 Large red center seal and large red "TEN" below seal.
Series 1880 Large brown center seal and large "X" below seal.

Face Design. Two signatures.

Series	Register	Treasurer	Seal in Center	Fine	VF	Ex. Fine	AU	CU	Ch. CU
Blue Serial numbers. Large "X" below center seal.									
1880	Scofield	Gilfillan		1,250	2,200	3,250	4,000	4,500	6,000
1880	Bruce	Gilfillan		1,250	2,200	3,250	4,000	4,500	6,000
1880	Bruce	Wyman		1,250	2,200	3,250	4,000	4,500	6,000

SILVER CERTIFICATES-TEN DOLLARS

Face Design, without large "X". Seal position lowered.

Series	Register	Treasurer	Seal in Center	Fine	VF	Ex. Fine	AU	CU	Ch. CU
Blue Serial numbers, without large "X" below center seal.									
1880	Bruce	Wyman	Lg. red	1,500	2,500	3,500	4,500	5,500	6,500

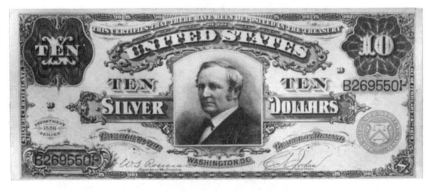

Face Design. Three different seals.

Back Design. Attractive green lathe-work.

SILVER CERTIFICATES-TEN DOLLARS

Series	Register	Treasurer	Seal at Right	Fine	VF	Ex. Fine	AU	CU	Ch. CU
1886	Rosecrans	Jordan	Sm. red	725.00	1,600	2,400	3,600	4,500	6,250
1886	Rosecrans	Hyatt	Sm. red	700.00	1,500	2,300	3,500	4,250	6,000
1886	Rosecrans	Hyatt	Lg. red	700.00	1,500	2,300	3,500	4,250	6,000
1886	Rosecrans	Huston	Lg. red	700.00	1,500	2,300	3,500	4,250	6,000
1886	Rosecrans	Huston	Lg. brown	700.00	1,500	2,300	3,500	4,250	6,000
1886	Rosecrans	Nebeker	Lg. brown	700.00	1,500	2,300	3,500	4,250	6,000
1886	Rosecrans	Nebeker	Sm. red	800.00	1,750	2,500	3,750	4,750	6,500

Face Design. Hendricks, with changed series date.

Back Design. More open than previous series.

Series	Register	Treasurer	Seal at Right	Fine	VF	Ex. Fine	AU	CU	Ch. CU
1891	Rosecrans	Nebeker	Sm. red	400.00	700.00	1,150	1,450	1,600	2,750
1891	Tillman	Morgan	Sm. red	400.00	700.00	1,150	1,450	1,600	2,750
1891	Bruce	Roberts	Sm. red	400.00	700.00	1,150	1,450	1,600	2,750
1891	Lyons	Roberts	Sm. red	400.00	700.00	1,150	1,450	1,600	2,750

SILVER CERTIFICATES-TEN DOLLARS

Face Design. Hendricks with Blue Seals.

Back Design. Same as series 1891.

Series	Register	Treasurer	Seal at Right	Fine	VF	Ex. Fine	AU	CU	Ch. CU
1908	Vernon	Treat	Sm. blue	**350.00**	**700.00**	**1,100**	**1,250**	**1,500**	**2,500**
1908	Vernon	McClung	Sm. blue	**350.00**	**700.00**	**1,100**	**1,250**	**1,500**	**2,500**
1908	Parker	Burke	Sm. blue	**350.00**	**700.00**	**1,100**	**1,250**	**1,500**	**2,500**

★ *A unique star replacement note exists for series 1908, Parker-Burke issue.*

TWENTY DOLLARS

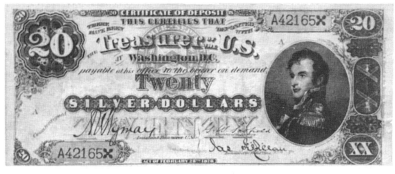

Face Design. Four types in the $20 denomination.
Above Type 3, three Signatures.

SILVER CERTIFICATES-TWENTY DOLLARS

Back Design. Black ink on white back.

Series	Countersigned by	Good	VG	Fine	VF
Scofield-Gilfillan signatures. Blue serial numbers. Countersigned by Assistant Treasurers.					
1878	J.C. Hopper	5,000	6,500	12,500	—
1878	A.U. Wyman	5,000	6,500	12,500	—
1878	T. Hillhouse	6,000	8,500	22,500	—
1880	T. Hillhouse	4,850	6,000	10,000	—

All are rare.

Types 1, 4 and 5 place of deposit: New York.
Type 3 place of deposit: Washington, D.C.
Series 1878 Large red "TWENTY" below red center seal.
Series 1880 Large "XX" below brown center seal.

Face Design. Not countersigned. Large "XX" below seal.

Series	Register	Treasurer	Seal in Center	Fine	VF	Ex. Fine	AU	CU	Ch. CU
1880	Scofield	Gilfillan	Lg. brown	3,000	4,600	8,750	12,000	17,500	—
1880	Bruce	Gilfillan	Lg. brown	3,000	4,600	8,750	12,000	17,500	—
1880	Bruce	Wyman	Lg. brown	3,000	4,600	8,750	12,000	17,500	—

SILVER CERTIFICATES-TWENTY DOLLARS

Face Design. "XX" removed. Small red seal.

Series	Register	Treasurer	Seal in Center	Fine	VF	Ex. Fine	AU	CU	Ch. CU
Large "XX" removed.									
1880	Bruce	Wyman	Sm. red, left	3,500	5,500	9,500	15,000	—	—

Face Design. Large seal left.

Back Design. Overall green lathe-work.

SILVER CERTIFICATES-TWENTY DOLLARS

Series	Register	Treasurer	Fine	VF	Ex. Fine	AU	CU	Ch. CU
Large red seal, left.								
1886	Rosecrans	Hyatt	**2,750**	**4,750**	**7,750**	**14,250**	**21,000**	—
Large brown seal, left.								
1886	Rosecrans	Huston	**2,500**	**4,500**	**7,500**	**14,000**	**20,000**	—
1886	Rosecrans	Nebeker	**2,500**	**4,500**	**7,500**	**14,000**	**20,000**	—
Small red seal, right.								
1886	Rosecrans	Nebeker	**3,000**	**5,000**	**8,000**	**14,500**	**22,000**	—

Small Red Seal. Daniel Manning on all Series 1886.

Face Design. Small scalloped seal.

Open Back Design to discourage counterfeiting.

SILVER CERTIFICATES-TWENTY DOLLARS

Series	Register	Treasurer	Seal at Right	Fine	VF	Ex. Fine	AU	CU	Ch. CU
"Series 1891" upper right, and lower left.									
1891	Rosecrans	Nebeker	Sm. red	900.00	1,500	2,100	2,750	3,750	4,500
1891	Tillman	Morgan	Sm. red	900.00	1,500	2,100	2,750	3,750	4,500
1891	Bruce	Roberts	Sm. red	900.00	1,500	2,100	2,750	3,750	4,500
1891	Lyons	Roberts	Sm. red	900.00	1,500	2,100	2,750	3,750	4,500
Large blue "XX" at left.									
1891	Parker	Burke	Sm. blue	850.00	1,400	2,000	2,600	3,500	4,250
1891	Teehee	Burke	Sm. blue	850.00	1,400	2,000	2,600	3,500	4,250

★ *Star replacement notes for series 1891 are extremely rare.*

FIFTY DOLLARS

Face Design. Three types. Above is Type 4, with three signatures.

Back Design. Black on white.

Series	Countersigned by	Good	V.G.	Fine
Scofield-Gilfillan signatures. Blue serial numbers. Countersigned by Assistant Treasurers.				
Large "FIFTY" below center seal.				
1878	A.U. Wyman	—	—	—
1878	T. Hillhouse	—	—	—
1878	R.M. Anthony	Unique		

Type 3 payable at Washington, D.C.
Type 4 payable in New York.
Type 6 payable at San Francisco-unknown.

SILVER CERTIFICATES-FIFTY DOLLARS

Face Design. Edward Everett. Minor variations and two signatures.

Back Design. Black on white.

Series	Register	Treasurer	Seal	Fine	VF	Ex. Fine	AU
Large "L" in center.							
1880	Scofield	Gilfillan	Lg. brown, center	Unique	—	—	—
1880	Bruce	Gilfillan	Lg. brown, center	12,000	17,500	22,000	—
1880	Bruce	Wyman	Lg. brown, center	17,500	22,000		—
Large "L" removed.							
1880	Rosecrans	Huston	Lg. brown, spikes	6,500	15,000	25,000	37,500
1880	Rosecrans	Nebeker	Sm. red, right	6,750	16,000	27,000	40,000

SILVER CERTIFICATES-FIFTY DOLLARS

Face Design. Minor variations.

More open back Design.

Series	Register	Treasurer	Seal at Right	Fine	VF	Ex. Fine	AU	CU	Ch. CU
1891	Rosecrans	Nebeker	Sm. red	2,200	3,400	4,500	6,000	8,000	12,500
1891	Tillman	Morgan	Sm. red	1,900	3,000	3,900	5,250	6,000	8,500
1891	Bruce	Roberts	Sm. red	1,850	2,800	3,750	5,000	5,750	8,000
1891	Lyons	Roberts	Sm. red	1,850	2,800	3,750	5,000	5,750	8,000
1891	Vernon	Treat	Sm. red	1,850	2,800	3,750	5,000	5,750	8,000
1891	Parker	Burke	Blue	1,800	2,750	3,500	4,750	5,500	7,500

SILVER CERTIFICATES-ONE HUNDRED DOLLARS
The Countersigned Series

Type 3 place of deposit: Washington, D.C.
Type 6 place of deposit: San Francisco
Type 7 place of deposit: New York

Face Design. Pres. James Monroe. Three types, Above Type 3.

Face Design Type 6, San Francisco.

Back Design. Black on white.

SILVER CERTIFICATES-ONE HUNDRED DOLLARS

Series	Countersigned by	VG	VF
Scofield-Gilfillan signatures. Blue serial numbers.			
1878	A.U. Wyman	—	—
1878	R.M. Anthony	**Extremely Rare**	
1878	W.G. White	**Possibly unique**	

All have large red "100" below center seal.

Face Design. Pres. James Monroe, two signatures.

Back Design. Black ink.

Series	Register	Treasurer	Seal	Fine	VF	Ex. Fine	AU
With Large "C" below center seal.							
1880	Scofield	Gilfillan	Lg. brown, center	**Unknown**	—	—	—
1880	Bruce	Gilfillan	Lg. brown, center	**10,000**	**20,000**	**34,000**	**52,000**
1880	Bruce	Wyman	Lg. brown, center	**9,500**	**18,000**	**28,000**	**47,500**
No "C" below center seal.							
1880	Rosecrans	Huston	Lg. brown, spikes	**9,000**	**17,500**	**28,500**	**45,000**
1880	Rosecrans	Nebeker	Sm. red, right	**9,700**	**19,000**	**30,000**	**50,000**

SILVER CERTIFICATES-ONE HUNDRED DOLLARS

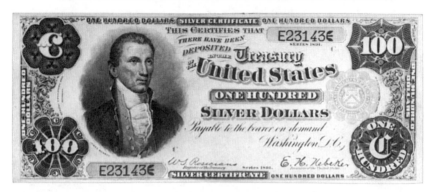

Face Design. Minor change.

Back Design. More open to discourage counterfeiters.

Series	Register	Treasurer	Seal at Right	VG	Fine	VF	Ex. Fine	AU
1891	Rosecrans	Nebeker	Sm. red	4,400	6,250	10,500	14,000	25,000
1891	Tillman	Morgan	Sm. red	4,200	6,000	10,000	13,500	22,500

The above series were extensively counterfeited. Genuine notes have fibers on the back of the note. Counterfeits have "ink drawn" threads or none.

SILVER CERTIFICATES-FIVE HUNDRED DOLLARS

Countersigned Series. One only, Type 3, payable at Washington, D.C. Scofield-Gilfillan signatures. Blue serial numbers.

Series	Countersigned by	Seal
1878	A.U. Wyman	Lg. red, center

Face Design.

Back Design. Black ink.

Series	Register	Treasurer	Seal
1880	Scofield	Gilfillan	Lg. brown, center
1880	Bruce	Gilfillan	Lg. brown, center
1880	Bruce	Wyman	Lg. brown, center

There have been no recent public sales. All are extremely rare. Some might not exist. Reportedly less than fifteen have not been redeemed of all the above.

SILVER CERTIFICATES-ONE THOUSAND DOLLARS

Series	Countersigned by	Seal
1878	A.U. Wyman	Lg. red, center

Series	Register	Treasurer	Seal
1880	Scofield	Gilfillan	Lg. brown, center
1880	Bruce	Gilfillan	Lg. brown, center
1880	Bruce	Wyman	Lg. brown, center
1891	Tillman	Morgan	Sm. red, right

Reportedly less than ten notes of this denomination, all series, have not been redeemed.

As with the $500 denomination, only Type 3 was issued in the Countersigned Series, Scofield-Gilfillan signatures and Blue Serial numbers.

The Silver Certificates series 1878 to 1923 include some of the finest engravings and most attractive designs used in the printing of United States paper money.

The memory of many great Americans has been perpetuated in the face designs: Martha Washington, General Winfield Scott, William Windom, Thos. A. Hendricks, Daniel Manning, Edward Everett, Wm. L. Marcy and former U.S. Presidents Washington, Lincoln, Grant and Monroe.

The Silver Dollar back design of series 1886 is exceptionally attractive. The well known and much sought after Educational series 1896 is outstanding for the designs and engraving on the face of the notes and the back designs honoring Martha and George Washington, inventors Robert Fulton and Samuel Morse and Generals U.S. Grant and Philip Henry Sheridan.

Our American Indians are honored by the face design of the series 1899 $5 certificate, commonly known as the "Onepapa" design.

NATIONAL BANK NOTES

Authorized by the National Currency Act, Feb. 25, 1863 and June 3, 1864. They were issued by Chartered Banks from 1863 to 1928 in large size.

During the Civil War, coins of gold and silver were hoarded and practically disappeared from circulation. The unsecured Legal Tender Notes, commonly known as "Greenbacks", were not popular and not readily accepted by skeptical persons having no confidence in the Government's promise to pay.

Although the National Currency Act was not passed until Feb. 26, 1863, Spencer M. Clark, Chief of Construction of the Treasury Department as early as April 1862, conceived the plan to have National Banks issue their own currency. The plan was endorsed by the then Secretary of the Treasury, Salmon P. Chase, who directed Clark to invite artists and engravers to submit proposals and designs.

Clark has previously suggested that historic pictures be used as back designs for the "Greenbacks" of 1862, claiming that these designs offered greater protection against counterfeiting. His proposed designs were not adopted for the Legal Tender notes, but were adopted for the National Bank Notes issued under Secretary of the Treasury, W.P. Fessenden. Clark suggested that these designs cover the entire back of the notes, but while the designs were adopted the size of each was reduced to allow space for denomination and legends.

Spencer M. Clark later became Chief of the Division and was largely responsible for the establishment of the Bureau of Engraving and Printing.

Under the original Act of Feb. 25, 1863, National Banks qualifying under the terms of the Act were granted 20 year charters to date from the enactment of the Act. The Act of June 1864 changed this procedure and permitted granting of charters for 20 years from the date of the charter. Changes in the original Act through the years provided for renewal of charters for 20 year periods. Banks so chartered were permitted to issue National Currency not to exceed 90% of the total of the U.S. Government Bonds deposited with the Treasurer of the United States.

The Act of 1863 provided for the issuance of denominations from $5 to $1000. The Act of 1864 added $1, $2 and $3 notes. The $3 note was never issued although a plate was engraved.

Early issues will be found with the imprint of American, Continental and National Bank Note Companies. These companies supplied the paper and delivered the printed notes to the Treasury. The Treasury number and Treasury seal were then imprinted by the Bureau.

The "History of the Bureau of Engraving and Printing" supplies this information: "National Bank Notes were printed exclusively by private contractors until Sept. 1875. Thereafter this type of currency was partially printed by the Bureau of Engraving and Printing. Beginning in Oct., 1877, the Bureau executed all work in connection with the printing of national currency."

Notes will be found bearing the imprint of one of the three bank note companies in the design and in very small type in the margin of the note the notation: "Printed at the Bureau of Engraving and Printing."

The dates appearing on National Bank Notes do not always indicate the date the Charter was granted nor the date the notes were issued. Nor do these dates denote the term of office of the Treasury Officials whose signatures appear on the notes. Plates engraved with the names of the U.S. Treasurer and Register of the Treasury were frequently used after the officials left office. The date appearing on the note is usually later than the granting of the Charter. Some banks, organized late in the First Charter period, continued to issue Series 1875 notes until Feb., 1902.

At the close of 1928, 13,269 banks had been chartered but many did not issue bank notes. Notes issued by banks in small communities are usually scarcer than those of large city banks. This thinking has at times been upset when a small town bank released a stock of notes which had been held in their reserve funds.

In addition to the engraved signatures of the two Treasury officials, National Bank Notes have the signatures of two bank officers, usually the president and cashier. Early issues did not carry the plate number on face or back.

The first Charter notes of $1 and $2 denominations were usually printed in sheets of three $1 notes and one $2 note. Check letters on notes so printed are A, B and C on the $1 notes and A on the $2 note. Known exceptions to "three ones' and a two" are:

The Westchester County National Bank, Peekskill, N.Y. Charter No. 1422.
The Merchants National Bank, Bangor, Maine. Charter No. 1437.
The City National Bank, Manchester, New Hampshire. Charter No. 1530.

The above three banks were supplied with sheets of two $1 notes, check letters A and B, and two $2 notes, check letters A and B.

The other known exception is the First National Bank of Philadelphia, with sheets of four $1 and sheets of four $2 notes.

The word "National" by law, must appear in the title of all Chartered banks. The exception is the Bank of North America, Philadelphia, Pa., which during its term of operation was allowed to retain the title used as a State bank.

REGIONAL LETTERS ON NATIONAL CURRENCY

To assist in sorting notes presented for redemption, a large letter was printed with the Charter numbers on National Currency for a period of about 25 years, approximately 1901-1925. These regional letters indicated the geographical area or region in which the issuing bank was located and may be found on Second and Third Charter notes. Six letters were used as follows:

E - Eastern Region   P - Pacific Region, including Hawaii and Alaska
M - Middle States Region   S - Southern Region
N - New England Region   W - Western Region

Many collectors endeavor to obtain at least one Bank Note from each of the six areas; Also a note with a regional letter and a note without the letter, issued by the same bank. Other collectors seek to obtain as many notes as are available with their own regional letter.

CHARTER NUMBERS

Bank Charter numbers were overprinted on Series 1875 and all later series and may also be found on some notes of the Original Series. The exact position varies on the face of the notes. These numbers on the First Issue are in red with the exception of a very few banks which were supplied with notes bearing BLACK Charter numbers.

Reported **"Black Charters"** are $5 notes of the following banks:

No. 1830 Minneapolis, Minn. Merchants Nat'l Bank. Allison-Spinner.
No. 2129 Central City, Colorado Territory, First Nat'l Bank. Allison-New.
No. 2130 Red Oak, Iowa. First National Bank. Allison-Spinner.
No. 2132 Green Bay, Wisconsin. Kellogg National Bank. Allison-Gilfillan.
No. 2137 Boyertown, Pa. First Nat'l Bank. Allison-Wyman.
No. 2138 Rochester, New Hampshire. National Bank. Allison-New.
No. 2141 Pontiac, Illinois. The National Bank. Allison-Wyman.
No. 2131 Possibly issued to the National Bank, Green Lane, Pennsylvania.

All the above are very rare and are valued conservatively at ten times the valuation of notes from the same states issued with red charter numbers.

66 YEAR RECORD OF CHARTERED NATIONAL BANKS

The following chart indicating the last Charter Number granted in each year from 1863 to the close of 1928 will be found helpful in determining the year in which any Charter was granted.

Year	No.	Year	No.	Year	No.	Year	No.
1863	179	1880	2498	1897	5108	1914	10672
1864	682	1881	2606	1898	5165	1915	10810
1865	1626	1882	2849	1899	5240	1916	10932
1866	1665	1883	3101	1900	5662	1917	11126
1867	1675	1884	3281	1901	6074	1918	11282
1868	1688	1885	3427	1902	6566	1919	11570
1869	1696	1886	3612	1903	7081	1920	11903
1870	1759	1887	3832	1904	7541	1921	12082
1871	1912	1888	3954	1905	8027	1922	12287
1872	2073	1889	4190	1906	8489	1923	12481
1873	2131	1890	4494	1907	8979	1924	12615
1874	2214	1891	4673	1908	9302	1925	12866
1875	2315	1892	4832	1909	9622	1926	13022
1876	2344	1893	4934	1910	9913	1927	13159
1877	2375	1894	4983	1911	10119	1928	13269
1878	2405	1895	5029	1912	10305		
1879	2445	1896	5054	1913	10472		

The record is not available as to the number of banks chartered early in 1929 before the issuance of small size notes in July of that year.

FIRST ISSUE NATIONAL BANK NOTES

First issue of National Bank Notes is known as the "Original Series." Followed by Series 1875. The two series comprise the issue of First Charter notes, denominations of $1 to $1000. Only two banks are known to have issued First Charter notes in denominations higher than $100.

The obligation to pay is by the issuing bank printed on the face of the notes and reads: "This note is secured by Bonds of the United States, deposited with the United States Treasurer at Washington. The...(Bank)...will pay the Bearer on Demand... Dollars."

FACE DESIGNS, First Charter Notes

$1   "Concordia." Two maidens clasping hands before an altar of earlier times which bears the Coat of Arms of the United States. The design represents the new Union brought about by the aid of Heaven, and the eventual return to peace. The vignette was designed by T.A. Liebler and engraved by Charles Burt.

$2   "Stars and Stripes" depicts a maiden unfurling the American flag. Engraved by James Smillie for the National Bank Note Co. Bank serial number at upper right. Treasury number at lower left in vertical position.

Known as the "Lazy 2" because of the large numeral "2" reclining on its side with the certification that Bonds have been deposited with the Treasurer of the U.S. at Washington. Similar large numerals were used on obsolete notes.

$5   "Columbus Sighting Land" showing the discoverer with some of his crew on the deck of the Caravel. The scene at lower right depicts Columbus introducing America, represented by an Indian Princess, to the Old World, Africa, Asia and Europe. Continental Bank Note Co. designer Fenton produced the design for engraving by Charles Burt.

$10   "Franklin and the Lightning" is the historical scene at left, symbolic of Benjamin Franklin experimenting with electrical energy and his assistant seated near him with a Leyden jar placed nearby. The year is marked by the figures "1752" in the corner. Eagle in flight bearing Liberty is shown at right, symbolizing "America Grasping the Lightning." Engraving by Alfred Jones.

$20   "Battle of Lexington 1775" depicts colonists in action, nurses attending the wounded and at right a symbolic design of "Loyalty." A procession for defense and preservation of the Union is led by Columbia with flag. The design is by Felix O.C. Darley. Engravings by Louis Delnoce and Alfred Jones.

$50   "Washington Crossing the Delaware" before his victorious battle at Princeton is the symbolical vignette at left. Engraved by Alfred Jones. "A Prayer for Victory" is depicted at right. Engraved by Louis Delnoce.

$100   Powell's painting "The Battle of Lake Erie" was the inspiration for the vignette at left engraved by Louis Delnoce. This shows Commodore Perry leaving his burning ship "The Lawrence." At right, Columbia is seated with a fasces and a bundle of rods with projecting ax handle. Inscribed are the words "The Union" and to the right "Maintain it." Engraving by James Bannister.

$500   Genius of the American Navy left and arrival of the Sirius 1838 right. James Mac Donough designer.

$1000   General Scott entering the City of Mexico is shown at left, after the painting by John Trubull. It was engraved by James Smillie and possibly Alfred Jones and A. Sealey. At right the Capitol Building, Washington, D.C. This note is believed to be non-existent.

BACK DESIGNS, First Charter Notes

The Coat of Arms of the State of issue appears in oval at left with the exception of notes issued by banks in the territories of Arizona, Nebraska, New Mexico, Oklahoma, Utah and Washington. The American eagle is shown in the oval at right. A rather lengthy inscription qualifying the acceptance of the note and the warning against counterfeiting "Punishable by $1000 fine, or fifteen years' imprisonment at hard labor, or both" is also part of the back design.

The border designs are green with center illustrations in black:

$1   "Landing of the Pilgrims" in center of back design depicts one of the memorable events in United States history. It is framed by the legend giving the legal value of the note and the purpose for which the note was intended and the warning to counterfeiters. Engraved by Elisha Hobart.

$2   Sir Walter Raleigh, with a long stem smoking pipe, demonstrates the use of tobacco brought from America. The King of England looks on with interest. Engraved by Louis Delnoce.

$5   "The Landing of Columbus" from the well known mural by John Vanderlyn. Louis Delnoce, Engraver.

$10   "DeSoto Discovering the Mississippi 1541" The beautiful mural by W.H. Powell shows a group of natives, soldiers and monks. A crucifix is being erected on the spot. Engraved by Girsch.

$20   "The Baptism of Pocahontas" at Jamestown, Virginia. The impressive scene shows Pocahontas kneeling, with John Smith and spectators, some of whom express interest and surprise. The painting is by John G. Chapman.

$50   "Embarkation of the Pilgrims" a reproduction of Robert W. Weir's mural which depicts the Pilgrims, before departing for America, kneeling to ask the Divine blessing. Engraved by W.W. Rice.

$100   "The Signing of the Declaration of Independence" July 4, 1776. One of John Trumbull's masterpieces showing Washington, Jefferson, Franklin and a dignified group assembled for the acceptance and signing of the historic document. Engraved by Girsch.

$500   "The Surrender of Burgoyne" Another mural by artist John Trumbull vividly portraying the surrender of the General to General Gates of the American Army at Saratoga, New York, Oct. 17, 1777. Engraved by Girsch.

$1000   "Washington Resigning his Commission" Dec. 23, 1783, at Annapolis, Maryland. John Trumbull's mural shows the Commander-in-Chief presenting his written resignation to the Congress. Engraved by Girsch and Louis Delnoce.

COMPARATIVE RARITY TABLE NATIONAL BANK NOTES

The following Rarity Table has been compiled after consultation with several ardent followers of this interesting series, plus the writer's experience in endeavoring to assemble a collection of National Bank Notes. *One hundred per cent accuracy is not to be expected* and changes will be made as new factual information is received. As with California notes, relative rarity for many states changes with the Charters.

Rarity 1	Rarity 2	Rarity 3
California, 3rd CH.	Indiana	Kansas
Illinois	Iowa	Kentucky
New York	Massachusetts	Michigan
Ohio	New Jersey	Minnesota
Pennsylvania	Texas	Missouri
		Wisconsin

Rarity 4	Rarity 5	Rarity 6
Alabama	California, 2nd CH.	Georgia
Connecticut	Colorado	Louisiana
Maryland	District of Columbia	Maine
Nebraska	New Hampshire	North Dakota
Tennessee	North Carolina	Oregon
Virginia	Oklahoma	South Carolina
	Washington	Vermont
	West Virginia	

Rarity 7	Rarity 8	Rarity 9
Arkansas	Arizona	California, 1st CH
Delaware	Idaho	District of Alaska
Florida	Hawaii	Territorial Notes
Montana	Mississippi	
Rhode Island	Nevada	**Rarity 10**
Utah	New Mexico	Puerto Rico
Wyoming	South Dakota	

Values listed for the various signature combinations throughout the three charter periods are for notes of RARITY ONE. No set rule can be given for every denomination of each charter period for each state.

Valuations for Rarity 1 may be increased for the various degree of rarity, approximately as follows:

Rarity Two	20%	Rarity Seven	Three to four times.
Rarity Three	30%	Rarity Eight	Four to five times.
Rarity Four	50%	Rarity Nine	Five to ten times.
Rarity Five	60%	Rarity Ten	Ten or more times.
Rarity Six	70%		

Notes of the high rarity groups are seldom offered and prices are largely a matter between buyer and seller.

NATIONAL BANK NOTES
FIRST CHARTER NOTES, issued 1862 and 1882

Original Series without Bank Charter number.

NATIONAL BANK NOTES-ONE DOLLAR
FIRST CHARTER NOTES, issued 1862 to 1882

Back Design "Landing of Pilgrims."

The early issues known as Original Series, with a few exceptions, bore no charter number and no series date. Additional information is given in the descriptive text in the preceding pages.

Series	Register	Treasurer	Seal	VG	VF	Ex. Fine	AU	CU	Ch. CU
Shield with rays at right.									
Original	Colby	Spinner	Sm. red	325.00	600.00	800.00	1,000	1,500	1,600
Original	Jeffries	Spinner	Sm. red	800.00	1,650	2,500	3,000	4,000	5,000
Original	Allison	Spinner	Sm. red	325.00	600.00	800.00	1,000	1,600	1,650
Charter number and "Series 1875" added. Shield with scallops.									
1875	Allison	New	Red, right	325.00	600.00	800.00	1,000	1,500	1,600
1875	Allison	Wyman	Red, right	325.00	600.00	800.00	1,000	1,500	1,600
1875	Allison	Gilfillan	Red, right	325.00	600.00	800.00	1,000	1,500	1,600
1875	Scofield	Gilfillan	Red, right	325.00	600.00	800.00	1,000	1,600	1,650

Signature combination Chittenden-Spinner not issued.
Gem well centered early Charters are difficult to find. Uncut sheets were cut apart by shear-happy tellers. Many New England notes were trimmed right down to the design.

TWO DOLLARS
"The Lazy Two" First Charter Notes

Original Series without Bank Charter number.

NATIONAL BANK NOTES-TWO DOLLARS

Back Design. "Sir Walter Raleigh demonstrating use of tobacco."

Series	Register	Treasurer	Seal	VG	VF	Ex. Fine	AU	CU
Shield with rays at right.								
Original	Colby	Spinner	Sm. red, right	1,000	2,200	3,200	4,000	5,000
Original	Jeffries	Spinner	Sm. red, right	1,750	2,750	4,000	5,200	6,500
Original	Allison	Spinner	Sm. red, right	1,000	2,200	3,200	4,000	5,000
Charter number and "Series 1875" added. Scalloped shield.								
1875	Allison	New	Red, right	1,000	2,200	3,200	4,000	5,000
1875	Allison	Wyman	Red, right	1,000	2,200	3,200	4,000	5,000
1875	Allison	Gilfillan	Red, right	1,000	2,200	3,200	4,000	5,000
1875	Scofield	Gilfillan	Red, right	1,000	2,200	3,200	4,000	5,000

Issuance of $1 and $2 National Bank Notes was discontinued in 1878. Latest date observed is July 30, 1878. First Charter Denominations of $5 and higher continued to be issued as late as 1909.

FIVE DOLLARS

Original Series with Bank Charter number.

NATIONAL BANK NOTES-FIVE DOLLARS

Back Design. "The Landing of Columbus."

Printed in sheets of four $5 notes from 1863 to 1909.

Series	Register	Treasurer	Seal	VG	VF	Ex. Fine	AU	CU
Original	Chittenden	Spinner	Sm. red, right	325.00	600.00	800.00	1,000	1,500
Original	Colby	Spinner	Sm. red, right	325.00	600.00	800.00	1,000	1,500
Original	Jeffries	Spinner	Sm. red, right	1,000	2,000	2,800	3,400	4,500
Original	Allison	Spinner	Sm. red, right	325.00	600.00	800.00	1,000	1,550

Charter number and "Series 1875" added.

Series	Register	Treasurer	Seal	VG	VF	Ex. Fine	AU	CU
1875	Allison	New	Red, right	325.00	600.00	800.00	1,000	1,550
1875	Allison	Wyman	Red, right	325.00	600.00	800.00	1,000	1,550
1875	Allison	Gilfillan	Red, right	325.00	600.00	800.00	1,000	1,550
1875	Scofield	Gilfillan	Red, right	325.00	600.00	800.00	1,000	1,550
1875	Bruce	Gilfillan	Red, right	325.00	600.00	800.00	1,000	1,550
1875	Bruce	Wyman	Red, right	375.00	650.00	850.00	1,100	1,600
1875	Bruce	Jordan	Red, right	900.00	1,800	2,750	3,400	4,250
1875	Rosecrans	Jordan	Red, right	325.00	600.00	800.00	1,050	1,600
1875	Rosecrans	Huston	Red, right	325.00	600.00	800.00	1,050	1,600

Signature combination Rosecrans-Hyatt not issued.

TEN DOLLARS

Series 1875, with Bank Charter number.

NATIONAL BANK NOTES-TEN DOLLARS

Back Design. "DeSoto discovering the Mississippi."

Sheets of four $10, three $10, one $20 and other combinations 1863 to 1909. Early issues have Continental Bank Note Co. in lower border. Later issues printed at Bureau.

Series	Register	Treasurer	Seal	VG	VF	Ex. Fine	AU	CU
Original	Chittenden	Spinner	Sm. red, right	500.00	1,000	1,400	2,000	2,800
Original	Colby	Spinner	Sm. red, right	500.00	1,000	1,400	2,000	2,800
Original	Jeffries	Spinner	Sm. red, right	750.00	1,750	3,000	4,000	4,750
Original	Allison	Spinner	Sm. red, right	500.00	1,000	1,400	2.000	2,800
1875	Allison	New	Red, right	500.00	1,000	1,400	2.000	2,800
1875	Allison	Wyman	Red, right	500.00	1,000	1,400	2.000	2,800
1875	Allison	Gilfillan	Red, right	500.00	1,000	1,400	2,000	2,800
1875	Scofield	Gilfillan	Red, right	500.00	1,000	1,400	2,000	2,800
1875	Bruce	Gilfillan	Red, right	500.00	1,000	1,400	2,000	2,800
1875	Bruce	Wyman	Red, right	500.00	1,000	1,400	2,000	2,800
1875	Rosecrans	Huston	Red, right	500.00	1,000	1,400	2,000	2,800
1875	Rosecrans	Nebeker	Red, right	500.00	1,000	1,400	2,000	2,800
1875	Tillman	Morgan	Possibly exists.					

See pages 82 and 83 for suggested valuations for all states.

TWENTY DOLLARS

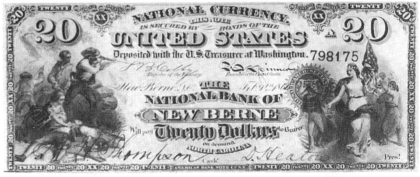

Original Series without Bank Charter Number. Blue Serial Number.

NATIONAL BANK NOTES-TWENTY DOLLARS

Back Design. "Baptism of Pocahontas."

Printed in sheets of several combinations, including three $10 and one $20, and four $20 from 1863 to 1902.

Series	Register	Treasurer	Seal	VG	Fine	VF	Ex. Fine
Original	Chittenden	Spinner	Sm. red, right	900.00	1,250	1,850	2,300
Original	Colby	Spinner	Sm. red, right	900.00	1,200	1,800	2,200
Original	Jeffries	Spinner	Sm. red, right	2,000	2,750	3,000	4,250
Original	Allison	Spinner	Sm. red, right	900.00	1,200	1,750	2,200
1875	Allison	New	Red, right	900.00	1,200	1,750	2,200
1875	Allison	Wyman	Red, right	900.00	1,200	1,750	2,200
1875	Allison	Gilfillan	Red, right	900.00	1,200	1,750	2,200
1875	Scofield	Gilfillan	Red, right	900.00	1,200	1,750	2,200
1875	Bruce	Gilfillan	Red, right	900.00	1,200	1,750	2,200
1875	Bruce	Wyman	Red, right	900.00	1,250	1,800	2,300
1875	Rosecrans	Huston	Red, right	925.00	1,250	1,800	2,300
1875	Rosecrans	Nebeker	Red, right	950.00	1,300	2,000	2,400
1875	Tillman	Morgan	Red, right	950.00	1,300	2,000	2,400

FIFTY DOLLARS

Series 1875 with Bank Charter number.

NATIONAL BANK NOTES-FIFTY DOLLARS

Back Design. "Embarkation of the Pilgrims."

Printed in sheets of three $50 and one $100 also sheets of two $50 and other combinations, from 1863 to 1902. Including one $50 and one $100 on a sheet of two.

Series	Register	Treasurer	Seal	Good	VG	Fine	VF
Original	Chittenden	Spinner	Sm. red, right	2,200	4,000	5,200	6,750
Original	Colby	Spinner	Sm. red, 0right	2,200	4,000	5,200	6,750
Original	Allison	Spinner	Sm. red, right	2,200	4,000	5,200	6,750
1875	Allison	New	Scalloped red	2,200	4,000	5,200	6,750
1875	Allison	Wyman	Scalloped red	2,200	4,000	5,200	6,750
1875	Allison	Gilfillan	Scalloped red	2,200	4,000	5,200	6,750
1875	Scofield	Gilfillan	Scalloped red	2,200	4,000	5,200	6,750
1875	Bruce	Gilfillan	Scalloped red	2,200	4,000	5,200	6,750
1875	Bruce	Wyman	Scalloped red	2,200	4,000	5,200	6,750
1875	Rosecrans	Huston	Scalloped red	2,200	4,000	5,200	6,750
1875	Rosecrans	Nebeker	Scalloped red	2,200	4,000	5,200	6,750
1875	Tillman	Morgan	Scalloped red	2,200	4,000	5,200	6,750

ONE HUNDRED DOLLARS

Series 1875 with Bank Charter number.

NATIONAL BANK NOTES-ONE HUNDRED DOLLARS

Back Design. "Signing of the Declaration of Independence."

Printed in sheets of one $100 and three $50, and sheets of two $100 or one $50 and one $100, and other combinations.

Series	Register	Treasurer	Seal	Good	VG	Fine	VF
Original	Chittenden	Spinner	Sm. red, right	4,250	5,200	6,750	9,200
Original	Colby	Spinner	Sm. red, right	4,250	5,200	6,750	9,200
Original	Allison	Spinner	Sm. red, right	4,250	5,200	6,750	9,200
1875	Allison	New	Red, right	4,250	5,200	6,750	9,200
1875	Allison	Wyman	Red, right	4,250	5,200	6.750	9,200
1875	Allison	Gilfillan	Red, right	4,250	5,200	6,750	9,200
1875	Scofield	Gilfillan	Red, right	4,250	5,200	6,750	9,200
1875	Bruce	Gilfillan	Red, right	4,250	5,200	6,750	9,200
1875	Bruce	Wyman	Red, right	4,250	5,200	6.750	9,200
1875	Rosecrans	Huston	Red, right	4,250	5,200	6.750	9,200
1875	Rosecrans	Nebeker	Red, right	4,250	5,200	6,750	9,200
1875	Tillman	Morgan	Red, right	4,250	5,200	6,750	9,200

All above are very scarce in any condition. It is doubtful that notes with some of the signature combinations issued still exist.

FIRST CHARTER NOTES-FIVE HUNDRED DOLLARS

Issued in the Original Series and some in Series 1875. Although over 150 notes remain unredeemed, only three have been reported. Possibly unique in private hands.

FIRST CHARTER NOTES-ONE THOUSAND DOLLARS

This denomination is unknown, although about 20 notes have not been redeemed.

Attractive tableau scenes are illustrated on the back designs of all notes of the First Charter period. The original murals decorated the rotunda of the Capitol Building in Washington and were the work of early American artists.

THE SECOND CHARTER PERIOD
Series 1882 Brown Backs, Series 1882-1908 and
Series 1882 with Denomination spelled out on back of note

First Issue: Series 1882. The well known and very popular Brown Backs.

Second Issue: Series 1882-1908 emergency issue. Whereas banks had previously been required to deposit United States Government bonds with the Treasurer, by Act of Congress, May 30, 1908, they were permitted to deposit other types of securities thus enabling the banks to place a larger number of notes into circulation.

Third Issue: Series 1882. Denomination spelled out on back. Scarcest of the three series of 1882 Nationals. Not all banks issued this series.

FACE DESIGNS, First, Second and Third Issues

The face designs of the three Second Charter issues are the same as the First Charter issues with the exception of the $5 notes. The bank obligation to pay is also the same.

The face design of the $5 denomination of all three issues of 1882 is distinctly different from the higher denominations of this series or the $5 First Charter notes. Portrait of James A. Garfield, 20th President, is in oval at left and possibly used to immortalize the Statesman following his assassination in 1881, the same year in which he assumed office. The design is by Geo. W. Casilear and engraved by Alonzo C. Hatch.

BACK DESIGNS, First Issue — 1882 Brown Backs

"Brown Backs" is the well known description of the First Series of Second Charter notes. The State Seals are in ovals at left in the back design, as on the First Charter notes, and the American Eagle is again shown in oval at right.

The striking change in the "Brown Backs" is in the center design which prominently features the Bank Charter Number in large numerals against a green background surrounded by a brown lathe-work design.

The legend appears in the top margin and the rather lengthy counterfeiting warning extends across bottom of the back design.

GREEN BACK DESIGNS, Second Issue — 1882-1908 Series

The back design of the Emergency Series, 1882-1908, shows various personages and designs in the small oval at left instead of the State Seals as used on the Brown Backs and First Charter notes. Various subjects are shown in the oval at right. Featured are the following:

$5   Washington at left; Capitol Building, Washington, D.C. at right.
$10   William P. Fessenden at left; right, Mechanics represented by seated workmen.
$20   American Eagle, two different poses, left and right ovals.
$50   Eagle with shield left and right.
$100   Eagle with flag at left and with Shield at right.

GREEN BACK DESIGNS, Third Issue — "Denomination Back"

The center design spells out in large letters the denomination of the notes. Vignettes in small ovals at left and right remain the same as the Second Issue, also legend at top and the counterfeiting warning at bottom.

NATIONAL BANK NOTES-SECOND CHARTER PERIOD
First Issue — "The Brown Backs"

All "Brown Backs" are series 1882. Many shades of brown seals in various positions, usually at right.

TYPE 1 FIVE DOLLARS
BLUE SERIAL NUMBERS

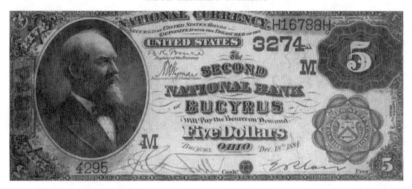

Brown Back. Charter Number with Regional Letter.

Type 1 Back Design. Bank Charter Number in Center.

Issued 1882-1909. Printed in sheets of four $5 notes.

Register	Treasurer	VG	VF	AU	CU	Ch. CU
Bruce	Gilfillan	225.00	350.00	625.00	800.00	1,000
Bruce	Wyman	225.00	350.00	625.00	800.00	1,000
Bruce	Jordan	225.00	350.00	625.00	800.00	1,000
Rosecrans	Jordan	225.00	350.00	625.00	800.00	1,000
Rosecrans	Hyatt	225.00	350.00	625.00	800.00	1,000
Rosecrans	Huston	225.00	350.00	625.00	800.00	1,000
Rosecrans	Nebeker	225.00	350.00	625.00	800.00	1,000
Rosecrans	Morgan	400.00	675.00	1,150	1,500	1,750
Tillman	Morgan	225.00	350.00	625.00	800.00	1,000
Tillman	Roberts	225.00	350.00	625.00	800.00	1,000
Bruce	Roberts	225.00	350.00	625.00	800.00	1,000
Lyons	Roberts	225.00	350.00	625.00	800.00	1,000
Lyons	Treat		Possibly Exists			
Vernon	Treat	275.00	400.00	725.00	875.00	1,200

See pages 82-83 for suggested valuations for all states.

NATIONAL BANK NOTES-SECOND CHARTER PERIOD
TYPE 1 TEN DOLLARS
RED SERIAL NUMBERS

Brown Back. Charter Number without Regional Letter.

Type 1 Back Design. Territorial Note. American Eagle instead of State Seal.

Issued 1882-1909. Printed in sheets of three $10 and one $20 and a few four $10.

Series 1882. Brown seal at right of center.

Register	Treasurer	VG	VF	AU	CU	Ch. CU
Bruce	Gilfillan	275.00	425.00	700.00	1,000	1,250
Bruce	Wyman	275.00	425.00	700.00	1,000	1,250
Bruce	Jordan	310.00	475.00	750.00	1,150	1,500
Rosecrans	Jordan	275.00	425.00	700.00	1,000	1,250
Rosecrans	Hyatt	275.00	425.00	700.00	1,000	1,250
Rosecrans	Huston	275.00	425.00	700.00	1,000	1,250
Rosecrans	Nebeker	275.00	425.00	700.00	1,000	1,250
Rosecrans	Morgan	550.00	950.00	1,350	1,950	2,400
Tillman	Morgan	275.00	425.00	700.00	1,000	1,250
Tillman	Roberts	275.00	425.00	700.00	1,000	1,250
Bruce	Roberts	275.00	425.00	700.00	1,000	1,250
Lyons	Roberts	275.00	425.00	700.00	1,000	1,250
Lyons	Treat	310.00	475.00	950.00	1,200	1,500
Vernon	Treat	310.00	475.00	950.00	1,200	1,500

Brown Back. Charter Number without Regional Letter.

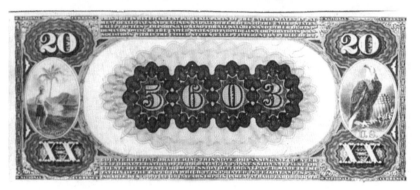

Type 1 Back Design. Charter Number in Large Numerals. State Seal at left.

Issued 1882-1909. Printed in sheets of one $20 and three $10.

Series 1882. Brown seal at right of center.

Register	Treasurer	VG	VF	AU	CU	Ch. CU
Bruce	Gilfillan	350.00	550.00	900.00	1,300	1,600
Bruce	Wyman	350.00	550.00	900.00	1,300	1,600
Bruce	Jordan	375.00	600.00	950.00	1,450	1,750
Rosecrans	Jordan	350.00	550.00	900.00	1,300	1,500
Rosecrans	Hyatt	350.00	550.00	900.00	1,300	1,500
Rosecrans	Huston	350.00	550.00	900.00	1,300	1,500
Rosecrans	Nebeker	350.00	550.00	900.00	1,300	1,500
Rosecrans	Morgan	575.00	1,100	1,950	2,350	2,850
Tillman	Morgan	350.00	550.00	900.00	1,300	1,600
Tillman	Roberts	350.00	550.00	900.00	1,300	1,600
Bruce	Roberts	350.00	550.00	900.00	1,300	1,600
Lyons	Roberts	350.00	550.00	900.00	1,300	1,600
Lyons	Treat	425.00	675.00	1,100	1,500	2,000
Vernon	Treat	400.00	625.00	1,000	1,450	1,850

$10 and $20 "brown-backs" have been found with Charter Numbers just to the right of the series date printed vertically instead of horizontally.

NATIONAL BANK NOTES-SECOND CHARTER PERIOD
TYPE 1 FIFTY DOLLARS
RED SERIAL NUMBERS

Brown Back. Charter Number without Regional Letter.

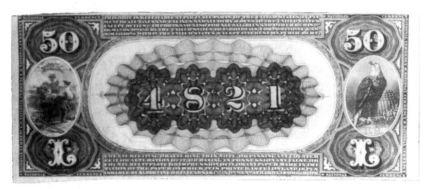

Type 1 Back Design. Charter Number in Large Numerals. State Seal at left.

Issued 1882-1909. Printed in sheets of three $50 and one $100.

Series 1882. Brown seal to right of center.

Register	Treasurer	VG	VF	AU	CU
Bruce	Gilfillan	1,200	1,850	4,000	5,000
Bruce	Wyman	1,200	1,850	4,000	5,000
Bruce	Jordan	1,250	2,000	4,250	5,250
Rosecrans	Jordan	1,200	1,850	4,000	5,000
Rosecrans	Hyatt	1,200	1,850	4,000	5,000
Rosecrans	Huston	1,200	1,850	4,000	5,000
Rosecrans	Nebeker	1,200	1,850	4,000	5,000
Rosecrans	Morgan	1,500	2,250	4,500	6,200
Tillman	Morgan	1,200	1,850	4,000	5,000
Tillman	Roberts	1,200	1,850	4,000	5,000
Bruce	Roberts	1,200	1,850	4,000	5,000
Lyons	Roberts	1,200	1,850	4,000	5,000
Vernon	Treat	1,500	2,250	4,500	6,200

Signature combination, Lyons-Treat, not issued.

NATIONAL BANK NOTES-SECOND CHARTER PERIOD
TYPE 1 ONE HUNDRED DOLLARS

Face Design. Series 1882 Brown Back.

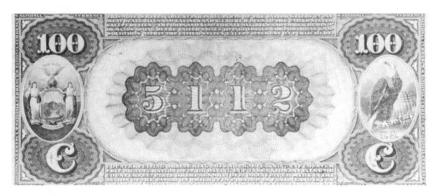

Type 1 Back Design. Charter Number in Large Numerals. State Seal at left.

Issued 1882-1909. Printed in sheets of one $100 and three $50.
Series 1882. Brown seal red serial numbers.

Register	Treasurer	VG	VF	AU	CU
Bruce	Gilfillan	1,550	2,500	5,000	6,200
Bruce	Wyman	1,550	2,500	5,000	6,200
Bruce	Jordan	1,550	2,500	5,000	6,200
Rosecrans	Jordan	1,550	2,500	5,000	6,200
Rosecrans	Hyatt	1,550	2,500	5,000	6,200
Rosecrans	Huston	1,550	3,000	5,000	6,200
Rosecrans	Nebeker	1,550	2,500	5,000	6,200
Rosecrans	Morgan	1,750	3,000	5,850	7,500
Tillman	Morgan	1,550	2,500	5,000	6,200
Tillman	Roberts	1,550	2,500	5,000	6,200
Bruce	Roberts	1,550	2,500	5,000	6,200
Lyons	Roberts	1,550	2,500	5,000	6,200
Vernon	Treat	1,750	3,000	5,850	7,500

Signature combination, Lyons-Treat, not issued.

NATIONAL BANK NOTES-SECOND CHARTER PERIOD
Second Issue-1882-1908 Green Backs
TYPE 2 FIVE DOLLARS

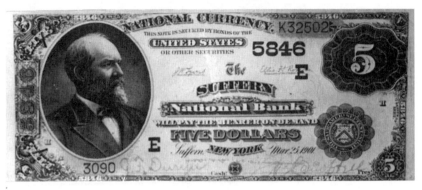

Type 2 Face Design. Very similar to Type 1.

Type 2 Back Design. The "Dated Back" in green ink.

Issued 1908-1916. Printed in sheets of four $5 notes.

Series 1882-1908. Blue seal, blue charter and serial numbers.

Register	Treasurer	VG	VF	AU	CU	Ch. CU
Rosecrans	Huston	225.00	350.00	600.00	850.00	950.00
Rosecrans	Nebeker	225.00	350.00	600.00	850.00	950.00
Rosecrans	Morgan	450.00	950.00	1,100	1,500	1,800
Tillman	Morgan	225.00	350.00	600.00	850.00	950.00
Tillman	Roberts	225.00	350.00	625.00	900.00	1,000
Bruce	Roberts	235.00	375.00	650.00	935.00	1,050
Lyons	Roberts	225.00	350.00	600.00	850.00	950.00
Vernon	Treat	235.00	375.00	700.00	935.00	1,050
Vernon	McClung			Possibly Exists		
Napier	McClung	450.00	950.00	1,100	1,500	1,800

Signature combination, Lyons-Treat, not issued.

See pages 82-83 for suggested valuations for all states.

NATIONAL BANK NOTES-SECOND CHARTER PERIOD
TYPE 2 TEN DOLLARS

Type 2 Back Design. The "Dated Back."

Issued 1908-1916. Printed in sheets of four $10, also three $10 and one $20.

Series 1882-1908, blue seal, blue charter and serial numbers.

Register	Treasurer	VG	VF	AU	CU	Ch. CU
Rosecrans	Huston	300.00	400.00	700.00	900.00	1,100
Rosecrans	Nebeker	300.00	400.00	700.00	900.00	1,100
Rosecrans	Morgan	575.00	900.00	1,400	1,650	2,000
Tillman	Morgan	300.00	400.00	700.00	900.00	1,100
Tillman	Roberts	300.00	400.00	700.00	950.00	1,150
Bruce	Roberts	300.00	400.00	700.00	950.00	1,150
Lyons	Roberts	300.00	400.00	700.00	900.00	1,100
Vernon	Treat	310.00	420.00	725.00	950.00	1,150
Vernon	McClung	325.00	435.00	750.00	1,000	1,200
Napier	McClung	325.00	435.00	750.00	1,000	1,200

Signature combination, Lyons-Treat, not issued.

TYPE 2 TWENTY DOLLARS

Issued 1908-1916. Printed in sheets of one $20 and three $10.

Series 1882-1908, blue seal, blue charter and serial numbers.

Register	Treasurer	VG	VF	AU	CU	Ch. CU
Rosecrans	Huston	360.00	600.00	950.00	1,300	1,400
Rosecrans	Nebeker	350.00	550.00	850.00	1,200	1,350
Rosecrans	Morgan	750.00	1,200	2,000	—	—
Tillman	Morgan	350.00	550.00	850.00	1,200	1,350
Tillman	Roberts	350.00	550.00	900.00	1,250	1,400
Bruce	Roberts	360.00	600.00	950.00	1,225	1,475
Lyons	Roberts	350.00	550.00	850.00	1,200	1,350
Vernon	Treat	375.00	600.00	950.00	1,300	1,475
Vernon	McClung			Possibly Exists		
Napier	McClung	400.00	650.00	1,100	1,500	1,850

Signature combination, Lyons-Treat, not issued.

NATIONAL BANK NOTES-SECOND CHARTER PERIOD
TYPE 2 FIFTY DOLLARS

Type 2 Back Design. The "Dated Back."

Issued 1908-1922. Printed in sheets of three $50 and one $100.

Series 1882-1908, blue seal, blue charter and serial numbers.

Register	Treasurer	VG	VF	AU	CU
Rosecrans	Huston	1,100	1,750	3,000	3,800
Rosecrans	Nebeker	1,100	1,750	3,000	3,800
Tillman	Morgan	1,100	1,750	3,000	3,800
Tillman	Roberts	1,200	2,000	3,250	4,200
Bruce	Roberts	1,135	1,850	3,125	4,050
Lyons	Roberts	1,100	1,750	3,000	3,800
Vernon	Treat	1,200	2,000	3,250	4,200
Napier	McClung	1,275	1,925	3,125	4,200

Signature combinations 16, 21 and 23 not issued.

TYPE 2 ONE HUNDRED DOLLARS

Issued 1908-1922. Printed in sheets of one $100 and three $50.

Series 1882-1908, blue seal, blue charter and serial numbers.

Register	Treasurer	VG	VF	AU	CU
Rosecrans	Huston	1,500	2,400	4,000	5,500
Rosecrans	Nebeker	1,500	2,400	4,000	5,500
Tillman	Morgan	1,500	2,400	4,000	5,500
Tillman	Roberts	1,500	2,400	4,000	5,500
Bruce	Roberts	1,500	2,400	4,000	5,500
Lyons	Roberts	1,500	2,400	4,000	5,500
Vernon	Treat	1,575	2,750	4,350	5,800
Napier	McClung	1,650	3,000	4,600	6,250

NATIONAL BANK NOTES-SECOND CHARTER PERIOD
Third Issue Green Back with Denomination
TYPE 3 FIVE DOLLARS

Type 3 Back Design. The "Denomination Back."

Issued 1916-1922. Printed in sheets of four $5 notes. All are scarce.

Series 1882, blue seal, blue charter and serial numbers.

Register	Treasurer	VG	VF	AU	CU	Ch. CU
Tillman	Morgan	240.00	350.00	650.00	800.00	1,300
Tillman	Roberts	300.00	500.00	975.00	1,600	2,200
Bruce	Roberts	300.00	500.00	975.00	1,600	2,200
Lyons	Roberts	240.00	350.00	650.00	800.00	1,300
Vernon	Treat	290.00	425.00	825.00	1,000	1,750
Napier	McClung	265.00	385.00	765.00	940.00	1,525
Teehee	Burke	325.00	700.00	1,000	1,600	2,100

TYPE 3 TEN DOLLARS

Type 3 Back Design. The "Denomination Back."

NATIONAL BANK NOTES-SECOND CHARTER PERIOD

TYPE 3 TEN DOLLARS

Issued 1916-1922. Printed in sheets of four $10; also three $10 and one $20.

Series 1882, blue seal, blue charter and serial numbers.

Register	Treasurer	VG	VF	AU	CU
Tillman	Morgan	300.00	625.00	1,100	1,300
Tillman	Roberts	250.00	500.00	850.00	1,000
Bruce	Roberts	300.00	625.00	1,100	1,300
Lyons	Roberts	250.00	500.00	850.00	1,000
Lyons	Treat		Possibly Exists		
Vernon	Treat	275.00	565.00	925.00	1,125
Napier	McClung	250.00	500.00	900.00	1,075
Teehee	Burke	300.00	625.00	1,100	1,300

TYPE 3 TWENTY DOLLARS

Issued 1916-1922. Printed in sheets of one $20 and three $10 notes.

Series 1882, blue seal, blue charter and serial numbers.

Register	Treasurer	VG	VF	AU	CU
Tillman	Morgan	375.00	550.00	1,500	1,700
Tillman	Roberts	350.00	750.00	1,900	2,200
Bruce	Roberts	350.00	750.00	1,900	2,200
Lyons	Roberts	350.00	500.00	1,500	1,700
Lyons	Treat	400.00	650.00	1,675	2,000
Vernon	Treat	400.00	650.00	1,675	2,000
Napier	McClung	375.00	550.00	1,500	1,825
Teehee	Burke	400.00	650.00	1,675	2,000

TYPE 3 FIFTY DOLLARS

Only five known. Four New Orleans, La., one Dayton, Ohio.
Only one signature combination, Lyons-Roberts.

TYPE 3 ONE HUNDRED DOLLARS

Only four now known. Two New Orleans, La., two Dayton, Ohio.
One signature combination, Lyons-Roberts.

THE THIRD CHARTER PERIOD

First Issue, Series 1902 — Red Seals and Charter Numbers. Blue Serial Numbers

Notes of this issue are scarce, having been issued by comparatively few Chartered banks. Red Seals were printed with only three signature combinations of Treasury Officials. Reference to the Table of Terms of Office will explain why the Lyons-Treat and Vernon-Treat signatures are less frequently found than those of Lyons-Roberts.

Second Issue, 1902-1908 — Blue Seals, Emergency Series, Dates on back

Authorized under Act of May 30, 1908, as were the Series 1882-1908 Second Charter Notes. They were first issued in 1908 and with two exceptions discontinued in 1916. The $50 and $100 denominations were issued through 1925.

Third Issue, 1902 — Blue Seals, No dates on back

First issued in 1916 and most common of the three issues of Third Charter notes. There were fifteen signature combinations, the scarcest being the Jones-Woods signatures. Edward E. Jones assumed the office of Register and Walter O. Woods the office of Treasurer in 1929, the same year in which large size notes were discontinued.

FACE DESIGNS, Third Charter Notes

The Treasury Seal is at right on all denominations of the three issues. Prominent Statesmen are featured in the oval, at left.

- $5   Benjamin Harrison, 23rd President of the United States.
- $10   William McKinley, 25th President, assassinated Buffalo, 1901.
- $20   Hugh McCulloch, Secretary of Treasury, 1865-69 and 1884-85.
- $50   John Sherman, Secretary of the Treasury 1877-1881; Secretary of State 1897-1898.
- $100   John J. Knox, Comptroller of Currency, 1872-1884. Later, President of the National Bank of the Republic, New York City.

Ostrander Smith designed all of the above. The $20 note was engraved by Charles Burt, all others by Geo. F.C. Smillie.

BACK DESIGNS, Third Charter Notes

Back designs of the three issues of Third Charter Notes feature:

- $5   Landing of the Pilgrims.
- $10   Female figure with ships in background.
- $20   Columbia and Capitol in Washington.
- $50   Allegorical Scene. Train and female figure at right. Primitive man reclining at left is a Walter Shirlaw design. Engraved by G.F.C. Smillie.
- $100   American Eagle on Shield, with two male figures.

The back design of all denominations bears a rather lengthy inscription:

"This note is receivable at par in all parts of the United States in payment of all taxes and excises and all other dues to the United States except duties on imports and also for all salaries and other debts and demands owing by the United States to individuals, corporations and associations within the United States except interest on public debt."

NATIONAL BANK NOTES-THIRD CHARTER PERIOD
First Issue — Red Seals
SERIES 1902. RED CHARTER NUMBERS. BLUE SERIAL NUMBERS.
Only three signature combinations.

TYPE 1 FIVE DOLLARS

Issued 1902-1922. Printed in sheets of four $5 notes.

Register	Treasurer	VG	VF	AU	CU	Ch. CU
Lyons	Roberts	250.00	350.00	600.00	800.00	1,200
Lyons	Treat	275.00	385.00	675.00	900.00	1,500
Vernon	Treat	285.00	435.00	775.00	1,100	1,750

Designs on Red Seal notes are the same as Type 3, Blue Seal, Third

TYPE 1 TEN DOLLARS

Issued 1902-1908. Printed in sheets of three $10 and one $20, also four $10 for some banks.

Lyons	Roberts	275.00	350.00	550.00	850.00	1,200
Lyons	Treat	300.00	400.00	585.00	950.00	1,275
Vernon	Treat	340.00	440.00	650.00	1,100	1,350

TYPE 1 TWENTY DOLLARS

Issued 1902-1908. Printed in sheets of three $10 and one $20.

Lyons	Roberts	350.00	600.00	900.00	1,200	1,500
Lyons	Treat	350.00	650.00	1,200	1,350	1,600
Vernon	Treat	350.00	650.00	1,200	1,425	1,750

TYPE 1 FIFTY DOLLARS

Issued 1902-1908. Printed in sheets of three $50 and one $100.

Lyons	Roberts	1,200	1,850	3,000	5,000	—
Lyons	Treat	1,300	2,000	3,600	6,000	—
Vernon	Treat	1,250	1,900	3,300	5,500	—

TYPE 1 ONE HUNDRED DOLLARS

Issued 1902-1908. Printed in sheets of one $100 and three $50.

Lyons	Roberts	1,600	2,400	4,000	6,000	
Lyons	Treat	1,700	2,600	4,750	6,850	
Vernon	Treat	1,800	2,800	5,000	7,500	

The $50 and $100 red seals are very rare in acceptable condition.

See pages 82-83 for suggested valuations for all states.

NATIONAL BANK NOTES-THIRD CHARTER PERIOD
Second Issue
BLUE SEALS — 1902-1908 BACK
TYPE 2 FIVE DOLLARS

Type 2 Back Design. Third Charter, 2nd Issue, 1902-1908.

Issued 1908-1916. Printed in sheets of four $5 notes.

Series 1902. Blue seal right. Blue serial and charter numbers.

Register	Treasurer	VG	VF	AU	CU	Ch. CU
Lyons	Roberts	120.00	150.00	225.00	300.00	400.00
Lyons	Treat	120.00	150.00	225.00	300.00	400.00
Vernon	Treat	120.00	150.00	225.00	300.00	400.00
Vernon	McClung	120.00	150.00	225.00	300.00	400.00
Napier	McClung	120.00	150.00	225.00	300.00	400.00
Napier	Thompson	165.00	225.00	325.00	500.00	600.00
Napier	Burke	125.00	160.00	240.00	320.00	425.00
Parker	Burke	125.00	160.00	240.00	320.00	425.00
Teehee	Burke	225.00	340.00	500.00	800.00	1,200

See pages 82-83 for suggested valuations for all states.

TYPE 2 TEN DOLLARS

Type 2 Back Design. Third Charter. Face Design same as Type 3.

NATIONAL BANK NOTES-THIRD CHARTER PERIOD
TYPE 2 TEN DOLLARS

Issued 1908-1916. Printed in sheets of four $10, also three $10 and one $20.

Series 1902. Blue seal right. Blue serial and charter numbers.

Register	Treasurer	VG	VF	AU	CU	Ch. CU
Lyons	Roberts	135.00	160.00	250.00	350.00	500.00
Lyons	Treat	135.00	160.00	250.00	350.00	500.00
Vernon	Treat	135.00	160.00	250.00	350.00	500.00
Vernon	McClung	135.00	160.00	250.00	350.00	500.00
Napier	McClung	140.00	175.00	275.00	365.00	520.00
Napier	Thompson	160.00	250.00	425.00	475.00	625.00
Napier	Burke	140.00	190.00	335.00	390.00	575.00
Parker	Burke	140.00	190.00	335.00	390.00	575.00
Teehee	Burke	180.00	250.00	475.00	550.00	750.00

TYPE 2 TWENTY DOLLARS

Type 2 Third Charter. Face Design same as Type 3.

Issued 1902-1908. Printed in sheets of one $20 and three $10.

Series 1902. Blue seal right. Blue serial and charter numbers.

Register	Treasurer	VG	VF	AU	CU	Ch. CU
Lyons	Roberts	160.00	200.00	275.00	425.00	500.00
Lyons	Treat	165.00	210.00	290.00	465.00	535.00
Vernon	Treat	160.00	200.00	275.00	425.00	500.00
Vernon	McClung	160.00	200.00	275.00	425.00	500.00
Napier	McClung	165.00	210.00	290.00	465.00	535.00
Napier	Thompson	190.00	240.00	400.00	625.00	675.00
Napier	Burke	190.00	220.00	320.00	500.00	600.00
Parker	Burke	190.00	220.00	320.00	500.00	600.00
Teehee	Burke	220.00	275.00	475.00	750.00	800.00

NATIONAL BANK NOTES-THIRD CHARTER PERIOD
TYPE 2 FIFTY DOLLARS

Issued 1908-1929. Printed in sheets of three $50 and one $100, also a limited number of sheets with one $50 and one $100.

Series 1902. Blue seal right. Blue serial and charter numbers.

Register	Treasurer	VG	VF	AU	CU
Lyons	Roberts	425.00	750.00	1,500	2,000
Lyons	Treat	425.00	750.00	1,500	2,000
Vernon	Treat	425.00	750.00	1,500	2,000
Vernon	McClung	425.00	750.00	1,500	2,000
Napier	McClung	425.00	750.00	1,500	2,000
Napier	Thompson	550.00	825.00	1,650	2,300
Napier	Burke	425.00	750.00	1,500	2,000
Parker	Burke	425.00	750.00	1,500	2,000
Teehee	Burke	585.00	875.00	1,850	2,750

TYPE 2 ONE HUNDRED DOLLARS

Type 2 Back Design. Face Design same as Type 3.

Issued 1908-1929. Printed in sheets of one $100 and three $50 and sheets of one $100 and one $50 in limited number.

Series 1902. Blue seal right. Blue serial and charter numbers.

Register	Treasurer	VG	VF	AU	CU
Lyons	Roberts	600.00	900.00	1,600	2,400
Lyons	Treat	600.00	900.00	1,600	2,400
Vernon	Treat	600.00	900.00	1,600	2,400
Vernon	McClung	600.00	900.00	1,600	2,400
Napier	McClung	600.00	900.00	1,600	2,400
Napier	Thompson	775.00	1,150	2,100	2,750
Napier	Burke	650.00	1,000	1,850	2,500
Parker	Burke	650.00	1,000	1,975	2,500
Teehee	Burke	685.00	1,150	2,350	2,875

NATIONAL BANK NOTES-THIRD CHARTER PERIOD
Third Issue
BLUE SEALS — WITHOUT 1902-1908 ON BACK
TYPE 3 FIVE DOLLARS

Face Design, Type 1, Type 2 and Type 3; Third Charter.

Back Design Type 3, Third Charter

Issued 1916-1929. Printed in sheets of four $5 notes.

Series 1902. Blue seal right. Blue serial and charter numbers.

Register	Treasurer	VG	VF	AU	CU	Ch. CU
Lyons	Roberts	120.00	135.00	220.00	300.00	350.00
Lyons	Treat	120.00	135.00	220.00	300.00	350.00
Vernon	Treat	120.00	135.00	220.00	300.00	350.00
Vernon	McClung	120.00	135.00	220.00	300.00	350.00
Napier	McClung	120.00	135.00	220.00	300.00	350.00
Napier	Thompson	140.00	190.00	325.00	435.00	685.00
Napier	Burke	125.00	145.00	225.00	325.00	400.00
Parker	Burke	125.00	145.00	225.00	325.00	400.00
Teehee	Burke	120.00	135.00	220.00	300.00	350.00
Elliott	Burke	120.00	135.00	220.00	300.00	350.00
Elliott	White	120.00	135.00	220.00	300.00	350.00
Speelman	White	120.00	135.00	220.00	300.00	350.00
Woods	White	125.00	145.00	240.00	400.00	575.00
Woods	Tate	130.00	200.00	275.00	435.00	685.00
Jones	Woods	230.00	275.00	385.00	500.00	800.00

NATIONAL BANK NOTES-THIRD CHARTER PERIOD
TYPE 3 TEN DOLLARS

Face Design Type 1, Type 2 and Type 3, Third Charter.

Back Design, Type 3, Third Charter.

Issued 1916-1929. Printed in sheets of four $10, also three $10 and one $20.

Register	Treasurer	VG	VF	AU	CU	Ch. CU
Lyons	Roberts	135.00	150.00	225.00	350.00	400.00
Lyons	Treat	135.00	150.00	225.00	350.00	400.00
Vernon	Treat	135.00	150.00	225.00	350.00	400.00
Vernon	McClung	135.00	150.00	225.00	350.00	400.00
Napier	McClung	135.00	150.00	225.00	350.00	400.00
Napier	Thompson	160.00	220.00	325.00	475.00	650.00
Napier	Burke	135.00	150.00	225.00	350.00	400.00
Parker	Burke	135.00	150.00	225.00	350.00	400.00
Teehee	Burke	135.00	150.00	225.00	350.00	400.00
Elliott	Burke	135.00	150.00	225.00	350.00	400.00
Elliott	White	135.00	150.00	225.00	350.00	400.00
Speelman	White	135.00	150.00	225.00	350.00	400.00
Woods	White	140.00	180.00	275.00	425.00	525.00
Woods	Tate	160.00	200.00	300.00	465.00	565.00
Jones	Woods	220.00	335.00	650.00	775.00	1,000

Register Edward E. Jones and Treasurer Walter O. Woods did not assume office until Jan. 22, 1929.
Only a few banks received large size National Currency with this signature combination.

Back Design Type 3, Third Charter.

Issued 1916-1929. Printed in sheets of one $20 and three $10.

Register	Treasurer	VG	VF	AU	CU	Ch. CU
Lyons	Roberts	150.00	200.00	275.00	400.00	460.00
Lyons	Treat	150.00	200.00	275.00	400.00	460.00
Vernon	Treat	150.00	200.00	275.00	400.00	460.00
Vernon	McClung	150.00	200.00	275.00	400.00	460.00
Napier	McClung	150.00	200.00	275.00	400.00	460.00
Napier	Thompson	165.00	250.00	475.00	550.00	650.00
Napier	Burke	150.00	200.00	275.00	400.00	460.00
Parker	Burke	150.00	200.00	275.00	400.00	460.00
Teehee	Burke	150.00	200.00	275.00	400.00	460.00
Elliott	Burke	150.00	200.00	275.00	400.00	460.00
Elliott	White	150.00	200.00	275.00	400.00	460.00
Speelman	White	150.00	200.00	275.00	400.00	460.00
Woods	White	175.00	285.00	465.00	575.00	675.00
Woods	Tate	220.00	350.00	625.00	850.00	1,100
Jones	Woods	350.00	575.00	800.00	1,000	1,300

NATIONAL BANK NOTES-THIRD CHARTER PERIOD
TYPE 3 FIFTY DOLLARS

Face Design Type 1, Type 2 and Type 3, Third Charter.

Issued 1916-1929. Printed in sheets of three $50 and one $100.

Register	Treasurer	VG	VF	AU	CU
Lyons	Roberts	425.00	750.00	1,400	1,800
Lyons	Treat	425.00	750.00	1,400	1,800
Vernon	Treat	425.00	750.00	1,400	1,800
Vernon	McClung	425.00	750.00	1,400	1,800
Napier	McClung	425.00	750.00	1,400	1,800
Napier	Thompson	550.00	850.00	1,600	2,000
Napier	Burke	425.00	750.00	1,400	1,800
Parker	Burke	425.00	750.00	1,400	1,800
Teehee	Burke	425.00	750.00	1,400	1,800
Elliott	Burke	425.00	750.00	1,400	1,800
Elliott	White	425.00	750.00	1,400	1,800
Speelman	White	425.00	750.00	1,400	1,800
Woods	White	475.00	850.00	1,550	2,200

NATIONAL BANK NOTES-THIRD CHARTER PERIOD
TYPE 3 ONE HUNDRED DOLLARS

Face Design Type 1, Type 2 and Type 3, Third Charter.

Back Design Type 3, Third Charter.

Issued 1916-1929. Printed in sheets of one $100 and three $50.

Register	Treasurer	VG	VF	AU	CU
Lyons	Roberts	600.00	900.00	1,600	1,800
Lyons	Treat	600.00	900.00	1,600	1,800
Vernon	Treat	600.00	900.00	1,600	1,800
Vernon	McClung	600.00	900.00	1,600	1,800
Napier	McClung	600.00	900.00	1,600	1,800
Napier	Thompson	750.00	1,000	1,750	2,000
Parker	Burke	600.00	900.00	1,600	1,800
Teehee	Burke	600.00	900.00	1,600	1,800
Elliott	Burke	600.00	900.00	1,600	1,800
Elliott	White	600.00	900.00	1,600	1,800
Speelman	White	600.00	900.00	1,600	1,800

Signature combination Woods-White, one note known.
Signature combinations Woods-Tate, if issued, not reported.
Signature combination Jones-Woods, not issued.

NATIONAL GOLD BANK NOTES OF CALIFORNIA
ISSUED 1870-1884 IN DENOMINATIONS OF $5 TO $1000
SERIES 1870-1872 AND 1874, BY NINE CALIFORNIA BANKS

Approximately $3,500,000 was issued in various denominations. About half of the total amount was issued by the National Gold Bank of San Francisco.

Charter	Bank	Charter Date
1741	First National Gold Bank, San Francisco	Nov. 30, 1870
1994	National Gold Bank & Trust Co., San Francisco	June 3, 1872
2014	National Gold Bank of D.O. Mills, Sacramento	July 19, 1872
2077	First National Gold Bank, Stockton	Jan. 27, 1873
2104	First National Gold Bank, Santa Barbara	May 7, 1873
2158	Farmers' National Gold Bank, San Jose	July 21, 1874
2193	First National Gold Bank, Petaluma	Oct. 12, 1874
2248	First National Gold Bank, Oakland	April 10, 1875
2266	Union National Gold Bank, Oakland	May 20, 1875

Although the National Currency Act was enacted in 1863 and over 1700 banks had been organized by 1870, no California bank had been chartered during that period. Hard money was preferred by Californians who did not readily accept National Bank notes of other states or Legal Tender notes then in circulation.

On July 12, 1870, Congress passed an amendment to the Act of 1863 which created the National Gold Banks and authorized them to issue currency redeemable in gold coin, up to 80% of the amount of Bonds deposited with the U.S. Treasurer. The First National Gold Bank of San Francisco became the first bank in California to be chartered as a National Bank or National Gold Bank.

Gold bank notes were issued from 1870 to 1884 in denominations of $5 to $1000 in series 1870, 1872 and 1874. Records of redemption were maintained until October 1914. After that date redemption of Gold Bank notes was not separated from redemption records of other National Currency.

The following table shows the total issue for all National Gold Banks and the number of notes outstanding as of Oct. 31, 1914, after which date no separate record of redemption was maintained.

Denomination	Number Issued	Number Outstanding Oct. 14, 1914
$ 5.00	72,828	3451
10.00	74,649	2481
20.00	38,129	806
50.00	8,097	113
100.00	8,097	84
500.00	685	4
1000.00	75	None

FACE DESIGNS, National Gold Bank Notes

The face designs of this series are the same as those of the First Issue of National Bank Notes. The inscription reads: "Redeemable in Gold Coin. This note is secured by Bonds of the United States deposited with the U.S. Treasurer at Washington." The obligation to pay is by the issuing bank and states that the bank "will pay to the Bearer on Demand...Dollars in Gold Coin."

BACK DESIGNS, National Gold Bank Notes

The back design of this series is very unusual. Printed in black, it features a liberal assortment of Gold Coins with a total face value of $211.00. Shown very prominently is a Double Eagle of 1871. The metallic appearance of the coins was produced by using extremely fine cut lines engraved by James Smillie for the American Bank Note Co. The border design is the same as First Charter notes with a warning against counterfeiting and lengthy legend.

All National Gold Bank Notes are extremely scarce and very seldom found in new condition.

The Kidder National Gold Bank of Boston

Records indicate that the Kidder National Gold Bank of Boston was the first National Gold Bank authorized under the new Act of 1870. Also that this bank received notes of $50, $100, $500 and $1000 denomination, and that these Gold Bank notes were never placed in circulation, the entire issue having been returned for cancellation. This bank was liquidated in 1872.

Included in the listing of notes issued to the Kidder National Gold Bank were 75 $1000 notes. Records show that only 75 notes of the $1000 denomination were issued for all banks authorized to issue these notes backed by gold. It is therefore logical to assume that no Gold Bank notes of $1000 denomination were ever placed in circulation. The Comptroller report of Oct. 31, 1914, shows no $1000 Gold Bank notes outstanding.

Allison-Spinner signatures appear on all issues, except the following:
Scofield-Gilfillan on Series 1875, $10 notes of Stockton and Petaluma.
Scofield-Gilfillan on Series 1875, $20 notes of Oakland.
Bruce-Gilfillan, 1875, $20 and $100, First National Gold Bank, San Francisco.

National Gold Bank Notes

Face Design similar to early issues National Bank Notes.

Back Design, all denominations. California State Seal and Gold Coins.

NATIONAL GOLD BANK NOTES-FIVE DOLLARS

Series	Issuing Bank	Location	Good	VG	Fine
1870	First National Gold Bank	San Francisco	**500.00**	**1,000**	**2,200**
1872	National Gold Bank & Trust Co.	San Francisco	**600.00**	**1,100**	**2,500**
1872	National Gold Bank of D.O. Mills	Sacramento	**550.00**	**1,200**	**2,350**
1873	First National Gold Bank	Stockton	**600.00**	**1,100**	**2,350**
1873	First National Gold Bank	Santa Barbara	**600.00**	**1,100**	**2,350**
1874	Farmers' National Gold Bank	San Jose	**600.00**	**1,100**	**2,350**

This denomination was not issued by the National Gold Banks in Petaluma and Oakland.

TEN DOLLARS

Face Design. Charter Numbers left and right.

Series	Issuing Bank	Location	Good	VG	Fine
1870	First National Gold Bank	San Francisco	**850.00**	**1,800**	**3,200**
1872	National Gold Bank & Trust Co.	San Francisco	**875.00**	**2,200**	**3,800**
1872	National Gold Bank of D.O. Mills	Sacramento	**900.00**	**2,250**	**3,500**
1873	First National Gold Bank	Stockton	**900.00**	**2,300**	**3,650**
1875	First National Gold Bank	Stockton	**950.00**	**2,300**	**3,650**
1873	First National Gold Bank	Santa Barbara	**950.00**	**2,400**	**4,500**
1874	Farmers' National Gold Bank	San Jose	**950.00**	**2,200**	**3,500**
1874	First National Gold Bank	Petaluma	**950.00**	**2,300**	**4,200**
1875	First National Gold Bank	Petaluma	**950.00**	**2,400**	**4,500**
1875	First National Gold Bank	Oakland	**950.00**	**2,400**	**4,500**
1875	Union National Gold Bank	Oakland	**1,000**	**2,600**	**5,250**

National Gold Bank Notes are seldom found in better than Fine condition. Above values should be increased for notes in better condition and decreased if note is only about Good or in Poor or Fair condition.

NATIONAL GOLD BANK NOTES-TWENTY DOLLARS

Face Design. Redeemable in gold coin clause.

Series	Issuing Bank	Location	Good	VG	Fine
1870	First National Gold Bank	San Francisco	2,800	6,000	12,000
1875	First National Gold Bank	San Francisco	2,800	5,000	14,000
1872	National Gold Bank & Trust Co.	San Francisco	None Reported		
1872	National Gold Bank of D.O. Mills	Sacramento	2,500	5,000	14,000
1873	First National Gold Bank	Stockton	2,500	5,000	14,000
1873	First National Gold Bank	Santa Barbara	2,750	6,000	18,500
1874	Farmers' National Gold Bank	San Jose	2,400	5,000	14,000
1875	First National Gold Bank	Petaluma	2,400	5,000	14,000
1875	First National Gold Bank	Oakland	2,600	5,500	15,000
1875	Union National Gold Bank	Oakland	2,600	5,500	15,000

See remarks on page 114 regarding condition and values.

NATIONAL GOLD BANK NOTES-FIFTY DOLLARS

Notes of this denomination were possibly issued by several National Gold Banks, although notes from only two banks are known. Allison-Gilfillan and Bruce-Gilfillan signatures appear on the known issues. Only six notes are known.

Series	Issuing Bank	Location	Good	VG
1870	First National Gold Bank	San Francisco	**10,000**	**20,000**
1874	National Gold Bank	San Jose	**12,000**	**22,000**

ONE HUNDRED DOLLARS

Face Design.
Series Issuing Bank Locations

1870	First National Gold Bank	San Francisco
1875	First National Gold Bank	San Francisco
1873	First National Gold Bank	Santa Barbara
1874	First National Gold Bank	Petaluma
1875	Union National Gold Bank	Oakland

As with the $50 denomination of this series, the $100 notes were possibly issued by National Gold Banks other than the above. A conservative valuation of $9,000 or more is justified for notes of $100 denomination from any issuing bank in this series. Less than ten notes are known to exist.

FIVE HUNDRED DOLLARS

Records indicate that $500 notes were issued by three National Gold Banks: First National Gold Bank and The National Gold & Trust Co. of San Francisco and The National Gold Bank of D.O. Mills, Sacramento.

Four notes have not been redeemed, but to date none have been reported.

FEDERAL RESERVE BANK NOTES, Series 1915 and 1918

Designated as National Currency, on face and back of notes, this series had a very limited issue. Total face value from the twelve Federal Reserve Banks, $1 to $50, amounted to $761,944,000. Of this total issue only $29,068 was reported outstanding on January 30, 1970.

The $50 denomination was issued by St. Louis only. Only 29 of these are known to exist today. See list of known serial numbers on page 123.

$1	1918	Twelve Federal Reserve Banks
$2	1918	Twelve Federal Reserve Banks
$5	1915	Atlanta, Chicago, Kansas City, Dallas, San Francisco
$5	1918	All Federal Reserve Banks, except Richmond
$10	1915	Atlanta, Chicago, Kansas City, Dallas
$10	1918	New York, Chicago, Atlanta, St. Louis
$20	1915	Atlanta, Chicago, Kansas City, Dallas
$20	1918	Atlanta, St. Louis
$50	1918	St. Louis only

The latter is a very scarce note, seldom found in uncirculated condition.

All bear the signature of the United States Treasurer, John Burke, and either Houston B. Teehee or Wm. S. Elliott, as Register of the Treasury. There are also signatures of two Federal Reserve Officers.

FACE DESIGNS, Federal Reserve Bank Notes 1915 and 1918

Presidents of the United States are featured on the left of the face design of these series. The blue seal is prominent on the right. Serial numbers have the prefix letter indicating bank of issue.

$1	George Washington		$10	Andrew Jackson
$2	Thomas Jefferson		$20	Grover Cleveland
$5	Abraham Lincoln		$50	Ulysses Grant

The inscription of the face of the note, 1918 series, reads: "Secured by United States Certificates of indebtedness or United States one-year Gold Notes, deposited with the Treasurer of the United States of America." There is a minor difference in the wording on series 1915.

The obligation to pay is by the issuing bank and reads: "The Federal Reserve Bank of…will pay to the Bearer on Demand (amount)."

BACK DESIGNS, Federal Reserve Bank Notes 1915 and 1918.

$1   The American flag in talons of large flying Eagle, series 1918 only.

$2   American Battleship, series 1918 only.

$5   Columbus in Sight of Land, at left, different from the same scene shown on the $5 First Charter National Currency. At right, the Landing of the Pilgrims as on the $1 First Charter Note, but a different engraving.

$10   Agriculture and Commerce. A reaper drawn by four horses and smoke from factory smokestacks indicate prosperity.

$20   Transportation. Various methods of sea and land travel.

$50   Female figure representing Panama shown between two oceans.

The rather lengthy inscription printed in a panel in the border at bottom of back designs reads: "This note is receivable at par in all parts of the United States in payment of all taxes and excises and all other dues to the United States except duties on imports and also for all salaries and other debts and demands owing by the United States to individuals, corporations and associations within the United States except interest on public debt."

FEDERAL RESERVE BANK NOTES-Series 1915

Act of Dec. 23, 1913, authorized $5, $10 and $20 notes.
Act of April 23, 1918, authorized $1 to $50 notes.

FIVE DOLLARS, SERIES 1915
BLUE SEAL RIGHT, BLUE SERIAL NUMBERS.

Bank	Register	Treasurer	Bank Officers		Fine	VF	Ex. Fine	CU
ATLANTA	Teehee	Burke	Bell	Wellborn	200.00	300.00	400.00	825.00
ATLANTA	Teehee	Burke	Pike	McCord	200.00	300.00	400.00	950.00
CHICAGO	Teehee	Burke	McLallen	McDougal	190.00	275.00	375.00	825.00
KANSAS CITY	Teehee	Burke	Anderson	Miller	190.00	275.00	375.00	825.00
KANSAS CITY	Teehee	Burke	Cross	Miller	190.00	275.00	375.00	825.00
KANSAS CITY	Teehee	Burke	Helm	Miller	200.00	300.00	400.00	825.00
DALLAS	Teehee	Burke	Hoopes	Van Zandt	220.00	335.00	425.00	825.00
DALLAS	Teehee	Burke	Talley	Van Zandt	275.00	400.00	450.00	875.00
SAN FRANCISCO	Teehee	Burke	Clerk	Lynch	200.00	300.00	400.00	825.00

TEN DOLLARS, SERIES 1915
BLUE SEAL RIGHT, BLUE SERIAL NUMBERS.

Bank	Register	Treasurer	Bank Officers		Fine	VF	Ex. Fine	CU
ATLANTA	Teehee	Burke	Bell	Wellborn	900.00	1,250	1,700	2,600
CHICAGO	Teehee	Burke	McLallen	McDougal	800.00	1,000	1,500	2,000
KANSAS CITY	Teehee	Burke	Anderson	Miller	800.00	1,000	1,500	2,000
KANSAS CITY	Teehee	Burke	Cross	Miller	800.00	1,000	1,500	2,000
KANSAS CITY	Teehee	Burke	Helm	Miller	800.00	1,000	1,500	2,000
DALLAS	Teehee	Burke	Hoopes	Van Zandt	800.00	1,000	1,500	2,000
DALLAS	Teehee	Burke	Gilbert	Van Zandt	1,000	1,300	1,700	3,000
DALLAS	Teehee	Burke	Talley	Van Zandt	800.00	1,000	1,500	2,000

TWENTY DOLLARS, SERIES 1915
BLUE SEAL RIGHT, BLUE SERIAL NUMBERS.

Bank	Register	Treasurer	Bank Officers		Fine	VF	Ex. Fine	CU
ATLANTA	Teehee	Burke	Bell	Wellborn	900.00	1,400	1,800	2,800
ATLANTA	Teehee	Burke	Pike	McCord	1,000	1,600	2,000	3,200
CHICAGO	Teehee	Burke	McLallen	McDougal	900.00	1,400	1,800	2,800
KANSAS CITY	Teehee	Burke	Anderson	Miller	900.00	1,400	1,800	2,700
KANSAS CITY	Teehee	Burke	Cross	Miller	900.00	1,400	1,800	2,700
DALLAS	Teehee	Burke	Hoopes	Van Zandt	950.00	1,500	1,900	2,900
DALLAS	Teehee	Burke	Gilbert	Van Zandt	1,000	1,600	2,000	3,000
DALLAS	Teehee	Burke	Talley	Van Zandt	950.00	1,500	1,800	2,800

The signature of M.W. Bell appears as Cashier on one issue of Atlanta notes and as Secretary on a later issue of this same bank. Values are about the same.

ONE DOLLAR, SERIES 1918

Face Design. Issued by all twelve Federal Reserve Banks.

FEDERAL RESERVE BANK NOTES-SERIES 1918
ONE DOLLAR, SERIES 1918

Back Design. American Eagle with Flag.

BLUE SEAL RIGHT, BLUE SERIAL NUMBERS.

Bank	Register	Treasurer	Bank Officers		VF	Ex. Fine	CU	Ch. CU
BOSTON	Teehee	Burke	Bullen	Morss	85.00	120.00	160.00	220.00
BOSTON	Teehee	Burke	Willett	Morss	110.00	165.00	300.00	475.00
BOSTON	Elliott	Burke	Willett	Morss	85.00	130.00	160.00	220.00
NEW YORK	Teehee	Burke	Sailer	Strong	85.00	120.00	160.00	220.00
NEW YORK	Teehee	Burke	Hendricks	Strong	85.00	120.00	160.00	220.00
NEW YORK	Elliott	Burke	Hendricks	Strong	85.00	120.00	160.00	220.00
PHILADELPHIA	Teehee	Burke	Hardt	Passmore	85.00	120.00	160.00	220.00
PHILADELPHIA	Teehee	Burke	Dyer	Passmore	85.00	120.00	160.00	250.00
PHILADELPHIA	Elliott	Burke	Dyer	Passmore	85.00	120.00	200.00	280.00
PHILADELPHIA	Elliott	Burke	Dyer	Norris	85.00	120.00	160.00	220.00
CLEVELAND	Teehee	Burke	Baxter	Fancher	85.00	120.00	160.00	220.00
CLEVELAND	Teehee	Burke	Davis	Fancher	85.00	120.00	170.00	250.00
CLEVELAND	Elliott	Burke	Davis	Fancher	85.00	135.00	160.00	220.00
RICHMOND	Teehee	Burke	Keesee	Seay	90.00	135.00	200.00	280.00
RICHMOND	Elliott	Burke	Keesee	Seay	90.00	135.00	200.00	280.00
ATLANTA	Teehee	Burke	Pike	McCord	90.00	130.00	160.00	220.00
ATLANTA	Teehee	Burke	Bell	McCord	95.00	150.00	220.00	310.00
ATLANTA	Teehee	Burke	Bell	Wellborn	90.00	130.00	160.00	220.00
ATLANTA	Elliott	Burke	Bell	Wellborn	90.00	130.00	160.00	220.00
CHICAGO	Teehee	Burke	McCloud	McDougall	85.00	120.00	160.00	220.00
CHICAGO	Teehee	Burke	Cramer	McDougall	85.00	120.00	160.00	220.00
CHICAGO	Elliott	Burke	Cramer	McDougall	85.00	120.00	160.00	220.00
ST. LOUIS	Teehee	Burke	Attebery	Wells	90.00	150.00	200.00	310.00
ST. LOUIS	Teehee	Burke	Attebery	Biggs	90.00	150.00	200.00	310.00
ST. LOUIS	Elliott	Burke	Attebery	Biggs	90.00	150.00	200.00	310.00
ST. LOUIS	Elliott	Burke	White	Biggs	90.00	165.00	200.00	335.00
MINNEAPOLIS	Teehee	Burke	Cook	Wold	115.00	180.00	275.00	425.00
MINNEAPOLIS	Teehee	Burke	Cook	Young	450.00	600.00	1,200	1,850
MINNEAPOLIS	Elliott	Burke	Cook	Young	115.00	180.00	275.00	450.00
KANSAS CITY	Teehee	Burke	Anderson	Miller	90.00	130.00	160.00	250.00
KANSAS CITY	Elliott	Burke	Anderson	Miller	90.00	135.00	200.00	280.00
KANSAS CITY	Elliott	Burke	Helm	Miller	90.00	130.00	160.00	250.00
DALLAS	Teehee	Burke	Talley	Van Zandt	90.00	130.00	160.00	250.00
DALLAS	Elliott	Burke	Talley	Van Zandt	175.00	300.00	400.00	650.00
DALLAS	Elliott	Burke	Lawder	Van Zandt	90.00	135.00	200.00	280.00
SAN FRANCISCO	Teehee	Burke	Clerk	Lynch	85.00	120.00	160.00	220.00
SAN FRANCISCO	Teehee	Burke	Clerk	Calkins	85.00	120.00	160.00	220.00
SAN FRANCISCO	Elliott	Burke	Clerk	Calkins	85.00	120.00	160.00	220.00
SAN FRANCISCO	Elliott	Burke	Ambrose	Calkins	85.00	120.00	160.00	220.00

★ *Star replacement notes for this series are valued at approximately double these prices.*

FEDERAL RESERVE BANK NOTES-SERIES 1918

TWO DOLLARS, SERIES 1918

Face Design. Issued by all twelve Federal Reserve Banks.

Back Design. World War I Battleship.

BLUE SEAL RIGHT. BLUE SERIAL NUMBERS.

Bank	Register	Treasurer	Bank Officers		VF	Ex. Fine	CU	Ch. CU
BOSTON	Teehee	Burke	Bullen	Morss	375.00	475.00	950.00	1,200
BOSTON	Teehee	Burke	Willett	Morss	470.00	600.00	1,100	1,600
BOSTON	Elliott	Burke	Willett	Morss	440.00	550.00	1,050	1,500
NEW YORK	Teehee	Burke	Sailer	Strong	375.00	475.00	1,000	1,350
NEW YORK	Teehee	Burke	Hendricks	Strong	375.00	475.00	1.000	1,350
NEW YORK	Elliott	Burke	Hendricks	Strong	375.00	475.00	1,000	1,350
PHILADELPHIA	Teehee	Burke	Hardt	Passmore	375.00	475.00	1,000	1,350
PHILADELPHIA	Teehee	Burke	Dyer	Passmore	375.00	475.00	1,000	1,350
PHILADELPHIA	Elliott	Burke	Dyer	Passmore	425.00	600.00	1,050	1,350
PHILADELPHIA	Elliott	Burke	Dyer	Norris	375.00	475.00	950.00	1,200
CLEVELAND	Teehee	Burke	Baxter	Fancher	375.00	525.00	1,000	1,250
CLEVELAND	Teehee	Burke	Davis	Fancher	375.00	550.00	1,025	1,300
CLEVELAND	Elliott	Burke	Davis	Fancher	375.00	525.00	950.00	1,200
RICHMOND	Teehee	Burke	Keesee	Seay	425.00	650.00	1,075	1,500
RICHMOND	Elliott	Burke	Keesee	Seay	425.00	600.00	1,050	1,350
ATLANTA	Teehee	Burke	Pike	McCord	385.00	550.00	1,000	1,325
ATLANTA	Teehee	Burke	Bell	McCord	450.00	680.00	1,100	1,600
ATLANTA	Elliott	Burke	Bell	Wellborn	425.00	600.00	1,050	1,350
CHICAGO	Teehee	Burke	McCloud	McDougall	375.00	475.00	950.00	1,200
CHICAGO	Teehee	Burke	Cramer	McDougall	375.00	475.00	950.00	1,200
CHICAGO	Elliott	Burke	Cramer	McDougall	375.00	475.00	950.00	1,200

FEDERAL RESERVE BANK NOTES-SERIES 1918

TWO DOLLARS, SERIES 1918

Bank	Register	Treasurer	Bank Officers		VF	Ex. Fine	CU	Ch. CU
ST. LOUIS	Teehee	Burke	Attebery	Wells	470.00	650.00	1,050	1,350
ST. LOUIS	Teehee	Burke	Attebery	Biggs	470.00	650.00	1,050	1,350
ST. LOUIS	Elliott	Burke	Attebery	Biggs	470.00	650.00	1,050	1,500
ST. LOUIS	Elliott	Burke	White	Biggs	500.00	550.00	1,300	1,700
MINNEAPOLIS	Teehee	Burke	Cook	Wold	470.00	650.00	1,100	1,500
MINNEAPOLIS	Elliott	Burke	Cook	Young	470.00	650.00	1,100	1,500
KANSAS CITY	Teehee	Burke	Anderson	Miller	470.00	650.00	1,050	1,450
KANSAS CITY	Elliott	Burke	Helm	Miller	470.00	650.00	1,050	1,450
DALLAS	Teehee	Burke	Talley	Van Zandt	470.00	650.00	1,050	1,450
DALLAS	Elliott	Burke	Talley	Van Zandt	470.00	650.00	1,050	1,450
SAN FRANCISCO	Teehee	Burke	Clerk	Lynch	470.00	650.00	1,025	1,350
SAN FRANCISCO	Elliott	Burke	Clerk	Calkins	470.00	650.00	1,025	1,350
SAN FRANCISCO	Elliott	Burke	Ambrose	Calkins	470.00	650.00	1,025	1,350

★ *Star replacement notes for this series are valued at approximately three times these prices.*

FIVE DOLLARS, SERIES 1918

Face Design Series 1915 and 1918 Issued all Districts, except Richmond.

BLUE SEAL RIGHT. BLUE SERIAL NUMBERS.

Bank	Register	Treasurer	Bank Officers		VF	Ex. Fine	CU	Ch. CU
BOSTON	Teehee	Burke	Bullen	Morss	1,000	1,300	2,600	3,500
NEW YORK	Teehee	Burke	Hendricks	Strong	275.00	400.00	825.00	1,000
PHILADELPHIA	Teehee	Burke	Hardt	Passmore	275.00	400.00	825.00	1,000
PHILADELPHIA	Teehee	Burke	Dyer	Passmore	275.00	400.00	825.00	1,000
CLEVELAND	Teehee	Burke	Baxter	Fancher	275.00	400.00	825.00	1,000
CLEVELAND	Teehee	Burke	Davis	Fancher	275.00	400.00	825.00	1,000
CLEVELAND	Elliott	Burke	Davis	Fancher	275.00	400.00	825.00	1,000
ATLANTA	Teehee	Burke	Pike	McCord	285.00	410.00	850.00	1,050
ATLANTA	Teehee	Burke	Bell	Wellborn	275.00	400.00	825.00	1,000
ATLANTA	Elliott	Burke	Bell	Wellborn	275.00	400.00	825.00	1,000
CHICAGO	Teehee	Burke	McLallen	McDougall	375.00	750.00	1,350	1,600
CHICAGO	Teehee	Burke	McCloud	McDougall	275.00	400.00	825.00	1,000
CHICAGO	Teehee	Burke	Cramer	McDougall	275.00	400.00	825.00	1,000
ST. LOUIS	Teehee	Burke	Attebery	Wells	320.00	450.00	950.00	1,100
ST. LOUIS	Teehee	Burke	Attebery	Biggs	320.00	450.00	950.00	1,100
ST. LOUIS	Elliott	Burke	White	Biggs	320.00	450.00	950.00	1,100
MINNEAPOLIS	Teehee	Burke	Cook	Wold	335.00	650.00	1,100	1,350
KANSAS CITY	Teehee	Burke	Anderson	Miller	320.00	425.00	950.00	1,100
KANSAS CITY	Elliott	Burke	Helm	Miller	320.00	425.00	950.00	1,100
DALLAS	Teehee	Burke	Talley	Van Zandt	320.00	425.00	1,000	1,150
SAN FRANCISCO	Teehee	Burke	Clerk	Lynch	325.00	750.00	1,100	1,200

Most San Francisco notes are dated May 20, 1914. One issue dated May 18, 1914 is scarce.

★ *Star replacement notes in this series are all very rare.*

FEDERAL RESERVE BANK NOTES-SERIES 1918

TEN DOLLARS, SERIES 1918

Face Design, Series date 1915 or 1918 upper right and left border.

BLUE SEAL RIGHT. BLUE SERIAL NUMBERS.

Bank	Register	Treasurer	Bank Officers		VF	Ex. Fine	CU
NEW YORK	Teehee	Burke	Hendricks	Strong	1,200	1,500	2,200
ATLANTA	Elliott	Burke	Bell	Wellborn	1,200	1,500	2,200
CHICAGO	Teehee	Burke	McLallen	McDougall	1,750	2,250	3,000
CHICAGO	Teehee	Burke	McCloud	McDougall	1,200	1,500	2,200
ST. LOUIS	Teehee	Burke	Attebery	Wells	1,350	1,650	2,350

★ *Star replacement notes in this series are all extremely rare.*

Boston, Philadelphia, Cleveland, Richmond, Minneapolis and San Francisco did not issue notes of $10 denomination. Kansas City and Dallas issued this denomination in series 1915 only. See 1915 listing on page 118.

TWENTY DOLLARS, SERIES 1918

BLUE SEAL RIGHT. BLUE SERIAL NUMBERS.

Bank	Register	Treasurer	Bank Officers		VF	Ex. Fine	CU
ATLANTA	Elliott	Burke	Bell	Wellborn	1,400	1,800	3,000
ST. LOUIS	Teehee	Burke	Attebery	Wells	1,500	1,950	3,350

★ *Star replacement notes of this denomination are unknown.*

Boston, New York, Philadelphia, Cleveland, Richmond, Minneapolis and San Francisco did not issue notes of $20 denomination. Kansas City and Dallas issued this denomination in series 1915 only. See page 118.

Face Design, issued by St. Louis bank only.

FEDERAL RESERVE BANK NOTES-SERIES 1918
FIFTY DOLLARS. SERIES 1918

Bank	Register	Treasurer	Bank Officers		VG	Fine	VF	Ex. Fine	CU
ST. LOUIS	Teehee	Burke	Attebery	Wells	2,400	4,500	6,250	8,750	12,500

The following serial numbers have been reported with condition ranging from very good to strictly uncirculated. Known existence of other serial numbers and condition will be appreciated.

103	122	608	682	774	3213
110	138	649	683	821	3299
115	151	656	689	898	3402
117	153	671	741	2128	3800
118	168	674	751	2923	

4,000 $50 St. Louis Federal Reserve Bank Notes were reportedly issued.

FEDERAL RESERVE NOTES, Series 1914 and 1918
Federal Reserve Act, Dec. 23, 1913
Series 1914, Red Seals, $5 to $100 Scarce

Signatures: John Burke, Treasurer of the United States; Wm. G. McAdoo, Secretary of the Treasury.

Blue Seals Series 1914 $5 to $100 and Series 1918 $500 to $10,000

Blue Seal signatures: John Burke-Wm. G. McAdoo; Burke-Carter Glass; Burke-D.F. Jouston; Frank White-A.W. Mellon.

There are three types of Blue seal notes with White-Mellon signatures.

Type One: District numeral and letter, rather large, lower left and upper right. Most common of the three types.

Type Two: Smaller letters and numerals at lower left, larger letters and numerals at upper right same as Type One.

Type Three: Larger numerals and letters, slightly to the left and higher. Seals closer to center of note. Scarcest of the three types.

Unlike the Federal Reserve *Bank* Notes, the obligation to pay is by the United States and reads: "The United States of America will pay the Bearer on Demand (amount)...Dollars."

FACE DESIGNS, Series 1914 — Red and Blue Seals

Portraits of presidents as on Federal Reserve Bank notes are featured in center oval on denominations $5 to $50. The $100 note has a portrait of Benjamin Franklin. The seal with number and letter of issuing bank is at left. Treasury seal is at right.

FACE DESIGNS, Series 1918 — all with Blue Seals

$500	John Marshall, Secretary of State and Jurist.
$1000	Alexander Hamilton, first Secretary of the Treasury.
$5000	James Madison, fourth President of the United States.
$10,000	Salmon P. Chase, Secretary of Treasury under Lincoln.

BACK DESIGNS, Series 1914 and 1918 — Red and Blue Seals

Series 1914 $5 to $50 have the same overall back designs as the Federal Reserve Bank notes with the designation National Currency removed. The back design of the $100 notes features five allegorical figures.

FEDERAL RESERVE NOTES

BACK DESIGNS, Series 1918 — Blue Seals

$500 "DeSoto Discovering the Mississippi 1541" as on the $10 First Charter, National Currency note.

$1000 American Eagle with Flag. A beautiful design.

$5000 "Washington Resigning his Commission" as on the $1000 First Charter note.

$10,000 "Embarkation of the Pilgrims" as on the $50 First Charter note.

The lengthy inscription in the lower border of the back design differs from that on the Federal Reserve *Bank* Notes. It stipulates that the note is payable in gold, and reads:

"This note is receivable by all national and member banks and the Federal Reserve Banks, and for all taxes, customs and other public dues. It is redeemable in gold on demand at the Treasury Department of the United States in the city of Washington, District of Columbia, or in gold or lawful money at any Federal Reserve Bank."

FEDERAL RESERVE NOTES, Series 1914 — Red Seals

Face and back designs the same as Blue Seal Federal Reserve Notes
All with signature combination Treasurer John Burke. Secretary Wm. G. McAdoo.

ALL WITH RED SEALS
FIVE DOLLARS

Bank	Fine	VF	Ex. Fine	AU	CU	Ch. CU
BOSTON	275.00	400.00	600.00	850.00	1,400	1,850
NEW YORK	275.00	400.00	600.00	850.00	1,400	1,850
PHILADELPHIA	275.00	400.00	600.00	850.00	1,400	1,850
CLEVELAND	275.00	400.00	600.00	850.00	1,400	1,850
RICHMOND	275.00	400.00	600.00	850.00	1,400	1,850
ATLANTA	275.00	400.00	600.00	850.00	1,400	1,850
CHICAGO	275.00	400.00	600.00	850.00	1,400	1,850
ST. LOUIS	275.00	400.00	600.00	850.00	1,400	1,850
MINNEAPOLIS	275.00	400.00	600.00	850.00	1,400	1,850
KANSAS CITY	275.00	400.00	600.00	850.00	1,400	1,850
DALLAS	275.00	400.00	600.00	850.00	1,400	1,850
SAN FRANCISCO	300.00	450.00	650.00	950.00	1,500	2,000

TEN DOLLARS

Bank	Fine	VF	Ex. Fine	AU	CU	Ch. CU
BOSTON	285.00	475.00	650.00	950.00	1,500	2,000
NEW YORK	285.00	475.00	650.00	950.00	1,450	2,000
PHILADELPHIA	285.00	475.00	650.00	950.00	1,450	1,900
CLEVELAND	285.00	475.00	650.00	950.00	1,450	1,900
RICHMOND	285.00	475.00	650.00	950.00	1,450	1,900
ATLANTA	285.00	475.00	650.00	950.00	1,450	1,900
CHICAGO	285.00	475.00	650.00	950.00	1,450	1,900
ST. LOUIS	285.00	475.00	650.00	950.00	1,450	1,900
MINNEAPOLIS	285.00	475.00	650.00	950.00	1,450	1.950
KANSAS CITY	285.00	475.00	650.00	950.00	1,450	1,900
DALLAS	290.00	485.00	675.00	1,000	1,500	2,200
SAN FRANCISCO	290.00	485.00	675.00	1,000	1,500	2,200

FEDERAL RESERVE NOTES, Red Seals

It would require a little patience and time to acquire a complete set of 12 Banks in any one denomination. Catalog values do not indicate the actual scarcity of **Red Seal Federal Reserve Notes** issued for a period of about one year, 1914-1915.

TWENTY DOLLARS

Bank	Fine	VF	Ex. Fine	AU	CU	Ch. CU
BOSTON	450.00	650.00	1,000	1,250	1,800	2,800
NEW YORK	450.00	650.00	1,000	1,250	1,800	2,800
PHILADELPHIA	450.00	650.00	1,000	1,250	1,800	2,800
CLEVELAND	450.00	650.00	1,000	1,250	1,800	2,800
RICHMOND	450.00	650.00	1,000	1,250	1,800	2,800
ATLANTA	465.00	675.00	1,050	1,300	1,850	3,000
CHICAGO	450.00	650.00	1,000	1,250	1,800	2,800
ST. LOUIS	465.00	675.00	1,050	1,300	1,850	3,000
MINNEAPOLIS	465.00	675.00	1,050	1,300	1,850	3,000
KANSAS CITY	465.00	675.00	1,050	1,300	1,850	3,000
DALLAS	465.00	675.00	1,050	1,300	1,850	3,000
SAN FRANCISCO	450.00	650.00	1,000	1,250	1,800	2,800

FIFTY DOLLARS

Bank	Fine	VF	Ex. Fine	AU	CU	Ch. CU
BOSTON	1,000	1,400	2,000	3,000	3,850	4,750
NEW YORK	1,000	1,400	2,000	3,000	3,850	4,750
PHILADELPHIA	1,000	1,400	2,000	3,000	3,850	4,750
CLEVELAND	1,000	1,400	2,000	3,000	3,850	4,750
RICHMOND	1,000	1,400	2,000	3,000	3,850	4,750
ATLANTA	1,050	1,450	2,100	3,100	3,900	5,000
CHICAGO	1,000	1,400	2,000	3,000	3,850	4.750
ST. LOUIS	1,050	1,450	2,100	3,100	3,900	5,000
MINNEAPOLIS	1,050	1,450	2,100	3,100	3,900	5,000
KANSAS CITY	1,050	1,450	2,100	3,100	3,900	5,000
DALLAS	1,050	1,450	2,100	3,100	3,900	5,000
SAN FRANCISCO	1,000	1,400	2,000	3,000	3,850	4,750

ONE HUNDRED DOLLARS

Bank	Fine	VF	Ex. Fine	AU	CU	Ch. CU
BOSTON	1,200	1,650	2,750	3,500	4,000	5,750
NEW YORK	1,200	1,650	2,750	3,500	4,000	5,750
PHILADELPHIA	1,200	1,650	2,750	3,500	4,000	5,750
CLEVELAND	1,200	1,650	2,750	3,500	4,000	5,750
RICHMOND	1,200	1,650	2,750	3,500	4,000	5,750
ATLANTA	1,250	1,700	2,900	3,700	4,200	6,000
CHICAGO	1,200	1,650	2,750	3,500	4,000	5,750
ST. LOUIS	1,250	1,700	2,900	3,700	4,200	6,000
MINNEAPOLIS	1,250	1,700	2,900	3,700	4,200	6,000
KANSAS CITY	1,250	1,700	2,900	3,700	4,200	6,000
DALLAS	1,250	1,700	2,900	3,700	4,200	6,000
SAN FRANCISCO	1,200	1,650	2,750	3,500	4,000	5,750

FEDERAL RESERVE NOTES, Blue Seals

Face Design. Back Designs same as Federal Reserve Bank Notes.

The designation "NATIONAL CURRENCY" has been removed from face and back.

BLUE SEALS AND SERIAL NUMBERS

Four signature combinations issued by each of the 12 Federal Reserve Banks

FIVE DOLLARS

Bank	Treasurer	Secretary	VF	Ex. Fine	CU	Ch. CU
BOSTON	Burke	McAdoo	65.00	77.00	105.00	165.00
BOSTON	Burke	Glass	75.00	85.00	125.00	210.00
BOSTON	Burke	Houston	65.00	77.00	105.00	165.00
BOSTON	White	Mellon Type One	60.00	75.00	100.00	160.00
BOSTON	White	Mellon Type Two	70.00	80.00	110.00	180.00

See Text describing three types of notes with White-Mellon signatures.

Bank	Treasurer	Secretary	VF	Ex. Fine	CU	Ch. CU
NEW YORK	Burke	McAdoo	65.00	77.00	105.00	160.00
NEW YORK	Burke	Glass	72.00	80.00	120.00	180.00
NEW YORK	Burke	Houston	65.00	77.00	105.00	160.00
NEW YORK	White	Mellon Type One	60.00	75.00	100.00	155.00
NEW YORK	White	Mellon Type Two	70.00	80.00	110.00	170.00
NEW YORK	White	Mellon Type Three	70.00	85.00	115.00	180.00
PHILADELPHIA	Burke	McAdoo	60.00	77.00	105.00	160.00
PHILADELPHIA	Burke	Glass	75.00	85.00	120.00	185.00
PHILADELPHIA	Burke	Houston	65.00	77.00	105.00	160.00
PHILADELPHIA	White	Mellon Type One	60.00	75.00	100.00	155.00
PHILADELPHIA	White	Mellon Type Two	70.00	80.00	110.00	170.00
PHILADELPHIA	White	Mellon Type Three	70.00	85.00	115.00	180.00
CLEVELAND	Burke	McAdoo	65.00	80.00	110.00	165.00
CLEVELAND	Burke	Glass	80.00	90.00	125.00	195.00
CLEVELAND	Burke	Houston	65.00	80.00	110.00	160.00
CLEVELAND	White	Mellon Type One	60.00	76.00	105.00	155.00
CLEVELAND	White	Mellon Type Two	70.00	85.00	115.00	175.00
CLEVELAND	White	Mellon Type Three	75.00	90.00	120.00	185.00
RICHMOND	Burke	McAdoo	70.00	85.00	115.00	165.00
RICHMOND	Burke	Glass	80.00	95.00	135.00	205.00
RICHMOND	Burke	Houston	70.00	85.00	115.00	165.00
RICHMOND	White	Mellon Type One	65.00	80.00	110.00	160.00
RICHMOND	White	Mellon Type Two	72.00	85.00	120.00	180.00

FEDERAL RESERVE NOTES, Blue Seals
$5 Federal Reserve Notes, Blue Seals Continued

Bank	Treasurer	Secretary	VF	Ex. Fine	CU	Ch. CU
ATLANTA	Burke	McAdoo	70.00	85.00	115.00	170.00
ATLANTA	Burke	Glass	85.00	100.00	150.00	205.00
ATLANTA	Burke	Houston	70.00	85.00	115.00	175.00
ATLANTA	White	Mellon Type One	70.00	82.00	110.00	170.00
CHICAGO	Burke	McAdoo	65.00	77.00	105.00	160.00
CHICAGO	Burke	Glass	72.00	80.00	120.00	180.00
CHICAGO	Burke	Houston	65.00	77.00	105.00	160.00
CHICAGO	White	Mellon Type One	60.00	75.00	100.00	155.00
CHICAGO	White	Mellon Type Two	70.00	80.00	110.00	170.00
CHICAGO	White	Mellon Type Three	70.00	85.00	115.00	180.00
ST. LOUIS	Burke	McAdoo	70.00	85.00	115.00	175.00
ST. LOUIS	Burke	Glass	85.00	100.00	150.00	205.00
ST. LOUIS	Burke	Houston	70.00	85.00	115.00	175.00
ST. LOUIS	White	Mellon Type One	70.00	82.00	110.00	165.00
ST. LOUIS	White	Mellon Type Two	75.00	90.00	120.00	170.00
MINNEAPOLIS	Burke	McAdoo	70.00	85.00	120.00	180.00
MINNEAPOLIS	Burke	Glass	85.00	100.00	160.00	220.00
MINNEAPOLIS	Burke	Houston	70.00	85.00	120.00	180.00
MINNEAPOLIS	White	Mellon Type One	70.00	82.00	115.00	170.00
KANSAS CITY	Burke	McAdoo	70.00	85.00	120.00	175.00
KANSAS CITY	Burke	Glass	85.00	100.00	140.00	205.00
KANSAS CITY	Burke	Houston	70.00	85.00	120.00	175.00
KANSAS CITY	White	Mellon Type One	70.00	85.00	115.00	170.00
KANSAS CITY	White	Mellon Type Two	75.00	90.00	125.00	180.00
DALLAS	Burke	McAdoo	70.00	85.00	115.00	170.00
DALLAS	Burke	Glass	85.00	100.00	150.00	220.00
DALLAS	Burke	Houston	70.00	85.00	115.00	180.00
DALLAS	White	Mellon Type One	70.00	85.00	110.00	170.00
DALLAS	White	Mellon Type Two	75.00	90.00	140.00	195.00
SAN FRANCISCO	Burke	McAdoo	70.00	80.00	110.00	170.00
SAN FRANCISCO	Burke	Glass	75.00	90.00	150.00	220.00
SAN FRANCISCO	Burke	Houston	70.00	80.00	110.00	170.00
SAN FRANCISCO	White	Mellon Type One	70.00	80.00	110.00	170.00
SAN FRANCISCO	White	Mellon Type Two	75.00	85.00	115.00	180.00
SAN FRANCISCO	White	Mellon Type Three	75.00	90.00	125.00	190.00

★ *Star replacement notes for this series are valued at approximately three times these prices.*

FEDERAL RESERVE NOTES, Blue Seals

TEN DOLLARS
BLUE SEALS AND SERIAL NUMBERS

Face Design. Andrew Jackson, 7th President of the United States

Back Design. Agriculture and Commerce.

Bank	Treasurer	Secretary	VF	Ex. Fine	CU	Ch. CU
BOSTON	Burke	McAdoo	55.00	65.00	110.00	185.00
BOSTON	Burke	Glass	65.00	75.00	130.00	200.00
BOSTON	Burke	Houston	55.00	65.00	110.00	185.00
BOSTON	White	Mellon Type One	55.00	65.00	110.00	175.00
BOSTON	White	Mellon Type Two	60.00	70.00	120.00	190.00
NEW YORK	Burke	McAdoo	55.00	65.00	110.00	185.00
NEW YORK	Burke	Glass	65.00	75.00	130.00	200.00
NEW YORK	Burke	Houston	55.00	65.00	110.00	185.00
NEW YORK	White	Mellon Type One	55.00	65.00	110.00	175.00
NEW YORK	White	Mellon Type Two	60.00	70.00	120.00	190.00
NEW YORK	White	Mellon Type Three	65.00	75.00	130.00	200.00
PHILADELPHIA	Burke	McAdoo	55.00	65.00	110.00	185.00
PHILADELPHIA	Burke	Glass	65.00	75.00	130.00	200.00
PHILADELPHIA	Burke	Houston	55.00	65.00	110.00	185.00
PHILADELPHIA	White	Mellon Type One	55.00	65.00	110.00	175.00
PHILADELPHIA	White	Mellon Type Three	65.00	75.00	130.00	200.00

FEDERAL RESERVE NOTES, Blue Seals
$10 Federal Reserve Notes, Blue Seals Continued

Bank	Treasurer	Secretary	VF	Ex. Fine	CU	Ch. CU
CLEVELAND	Burke	McAdoo	55.00	65.00	110.00	185.00
CLEVELAND	Burke	Glass	65.00	75.00	130.00	210.00
CLEVELAND	Burke	Houston	55.00	65.00	110.00	185.00
CLEVELAND	White	Mellon Type One	55.00	65.00	110.00	175.00
CLEVELAND	White	Mellon Type Two	60.00	60.00	120.00	190.00
CLEVELAND	White	Mellon Type Three	65.00	75.00	130.00	210.00
RICHMOND	Burke	McAdoo	55.00	65.00	110.00	185.00
RICHMOND	Burke	Glass	65.00	75.00	135.00	210.00
RICHMOND	Burke	Houston	55.00	65.00	110.00	185.00
RICHMOND	White	Mellon Type One	55.00	65.00	110.00	175.00
ATLANTA	Burke	McAdoo	60.00	60.00	120.00	190.00
ATLANTA	Burke	Glass	70.00	80.00	140.00	220.00
ATLANTA	Burke	Houston	60.00	60.00	120.00	190.00
ATLANTA	White	Mellon Type One	55.00	65.00	110.00	190.00
ATLANTA	White	Mellon Type Two	65.00	75.00	125.00	220.00
CHICAGO	Burke	McAdoo	55.00	65.00	110.00	185.00
CHICAGO	Burke	Glass	65.00	75.00	130.00	210.00
CHICAGO	Burke	Houston	55.00	65.00	110.00	185.00
CHICAGO	White	Mellon Type One	55.00	65.00	110.00	175.00
CHICAGO	White	Mellon Type Two	60.00	60.00	120.00	185.00
CHICAGO	White	Mellon Type Three	65.00	75.00	140.00	210.00
ST. LOUIS	Burke	McAdoo	60.00	60.00	120.00	190.00
ST. LOUIS	Burke	Glass	75.00	80.00	140.00	220.00
ST. LOUIS	Burke	Houston	60.00	60.00	120.00	190.00
ST. LOUIS	White	Mellon Type One	55.00	65.00	110.00	185.00
MINNEAPOLIS	Burke	McAdoo	60.00	60.00	120.00	190.00
MINNEAPOLIS	Burke	Glass	70.00	85.00	160.00	230.00
MINNEAPOLIS	Burke	Houston	60.00	75.00	125.00	210.00
MINNEAPOLIS	White	Mellon Type One	60.00	60.00	120.00	190.00
KANSAS CITY	Burke	McAdoo	60.00	75.00	125.00	210.00
KANSAS CITY	Burke	Glass	70.00	85.00	160.00	230.00
KANSAS CITY	Burke	Houston	60.00	75.00	125.00	200.00
KANSAS CITY	White	Mellon Type One	60.00	60.00	120.00	190.00
DALLAS	Burke	McAdoo	60.00	75.00	125.00	210.00
DALLAS	Burke	Glass	70.00	85.00	150.00	230.00
DALLAS	Burke	Houston	60.00	75.00	125.00	200.00
DALLAS	White	Mellon Type One	60.00	60.00	120.00	190.00
SAN FRANCISCO	Burke	McAdoo	55.00	65.00	110.00	185.00
SAN FRANCISCO	Burke	Glass	60.00	80.00	140.00	220.00
SAN FRANCISCO	Burke	Houston	55.00	60.00	120.00	190.00
SAN FRANCISCO	White	Mellon Type One	55.00	65.00	110.00	185.00
SAN FRANCISCO	White	Mellon Type Two	60.00	60.00	125.00	210.00
SAN FRANCISCO	White	Mellon Type Three	65.00	75.00	135.00	225.00

★ *Star replacement notes for this series are valued at approximately three times these prices.*

FEDERAL RESERVE NOTES, Blue Seals

TWENTY DOLLARS
BLUE SEALS AND SERIAL NUMBERS

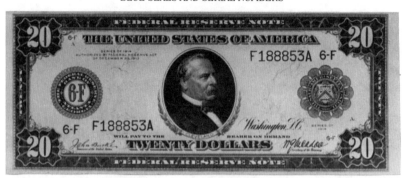

Face Design. Stephen Grover Cleveland.

Back Design. Various means of transportation.

Bank	Treasurer	Secretary	VF	Ex. Fine	CU	Ch. CU
BOSTON	Burke	McAdoo	85.00	100.00	160.00	275.00
BOSTON	Burke	Glass	95.00	120.00	175.00	300.00
BOSTON	Burke	Houston	85.00	100.00	160.00	275.00
BOSTON	White	Mellon Type One	80.00	95.00	150.00	275.00
NEW YORK	Burke	McAdoo	80.00	100.00	160.00	275.00
NEW YORK	Burke	Glass	90.00	120.00	170.00	300.00
NEW YORK	Burke	Houston	85.00	100.00	160.00	275.00
NEW YORK	White	Mellon Type One	75.00	95.00	150.00	265.00
NEW YORK	White	Mellon Type Two	85.00	110.00	160.00	280.00
PHILADELPHIA	Burke	McAdoo	85.00	100.00	160.00	275.00
PHILADELPHIA	Burke	Glass	90.00	120.00	175.00	290.00
PHILADELPHIA	Burke	Houston	80.00	100.00	160.00	275.00
PHILADELPHIA	White	Mellon Type One	75.00	95.00	150.00	270.00
CLEVELAND	Burke	McAdoo	85.00	100.00	160.00	275.00
CLEVELAND	Burke	Glass	90.00	120.00	175.00	300.00
CLEVELAND	Burke	Houston	80.00	100.00	160.00	275.00
CLEVELAND	White	Mellon Type One	75.00	95.00	150.00	270.00
CLEVELAND	White	Mellon Type Two	85.00	110.00	160.00	280.00

FEDERAL RESERVE NOTES, Blue Seals
$20 Federal Reserve Notes, Blue Seals Continued

Bank	Treasurer	Secretary	VF	Ex. Fine	CU	Ch. CU
RICHMOND	Burke	McAdoo	85.00	110.00	165.00	275.00
RICHMOND	Burke	Glass	95.00	120.00	185.00	300.00
RICHMOND	Burke	Houston	85.00	105.00	165.00	275.00
RICHMOND	White	Mellon Type One	80.00	100.00	160.00	275.00
ATLANTA	Burke	McAdoo	90.00	115.00	170.00	300.00
ATLANTA	Burke	Glass	100.00	130.00	200.00	325.00
ATLANTA	Burke	Houston	90.00	115.00	170.00	300.00
ATLANTA	White	Mellon Type One	85.00	105.00	165.00	275.00
CHICAGO	Burke	McAdoo	80.00	105.00	160.00	280.00
CHICAGO	Burke	Glass	90.00	120.00	170.00	300.00
CHICAGO	Burke	Houston	80.00	105.00	160.00	275.00
CHICAGO	White	Mellon Type One	75.00	100.00	150.00	265.00
CHICAGO	White	Mellon Type Two	85.00	110.00	160.00	275.00
CHICAGO	White	Mellon Type Three	95.00	120.00	170.00	300.00
ST. LOUIS	Burke	McAdoo	90.00	115.00	170.00	300.00
ST. LOUIS	Burke	Glass	100.00	130.00	200.00	325.00
ST. LOUIS	Burke	Houston	90.00	115.00	170.00	300.00
ST. LOUIS	White	Mellon Type One	85.00	110.00	165.00	275.00
MINNEAPOLIS	Burke	McAdoo	90.00	120.00	175.00	300.00
MINNEAPOLIS	Burke	Glass	100.00	140.00	210.00	325.00
MINNEAPOLIS	Burke	Houston	90.00	120.00	175.00	300.00
MINNEAPOLIS	White	Mellon Type One	85.00	115.00	170.00	275.00
KANSAS CITY	Burke	McAdoo	90.00	120.00	175.00	300.00
KANSAS CITY	Burke	Glass	100.00	140.00	210.00	325.00
KANSAS CITY	Burke	Houston	90.00	120.00	175.00	300.00
KANSAS CITY	White	Mellon Type One	85.00	115.00	170.00	275.00
KANSAS CITY	White	Mellon Type Two	95.00	125.00	180.00	300.00
DALLAS	Burke	McAdoo	90.00	120.00	175.00	300.00
DALLAS	Burke	Glass	100.00	140.00	210.00	325.00
DALLAS	Burke	Houston	90.00	120.00	175.00	300.00
DALLAS	White	Mellon Type One	85.00	115.00	170.00	275.00
DALLAS	White	Mellon Type Two	95.00	125.00	180.00	300.00
SAN FRANCISCO	Burke	McAdoo	85.00	115.00	165.00	275.00
SAN FRANCISCO	Burke	Glass	95.00	130.00	185.00	300.00
SAN FRANCISCO	Burke	Houston	85.00	115.00	160.00	275.00
SAN FRANCISCO	White	Mellon Type One	80.00	110.00	155.00	275.00
SAN FRANCISCO	White	Mellon Type Two	90.00	120.00	165.00	300.00
SAN FRANCISCO	White	Mellon Type Three	100.00	130.00	175.00	300.00

★ *Star replacement notes for this series are valued at from three to four times these prices.*

FEDERAL RESERVE NOTES, Blue Seals

FIFTY DOLLARS
BLUE SEALS AND SERIAL NUMBERS

Face Design. Ulysses S. Grant, General and President.

Back Design. Panama represented by female figure, with two oceans.

Bank	Treasurer	Secretary	VF	Ex. Fine	CU	Ch. CU
BOSTON	Burke	McAdoo	260.00	375.00	645.00	1,200
BOSTON	Burke	Glass	275.00	410.00	675.00	1,250
BOSTON	Burke	Houston	260.00	375.00	645.00	1,200
BOSTON	White	Mellon Type One	260.00	375.00	625.00	1,200
NEW YORK	Burke	McAdoo	260.00	375.00	645.00	1,200
NEW YORK	Burke	Glass	275.00	410.00	675.00	1,250
NEW YORK	Burke	Houston	260.00	375.00	645.00	1,200
NEW YORK	White	Mellon Type One	260.00	375.00	625.00	1,200
NEW YORK	White	Mellon Type Two	265.00	400.00	655.00	1,250
PHILADELPHIA	Burke	McAdoo	260.00	375.00	645.00	1,200
PHILADELPHIA	Burke	Glass	275.00	410.00	675.00	1,250
PHILADELPHIA	Burke	Houston	260.00	375.00	645.00	1,200
PHILADELPHIA	White	Mellon Type One	260.00	375.00	625.00	1,200
CLEVELAND	Burke	McAdoo	260.00	375.00	645.00	1,200
CLEVELAND	Burke	Glass	275.00	410.00	675.00	1,250
CLEVELAND	Burke	Houston	260.00	375.00	645.00	1,200
CLEVELAND	White	Mellon Type One	260.00	375.00	625.00	1,200
CLEVELAND	White	Mellon Type Two	265.00	400.00	660.00	1,200

FEDERAL RESERVE NOTES, Blue Seals
$50 Federal Reserve Notes, Blue Seals Continued

Bank	Treasurer	Secretary	VF	Ex. Fine	CU	Ch. CU
RICHMOND	Burke	McAdoo	260.00	375.00	650.00	1,200
RICHMOND	Burke	Glass	275.00	400.00	675.00	1.300
RICHMOND	Burke	Houston	260.00	375.00	650.00	1.200
RICHMOND	White	Mellon Type One	250.00	370.00	650.00	1.200
ATLANTA	Burke	McAdoo	265.00	380.00	700.00	1.300
ATLANTA	Burke	Glass	285.00	410.00	720.00	1,400
ATLANTA	Burke	Houston	265.00	380.00	650.00	1,300
ATLANTA	White	Mellon Type One	260.00	375.00	650.00	1,200
CHICAGO	Burke	McAdoo	260.00	375.00	650.00	1,200
CHICAGO	Burke	Glass	275.00	400.00	675.00	1,300
CHICAGO	Burke	Houston	260.00	375.00	625.00	1,200
CHICAGO	White	Mellon Type One	260.00	375.00	625.00	1,200
ST. LOUIS	Burke	McAdoo	265.00	380.00	650.00	1,300
ST. LOUIS	Burke	Glass	285.00	410.00	700.00	1,400
ST. LOUIS	Burke	Houston	265.00	375.00	650.00	1,300
ST. LOUIS	White	Mellon Type One	260.00	375.00	650.00	1,300
MINNEAPOLIS	Burke	McAdoo	265.00	380.00	650.00	1,300
MINNEAPOLIS	Burke	Glass	285.00	410.00	700.00	1,400
MINNEAPOLIS	Burke	Houston	265.00	380.00	650.00	1,300
MINNEAPOLIS	White	Mellon Type One	260.00	375.00	650.00	1,200
KANSAS CITY	Burke	McAdoo	265.00	385.00	650.00	1,300
KANSAS CITY	Burke	Glass	285.00	410.00	700.00	1,400
KANSAS CITY	Burke	Houston	265.00	385.00	650.00	1,300
KANSAS CITY	White	Mellon Type One	260.00	375.00	650.00	1,200
DALLAS	Burke	McAdoo	265.00	375.00	650.00	1,300
DALLAS	Burke	Glass	285.00	410.00	700.00	1,400
DALLAS	Burke	Houston	265.00	380.00	650.00	1,300
DALLAS	White	Mellon Type One	260.00	375.00	650.00	1,200
SAN FRANCISCO	Burke	McAdoo	260.00	375.00	650.00	1,200
SAN FRANCISCO	Burke	Glass	275.00	410.00	675.00	1,400
SAN FRANCISCO	Burke	Houston	260.00	375.00	650.00	1,200
SAN FRANCISCO	White	Mellon Type One	260.00	375.00	650.00	1,200

★ *Star replacement notes for this series are very rare.*

ONE HUNDRED DOLLARS
BLUE SEALS AND SERIAL NUMBERS

Face Design. Benjamin Franklin.

FEDERAL RESERVE NOTES, Blue Seals
ONE HUNDRED DOLLARS

Back Design. Not issued in Federal Reserve Bank Notes.

All of this denomination are Type One

Bank	Treasurer	Secretary	VF	Ex. Fine	CU	Ch. CU
BOSTON	Burke	McAdoo	475.00	525.00	900.00	1,250
BOSTON	Burke	Glass	500.00	550.00	950.00	1,350
BOSTON	Burke	Houston	475.00	525.00	900.00	1,250
BOSTON	White	Mellon	450.00	500.00	850.00	1,200
NEW YORK	Burke	McAdoo	475.00	525.00	900.00	1,250
NEW YORK	Burke	Glass	500.00	550.00	950.00	1,350
NEW YORK	Burke	Houston	475.00	525.00	900.00	1,250
NEW YORK	White	Mellon	450.00	500.00	850.00	1,200
PHILADELPHIA	Burke	McAdoo	475.00	525.00	900.00	1,250
PHILADELPHIA	Burke	Glass	530.00	550.00	950.00	1,350
PHILADELPHIA	Burke	Houston	475.00	525.00	900.00	1,250
PHILADELPHIA	White	Mellon	450.00	500.00	850.00	1,200
CLEVELAND	Burke	McAdoo	475.00	525.00	900.00	1,250
CLEVELAND	Burke	Glass	500.00	550.00	950.00	1,350
CLEVELAND	Burke	Houston	475.00	550.00	900.00	1,250
CLEVELAND	White	Mellon	450.00	500.00	850.00	1,200
RICHMOND	Burke	McAdoo	475.00	525.00	900.00	1,250
RICHMOND	Burke	Glass	500.00	550.00	950.00	1,350
RICHMOND	Burke	Houston	475.00	525.00	900.00	1,250
RICHMOND	White	Mellon	450.00	500.00	850.00	1,200
ATLANTA	Burke	McAdoo	475.00	525.00	900.00	1,250
ATLANTA	Burke	Glass	500.00	550.00	950.00	1,350
ATLANTA	Burke	Houston	475.00	525.00	900.00	1,250
ATLANTA	White	Mellon	450.00	500.00	850.00	1,200
CHICAGO	Burke	McAdoo	475.00	525.00	900.00	1,250
CHICAGO	Burke	Glass	500.00	550.00	950.00	1,350
CHICAGO	Burke	Houston	475.00	525.00	900.00	1,250
CHICAGO	White	Mellon	450.00	500.00	850.00	1,200
ST. LOUIS	Burke	McAdoo	485.00	525.00	900.00	1,250
ST. LOUIS	Burke	Glass	510.00	550.00	950.00	1,350
ST. LOUIS	Burke	Houston	475.00	525.00	900.00	1,250
ST. LOUIS	White	Mellon	475.00	500.00	850.00	1,250

FEDERAL RESERVE NOTES, Blue Seals

$100 Federal Reserve Notes, Blue Seals Continued

Bank	Treasurer	Secretary	VF	Ex. Fine	CU	Ch. CU
MINNEAPOLIS	Burke	McAdoo	485.00	525.00	900.00	1,250
MINNEAPOLIS	Burke	Glass	510.00	550.00	950.00	1,350
MINNEAPOLIS	Burke	Houston	485.00	525.00	900.00	1,250
MINNEAPOLIS	White	Mellon	475.00	500.00	875.00	1,200
KANSAS CITY	Burke	McAdoo	485.00	525.00	900.00	1,250
KANSAS CITY	Burke	Glass	510.00	550.00	950.00	1,350
KANSAS CITY	Burke	Houston	485.00	525.00	900.00	1,250
KANSAS CITY	White	Mellon	475.00	500.00	875.00	1,200
DALLAS	Burke	McAdoo	485.00	525.00	900.00	1,250
DALLAS	Burke	Glass	510.00	550.00	950.00	1,350
DALLAS	Burke	Houston	485.00	525.00	900.00	1,250
DALLAS	White	Mellon	475.00	500.00	875.00	1,200
SAN FRANCISCO	Burke	McAdoo	475.00	525.00	900.00	1,250
SAN FRANCISCO	Burke	Glass	500.00	550.00	950.00	1,350
SAN FRANCISCO	Burke	Houston	475.00	525.00	900.00	1,250
SAN FRANCISCO	White	Mellon	450.00	500.00	850.00	1,200

★ *Star replacement notes of this denomination are extremely rare.*

FIVE HUNDRED DOLLARS
BLUE SEALS AND SERIAL NUMBERS

Face Design. John Marshall, Chief Justice Supreme Court.

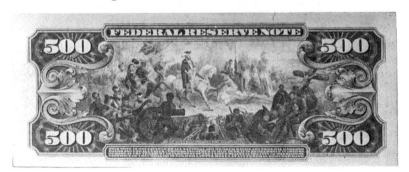

Back Design. "DeSoto Discovering the Mississippi."

Issued by Federal Reserve Banks in all districts except Richmond and Minneapolis.

Bank	Fine	VF	Ex. Fine	CU
BOSTON or NEW YORK - Others are rare	4,500	6,250	8,750	15,000

FEDERAL RESERVE NOTES, Blue Seals
ONE THOUSAND DOLLARS
BLUE SEALS AND SERIAL NUMBERS

Face Design. Alexander Hamilton, first Secretary of the Treasury.

Back Design. American Eagle with Flag. Much admired design.

Issued by Federal Reserve Banks in all districts except Boston and Richmond. Values shown are for the more common notes of New York, Chicago, St. Louis, Kansas City and Dallas.

	Fine	VF	Ex. Fine
Common Banks	5,500	9,000	13,500

FIVE THOUSAND DOLLARS

Face Design: James Madison, fourth President of the United States.
Back Design: Washington resigning his commission.

TEN THOUSAND DOLLARS

Face Design: Salmon P. Chase, Secretary of the Treasury under Lincoln.
Back Design: Embarkation of the Pilgrims, as on the $50 First Charter.

GOLD CERTIFICATES
Acts of Mar. 3, 1863, July 12, 1882, Mar. 14, 1900, Dec. 24, 1919

FIRST, SECOND and THIRD ISSUES

The above issues may be considered to be non-collectible, having been used principally in transactions between banks. Some of these issues were uniface. In the First Issue, denominations ranged from $20 to $10,000. In later issues $100 to $10,000. The $20 and $100 certificates of these issues are extremely rare. The higher denominations have not been discovered. Dates of issue were filled in with pen and ink on these three issues. Two $20 first issue certificates are known.

FOURTH ISSUE, Series 1882

$20 to $10,000 denomination. As with the first three issues, denominations higher than $100 are extremely rare, practically unknown.

The obligation to pay in gold is on the face of the note. It reads: "This certifies that there have been deposited in the Treasury of the United States…Dollars in Gold Coin, payable to the Bearer on Demand." This issue is indicated as "Department Series" on the face of the certificates.

FACE DESIGNS, Series 1882

$20	James A. Garfield, twentieth President. Assassinated six months after his inauguration in 1881. Portrait at right.
$50	Silar Wright, U.S. Senator 1833-1834. New York State Governor 1845-1846. Portrait at left.
$100	Thomas H. Benton, left. U.S. Senator for over thirty years.
$500	Abraham Lincoln. Portrait at left.
$1000	Alexander Hamilton, at right.
$5000	James Madison, at left, engraved by A. Sealey.
$10,000	Andrew Jackson, at left.

Some notes of the 1882 series, bearing Bruce-Gilfillan signatures and a brown seal, were countersigned by Thomas C. Acton, Assistant Treasurer, and were payable in New York. Notes so countersigned are rare.

BACK DESIGNS, Series 1882

The American Eagle in various poses is featured on the back design of all denominations of this series. There is no legend or inscription. Large Roman numerals "C", "D" and "M" in the back design indicate the $100, $500 and $1000 denominations. "United States" without "of America" is used on all back designs of this series.

FIFTH ISSUE, Series 1888

Two denominations only:

$5,000	James Madison, portrait at left. Back design: "5000" and eagle.
$10,000	Andrew Jackson, portrait at left. Back design: "10000" and Eagle with flag.

SIXTH ISSUE, Series 1900

$10,000 only. Andrew Jackson, as on Series 1888. Back design same as 1888.

GOLD CERTIFICATES

SEVENTH ISSUE, Series 1905, 1906 and 1907

$10   Series 1907. Michael Hillegas, center, U.S. Treasurer 1777-1789. Large "X" Roman equivalent of "10" at left.

$20   Series 1905, George Washington. The beautiful blending of gold, red, black and white has caused this note to be known as the "technicolor" note.

$20   Series 1906, George Washington. Gold and black design with Roman numeral "XX."

The back design of gold for this series carries no inscription. Simply the designation "Gold Certificate," the denomination and the Seal.

EIGHTH ISSUE, Series 1907

$1000   Alexander Hamilton. One denomination.

NINTH ISSUE, Series 1913

$50   Series 1913. Portrait of Grant. Issued with two signature combinations, both of which were offered in the Grinnell sale in 1945. Series 1913 and Series 1922 were the only two issues of the $50 denomination.

LAST ISSUE, Series 1922

$10 to $1000 denominations. All bear signature combination 31, Speelman-White.

A legend was added to the face of the notes: "This certificate is a Legal Tender in the amount thereof, in payment of all debts and dues public and private. Acts of March 14, 1900, as amended, and December 24, 1919."

$10   Michael Hillegas, first U.S. Treasurer.

$20   George Washington.

$50   Ulysses Grant.

$100   Thomas H. Benton.

$500   Abraham Lincoln.

$1000   Alexander Hamilton.

The back designs in gold feature the Seal, the denomination and United States of America. There is no legend or inscription.

First, Second and Third Issues, Act of March 3, 1863 — Issued 1865 to 1876

Signatures Colby-Spinner or Allison-Spinner — Countersignature and date added with pen and ink.

FIRST ISSUE $20 and $100 Extremely rare — $500 to $5000 Non-collectible.

SECOND ISSUE $100 to $10,000 Non-collectible.

THIRD ISSUE $100 series 1875, Allison-New, Extremely rare. $500 to $10,000 Non-collectible.

GOLD CERTIFICATES-FOURTH ISSUE

FOURTH ISSUE, Series 1882
TWENTY DOLLARS, SERIES 1882

Face Design. Fourth Issue Series 1882. James A. Garfield.

Back Design. American Eagle.

Register	Treasurer	Seal	Fine	VF	Ex. Fine	CU
Bruce	Gilfillan	Brown, right	—	Rare	—	—
Countersigned Thos. C. Acton, Asst. Treas.						
Bruce	Gilfillan	Brown, right	2,000	4,250	7,800	—
Bruce	Wyman	Brown, right	1,800	3,900	6,750	—
Rosecrans	Huston	Lg. brown, right	1,750	3,750	6,250	—
Lyons	Roberts	Sm. red, right	550.00	1,000	1,750	2,400

GOLD CERTIFICATES-FOURTH ISSUE

FIFTY DOLLARS, SERIES 1882

Register	Treasurer	Seal	Fine	VF	Ex. Fine	CU
Countersigned notes of this issue are very rare.						
Bruce	Gilfillan	Brown, right	6,000	8,500	13,500	—
Bruce	Wyman	Brown, right		Very Rare		
Rosecrans	Hyatt	Lg. Red, right		Very Rare		
Rosecrans	Huston	Lg. Brown, right		Rare		
Lyons	Roberts	Sm. Red, right	900.00	1,500	2,500	4,500
Lyons	Treat	Sm. Red, right	900.00	1,500	2,500	4,500
Vernon	Treat	Sm. Red, right	900.00	1,500	2,500	4,500
Vernon	McClung	Sm. Red, right	900.00	1,500	2,500	4,500
Napier	McClung	Sm. Red, right	900.00	1,500	2,500	4,500

ONE HUNDRED DOLLARS, SERIES 1882

Register	Treasurer	Seal	Fine	VF	Ex. Fine	CU
Countersigned notes of this issue are very rare.						
Bruce	Gilfillan	Brown, right		Only 3 in private hands.		
Bruce	Wyman	Brown, right		Very Rare		
Rosecrans	Hyatt	Lg. Red, right		Very Rare		
Rosecrans	Huston	Lg. Brown, right		Rare		
Lyons	Roberts	Sm. Red, right	700.00	1,000	1,500	3,200
Lyons	Treat	Sm. Red, right	700.00	1,000	1,500	3,200
Vernon	Treat	Sm. Red, right	700.00	1,000	1,500	3,200
Vernon	McClung	Sm. Red, right	700.00	1,000	1,500	3,200
Napier	McClung	Sm. Red, right	700.00	1,000	1,500	3,200
Napier	Thompson	Sm. Red, right	850.00	1,350	2,400	4,000
Napier	Burke	Sm. Red, right	700.00	1,000	1,500	3,200
Parker	Burke	Sm. Red, right	700.00	1,100	1,750	3,750
Teehee	Burke	Sm. Red, right	700.00	1,100	1,750	3,750

FIVE HUNDRED DOLLARS, SERIES 1882

Register	Fine	VF	Ex. Fine	CU
Various signature combinations	8,500	12,000	15,000	—

Series 1882 $1000, $5000 and $10,000 were issued but may be considered non-collectible, although notes of each denomination do exist.

GOLD CERTIFICATES FIFTH AND SIXTH ISSUES

Series 1888 — $5000 and $10,000
Series 1900 — $10,000

As with the high denomination Gold Certificates of 1882, notes of Series 1888 and 1900 reportedly exist, but may be considered to be non-collectible. See text page 137 for additional descriptions.

TEN DOLLARS, SERIES 1907 and 1922
All have Gold Seals and Gold Backs

Face Design. Series 1907 and 1922, with minor addition.

Back Design. Series 1907 and 1922.

Series	Register	Treasurer	VF	Ex. Fine	AU	CU	Ch. CU
1907	Vernon	Treat	140.00	250.00	350.00	450.00	750.00
1907	Vernon	McClung	140.00	250.00	350.00	450.00	750.00
1907	Napier	McClung	140.00	250.00	350.00	450.00	750.00
1907	Napier	Thompson	175.00	300.00	400.00	550.00	900.00
1907	Parker	Burke	140.00	250.00	350.00	450.00	750.00
1907	Teehee	Burke	140.00	250.00	350.00	450.00	750.00
1922	Speelman	White	120.00	210.00	300.00	400.00	700.00

★ *Star replacement notes for Series 1907 are very scarce. Those for Series 1922 are valued at approximately double prices shown here.*

GOLD CERTIFICATES

TWENTY DOLLARS, SERIES 1905, 1906 and 1922

Face Design. Series 1905, 1906 and 1922. Legend added to 1922.

Back Design. Series 1905, 1906 and 1922.

Series 1905 have Red Seals, others have Gold Seals, and a few orange Seals.

Series	Register	Treasurer	VF	Ex. Fine	AU	CU	Ch. CU
1905	Lyons	Roberts	1,800	3,200	5,000	6,000	8,600
1905	Lyons	Treat	1,800	3,200	5,000	6,000	8,600
1906	Vernon	Treat	290.00	425.00	600.00	650.00	1,000
1906	Vernon	McClung	290.00	425.00	600.00	650.00	1,000
1906	Napier	McClung	290.00	425.00	600.00	650.00	1,000
1906	Napier	Thompson	325.00	500.00	800.00	1,000	1,350
1906	Parker	Burke	290.00	425.00	600.00	650.00	1,000
1906	Teehee	Burke	290.00	425.00	600.00	650.00	1,000
1922	Speelman	White	265.00	375.00	500.00	600.00	950.00

★ *Star replacement notes for Series 1906 are rare. Those for Series 1922 are valued at approximately three times the prices shown here.*

GOLD CERTIFICATES
FIFTY DOLLARS, SERIES 1913 and 1922, GOLD SEALS

Face Design. Series 1913 and 1922. Minor change on 1922.

Series	Register	Treasurer	VF	Ex. Fine	AU	CU
1913	Parker	Burke	**1,000**	**1,350**	**1,750**	**2,500**
1913	Teehee	Burke	**850.00**	**1,000**	**1,500**	**1,750**
1922	Speelman	White	**600.00**	**900.00**	**1,250**	**1,500**

★ *Star replacement notes for this series are rare.*

ONE HUNDRED DOLLARS, SERIES 1922, GOLD SEAL

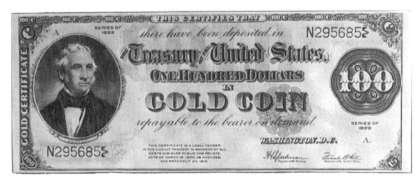

Face Design. With legend added as on all Series 1922.

Series	Register	Treasurer	VF	Ex. Fine	AU	CU
1922	Speelman	White	**800.00**	**1,200**	**2,000**	**2,500**

★ *Star replacement notes for this series are rare.*

$500 and $1000 notes were also issued in Series 1922. All are rare.

TREASURY OR COIN NOTES, 1890-1891

Act of July 14, 1890

Under the above Act, Congress authorized the Secretary of the Treasury to issue notes which would be payable in coin on demand. Although backed by deposits of silver bullion, redemption in either silver or gold was left to the discretion of the Secretary of the Treasury.

Two series were issued, 1890 and 1891, in denominations from $1 to $1000, the $50 note being issued only, in series 1891. The issue is characterized as having the smallest number of signatures, seals and varieties in design of any other type of United States currency.

It is important to note that all serial numbers of both series were followed by a star. This star does not indicate a replacement note. It is merely a printing embellishment as on series 1869 Legal Tender notes.

FACE DESIGNS, Series 1890-1891

$1	Edwin M. Stanton, Secretary of War 1862-1868, serving under Presidents Lincoln and Andrew Johnson.
$2	General James D. McPherson, killed in action, 1864.
$5	General George H. Thomas, Civil War hero.
$10	General Philip H. Sheridan, Civil War and later in Indian Wars.
$20	John Marshall, Secretary of State under President John Adams, 1800-1801. Chief Justice of the Supreme Court, for thirty years.
$50	1891 only. William H. Seward, admitted to the Bar in Utica, New York, in 1822. Secretary of State 1860-1869. Negotiated purchase of Alaska from Russia, at the time called "Seward's Folly", for the sum of $7,200,000.
$100	David Glasgow Farragut, first Admiral of the U.S. Navy.
$500	General Wm. T. Sherman. Designed for Series 1891 but probably never printed. There are no known specimens. A proof exists and is illustrated on page 152.
$1000	General George Gordon Meade, active in the Seminole Indian War, the War with Mexico, and the Civil War.

The obligation to pay on the face of the notes, both series, reads very simply: "The United States will Pay to the Bearer on Demand…Dollars in Coin."

BACK DESIGNS, Series 1890-1891

The brilliant green lathe-work back design of the 1890 series is most attractive. It was changed to a more open design on the 1891 series due to the belief that the first design was more easily counterfeited by means of photography.

The inscription on both back designs reads: "This Note is Legal Tender at its Face Value in Payment of Debts Public and Private Except When Otherwise Expressly Stipulated in the Contract."

The large zeros in the back design of series 1890 $100 note have caused it to be known as the "watermelon note." It ranks high in the rarity tables of United States currency.

TREASURY NOTES
ONE DOLLAR, SERIES 1890-1891

Face Design, Series 1890 and 1891.

Back Design, Series 1890.

Treasury Notes of all denominations are very scarce. This is especially true of Series 1890 with the brilliant green lathe-work back designs. The 1890 series was printed for less than two years, quickly being replaced by Series 1891 which also had a comparatively short life.

Series 1890 Large Brown or Small Red Seals. Series 1891 Small Red Seals.

Series	Register	Treasurer	Seal	Fine	VF	Ex. Fine	AU	CU
1890	Rosecrans	Huston	Lg. Brown, right	425.00	750.00	1,000	1,500	2,000
1890	Rosecrans	Nebeker	Lg. Brown, right	450.00	800.00	1,100	1,600	2,200
1890	Rosecrans	Nebeker	Sm. Red, right	425.00	750.00	1,000	1,500	2,000

Back Design, Series 1891.

TREASURY NOTES
ONE DOLLAR, SERIES 1890-1891 Continued

Series	Register	Treasurer	Seal	Fine	VF	Ex. Fine	AU	CU
1891	Rosecrans	Nebeker	Sm. Red, right	150.00	225.00	350.00	450.00	550.00
1891	Tillman	Morgan	Sm. Red, right	150.00	225.00	350.00	450.00	550.00
1891	Bruce	Roberts	Sm. Red, right	150.00	225.00	350.00	450.00	550.00

TWO DOLLARS, SERIES 1890-1891

Face Design, Series 1890 and 1891.

Back Design, Series 1890.

Series	Register	Treasurer	Seal	Fine	VF	Ex. Fine	AU	CU
1890	Rosecrans	Huston	Lg. Brown, right	650.00	1,500	2,850	4,000	4,600
1890	Rosecrans	Nebeker	Lg. Brown, right	675.00	1,600	3,000	4,200	4,800
1890	Rosecrans	Nebeker	Sm. Red, right	650.00	1,500	2,850	4,000	4,600

TREASURY NOTES
TWO DOLLARS, SERIES 1890-1891 Continued

Back Designs, Series 1891.

Series	Register	Treasurer	Seal	Fine	VF	Ex. Fine	AU	CU
1891	Rosecrans	Nebeker	Sm. Red, right	275.00	600.00	850.00	1,000	1,200
1891	Tillman	Morgan	Sm. Red, right	275.00	600.00	850.00	1,000	1,200
1891	Bruce	Roberts	Sm. Red, right	285.00	625.00	900.00	1,100	1,400

FIVE DOLLARS, SERIES 1890-1891

Face Designs, Series 1890 and 1891.

Back Design, Series 1890.

FIVE DOLLARS, SERIES 1890-1891 Continued

Series	Register	Treasurer	Seal	Fine	VF	Ex. Fine	AU	CU
1890	Rosecrans	Huston	Lg. Brown, right	400.00	850.00	1,500	2,400	2,500
1890	Rosecrans	Nebeker	Lg. Brown, right	450.00	950.00	1,750	2,750	3,500
1890	Rosecrans	Nebeker	Sm. Red, right	400.00	850.00	1,500	2,400	2,500

Back Design, Series 1891.

Series	Register	Treasurer	Seal	Fine	VF	Ex. Fine	AU	CU
1891	Rosecrans	Nebeker	Sm. Red, right	275.00	450.00	650.00	775.00	900.00
1891	Tillman	Morgan	Sm. Red, right	275.00	450.00	650.00	775.00	900.00
1891	Bruce	Roberts	Sm. Red, right	300.00	475.00	700.00	825.00	1,000
1891	Lyons	Roberts	Sm. Red, right	400.00	600.00	800.00	1,100	1,250

TEN DOLLARS, SERIES 1890-1891

Face Design, Series 1890 and 1891.

TREASURY NOTES
TEN DOLLARS, SERIES 1890-1891 Continued

Back Design, Series 1890.

Series	Register	Treasurer	Seal at Right	Fine	VF	Ex. Fine	AU	CU
1890	Rosecrans	Huston	Lg. Brown	750.00	1,400	2,200	2,750	3,200
1890	Rosecrans	Nebeker	Lg. Brown	750.00	1,400	2,200	2,750	3,200
1890	Rosecrans	Nebeker	Sm. Red	750.00	1,400	2,200	2,750	3,200

Back Design, Series 1891.

Series	Register	Treasurer	Seal at Right	Fine	VF	Ex. Fine	AU	CU
1891	Rosecrans	Nebeker	Sm. Red	450.00	800.00	1,100	1,500	1,800
1891	Tillman	Morgan	Sm. Red	450.00	800.00	1,100	1,500	1,800
1891	Bruce	Roberts	Sm. Red	475.00	850.00	1,150	1,600	2,000

TREASURY NOTES
TWENTY DOLLARS, SERIES 1890-1891

Face Design, Series 1890 and 1891.

Back Design, Series 1890.

Series	Register	Treasurer	Seal at Right	Fine	VF	Ex. Fine	AU	CU
1890	Rosecrans	Huston	Lg. Brown	2,750	5,000	6,000	8,500	12,000
1890	Rosecrans	Nebeker	Lg. Brown	4,750	8,000	12,000	—	—
1890	Rosecrans	Nebeker	Sm. Red	2,750	5,000	6,000	8,500	12,000

Series 1891 with modified back design.

Series	Register	Treasurer	Seal at Right	Fine	VF	Ex. Fine	AU	CU
1891	Tillman	Morgan	Sm. Red	2,750	4,500	6,500	8,000	10,000
1891	Bruce	Roberts	Sm. Red	Very Rare (only 2 known)				

FIFTY DOLLARS, SERIES 1890-1891

Face Design, Series 1891.

Series	Register	Treasurer	Seal at Right	VG	Fine	VF	Ex. Fine	AU
1891	Rosecrans	Nebeker	Sm. Red	8,000	13,500	18,500	30,000	—

Only one signature combination issued.

ONE HUNDRED DOLLARS, SERIES 1890-1891

Face Design, Series 1890 and 1891.

Back Design, Series 1890. The "Watermelon Back."

Series	Register	Treasurer	Seal at Right	VG	Fine	VF	Ex. Fine	AU
1890	Rosecrans	Huston	Lg. Brown	10,000	15,000	20,000	27,500	—
1891	Rosecrans	Nebeker	Sm. Red	15,000	25,000	30,000	40,000	—

Records indicate 120,000 series 1890 issued and only 16,000 Series 1891. Only one signature combination was issued in each series.

TREASURY NOTES
FIVE HUNDRED DOLLARS, SERIES 1890-1891

Photograph of $500 Proof Note courtesy of Morey Perlmutter and W.T. Anton, Jr.

It is believed that the above note was designed as a memorial to General William T. Sherman who died in 1891. For some reason it was never issued. General Sherman is best known for his "march to the sea" in 1864 and for originating the saying "War is Hell," which is still in use.

ONE THOUSAND DOLLARS, SERIES 1890-1891

Series	Register	Treasurer	Seal
1890	Rosecrans	Huston	Lg. Brown, right
1890	Rosecrans	Nebeker	Sm. Red, right (unique)
1891	Rosecrans	Nebeker	Sm. Red, right
1891	Tillman	Morgan	Sm. Red, right

The above denomination may be considered non-collectible. Reportedly less than 25 notes have not been redeemed.

DEMAND NOTES OF 1861
Issued under Acts of Congress, July 17 and Aug. 5, 1861

Denominations $5, $10 and $20 only. All bear the date of the first authorization and also the date of issue, August 10, 1861. These notes were not originally Legal Tender, but later were so specified and were the first notes authorized by Congress to circulate as money.

With the exception of early issues of Fractional Currency, this is the only issue of United States paper money that does not bear the Treasury Seal. The names of the United States Treasurer and the Register of the Treasury were not engraved or printed on Demand notes. Clerks in the Treasury Department signed the notes with the added notation "for the" Register and "for the" Treasurer. Subsequently the words "for the" were engraved on the plates. Notes with "for the" handwritten, are quite rare.

The major portion of the face designs are the same as the Legal Tender notes of the $5, $10 and $20 denominations. See description under "United States Legal Tender Notes."

Notes were payable on demand by the Assistant Treasurer of the United States, at Boston, New York, Philadelphia, St. Louis and Cincinnati. All bear the following obligation to pay: "The United States Promise to pay the Bearer...Dollars on Demand." In the border design on the face of the notes, is the inscription: "Receivable in Payment of all Public Dues."

The term "greenback" originated from the back design of the Demand Notes which have an over-all lathe work design in vivid green. The denomination is shown in large letters and numerals. There is no other legend.

DEMAND NOTES OF 1861

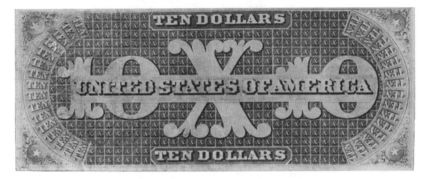

All-over designs were used on the three denominations.

FIVE DOLLARS

Face Design, Type One, "for the" Handwritten.

No Treasury Seal. No signatures of Register and Treasurer.
TYPE ONE has "for the" handwritten. TYPE TWO "for the" is printed.

Payable at	Type	Good	VG	Fine
BOSTON	Type One	Rare	—	—
BOSTON	Type Two	550.00	900.00	1,600
NEW YORK	Type One	Rare	—	—
NEW YORK	Type Two	550.00	900.00	1,600
PHILADELPHIA	Type One	Not Issued		
PHILADELPHIA	Type Two	600.00	950.00	1,700
ST. LOUIS	Type One	Unknown	—	—
ST. LOUIS	Type Two	6,000	12,000	—
CINCINNATI	Type One	Unknown	—	—
CINCINNATI	Type Two	6,000	12,000	—

DEMAND NOTES OF 1861
TEN DOLLARS

Face Design, Type Two, "for the" printed.

Payable at	Type	Good	VG	Fine
BOSTON	Type One	Rare	—	—
BOSTON	Type Two	1,000	1,600	3,000
NEW YORK	Type One	1,800	6,000	—
NEW YORK	Type Two	1,000	1,600	3,000
PHILADELPHIA	Type One	Rare	—	—
PHILADELPHIA	Type Two	1,200	1,750	3,500
ST. LOUIS	Type One	Rare	—	—
ST. LOUIS	Type Two	Rare	—	—
CINCINNATI	Type One	Rare	—	—
CINCINNATI	Type Two	Rare	—	—

TWENTY DOLLARS

Face Design, Type Two, "for the" printed.

Payable at	Type	Good	VG	Fine
BOSTON	Type One	Rare	—	—
BOSTON	Type Two	6,500	13,000	—
NEW YORK	Type One	Rare	—	—
NEW YORK	Type Two	6,000	11,500	—
PHILADELPHIA	Type One	Unknown	—	—
PHILADELPHIA	Type Two	6,500	12,000	—
ST. LOUIS	Type One	None Reported		—
ST. LOUIS	Type Two	None Reported		
CINCINNATI	Type One	Unknown	—	—
CINCINNATI	Type Two	Rare	—	—

INTEREST BEARING NOTES

As an emergency measure to alleviate the financial condition of the U.S. Treasury caused by the Civil War, Congress, by Acts of July 17, 1861, June 30, 1864 and March 3, 1865, authorized various issues of paper money which would bear interest and would also circulate as Legal Tender.

THREE YEAR 7 and 3/10% INTEREST BEARING NOTES

Act of Congress, July 17, 1861

The first Interest Bearing Notes and now the rarest were the Three Year Notes first authorized by the above act. This issue paid the highest rate of interest, a very attractive 7-3/10 per cent.

Only the higher denominations of $50 to $5000 were issued in this series. Five coupons were attached to each note which could be presented for payment as the interest became due with final interest payment upon redemption of the note itself. Due to this factor and the tight money situation, it is understandable that very few notes of this issue were preserved with coupons or minus coupons to be handed down to present day collectors.

By Act of August 5, 1861, the Three Year Notes were convertible into 20 year Government Bonds with interest @ 6%, in units of $500 and $1000.

Signatures: Chittenden-Spinner or Colby-Spinner

All Extremely Rare, Unique or Non-Collectible.

		Good
$50	American Eagle with Shield in center	—
$100	General Winfield Scott	
$500	George Washington	
$1000	Salmon P. Chase	
$5000	Justice and Indian Maid with Shield and Eagle.	

Issued under the Act of June 30, 1864

$50	Eagle with Shield	—

Convertible into 6% Bonds at option of Bearer

Issued under Act of March 3, 1865

$50	Eagle with Shield	—
$100	General Winfield Scott	—
$500	Unknown, if issued	
$1000	Justice Seated with Shield	

At left end on face of this issue was the inscription: "The Government reserves the right of paying in coin the interest on this note at the rate of 6% per annum."

Printed by American Bank Note Co., three notes to each sheet.

TWO YEAR 5% INTEREST BEARING NOTES

Act of Congress, March 3, 1863

The $500 note of this issue had three coupons attached which could be presented for 5% interest payment in six month periods. Interest on other denominations, was payable upon redemption of the notes.

INTEREST BEARING NOTES

	VG	Fine	VF	
$50	Three female figures, Justice in center.	—	—	—
$100	Vignettes representing Farming and Mechanics.	—	—	—
$500	American Eagle and Liberty with flag & anchor.	—	—	—
$1000	"DeSoto Discovering the Mississippi 1541" and ships Constitution and Guerriere.	—	—	—

All of the above are Extremely Rare, Unknown or Non-Collectible.

ONE YEAR 5% INTEREST BEARING NOTES
Act of Congress, March 3, 1863

The $10 and $20 denominations were added to this issue undoubtedly to attract investors with limited funds. The $5000 denomination was also added and probably was not too popular. No coupons were attached to the One Year Notes.

$10	Eagle with Flag, center. Salmon P. Chase at left. Peace holding sheaf of wheat at right.	**1,300**	**2,800**	**3,800**
$20	Mortar firing, center. Figure of Victory at left. Abraham Lincoln at right.	**1,800**	**4,600**	**6,750**
$50	Alexander Hamilton, right. Allegorical Loyalty at left.	—	—	—
$100	George Washington, center. "The Guardian" at left. Justice with shield right.	—	—	—
$500	Vignette "Standard Bearer" and the ship "New Ironsides."	—	—	—
$1000	Eagles and Shield, center. Justice, left. Liberty at right.	—	—	—
$5000	"The Altar of Liberty" represented by vignette of female figure.	—	—	—

There are no recent records of any of this series being recently offered. The $10 note sold in the Grinnell sale, Nov. 1944, for $65 and more recently at $500 to $1000. Condition was stated to be fine to very fine.

The $20 note sold in same Grinnell sale for $145 extra fine. Later at $750 and up.

The $50 denomination brought $125 in the Grinnell sale. It was described as "good, re-inforced."

6% COMPOUND INTEREST TREASURY NOTES
Issued under Acts of March 3, 1863 and June 30, 1864
Signatures: Chittenden-Spinner or Colby-Spinner

This issue, as with other Interest Bearing issues, freely circulated as legal tender. Interest was compounded semi-annually and the accumulated interest for each six month period was indicated in a table in the center of the green lathe-work design on the back of the note.

Denomination	Interest	Redemption Value
$10	1.94	11.94
$20	3.88	23.88
$50	9.70	59.70
$100	19.40	119.40
$500	97.03	597.03
$1000	194.06	1,194.06

INTEREST BEARING NOTES

The Treasury Seal was in red. The obligation to pay, with interest, appeared on the face of the note, which also bore in prominent gold letters the surcharge "Compound Interest Note." On some existing specimens the gold surcharge has eaten through the paper, possibly caused by oxidation.

With interest at 6% payable only upon redemption of the notes, very few escaped redemption. Interest Bearing notes of all issues are still redeemable at face value plus interest for the period stated on the note. Due to the present numismatic value, it is doubtful that many will be redeemed.

6% Compound Interest notes were issued as follows:

		VG	Fine	VF
$10	Salmon P. Chase, usually found fair to Very Fine.	**1,250**	**3,750**	**6,000**
$20	Abraham Lincoln, seldom found better than Fine.	**2,500**	**5,000**	**9,000**
$50	Alexander Hamilton, extremely rare, any cond. Two varieties exist, one with Chittenden-Spinner, the other Colby-Spinner.	—	—	—
$100	George Washington, extremely rare, any cond.	**Rare**	—	—
$500	New Ironsides, believed non-collectible.	—	—	—
$1000	Liberty and Justice, believed non-collectible.	—	—	

Face Design. Lincoln, as on One Year Interest Bearing Note.

4% REFUNDING CERTIFICATES

Act of Congress, Feb. 26, 1879

$10 denomination only. Signatures: G.W. Scofield and James Gilfillan.

Issued in the low denomination to attract investors with lower incomes. Two Types were issued, both earning 4% interest and originally with no time limit set for redemption. By Act of Congress, April 1907, interest was discontinued as of July 1, 1907. On that date the total redemption value was $21.30 and remains at that figure.

Type One was payable to Order with name of person to whom issued on the face of the note. The certifications read: "This certifies that (name)…has deposited with the Treasurer of the United States the sum of Ten Dollars under Act of Feb. 26th 1879." Space was provided for endorsement by the purchaser. This was printed in black, vertically across the back of the note, with lengthy inscription.

Type Two provided no name space and was payable to Bearer. The certification was changed to read: "This certifies the sum of Ten Dollars has been deposited under Act of Feb. 26th, 1879."

INTEREST BEARING NOTES

The three line inscription across the lower portion of the face of both Types reads: "Convertible with accrued interest of 4% per annum into 4% bonds of the United States, issued under the Acts of July 14, 1870 and January 20, 1871, upon presentation properly endorsed, at the Office of the Treasurer of the U.S., Washington, D.C. in sums of $50 or multiples thereof." The words "properly endorsed" were eliminated on Type Two.

Type Two back design was in black and was printed horizontally as are most notes. The denomination "TEN" was prominent, and an explanatory table showed earned interest:

Interest on this note will accrue as follows:

For each 9 days, or 1/10 of a quarter ....1 cent
For each quarter year...10 cents
For each entire year...40 cents

	VG	Fine	VF	AU
The Type Two notes are valued at......................................	1,000	1,200	1,500	3,000

Only 2 of the Type One notes are known.

ERRORS OR MISPRINTED NOTES

Probably no branch of manufacturing or printing has such rigid rules and inspection methods as the printing of United States paper money. When one considers the millions of notes coming off the presses at the Bureau of Engraving and Printing, it is understandable that misprints and errors do occur. The infrequency in which these misprints escape into circulation is a tribute to the efficiency of the "check and double check" system in the Bureau.

In the printing of U.S. large size paper money, more operations were involved and perhaps imperfections were more readily detected by pressmen and inspectors. Possibly this is the explanation for comparatively few errors or misprinted notes being found in our large size paper money. When found and offered for sale, the valuation is largely a matter between buyer and seller. A sufficient number do exist to make possible the acquisition of some interesting and possibly unique varieties.

ERRORS OR MISPRINTED NOTES

THE "DOUBLE DENOMINATION" NOTE

The error most coveted and which is now valued well into four figures is the Double Denomination Note with the face of one denomination and the back of another.

Large size National Bank Notes were printed customarily in sheets of three "tens" and a "twenty," or three "fifties" and one "one hundred." If a sheet of printed backs were turned end for end before printing the face, the $20 back would be imprinted with the $10 face and the $10 back would also become a Double Denomination with a $20 face design.

On this same sheet of four notes the second and third notes would have inverted faces. Notes so misprinted have been called "Inverted Backs;" however this is a misnomer as it is the face of the note which was actually inverted. Perhaps the term "Inverted Design" would be more appropriate.

When Double Denomination notes are found in series other than National Bank Notes, the error was probably caused by a sheet of one denomination with previously printed back being removed for inspection and then through error replaced in a rack of another denomination. To this writer's knowledge a complete uncut or cut sheet of large size Double Denomination notes is unknown.

Other misprints include notes with white streaks on face or back caused by a fold in the paper at time of printing. Also notes to which a piece of paper adhered during printing caused a blank white space and notes with seals and signatures well out of position was caused by improper alignment of the sheet before the addition of seals and signatures. Inverted seals and signatures were caused by a sheet being turned end for end before these imprints were added.

Double Denomination, National Bank Note, Barry, Ill.
$10 Face, $20 Back. Top note of the sheet.

ERRORS OR MISPRINTED NOTES

Double Denomination, $20 Face, $10 Back.
This is the bottom note of the sheet of four.

Misprint. Bank Charter numbers were added after design was printed
and Serial Number imprinted. A half turn of the note or sheet of
notes caused this error when Charter number was added.

Double Denomination Federal Reserve Bank Note.
$2 Face, $1 Back.

ERRORS OR MISPRINTED NOTES

Double Denomination Federal Reserve Note
$5 Face, $10 Back.

STAR NUMBERED NOTES

Star numbered notes were not substituted for mis-printed or damaged notes prior to 1910. Defective notes of early issues were either replaced by notes of an entirely different sequence of numbers, which caused considerable confusion in record keeping, or they were replaced by a specially numbered note which duplicated the number of the spoiled note.

This time-consuming procedure gave way in 1910 to the present system of star numbered notes as replacements. The "star" system was developed by Register of the Treasury Wm. T. Vernon and Treasurer Lee McClung with the cooperation of J.T. Ralph, Director of the Bureau of Engraving and Printing.

The earliest star numbered notes were used in July, 1910, as replacements for any damaged notes in the $5 Silver Certificates Series 1899, the well-known and popular "ONEPAPA" notes. Then followed star numbers replacing misprinted notes of the Legal Tender notes and others.

As with the small size U.S. paper money, the star on large size notes was used as a prefix to the serial number with the exception of Federal Reserve notes, where as now, it was placed after the serial number, replacing the suffix letter.

FRACTIONAL CURRENCY
United States Fractional Currency by Matt Rothert.

INTRODUCTION

The general public is usually surprised to know that we Americans used paper for such small amounts as three cents, five cents and ten cents, and that it is still redeemable at full face value today. In the fourteen years of issue (1862-1876) about 369 million dollars of Fractional Currency was printed, yet very little exists today and the average person has never seen any of it. It is estimated that $1.8 million is now in existence.

Collectors like Fractional Currency because it is a short yet varied series. A denominational collection consists of only six notes. A type collection can be made with only twenty-five notes and a collection of about one hundred forty notes and fifty Specimens would be practically complete. Fractional Currency has its error notes, too. In addition one can collect sheets, pairs, strips, blocks and a Fractional Currency Shield. This series also has many unusual varieties and was printed on many types of paper as part of the experimentation to discourage counterfeiting.

Fractional Currency is a most important and vital part of numismatics — a bridge between the all metal "hard money" period before 1861 and the metal and paper money combination period after 1862. It is an interesting series to collect because it is the product of a period of our history full of important events — the years 1862 to 1876. It exemplifies the need for small change, the "Necessity" money born of the scarcity of hard money in these troubled times.

It is said that there are no large stocks of Fractional Currency. A letter from the Treasury Department in February, 1962, disclosed that there is less than one half of one per cent of the amount issued still outstanding. There are undoubtedly many "sleepers," many rare notes, in this series. The history and romance that could be connected with every single note should stir the spirit of the thoughtful collector. These notes are easy to keep in albums or individual holders, and when displayed they obtain the attention and invite the interest of non-collectors with that same indefinable intrigue that holds the admiration of the most advanced numismatist.

The author became interested in United States Fractional Currency many years ago and has made an extensive study of this subject. A small collection was obtained in one purchase from the relative of a man who had worked in the "Department" at the time is was printed. These uncirculated notes were the nucleus of an exciting search for others.

All photos of regular issue notes were made from those in the author's collection.

Matt Rothert, 1963.

SPECIMEN NOTES

The term "Specimen" as used generally in this book refers to a note other than one issued for general circulation and may include "proof," "essay," "Specimen" notes and experimental pieces. These should come only in new condition.

The Specimen notes listed in the catalog section consist specifically of separately printed fronts or backs with plain margins on all four sides. The backs are blank, or they may have the word "SPECIMEN" on them.

Some of the Specimen notes are on paper watermarked CSA. This paper, made in England for the Confederate States of America, was captured on a blockade runner by a Union ship. No single Specimen note is known with all three of these letters, though many have two.

Values shown in the catalog section are for wide margin notes. Those with close margin are worth less than the listed prices.

FRACTIONAL CURRENCY

Typical Specimen Note, Wide Margin.

Typical Back of a Specimen Note.

Backs of Specimen Notes
Showing CSA Watermark.

FRACTIONAL CURRENCY

VALUATIONS

The valuations in this book are based on the realistic retail value of these notes as obtained from auction sales, from dealers, and from actual sales when and if the dealers have them in stock. Perfectly centered, bright new specimens are worth an extra premium while closely cut edges and off centered notes are worth slightly less. Many of these notes were destroyed by fire or simply worn out in the pockets of past generations. Thus, some of them may be "sleepers" and the prices shown may be low on those particular notes.

The notes that are known to be extremely rare are not priced because they come up for sale so seldom that their price is an individual matter between buyer and seller.

Prices shown for "Specimen" notes are for narrow margin type only. Notes with wide margins are generally valued at 30% to 50% more.

HISTORY

On the eve of the Civil War in 1861, trade and commerce seemed to be coming to a sudden stop; for almost overnight all the gold, silver and copper money in the United States had disappeared.

The prospect of a long struggle between the North and South caused the hoarding of coins. Large amounts of silver coins were sent to Canada, and a premium of from 10 to 12 per cent was offered by businessmen for them. It was reported that one building in New York had so many copper coins stored in it that the floors collapsed!

Even the heavy discounting of the "wild cat" notes and the State Bank notes then in circulation failed to bring the coins out of their hiding places. Throughout the country it was a serious problem to make change. In fact, if a person had a five-dollar gold piece, he would probably have had to take change for a purchase in potatoes, corn or some other commodity.

Merchants' "tickets," metal tokens or anything having any apparent value were pressed into service to make change. Many firms and individual merchants issued their own notes of small value, generally less than one dollar, redeemable at their place of business. These were often called "shinplasters," a term said to have originated during the Revolutionary War when Continental Currency had become almost worthless. (These bills were used in the absence of bandages to protect minor cuts and bruises on the shins. The name came into early use in the United States for notes without legal security.)

Private notes were practically worthless to most people because they could be redeemed only by the firm or person that issued them. They were prohibited by law on July 17, 1862, but were nevertheless issued as the need arose through 1863.

5¢ Note of Newport, Rhode Island
Photo Courtesy H.K. Crofoot Collection

FRACTIONAL CURRENCY

Postage stamps were next turned to as a form of relief from the severe dearth of small coins. Some firms put various amounts of stamps in small envelopes and issued them as change. Henry Russell Drowne, an early collector of Fractional Currency, published an important article on these postage stamp envelopes in the "American Journal of Numismatics," Volume LII, 1918, page 63. He records 90 separate issues of different designs with the names and addresses of sixty of the business firms, stationers, printers, etc. printed on these envelopes.

Photos of some of the envelopes are shown below:

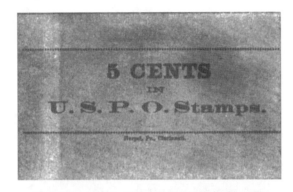

The stamps soon stuck to each other inside the envelopes and the envelopes themselves became torn, so this substitute for coins proved unsatisfactory.

Stamps were also enclosed in brass holders with mica fronts. This idea, patented by J. Gault in 1862, was used by firms as a convenient means of advertising. The name of the business or the product was embossed on the back of the holder. Their denominations were 1¢, 3¢, 5¢, 10¢, 12¢, 24¢, 30¢, and 90¢. Since this was a relatively expensive undertaking, plus the fact that the mica front was easily cracked, the encased postage stamps did not see very wide circulation.

Obverse and Reverse of Encased Postage Stamp.

FRACTIONAL CURRENCY

Typical Examples of Casings Used for Encased Postage Stamps.

Out of this confusion was born one of the most interesting types of paper money — United States Fractional Currency. These beautiful little bills, ranging in denominations from 3¢ to 50¢, played their part to help carry on commerce during and after the Civil War.

The first of the five issues was known as "Postage Currency," and was issued in 1862 and 1863. The next four issues, 1863 to 1876, were called "Fractional Currency." As the term Fractional Currency has been widely used to refer to all U.S. issues of less than one dollar, the author will continue its use for both Postage Currency and Fractional Currency.

FIRST GENERAL ISSUE — Denominations: 5¢, 10¢, 25¢, 50¢

The country was really hard put to carry on even the simplest commercial activities by early 1862. On July 14 of that year, Secretary of the Treasury Salmon P. Chase finally got around to suggesting two alternative proposals to Congress. The first outlined a plan for the reduction in size of silver coins, and the second asked for the authority to issue and use ordinary postage stamps as circulating change. Incredibly enough, Chase himself favored the proposal that would legalize the circulation of small squares of gummed paper as a national medium of exchange!

Congress went ahead and adopted the postage stamp idea, and it actually became law when President Lincoln signed it on July 17, 1862. The immediate effect of the law was a run on stamps at the post offices, since they were needed everywhere and no way had been provided for the Treasury Department to acquire and release the stamps as money. The volume of stamp purchases was very greatly increased. In New York, for example, stamp sales jumped from a daily normal of $3,000 to over $20,000 soon after the new law was announced.

The supply of stamps was soon exhausted. Postmaster General Blair was understandably irritated, since he had not been consulted beforehand. He therefore refused to permit further sale of stamps to be used as money. The Treasury Department then called on Commissioner of Internal Revenue Boutwell to settle things with Blair. In short, Boutwell's suggestions were that specially marked stamps be made, that the Treasury   sell and redeem them, that post offices accept them as postage, and that either party be free to withdraw from such an agreement. Blair accepted these proposals and went ahead with arrangements to print these special stamps for the Treasury.

Meanwhile, a great many stamps had been placed in circulation, and almost immediately they became unfit for further use either as a substitute for coin or as postage. Blair refused to allow their redemption at first. The Treasury was also unwilling to redeem them since it had never sold any stamps to the public in the first place. Blair then gave in, announcing that in the public interest he would redeem the crumpled, sticky messes that were held by so many people.

As previously noted, a special issue of ordinary stamps was agreed upon by Boutwell and Blair to be distributed by the Treasury. This was in accordance with the law of

FRACTIONAL CURRENCY

July 17. Just before their manufacture, it was happily decided to issue them in sizes more convenient to handle than the diminutive postage stamps, and the backs were to be left ungummed. Thus they ceased to be stamps altogether, for in this form they were no less than fractional Federal promissory notes. They bore the authorization date of July 17, 1862, but this was not true. That law referred only to stamps and not to notes; therefore, these small notes were made and issued without any legal authorization whatsoever! (It was not until the law of March 3, 1863 which provided for the government to print fractional notes that the Postage Currency already in use was legally recognized and sanctioned.)

The original format for the Postage Currency was conceived by General F.E. Spinner, then U.S. Treasurer, who pasted unused U.S. postage stamps on bits of treasury paper cut to uniform size for convenience in handling.

The purpose of Spinner's pasted stamps was primarily to develop the idea of what "Postage Currency" might actually look like. It is doubtful whether his pieces ever circulated. All known specimens are unique.

FRACTIONAL CURRENCY

Stamps Pasted on Treasury Paper, Made by General Spinner
Photos Courtesy H.K. Crofoot Collection

An article in the "Washington Star" of this period states:

"...In 1862 small change became very scarce...It was more than a day's search to find a five-cent silver piece...General Spinner was then Treasurer of the United States. He was constantly appealed to from all quarters to do something to supply the demand for small change. In his dilemma he bethought him of the postage stamp. He sent down to the Post Office Department and purchased a quantity of stamps. He then ordered up a package of the paper upon which Government Securities were printed. He cut this into various sizes and on the pieces he pasted stamps to represent different amounts. He thus invented a substitute for fractional silver."

The "Savannah Republican," Savannah, Ga., March 27, 1863, contained this article:

"The Yankee Post Office Department is having postage stamps printed...on ungummed paper, to be used for general circulation as a substitute for specie."

It is interesting to observe that early trial designs carry the heading "Postage Stamps" at the top. This was changed on the actual notes to read "Postage Currency," another step farther from the original law which had called for stamps.

The following illustrations are the Artist's Models or Designs, with corrections, from which the first plates were engraved. They were made "in the similitude" of General Spinner's original pasted bills, and are unique.

FRACTIONAL CURRENCY

Artist's Models labeled "Postage Stamps"
Photos Courtesy H.K. Crofoot Collection

FRACTIONAL CURRENCY

Artist's Models labeled "Postage Stamps"
Photos Courtesy H.K. Crofoot Collection

The fronts of this First Issue were designed under the direction of James Macdonough, a master in bank note designing who was then Secretary of the National Bank Note Company at 1 Wall Street. The lettering was probably engraved by W.D. Nichols, who at an earlier period did similar work for Danforth, Perkins and Company.

The portraits were engraved by W. Marshall, one of the best in the business. The transfer rolls for the postage stamps of the 1861 issue were used to lay down the multiple values on the fronts of the Postage Currency. The lathe work was done by Cyrus Durand.

The backs were designed under the direction of James P. Major, head of the Designing and Engraving Department of the American Bank Note Company, then at 55 Wall Street. Mr. Major was assisted by Nathaniel Jocelyn, formerly of N. & S.S. Jocelyn, a firm which consolidated with the American Bank Note Company in 1858.

The lettering for the back of the five-cent note was engraved by J.E. Van Houten, American Bank Note Company, as shown by the records of Thomas F. Morris, Sr.

The National Currency Bureau was a new department of the government when the First Issue appeared on August 21, 1862. The notes themselves were printed by two bank note companies. The American Bank Note Company printed the back side and the National Bank Note Company printed the front. (It is thought that when the National Bank Note Company printed both the front and the back, the monogram of the American Bank Note Company was removed from the back.) These two concerns were closely related, and contracts were given to both of them in this manner not to prevent the fraudulent issue of money but to prevent possible wrongdoing by individual employees. As notes were needed quickly and time was short, it was desirable that both companies work on this project at the same time. (The New York Bank Note Company, another firm, was busy printing the demand notes of 1861 and postage stamps for the government.)

D.W. Valentine in his book "Fractional Currency" states that Mrs. Whitman, daughter of Thomas Cunningham, neighbor of General F.E. Spinner, recalled conversations between her father and Spinner regarding objections raised against the perforated edges of the First issue. This situation was soon rectified when edges were made straight.

There are no signatures and no Treasury seals on the First Issue. A few sheets made for the government were stamped "Treasury Dept." on the upper right hand corner of the front.

FRACTIONAL CURRENCY

SECOND GENERAL ISSUE — Denominations: 5¢, 10¢, 25¢, 50¢

The Second Issue was authorized by Congress on March 3, 1863 and the name was officially changed to "Fractional Currency." The many counterfeits that had so quickly appeared dictated changes in the design, size and paper.

The cost of producing the First Issue under the contracts with the bank note companies was excessive as compared with the plans for production of the Second Issue by the Treasury Department. Secretary Chase said the price paid for the postal currency to the companies was much greater than their actual cost of production. In his own language —"...though bearing no interest, it was the dearest loan."

When the Second Issue was being considered, therefore, we find the following correspondence dated October 7, 1862 from S.M. Clark, then Chief Clerk of the Treasury Department Bureau of Construction to the Honorable S.P. Chase, Secretary of the Treasury:

"Sir: I have the honor to report that I have matured the details for carrying out the Secretary's plan of supplying the place of the present Postage Currency, with a currency based on the issue of revenue stamps, as follows:

Upon the Secretary's suggestion that the size of all denominations shall be the same as the present 10 cent Postage Currency, I respectfully recommend that —

A sheet of 5 cent stamps contain ....50 or $ 2.50
A sheet of 10 cent stamps contain ....50 or   5.00
A sheet of 25 cent stamps contain ....40 or   10.00
A sheet of 50 cent stamps contain ....40 or   20.00

and that the proposed issue of $100,000 per day be divided as follows:

8,000 sheets, 14 x 19 inches, of 5 cents ....$ 20,000
4,000 sheets, 14 x 19 inches, of 10 cents 20,000
2,000 sheets, 14-1/2 x16 inches, of 25 cents 20,000
2,000 sheets, 14-1/2 x 16 inches, of 50 cents 40,000

16,000 ....$ 100,000

The obverse of all denominations I would print in black, and the reverse in four different colors; say 50's red, 25's purple, 10's green, and 5's tan color.

To print 16,000 sheets per day, (if the obverse is of plate-printing, and the reverse of surface-printing, which I very decidedly recommend) there would be required —

Thirty 22-inch copper-plate presses.
Ten 18-inch copper-plate presses.
Four Gordon presses for surface-printing, similar to those now in use for Bonds.

To trim and separate 16,000 sheets per day, there would be required five trimmers and ten separators.

The power presses, with the trimmers and separators, could be moved by the same power, and in the same room, now used for the small note machinery, without disturbing the present arrangements, except that the present work would require to be suspended for a few days, while the additional machinery was being put in place.

The plate presses, which would be worked by hand, (and for which I do not think machinery can be substituted, as it requires the varied action of the brain as well as the hand at each printing,) could be placed in a portion of the new attic, designed for the west wing, to and from which the paper could be elevated, and the printed sheets lowered, by a dumb waiter, constructed in the southeast corner, on the extreme court yard side.

The engraving of the bed-plates could all be done in the Department by three artists, and would take about thirty days. After the bed-plates were made, eighty-four plates would be required; these could be made by one transfer press, to be worked day and night, which would make one plate by day and one by night; taking forty-two days in all; but in view of possible failures, I should think it safe to say it would take three months.

FRACTIONAL CURRENCY

I have a design prepared for the Secretary's inspection, whenever he has the time to examine it.

The trimmers and separators, with the paper, etc., could all be prepared within the same period.

The cost of the whole, presses, cutters, separators, etc., with fixtures, I estimate, will be less than $20,000. The machinery I make about $16,000, and allow $4,000 for fixtures and contingencies. Making the paper would be in addition to this.

I respectfully suggest that the product be packed in neat paper boxes, in packages of $10, $20, and $50 each, which boxes, for transmission could be packed in hermetically sealed tin boxes, in such quantities as may be required, and then enclosed in wooden cases for transportation.

If these details meet the Secretary's approval, I respectfully recommend that Mr. Neale be placed in charge of the printing department, at a proper compensation, to be under my general direction, and that he be immediately detailed to go to Philadelphia and New York, etc., to secure the necessary plate presses and workmen. The press workmen would be hired 'by the piece,' probably at not over 75¢ to $1 per 100 sheets. (The Secretary can compare this price with the price paid for printing to the Bank Note Companies.)

I further respectfully recommend, as it is impossible for me to get away from Washington until the small-note room is more perfectly systematized, and operatives more experienced than now, that I be authorized to send for such parties to confer with as may be necessary, or to send parties to them if desirable.

I respectfully suggest to the Secretary, if these details are to be carried out, that he should give me some title — (not to carry any pay — but) to give more of an air of official authority, than a naked signature will carry.

If the Secretary approves this project, and endorses it, I will take immediate steps for its prosecution. How soon Mr. Rogers will get his new roof ready, so that the attic can be occupied, I can only conjecture; he will, doubtless, anticipate finishing it before it will be needed, but I have much fear that he will be disappointed.

I have the honor to be, very respectfully, your obedient servant,

S.M. Clark,

Chief Clerk, Bureau of Construction."

The Secretary adopted the report on the 10th of October, 1862, and approved the design.

By October 1, 1864, the Division had printed and finished 3,529,064 sheets of the Second Issue of Fractional Currency, amounting to $13,851,859, issued under act of March 3, 1863.

To give some idea of the amount of fiber paper notes of the Second Issue that was printed to October 1, 1864, S.M. Clark gives these figures:

Fractional Currency on Membrane Paper, printed dry:

5¢	$ 14,821.25
10¢	42,745.00
25¢	293,445.00
50¢	623,000.00
Total on membrane paper	$974,011.25

FRACTIONAL CURRENCY

Printed on Regular Bank Note Paper:

	Printed Dry	Printed Wet
5¢	$ 8,125.00	$ 1,245,005.50
10¢	22,500.00	3,123,237.50
25¢	325,000.00	2,379,230.00
50¢	41,000.00	5,733,750.00
	$396,625.00	12,481,223.00
		396,625.00

Total on regular paper...$12,877,848.00

The cost of printing for the First Issue of Postage Currency by the bank note companies as compared with the Second Issue was noted in 1864 by Clark as follows: "The cost of the issues produced in the department has generally been about one-fourth the amount which the same issues would cost under the former contracts with the New York Bank Note Companies. The amount paid these companies for printing the United States notes, for 14,245,552 impressions, was $1,516,297.38. The cost of the same work, if done in the department, as ascertained and made record of on the 13th of November, 1863, would have been $413,899.93."

THIRD GENERAL ISSUE — Denominations: 3¢, 5¢, 10¢, 25¢, 50¢

The Third General Issue of Fractional Currency came about through provisions of the law of June 30, 1864. S. M. Clark in his report stated that "To protect that portion of the public which will not protect itself by the exercise of ordinary diligence in scrutinizing paper money, the only course of my judgment when a counterfeit gets into the channels of circulation is therefore to make a new issue and withdraw the latter from circulation."

Valentine has this to say regarding the Third General Issue. "Counterfeits of the Second General Issue were more numerous than those of the First Issue and of much better workmanship; this and the increased demand for Fractional Currency necessitated the change of type and created two additional denominations, though one of these, the fifteen-cent denomination, was only made as an "essay," the other, the three-cent denomination, is the first and the only one of such denomination in all issues, and was only printed with the green back. It is the only variety of this issue that has no signature, though none has a seal. The need of this denomination was afterwards eliminated by an Act of Congress March 3, 1865, providing for the coinage of a three-cent coin of nickel."

An Act of Congress May 17, 1866, provided for the coinage of the five-cent nickel and prohibited the issue of any bill with a denomination of less than ten cents.

Valentine and others cannot understand why notes with the likeness of a living person could be issued after the act of April 7, 1866 was passed. However, a careful reading of this act passed by the first session of the thirty-ninth Congress gives the answer. It states:

"Section 12. And be it further enacted, that the following sums be, and the same are hereby appropriated to supply deficiencies in the appropriations for the fiscal year ending the thirtieth of June, eighteen hundred and sixty-five, out of any money in the treasury not otherwise appropriated:

For plates, engraving, printing, and paper for national currency notes, two hundred and fifty thousand dollars: Provided, That no portrait or likeness of any living person hereafter engraved, shall be placed upon any of the bonds, securities, notes, Fractional or Postal Currency of the United States." In other words, if the plates had already been prepared, then the notes could be issued.

FRACTIONAL CURRENCY

The portrait of the controversial S.M. Clark was not eliminated by this act. It was only upon the abolishment of the manufacture of all denominations under Ten Cents that Clark's portrait was permanently removed from U.S. Currency.

All notes of the Third Issue were made by the Treasury Department.

FOURTH GENERAL ISSUE — Denominations: 10¢, 15¢, 25¢, 50¢

There are further improvements in the Fourth General Issue. For the first time the Treasury seal appears on all varieties, bronze surcharges are left off, and the paper is more artistic.

The American Bank Note Company made plates for the fronts of the ten-cent and the "Fifty-Cent Lincoln," and the plates for the backs of the fifteen-cent, twenty-five cent and "Fifty-Cent Stanton." The National Bank Note Company made the plates for the fronts of the fifteen and twenty-five-cent notes and the plates for the backs of the ten-cent note, the "Fifty-Cent Lincoln" and the "Fifty-Cent Dexter." The Bureau of Engraving and Printing made the plates for the fronts of the "Fifty-Cent Stanton" and the "Fifty-Cent Dexter." Mr. C. Burt engraved the portrait of Lincoln. The Columbia and the portrait of Washington were engraved by Douglas C. Romerson.

The bust of Liberty on the ten-cent note is said to be the portrait of a girl named Mary Hull, engraved by C. Burt.

FIFTH GENERAL ISSUE — Denominations: 10¢, 25¢, 50¢

The Fifth and last General Issue was the simplest. Appropriations to print more were about exhausted, and an Act of Congress of April 17, 1876 called for the issuance of fractional silver coins to redeem Fractional Currency.

The few varieties include the green seal ten cents, and the "long key" and "short key" ten and twenty-five cent notes.

All front plates were made at the Bureau of Engraving and Printing. Plates for the backs of the ten and twenty-five cent notes were made by the Columbian Bank Note Company of Washington, D.C., and the back of the fifty-cent note came from the firm of Joseph R. Carpenter of Philadelphia.

The retirement of Fractional Currency has been carried on since 1876. It is estimated that less than one-half of one per cent of the total amount issued of all series is outstanding.

POSTAGE CURRENCY

FIRST ISSUE-August 21, 1862 to May 27, 1863

Illegally issued under the Act of Congress of July 17, 1862, the notes were made by privately operated bank note companies while the new National Currency Bureau was getting organized. Both perforated and unperforated or straight edge notes were issued, the straight edge with monogram being the most common although all are scarce. The monogram ABNCo stands for the American Bank Note Company. Notes of this issue without the monogram are believed to have been printed solely by the National Bank Note Company.

No signatures appear on notes of the First Issue.

POSTAGE CURRENCY
FIRST ISSUE-FIVE CENTS

Brown Face

Black Back, ABNCo Monogram

This note comes in various shades of brown and tan on pale yellow, bright yellow, grayish yellow, orange and buff colored paper. Collectors do not set different values on these shades, but the brightest, cleanest notes are most valuable. It was printed in sheets of twenty notes. These notes have been found with inverted backs, which are of course rare.

	Fine	VF	AU	CU	Ch. CU
Perforated edges, with ABNCo on back	25.00	40.00	65.00	100.00	200.00
Perforated edges, without monogram on back	30.00	45.00	75.00	125.00	270.00
Straight edges, with ABNCo on back	25.00	40.00	50.00	65.00	85.00
Straight edges, without monogram on back	30.00	50.00	80.00	130.00	260.00

Specimen Notes of Five Cents
White or Buff Paper

POSTAGE CURRENCY
FIRST ISSUE-FIVE CENTS

Values are for narrow margin specimens	AU	CU	Ch. CU
Specimen of face	50.00	100.00	150.00
Specimen of back	50.00	100.00	150.00

FIRST ISSUE-TEN CENTS

Green Face   Black Back

This denomination comes in various shades of green on shades of white and grayish white paper. It was printed in sheets of twenty notes. Inverted backs are known and are very rare.

	Fine	VF	AU	CU	Ch. CU
Perforated edges, with ABNCo on back	25.00	40.00	65.00	100.00	200.00
Perforated edges, without monogram on back	30.00	45.00	75.00	125.00	250.00
Straight edges, with ABNCo on back	20.00	35.00	45.00	60.00	85.00
Straight edges, without monogram on back	30.00	50.00	80.00	130.00	270.00

Specimen Notes of Ten Cents
White or Gray Paper.

POSTAGE CURRENCY
FIRST ISSUE-FIVE CENTS

White or Gray Paper. Notice Engraver's Ruling Marks.

	AU	CU	Ch. CU
Specimen of face	50.00	100.00	150.00
Specimen of back	50.00	100.00	150.00

FIRST ISSUE-TWENTY-FIVE CENTS

Brown Face

Black Back

POSTAGE CURRENCY

FIRST ISSUE-TWENTY-FIVE CENTS

This note comes in various shades of brown and on various shades of paper similar to the five-cent denomination. It was printed in sheets of sixteen notes. Inverted backs are known and are rare.

	Fine	VF	AU	CU	Ch. CU
Perforated edges, with ABNCo on back	30.00	45.00	75.00	110.00	250.00
Perforated edges, without monogram on back	35.00	55.00	95.00	165.00	300.00
Straight edges, with ABNCo on back	20.00	30.00	40.00	60.00	110.00
Straight edges, without monogram on back	40.00	60.00	115.00	210.00	350.00

Specimen Notes of Twenty-Five Cents
White or Buff Paper

	AU	CU	Ch. CU
Specimen of face	50.00	150.00	200.00
Specimen of back	50.00	135.00	170.00

POSTAGE CURRENCY
FIRST ISSUE-FIFTY CENTS

Green Face

Black Back

This denomination comes in various shades of green on white, cream and grayish white paper. It was printed in sheets of sixteen notes. Inverted backs are rare.

	Fine	VF	AU	CU	Ch. CU
Perforated edges, with ABNCo on back	35.00	50.00	125.00	225.00	350.00
Perforated edges, without monogram on back	45.00	75.00	140.00	300.00	450.00
Straight edges, with ABNCo on back	22.00	35.00	60.00	100.00	225.00
Straight edges, without monogram on back	50.00	85.00	150.00	340.00	500.00

POSTAGE CURRENCY
FIRST ISSUE-FIFTY CENTS

Specimen Notes of Fifty Cents
White or Gray Paper

	AU	CU	Ch. CU
Specimen of face	50.00	175.00	235.00
Specimen of back	50.00	140.00	180.00

SECOND ISSUE
October 10, 1863 to February 23, 1867

The Act of March 3, 1863 authorized this issue of Fractional Currency and provided that the Treasury Department print its own notes. In line with the suggestion made by Mr. S.M. Clark, Superintendent of the National Currency Bureau, all notes of this issue have the same design, the head of Washington in a bronze oval frame, and each denomination has a different color on the back. This bronze overprint sometimes turns green with age making the notes less valuable than bright ones. Various ideas were incorporated to discourage counterfeiting and to test different kinds of paper. This issue was printed in sheets of twenty notes. Inverted backs and inverted back surcharges are known, but are rare.

Some Specimen notes of the Second Issue are found on paper watermarked CSA.

There are no signatures on notes of the Second Issue.

FRACTIONAL CURRENCY
SECOND ISSUE-FIVE CENTS

Face: Slate Color
with Bronze Oval Frame

Back: Brown with
Bronze Overprint

The surcharges on the reverse place the figure 18 in the lower left corner, the figure 63 in the lower right corner, the letter in upper left corner and the 1 in the upper right corner. Some back surcharges are blurred, and some even seem to be missing.

	Fine	VF	AU	CU	Ch. CU
Without small surcharge on corners of back	16.00	23.00	35.00	45.00	75.00
With surcharge 18-63	18.00	26.00	37.00	50.00	85.00
With surcharge S-18-63	20.00	30.00	40.00	70.00	110.00
With surcharge R-1-18-63. Fiber paper	30.00	50.00	110.00	200.00	400.00

This note is found with surcharge "18" only or surcharge "63" only. A double denomination note with 5¢ face and 50¢ back has been found.

Specimen Notes of Five Cents
White or Parchment Paper

FRACTIONAL CURRENCY
SECOND ISSUE-FIVE CENTS

	AU	CU	Ch. CU
Specimen of face	50.00	100.00	150.00
Specimen of back	50.00	90.00	130.00

SECOND ISSUE-TEN CENTS

Face: Slate Color with Bronze Oval Frame

Back: Green with Bronze Overprint

	Fine	VF	AU	CU	Ch. CU
Without small surcharge on corners of back	15.00	20.00	33.00	45.00	75.00
With surcharge 18-63	16.00	25.00	38.00	55.00	85.00
With surcharge S-18-63	18.00	28.00	45.00	70.00	100.00
With surcharge 1-18-63	25.00	65.00	125.00	200.00	300.00

Rare. Only One or Two Sheets Issued.

	Fine	VF	AU	CU	Ch. CU
With surcharge 0 in upper left, 63 in upper right	550.00	1,000	1,450	2,000	2,850
With surcharge T-1-18-63. Fiber paper	22.00	50.00	100.00	225.00	425.00

This denomination is known with surcharge "18" only and "63" only. It is also found surcharged 63-63, with individual surcharge figures and letters inverted and with the back printing inverted. These are classed as misprints and not priced, as they are rare and appear so seldom that the price is determined on an individual basis.

FRACTIONAL CURRENCY
SECOND ISSUE-TEN CENTS

Specimen Notes of Ten Cents
White or Cream Paper

	AU	CU	Ch. CU
Specimen of face	50.00	110.00	160.00
Specimen of back	50.00	100.00	150.00

A few of these Specimens are printed on fiber paper.

SECOND ISSUE-TWENTY-FIVE CENTS

Face: Slate Color with
Bronze Oval Frame

Back: Purple with Bronze Overprint.
A few are found with a
Steel Colored Back

FRACTIONAL CURRENCY
SECOND ISSUE-TWENTY-FIVE CENTS

	Fine	VF	AU	CU	Ch. CU
Without small surcharge on corners of back	18.00	25.00	40.00	65.00	120.00
With surcharge 18-63	20.00	30.00	50.00	75.00	110.00
With surcharge S-18-63	18.00	25.00	40.00	65.00	110.00
With surcharge 2-18-63	25.00	40.00	65.00	130.00	150.00
With surcharge A-18-63	26.00	38.00	60.00	85.00	120.00
With surcharge T-1-18-63. Fiber paper	35.00	50.00	100.00	300.00	450.00
With surcharge T-2-18-63. Fiber paper	33.00	45.00	90.00	275.00	450.00

This note is also found surcharged 1-S-63, "18" only and "63" only. These are rare and are not considered regular issues. S-18-63 comes with inverted "S" only, the balance of the surcharge not being inverted.

Specimen Notes of Twenty-Five Cents
White or Cream Paper. Note Plate Number 8.

	AU	CU	Ch. CU
Specimen of face	50.00	125.00	150.00
Specimen of back	50.00	110.00	130.00

FRACTIONAL CURRENCY
SECOND ISSUE-FIFTY CENTS

Face: Slate Color with Bronze Oval Frame	Back: Red with Bronze Overprint. Some are Reddish Orange.

	Fine	VF	AU	CU	Ch. CU
Without small surcharge on corners of back			**Unconfirmed**		

Beware of forgeries or notes with the surcharge removed. Here is one case where the Specimen note is not as valuable as the regular note.

	Fine	VF	AU	CU	Ch. CU
With surcharge 18-63. (Also comes with 18 only or 63 only)	32.00	45.00	75.00	175.00	275.00
With surcharge 1-18-63	32.00	45.00	75.00	175.00	275.00

Surcharge A-18-63	Surcharge T-18-63

	Fine	VF	AU	CU	Ch. CU
With surcharge A-18-63	32.00	45.00	75.00	175.00	275.00
With surcharge O-1-18-63. Fiber paper	40.00	60.00	175.00	250.00	400.00
With surcharge R-2-18-63. Fiber paper	45.00	75.00	210.00	300.00	475.00
With surcharge T-1-18-63. Fiber paper	40.00	60.00	175.00	250.00	400.00
Also known with T-18-63 (no 1). Fiber paper					**Rare**

Specimen Notes of Fifty Cents
White or Cream Paper

	AU	CU	Ch. CU
Specimen of face	50.00	130.00	225.00
Specimen of back (no surcharge)	50.00	125.00	170.00

FRACTIONAL CURRENCY
THIRD ISSUE
December 5, 1864 to August 16, 1869

The Third Issue includes the first three-cent note. The designs of this issue are different for each denomination. They are more intricate than the first two issues. The five-cent notes and higher denominations have the signatures of the Register and the Treasurer, and also have sheet position check letters and numbers. Those with green backs have printed signatures but the red back notes of ten, fifteen and fifty cents have both printed and autographed signatures. This is one of the rare instances of autographed signatures appearing on United States regular issue notes.

Though the larger U.S. notes carried some form of signature from their inception in 1861, it was not until the Third Issue of Fractional Currency that signatures were placed on the smaller notes. All denominations except the three-cent note carry either printed or autographed signatures, as indicated in the listings for each type and denomination. The names of the officials whose signatures appear on the notes are: S.B. Colby, N.L. Jeffries or John Allison as Register, and F.E. Spinner or John C. New as Treasurer.

Some of the Specimens of this series are on paper watermarked CSA.

THIRD ISSUE–THREE CENTS

Face
Dark Background

Face
Light Background

Back Green

These were printed in sheets of twenty-five notes. These notes are made on thick or thin paper and are occasionally found with inverted backs.

	Fine	VF	AU	CU	Ch. CU
With light background to Washington's portrait	35.00	42.00	75.00	120.00	110.00
With dark background to Washington's portrait	30.00	38.00	65.00	90.00	175.00

FRACTIONAL CURRENCY
THIRD ISSUE-THREE CENTS

Specimen Note of Three Cents
White or Cream Paper

	AU	CU	Ch. CU
Specimen of face with dark background	50.00	100.00	150.00
Specimen of face with light background	—	—	—
Specimen of back	50.00	70.00	110.00

THIRD ISSUE–FIVE CENTS

Face Black Back Red or Green

FRACTIONAL CURRENCY
THIRD ISSUE-FIVE CENTS

These were printed in sheets of twenty notes. Spencer M. Clark (1810-1890) was Superintendent of the National Currency Bureau and had his likeness put on this note without authority from his superiors. This action caused a law to be passed forbidding the unauthorized portrait of a living person to appear on United States currency. (See History, page 173).

	Fine	VF	AU	CU	Ch. CU
With red back	35.00	60.00	100.00	125.00	175.00
Same with position letter "a" on face	45.00	65.00	110.00	150.00	250.00
With green back	20.00	30.00	55.00	90.00	110.00
Same with position letter "a" on face	25.00	35.00	75.00	100.00	145.00

a				
a				
a				
a				

Location of Sheet Position of Letter "a"

The letter "a" is not always the same size nor in exactly the same position.

FRACTIONAL CURRENCY
THIRD ISSUE-FIVE CENTS

Specimen Note of Five Cents
White or Cream Paper

	AU	CU	Ch. CU
Specimen of face	50.00	100.00	150.00
Specimen of red back	50.00	90.00	120.00
Specimen of green back	50.00	70.00	115.00

THIRD ISSUE-TEN CENTS

Face Black

Back Red or Green

FRACTIONAL CURRENCY
THIRD ISSUE-TEN CENTS

These were printed in sheets of sixteen. Through an inexcusable error, the word "CENTS" does not appear anywhere on this note. The numeral 1 comes in both large and small size and its position varies slightly.

	Fine	VF	AU	CU	Ch. CU
Red back with printed signatures	25.00	35.00	75.00	125.00	170.00
Same with position numeral "1" on face	35.00	50.00	100.00	150.00	200.00
Red back with autographed signatures					
"Colby" and "Spinner"	55.00	80.00	125.00	175.00	250.00
Same with autographed signatures					
"Jeffries" and "Spinner"	70.00	95.00	140.00	300.00	375.00
Green back with printed signatures	20.00	30.00	50.00	80.00	100.00
Same with position numeral "1" on face	26.00	38.00	65.00	90.00	115.00

TEN CENTS

1		
1		
1		
1		

Location of Position Numeral "1"

The numeral "1" comes in both large and small sizes, and its position varies slightly.

FRACTIONAL CURRENCY
THIRD ISSUE-TEN CENTS

Specimen Notes of Ten Cents

Values are for narrow margin specimens	AU	CU	Ch. CU
Specimen of face with printed signatures "Colby" and "Spinner"	50.00	110.00	135.00
Specimen of face with autographed signatures "Colby" and "Spinner"	100.00	200.00	300.00
Same with autographed signatures "Jeffries" and "Spinner"	50.00	110.00	135.00
Specimen of red back	50.00	110.00	135.00
Specimen of green back	50.00	100.00	120.00

THIRD ISSUE-FIFTEEN CENTS

Wide Margin, Face Black Only

FRACTIONAL CURRENCY
THIRD ISSUE-FIFTEEN CENTS

Back Red or Green

This denomination was made only in uniface Specimens and was not placed in actual circulation. As previously mentioned under the five-cent note of this issue, a law was passed making it illegal to place the likeness of a living person on currency before this note had been produced in quantity for circulation, and while Grant and Sherman were alive. The notes produced with wide margins are the first Specimens or essays. Those with narrow margins were printed or cut for the Fractional Currency Shields which were being assembled at this same time. They were probably cut from the wide margin notes. (See Fractional Shields.) Many of the wide margin Specimens show engraver's ruling marks. Prices are for the narrow margin notes. Wide margin notes are considerably more valuable.

	AU	CU	Ch. CU
Specimen of face with autographed signatures "Colby" and "Spinner"	700.00	1,750	2,000
Same with autographed signatures "Jeffries" and "Spinner"	200.00	325.00	400.00
Same with autographed signatures "Allison" and "Spinner"	300.00	400.00	600.00

Narrow Margin Face, No signatures

	AU	CU	Ch. CU
Same without any signatures		Rare	—
Specimen of red back	90.00	175.00	250.00
Specimen of face with printed signatures "Colby" and "Spinner"	300.00	400.00	500.00
Specimen of green back	90.00	175.00	225.00

The Allison signature is found as "Allison" or "Alleson." Jeffries is written "Jeffus" or "Jeffries."

FRACTIONAL CURRENCY
THIRD ISSUE-TWENTY-FIVE CENTS

Face Black

William Pitt Fessenden (1806-1869) was Secretary of the Treasury in 1864-65. He was a United States Senator from Maine.

Back Red or Green

These were printed in sheets of twelve notes.

	Fine	VF	AU	CU	Ch. CU
Red back with printed signatures	20.00	35.00	70.00	125.00	175.00
Same with position letter "a" on face	30.00	50.00	90.00	150.00	200.00
Green back with printed signatures	16.00	30.00	60.00	85.00	110.00
Same with position letter "a" on face	26.00	45.00	80.00	110.00	150.00
Green back with surcharge M-2-6-5. (Fiber paper)	30.00	60.00	150.00	200.00	300.00
Same with position letter "a" on face	40.00	80.00	170.00	250.00	350.00

Solid Surcharge, and Position Letter "a"

	CU	Ch. CU
Same as above, the two ornamental designs on the face surcharged in heavy solid bronze instead of outlined. Fiber paper		Rare
Same as above, with position letter "a" on face		Very Rare

FRACTIONAL CURRENCY
THIRD ISSUE-TWENTY-FIVE CENTS

a		
a		
a		
a		

Location of Position Letter "a" on face.

The letter "a" comes in both large and small sizes.

FRACTIONAL CURRENCY
THIRD ISSUE-TWENTY-FIVE CENTS

Specimen Notes of Twenty-Five Cents

	AU	CU	Ch. CU
Specimen of face	70.00	100.00	150.00
Specimen of red back	75.00	125.00	175.00
Specimen of green back	70.00	100.00	150.00

THIRD ISSUE-FIFTY CENTS — TYPE 1

Face in Black, Justice Seated

FRACTIONAL CURRENCY
THIRD ISSUE-FIFTY CENTS-TYPE 1

Back Red or Green

These were printed in sheets of twelve notes.

	VG	VF	Ex. Fine	AU	CU
Red back with printed signatures and no surcharge	65.00	80.00	135.00	250.00	375.00
Same with position figures "1" and "a" on face	225.00	450.00	800.00	1,300	2,400
Same with position figure "1" only	75.00	100.00	160.00	275.00	425.00
Same with position letter "a" only	90.00	125.00	180.00	290.00	450.00
Red back, printed signatures with surcharge S-2-6-4 on back. Fiber paper	3,000	5,000	7,000	9,000	12,000
Same with position figures "1" and "a" on face. Fiber paper	—	—	—	—	—
Same with position figure "1" only. Fiber paper	4,000	6,000	8,000	1,000	13,000
Same with position letter "a" only. Fiber paper	5,000	7,000	9,000	11,000	14,000
Red back, printed signatures, with surcharge A-2-6-5 on back. Plain paper	75.00	100.00	145.00	250.00	390.00
These surcharge letters come in two slightly different sizes.					
Same with position figures "1" and "a" on face. Plain paper	450.00	750.00	950.00	1,400	2,200
Same with position figure "1" only. Plain paper	105.00	135.00	175.00	300.00	425.00
Same with position letter "a" only. Plain paper	115.00	145.00	185.00	320.00	450.00
Red back without surcharge or position figures, with autographed signatures of "Colby" and "Spinner."	80.00	110.00	150.00	260.00	390.00
Red back with surcharge S-2-6-4, with autographed signatures of "Colby" and "Spinner." Fiber paper	250.00	400.00	600.00	900.00	1,200
Red back with surcharge A-2-6-5, with autographed signatures of "Colby" and "Spinner." Plain paper	90.00	125.00	165.00	280.00	425.00
Green back (all green back notes have printed signatures). No surcharge or position figures	60.00	90.00	120.00	190.00	275.00

FRACTIONAL CURRENCY
THIRD ISSUE-FIFTY CENTS-TYPE 1

	VG	VF	Ex. Fine	AU	CU
Same with position figures "1" and "a" on face	400.00	700.00	1,200	1,600	2,300
Same with position figure "1" only on face	70.00	100.00	130.00	200.00	285.00
Same with position letter "a" only on face	80.00	110.00	140.00	230.00	300.00
Green back with surcharge A-2-6-5 on back, compactly spaced	65.00	95.00	120.00	190.00	260.00

Surcharge A-2-6-5 Compactly Spaced

	VG	Fine	Ex. Fine	AU	CU
Same with position figures "1" and "a" on face	175.00	275.00	425.00	650.00	950.00
Same with position figure "1" only on face	80.00	110.00	140.00	240.00	325.00
Same with position letter "a" only on face	100.00	120.00	160.00	260.00	350.00

Surcharge A-2-6-5 Widely Spaced

	VG	Fine	Ex. Fine	AU	CU
Green reverse with surcharge A-2-6-5 on back, widely spaced	75.00	110.00	165.00	225.00	360.00
Same with position figures "1" and "a" on face	450.00	750.00	1,100	2,300	3,800
Same with position figure "1" only on face	90.00	170.00	250.00	400.00	525.00
Same with position letter "a" only on face	100.00	180.000	270.00	430.00	560.00

FRACTIONAL CURRENCY
THIRD ISSUE-FIFTY CENTS-TYPE 1

Back Surcharge S-2-6-4

	VG	Fine	Ex. Fine	AU	CU
Green back with surcharge S-2-6-4. Fiber paper. Only a few known			**Extremely Rare**		
Green back with surcharge A-2-6-5. Fiber paper	100.00	150.00	335.00	450.00	650.00
Same with position figures "1" and "a" on face. Fiber paper	350.00	450.00	1,500	2,500	3,500
Same with position figure "1" only. Fiber paper	145.00	210.00	375.00	525.00	750.00
Same with position letter "a" only. Fiber paper	175.00	245.00	435.00	575.00	850.00

1 a	a	a
1		
1		
1		

Location of Position Figures "1" and "a"

The "1" and "a" come large and small; their position may vary slightly.

Specimen Notes of Fifty Cents
Justice Face

FRACTIONAL CURRENCY
THIRD ISSUE-FIFTY CENTS-TYPE 1

Back

	AU	CU	Ch. CU
Specimen of obverse with autographed signatures of "Colby" and "Spinner"	75.00	180.00	275.00
Same with autographed signatures "Jeffries" and "Spinner"	125.00	250.00	400.00
Specimen of red back	50.00	150.00	250.00
Specimen of face with printed signatures	75.00	125.00	200.00
Specimen of green back	50.00	150.00	250.00

THIRD ISSUE-FIFTY CENTS-TYPE 2

Face Black

General F.E. Spinner (1802-1890), the "father of Fractional Currency," is portrayed on this note. He was Treasurer of the United States from 1861 to 1875. (See History.)

FRACTIONAL CURRENCY
THIRD ISSUE-FIFTY CENTS-TYPE 2

Back Red or Green

These were printed in sheets of twelve notes. The location of position figures and letters is the same as the previous note. Some of the autographed notes come with only one signature.

	VG	VF	Ex. Fine	AU	CU
Red back with printed signatures and with surcharge A-2-6-5 on back	80.00	100.00	150.00	200.00	275.00
Same with position figures "1" and "a" on face	190.00	300.00	500.00	675.00	850.00
Same with position figure "1" only on face	100.00	125.00	175.00	230.00	285.00
Same with position letter "a" only on face	110.00	140.00	190.00	250.00	310.00
Red back with surcharge A-2-6-5, with autographed signatures of "Colby" and "Spinner." This note is also found with one signature.	70.00	95.00	145.00	200.00	265.00

One Signature — Spinner. Rare.

	VG	VF	Ex. Fine	AU	CU
Red back with surcharge A-2-6-5, with autographed signatures of "Allison" and "Spinner"	110.00	175.00	275.00	400.00	600.00

Signatures of Allison and New

	VG	VF	Ex. Fine	AU	CU
Red back with surcharge A-2-6-5, with autographed signatures of "Allison" and "New." This is another rare note; only about twenty are known, possibly only twenty-four issued			**Extremely Rare**		
Green back, without surcharge or position figures	65.00	85.00	115.00	150.00	235.00
Same with position figures "1" and "a" on face	95.00	115.00	165.00	210.00	290.00
Same with position figure "1" only	110.00	125.00	175.00	225.00	265.00
Same with position letter "a" only	120.00	135.00	185.00	235.00	275.00
Green back with surcharge A-2-6-5 on back	135.00	165.00	185.00	265.00	325.00
Same with position figures "1" and "a" on face	500.00	900.00	1,400	2,100	2,900
Same with position figure "1" only	135.00	170.00	200.00	300.00	360.00
Same with position letter "a" only	145.00	180.00	220.00	320.00	380.00

FRACTIONAL CURRENCY
THIRD ISSUE-FIFTY CENTS-TYPE 2

Specimen Notes of Fifty Cents

	AU	CU	Ch. CU
Specimen of face with autographed signatures of "Colby" and "Spinner"	100.00	150.00	300.00
Same with autographed signatures of "Jeffries" and "Spinner"	2,000	3,800	5,000
Specimen of red back	75.00	175.00	250.00
Specimen of face with printed signatures	75.00	125.00	200.00
Specimen of green back	75.00	125.00	200.00

THIRD ISSUE-FIFTY CENTS-TYPE 3

Face Black

FRACTIONAL CURRENCY
THIRD ISSUE-FIFTY CENTS-TYPE 3

Back Green

These were printed in sheets of twelve notes. The notes are found on regular paper or heavier cream paper.

	VG	VF	Ex. Fine	AU	CU
Green back without surcharge or position figures	90.00	100.00	150.00	240.00	325.00
Same with position figures "1" and "a" on face	100.00	175.00	225.00	400.00	650.00
Same with position figure "1" only	70.00	95.00	125.00	200.00	330.00
Same with position letter "a" only	70.00	110.00	150.00	225.00	350.00

	AU	CU	Ch. CU
Specimen of face with printed signatures	70.00	125.00	175.00
Specimen of back, green	50.00	100.00	200.00

FOURTH ISSUE
July 14, 1869 to February 16, 1875

Each of the notes of this issue is of a different design. The United States Treasury Seal was added to the faces for the first time. A new improved type of bank note paper containing silk fibers was used. All backs and most faces of these notes were printed by the American Bank Note Company and the National Bank Note Company, both of New York.

Some notes were issued without the seal, through error. No Specimen notes of the Fourth Issue were printed.

All notes of this issue carry printed signatures of John Allison, Register and F.E. Spinner, Treasurer.

Some notes of the Fourth and Fifth Issues come with a bright pink color over the entire face. These are worth a premium.

TEN CENTS

Face Black

FRACTIONAL CURRENCY
FOURTH ISSUE-TEN CENTS

Back Green

These were printed in sheets of sixteen notes. The face design shows a bust of Liberty. "Allison" is spelled with an "i," an "e" with a dot over it or with a closed "e."

	Fine	VF	AU	CU	Ch. CU
Large red seal (40 millimeters),watermarked	16.00	24.00	30.00	50.00	70.00
Same large seal, paper with pink silk fibers	18.00	27.00	35.00	55.00	75.00
Same large seal, paper with violet fibers and blue ends	20.00	32.00	40.00	60.00	80.00
Smaller red seal (38 millimeters), paper with violet fibers and blue ends.	22.00	35.00	45.00	65.00	85.00

Note: The lines making up the design of the large seal are finer and closer together than those of the small seal, especially noticeable in the border of the shield inside the seal. The color of these seals varies from red to pink. Some have an orange tinge.

FOURTH ISSUE-FIFTEEN CENTS

Face Black — Bust of Columbia

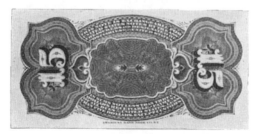

Back Green

FRACTIONAL CURRENCY
FOURTH ISSUE-FIFTEEN CENTS

These were printed in sheets of twelve notes. Allison spelled as before.

	Fine	VF	AU	CU	Ch. CU
Large red seal (40 millimeters), watermarked	45.00	60.00	90.00	140.00	160.00
Same large seal, paper with pink fibers	65.00	85.00	125.00	175.00	225.00
Same, paper with violet fibers and blue ends	60.00	80.00	110.00	165.00	185.00
Smaller red seal (38 millimeters), paper with violet fibers and blue ends.	65.00	80.00	120.00	175.00	195.00

On a few notes Columbia seems to have a hairpin in her hair under the third star.

FOURTH ISSUE-TWENTY-FIVE CENTS

Face Black — Bust of Washington

Back Green

These were printed in sheets of twelve notes.

	Fine	VF	AU	CU	Ch. CU
Large red seal (40 millimeters), watermarked	17.00	26.00	32.00	48.00	75.00
Same seal, paper with pink fibers	20.00	28.00	38.00	60.00	80.00
Same seal, paper with violet fibers and blue ends	26.00	35.00	45.00	70.00	95.00
Smaller red seal (38 millimeters), paper with violet fibers and blue ends	28.00	37.00	47.00	68.00	90.00

Face Black — Bust of Lincoln

Back Green

These were printed in sheets of twelve notes.

	Fine	VF	AU	CU	Ch. CU
Large red seal (40 millimeters), watermarked paper with pink fibers	60.00	90.00	200.00	300.00	400.00

FIFTY CENTS — TYPE 2

Face Black

These were printed in sheets of twelve notes. The bust of E.M. Stanton (1814-1869), Secretary of War under Lincoln, appears on the face.

FRACTIONAL CURRENCY
FOURTH ISSUE-FIFTY CENTS-TYPE 2
E. M. Stanton

Back Green

	Fine	VF	AU	CU	Ch. CU
Small red seal, paper with violet fibers and blue ends	28.00	55.00	90.00	175.00	225.00

FIFTY CENTS — TYPE 3

Face Black

Bust of Samuel Dexter (born at Boston May 14, 1761, died May 4, 1816). Dexter served as Secretary of War and Secretary of the Treasury under President John Adams.

Back Green

FRACTIONAL CURRENCY
FOURTH ISSUE-FIFTY CENTS-TYPE 3
Samuel Dexter

These were printed in sheets of twelve notes.

	Fine	VF	AU	CU	Ch. CU
Green seal, paper has violet fibers and blue ends. Some notes have a very light trace of blue on the ends. This seal comes in various shades of green	23.00	40.00	75.00	100.00	140.00

FIFTH ISSUE
February 26, 1874 to February 15, 1876

The Fifth and last issue was short; it contained only three notes, each of a different design. The appropriations for printing Fractional Currency were exhausted with this issue. No new funds for this purpose were provided.

No Specimen notes were made of the Fifth Issue. Some notes were issued without seals, through error.

All notes of the Fifth Issue carry printed signatures. The Ten Cent and Twenty-Five Cent notes have John Allison, Register and F.E. Spinner, Treasurer. The Fifty Cent notes have John C. New as Treasurer.

TEN CENTS

Face Black — Showing Long Key

Short Key

Bust of William M. Meredith (1799-1873), Secretary of the Treasury 1849-1850.

FRACTIONAL CURRENCY
FIFTH ISSUE-TEN CENTS

Back Green

	Fine	VF	AU	CU	Ch. CU
Green seal, printed on bank note paper. This note is always found with the long key	18.00	28.00	40.00	60.00	70.00
Red seal with long key, 5 millimeters	17.00	24.00	30.00	35.00	45.00
Red seal with short key, 4 millimeters	17.00	20.00	24.00	32.00	40.00

FIFTH ISSUE-TWENTY-FIVE CENTS

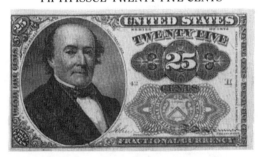

Face Black

Bust of Robert J. Walker, (born at Northumberland, Pennsylvania, July 23, 1801 and died November 11, 1869.) He was Secretary of the Treasury under President Polk from 1845-1849.

Back Green

FRACTIONAL CURRENCY
FIFTH ISSUE-TWENTY-FIVE CENTS

	Fine	VF	AU	CU	Ch. CU
Red seal with long key, 5 millimeters	16.00	22.00	30.00	43.00	50.00
Red seal with short key, 4 millimeters	16.00	22.00	30.00	43.00	50.00

FIFTH ISSUE-FIFTY CENTS

Face Black
Bust of William H. Crawford (1722-1834), Secretary of War and Treasury Departments from 1815-1825.

Back Green

	Fine	VF	AU	CU	Ch. CU
Red seal, white paper with silk fibers and blue ends. Some notes have a very slight trace of blue on the ends and some have a pink face	25.00	32.00	45.00	65.00	90.00

The backs of this issue have various shades of green caused by yellow-green and blue-green ink. The seal is found in various shades of red, from an orange to a dark red color.

FRACTIONAL SHIELDS

The Fractional Shield was first issued in 1866 as an aid in the detection of counterfeits. It contains 39 Specimen notes of the first three issues of Postage and Fractional Currency including the Grant and Sherman essays.

The Specimen notes were printed on one side and some were trimmed with very narrow margins before being pasted on the shields. Girls employed in the Treasury Department prepared these shields. They placed the notes on a cardboard back, size 20-5/8 inches by 24-5/8 inches. The shape of the shield with the eagle and stars above it was printed on this cardboard. Another piece of cardboard was placed behind this and both were then put under glass in a frame. The frame is a beautiful example of early wood moulding made of solid walnut.

The notes were not always placed in the same order but the face value of the face Specimens was the same, $4.66. The Fourth and Fifth Issues were not included since the shields were completed before these were issued.

Shields were made available to banks and other institutions to show type sets of Fractional Currency which could be checked against those offered over their counters. In a letter written by the Treasurer of the United States on May 28, 1868, he stated that the shields were "sent free of express charges for Four and 50/100 dollars each."

FRACTIONAL SHIELDS

The demand for the shields was not as great as anticipated; therefore, some were stored in Washington for a number of years. Most of the boards seen today are stained, and seem to be water damaged. Some shields remaining unsold reportedly were destroyed about 1869.

The 39 notes on the shield are composed of 20 faces and 19 backs. There are two faces of the 3¢ note, one with the light curtain and one with the dark curtain, but only one three-cent back.

An eagle and thirteen stars appear at the top of the shield. The size of the actual shield is approximately 19-1/2 by 23-1/2 inches. The original frames were 24-1/2 by 28-1/4 inches. All these shields are rare, the gray background type being somewhat more available than the pink or green type.

Valentine, in his book "Fractional Currency of the United States," gives this description of the shield:

"A 'shield' is an assortment of 39 closely trimmed specimens that the government mounted on a mat of heavy paper on which was engraved a large shield, surmounted by an eagle standing on a shield, in the talons of the eagle, at the right is a number of arrows, and at the left is an olive branch with leaves and berries on it and a streamer on which is 'E pluribus unum.' Above the eagle are 13 stars in two curved rows, 9 in the upper and 4 in the lower. The engraved shield seems to have been spaced as for stars and bars, in the space where the stars would have been are 13 specimens in three rows, 4 in each of the upper two and 5 in the third row; in the space where the bars would have been are 26 specimens arranged in 6 rows of 4 in each row and below these under the second and third columns are the other 2, to fill out the space under the first and fourth columns is the Treasury seal. The assortment of 39 specimens were not all the same, on each shield, though the arrangement of denominations did not vary."

		VF
Shield with Gray Background	RARE	$ 2,800
Shield with Pink Background	VERY RARE	8,000
Shield with Green Background	VERY RARE	—

COUNTERFEITS AND COUNTERFEITING

It did not take long for counterfeits of Fractional Currency to appear. The First Issue was counterfeited quickly and rather successfully, therefore the Second Issue was prepared with a more intricate design. The paper was changed from regular bank note paper. Various types of fiber paper (or as it was called in that day, membrane paper) were tried. Each new issue employed other methods or new ideas, such as surcharges on the face and back, to discourage counterfeiters. Before the use of membrane and other special papers it was reported that about three hundred and fifty dollars of counterfeit Fractional Currency was uncovered daily.

Heath's Counterfeit Detector, issued at that time, pictured examples of Fractional Currency so that the originals could be distinguished. The following comment appeared in the Second Edition of the pocket size edition:

"In presenting to the public two plates of Scrip, or Fractional Currency, we wish to say that the 50¢ Scrip (which is the first on the plates) is the best executed counterfeit ever issued. It was engraved by a man who was an expert in the art, as thousands who have been made dupes to his nefarious designs can testify. He was finally arrested by the Secret Service Division, convicted, his plates secured, and his illegal business broken up."

COUNTERFEITS AND COUNTERFEITING

50 Cents Counterfeit

25 Cents Counterfeit

10 Cents Counterfeit

50 Cents Counterfeit

COUNTERFEITS AND COUNTERFEITING

In the December, 1862, issue of the "Connecticut Bank Note List," Hartford, Connecticut, the counterfeiting of Postage Currency was noted with the following article:

"There are counterfeit 50 cents of the Postage Currency in circulation, and as they are quite well executed, we desire to put the public on their guard against them. There are four distinct and easily noted marks by which they may be detected. 1st. The paper is thinner than the genuine. 2d. The five faces of Washington vary considerably from each other in the counterfeit — so much so, that two or three of them,if standing alone, would hardly be taken to be the portraits of Washington — while on the genuine they closely resemble each other. 3d. The linked letters "U.S." under the middle face of Washington in the counterfeit do not show the lower end of the "S" inside of the leg of the "U" while in the genuine they do. The mark is easily seen. 4th. The border around the lettering and "50" on the back of the counterfeit is dark, and the lines are crowded, while in the genuine the border is open which includes a line of light dots running though the middle. In the counterfeit the middle line is almost invisible, while in the genuine it is so distinct as to catch the eye at once. By these marks one will be enabled to detect the counterfeit."

Mr. Thomas Cunningham, Mohawk, N.Y., an intimate friend of Spinner, listed thirteen counterfeit fractional notes in his article appearing in 1893 in the American Journal of Numismatics, Volume XXVII No. 4. His actual collection as examined by the author contained fifteen counterfeits.

A counterfeit is known of the 25¢ Fessenden, Third Issue, that is almost perfect to the last detail; but it did not have the bronze surcharges on the obverse, as this surcharge was hard to duplicate. Many rather crude counterfeits have been found in some of the old Fractional Currency still floating around. Most of these are of the various denominations of the First, Second and Third Issues.

The United States Secret Service must take up all counterfeit U.S. currency so naturally these counterfeits are non-collectible. However, they are mentioned because they explain why this series contains so many varieties, so many types of paper and so many designs. Much time and effort was spent on each new issue to prevent counterfeiting.

GLOSSARY OF TERMS

The following diagram illustrates the respective positions of various characters and symbols found on modern U.S. currency issues. The nomenclature will be fully explained in succeeding sections of this book.

1. TYPE OF NOTE — Federal Reserve Note, Silver Certificate, United States Note, National Currency.*

2. SERIAL NUMBER — Every note has two identical serial numbers.

3. PORTRAIT — Each denomination carries a distinctive portrait. On notes of Series 1990 and later, the portrait has a security border of microprinting.

4. SERIES DATE — The indicated position is for notes of later issue. Earlier printings carry the series date two times on the face, and in varying positions.

5. SIGNATURE — Treasurer of the United States.

6. SIGNATURE — Secretary of the Treasury.

7. TREASURY SEAL — Blue, green, red, brown, gold or yellow.

8. CHECK LETTERS — Sheet-fed notes printed in Washington have two identical check letters which indicate the position on a full printed sheet. On sheet-fed notes printed at Fort Worth small letters FW are added before the check letter. Web-fed notes printed in Washington do not have a check letter.

9. FACE PLATE SERIAL NUMBER — On sheet-fed notes the plate number is positioned at the lower right adjacent to a check letter. It designates the specific plate from which the note was printed. The small number in this position on web-fed notes is a face check number used in place of a check letter.

10. QUADRANT NUMBER — Going from 1 to 4, this is found only on sheet-fed issues printed in sheets of 32 notes.

11. FEDERAL RESERVE BANK SEAL — Found only on Federal Reserve Notes.

12. FEDERAL RESERVE DISTRICT NUMBERS — Found only on Federal Reserve Notes.

*Gold Certificates do not have the Type Heading in the usual position at the top

TABLE OF PORTRAITS AND DESIGNS

Denomination	Portrait on Face	Design on Back
$1	George Washington	Great Seal
$2	Thomas Jefferson	Monticello
$5	Abraham Lincoln	Lincoln Memorial
$10	Alexander Hamilton	U.S. Treasury
$20	Andrew Jackson	White House
$50	Ulysses S. Grant	U.S. Capitol
$100	Benjamin Franklin	Independence Hall
$500	William McKinley	Value
$1000	Grover Cleveland	Value
$5000	James Madison	Value
$10,000	Salmon P. Chase	Value
$100,000	Woodrow Wilson	Value

Papers and Inks

To guard against counterfeiting, United States paper money is printed by engraved intaglio steel plates on distinctive paper. The currency paper for dry printing is made of 75% cotton and 25% linen, and contains small segments of red and blue fibers which are imbedded during manufacture. Strict government control is exercised during the preparation of this paper.

For 85 years (1879-1964) the firm of Crane and Company, Dalton, Massachusetts, was the sole producer of currency paper for the Bureau. From 1964 to 1969 the Bureau has had contracts with the Gilbert Paper Company of Menasha, Wisconsin (a subsidiary of the Meade Paper Corporation of Dayton, Ohio) to furnish some of its paper needs. Since then Crane has been the exclusive supplier.

Until 1980, all inks used in plate and surface printing were manufactured in the Bureau by blending dry colors, oils and extenders of the highest quality obtainable in huge mixers. The blended ink mixtures were ground under extreme pressure in large mills between water-cooled heavy steel rollers to ensure the proper texture. From 1980 to 1983, the Bureau withdrew from manufacturing its own ink. During that period SICPA of Lausanne, Switzerland, gradually undertook the supply of currency ink.

Plate Manufacture

To afford the best protection against counterfeiting, all United States paper money, as well as nearly all postage stamps and other evidences of a financial character issued by the United States Government, are printed from plates made from steel engravings. This type of printing is known as intaglio. Of all the printing processes, intaglio is the most difficult to produce and to counterfeit. Other processes lack the fidelity of fine line engraving and the distinctive third dimensional effect of raised line on paper inherent in intaglio printing. Another outstanding element of protection is the portrait. The use of portraits in security design takes full advantage of the characteristics of intaglio printing since even a slight alteration in breadth, spacing or depth of line on the part of a counterfeiter will cause a perceptible facial change.

In the intaglio-plate manufacturing process the individual features of a chosen design are hand-tooled by highly skilled engravers who carve dots and lines of varying depths into soft pieces of steel with delicate steel-cutting instruments called gravers. With infinite care each feature, such as the portrait, the vignette, the numerals, the lettering, the script and the scroll work, is hand-engraved by a different master craftsman expertly trained in his own particular skill. The fine crosshatched lines in the background of the portrait are precisely etched from lines ruled in wax on a ruling machine. An unlimited number of intricate lacy patterns for use as borders and ornamentation are deftly cut by means of a geometric lathe. It takes years to acquire the skill of an engraver and it is impossible for him to exactly reproduce his own work, much less that of another engraver. It takes several engravers to prepare the hand-engraved pieces of steel, or dies, as they are called, that are used to make up a master roll or plate.

Currency Manufacture

The Bureau printed all currency by the wet intaglio process on sheet-fed flatbed presses until 1957. As part of an extensive modernization program which has been in progress since 1950, nine high-speed sheet-fed rotary intaglio printing presses, using one plate per press, were procured during the calendar year 1957 and one more in 1964 for printing currency by the dry intaglio process from plates bearing 32 notes (or subjects) to a sheet. These high-speed presses were first used to print one dollar Silver Certificates, Series 1957. Since new dies were adopted and new plates had to be made, these certificates were the first to include in the back design the motto "In God We Trust" in accordance with Public Law 140 of the 84th Congress. Early in 1965, four additional sheet-fed presses having four plates each and capable of printing high-quality 32-subject currency by the dry intaglio process at greatly increased production rates were purchased and placed in operation. By April of 1968, the transition to the dry process was completed.

The major components of these high-speed presses include an intaglio plate cylinder, an impression cylinder, an ink fountain and an automatic sheet-feeding device capable of holding 10,000 sheets in one loading. Each sheet of paper passes between the plate and impression cylinder, under extremely heavy pressure, forcing it down into the fine engraved lines of each plate to pick up the ink. The printed sheets are automatically delivered and deposited one on another in a well-aligned pile.

The backs of the notes are printed with green ink on one day and the faces are printed with black ink on the following day. After the intaglio printing operation, the stacks of 32-subject sheets are trimmed to a uniform dimension. The Treasury seal and serial numbers are then simultaneously overprinted on the face of each of the 32 notes on the sheet by the typographic process on two-color rotary presses.

For many years this overprinting also included the series date and the two signatures of Treasury officials, but with the complete conversion to the dry printing process in April of 1968, it was found more efficient to engrave these features once again on the plate itself. This was first accomplished on the $100 United States Note Series 1966 (issued in 1968). Next were the $1 Federal Reserve Notes Series 1963 B with Joseph W. Barr's signature as Secretary of the Treasury. All notes series dated 1969 and later have been made in a similar fashion.

A Federal Reserve district seal is also overprinted on the face of each Federal Reserve Note. The district seal and number are always overprinted in black ink. A detailed examination is then made in 16-subject form (1/2 of a full-size sheet) and the defective notes marked or identified for subsequent removal. When examined, the sheets are separated into stacks of individual notes on paper cutting machines. After a final note examination — in units of 100 each — for the removal of imperfect notes and the replacement with "star" notes, the currency is securely banded and wrapped for delivery to the vaults of the customer agencies. Each currency package or "brick" contains 40 units of 100 notes each, or 4,000 notes, and weighs about 8-1/2 pounds.

The COPE Process

During the past several years the Bureau has taken yet another giant step forward in its continuing program of modernization. A revolutionary new currency processing machine designed to automate the largely manual final steps in preparing paper money for issue has been activated for part of the Bureau's production. The Currency Overprinting and Processing Equipment (COPE), built to Bureau specifications by a German firm, is destined to save more than two million dollars a year in production costs. The machine starts with two stacks of 10,000 engraved 16-subject sheets which have been inspected for errors. This is the final human inspection, as COPE is designed to catch its own mistakes.

The sheets are fed simultaneously, one at a time, from each stack, into a letterpress overprinting unit which adds the seals and serial numbers. Sheets are accumulated into stacks of 100, then cut into two-subject units and finally into individual notes. Units of 100 notes each are banded and packaged into "bricks" containing 40 units. Each "brick" contains 4,000 notes and weighs approximately 8-1/2 pounds.

After the COPE operations and a final examination, the "bricks" are compressed and banded, then plastic shrink-wrapped and placed in pouches for shipment.

"Notes" From Test Plates

Several years ago some curious-looking items appeared which at first glance seem to be some sort of United States paper money. This is because they are test prints from special 32-subject plates showing portions of design elements from various regular notes. The plates were made by the Bureau of Engraving and Printing and were sent to Germany for test runs on new Giori presses which were subsequently purchased for use by the Bureau.

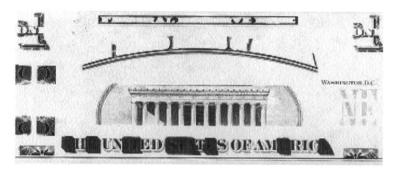

This is a test 'note', made in Germany.

Two color varieties are presently known: the first is printed in black on the face side and reddish brown on the back, and the second has a slate green face side and black printing on the back. All such special printings should have been destroyed, according to Bureau officials, even though they cannot be construed as obligations of the United States government. Thus, they may legally be held by collectors since they are test prints and not special notes.

When available, which is very seldom, the green/black piece will bring about $250. The rarer black/reddish brown piece has not been seen for sale publicly.

Another similar test 'note' believed to have been made in 1976 at Geneva, New York is being offered with increasing frequency on the market. Printed uniface and in 32-subject sheets, the design closely resembles the earlier version except for one portrait change (Washington for Jefferson) and some border elements which are different. Face and back designs are printed side by side on the sheets.

Miscellaneous Information

The cost of producing United States currency is 1¢ a note regardless of denomination. Two-thirds of the currency notes produced are of the $1 denomination. The life of the dry-printed $1 Federal Reserve Note averages about 18 months. Other denominations remain in circulation longer. The size of a currency note is 2.61 inches x 6.14 inches and the thickness is .0043 inch. There are 233 new notes to an inch (not compressed) and 490 to a pound. A million notes of any denomination weigh approximately 2,000 pounds and occupy approximately 42 cubic feet of space (with moderate pressure). Approximately 3,500 tons of paper and 1,000 tons of ink are used each year in producing the Government securities.

THE SERIAL NUMBER SYSTEM FOR U.S. CURRENCY

The system of numbering paper money must be adequate to accommodate a large volume of notes. For security and accountability purposes, no two notes of any one type, denomination and series may have the same serial number. The serial numbers on each note have a full complement of eight digits and an alphabetical prefix and suffix letter. When necessary, ciphers are used at the left of the number to make a total of eight digits. Every note has two identical serial numbers.

This note is the 100 millionth in its run and should never have been released.
It is probably unique in collectors' hands.
For further information see text below.

Whenever a new numbering sequence is used for United States Notes, Silver or Gold Certificates, the first note is numbered A00 000 001A; the second A00 000 002A; the hundredth A00 000 100A; the thousandth A00 001 000A; and so on through A99 999 999A.* The suffix letter "A" will remain the same until a total of 25 groups of 99,999,999 notes are numbered, each group having a different *prefix* letter from A to Z. The letter "O" is omitted, either as a prefix or as a suffix, because of its similarity to zero. The 100,000,000th note in each group will be a star note, since eight digits are the maximum practicable for the numbering machines.† Further testimony to modern numbering machines' inability to produce the nine-digit number is seen in the late discovery of a note with a serial number of eight zeros.

At this point, the *suffix* letter changes to "B" for the next 25 groups of 99,999,999 notes, and numbering proceeds the same as with suffix letter "A." A total of 62,500,000,000 notes could be numbered before a duplication of serial numbers would occur. However, the Bureau has never been required to number that many notes of any one type, denomination and series.

The Federal Reserve Notes printed for the twelve Districts are numbered the same way as United States Notes and Silver Certificates, except that the letter identifying each District is used as a *prefix* letter at the beginning of the two serial numbers, and it does not change. Only the suffix letter changes in the serial numbers on Federal Reserve currency.

The numbering system used for National Currency and Federal Reserve Bank Notes is illustrated and described in detail on pages 322-323.

STAR, OR REPLACEMENT NOTES

As mentioned previously on page 219, if during the course of examination a note is found to be imperfect, it is removed and replaced by a "star" note.

Typical star note

Star notes are exactly the same as regular notes except that an independent series of serial numbers is assigned. Instead of the usual prefix letter, a star appears with the serial numbers on Gold Certificates, United States Notes and Silver Certificates; on Federal Reserve Notes and Federal Reserve Bank Notes the star appears in place of the suffix letter since the prefix letter is the Bank letter as well. No star notes were used in connection with the National Bank Note issues.

As explained above, the 100,000,000th note of any group will also be a star note because the numbering machines are not geared to print over eight digits.*

* Serial numbers start from the beginning when a completely new issue and series date is printed. For minor changes within a series date, the numbers usually continue undisturbed. This is not always the case; as an instance, the $1 Silver Certificate Series 1957 has numbers starting from the beginning, but the *same* is true for the Series 1957 A notes as well. The 1957 B notes, however, do *not* start over but simply continue where the 1957 A notes leave off.

† Apparently in earlier issues of modern-size notes, the 100,000,000th piece *was* prepared with nine digits. Such a note ($1 1928 A) was rediscovered and reported late in 1966 by Thomas B. Ross. The famed Grinnell sale of 1946 also contained one of these, as well as a specimen of the 1928 B series and two dated 1934.

Star Note Totals

A given total for any issue of star notes during the last few years refers only to the quantity of that series that was *printed,* not to the quantity issued. The practice has been to make star notes in anticipation of spoilage, with their actual issuance only as necessary. Thus they may or may not be released with their regular issue counterparts.

As cases in point, Fowler star notes were still available at the time the regular Barr series was issued, and were interspersed with them as required. Similarly, Barr star notes were mixed into early releases of the Kennedy series. Another good example is the $100 U.S. Note Series 1966. There were 120,000 star notes printed but very few were released as not many were needed. In any case, regular issue totals include all star notes (of whatever series) used to make up those totals, as no figures are available for the number of defective regular notes replaced by star notes in a given series.

Occasionally whole decks (100) of star notes are "dumped" out when new notes have been printed.

Scarcity and Valuation

Recently a great deal of attention has been focused on star printings with demand centering chiefly on the better issues. Earlier issues of star notes are generally scarce, and certain ones are rare. The most popular of these are each listed in the catalog immediately after their regular issue counterparts.

Selected later issues are also in demand; these are shown where possible.

Example: ★28 on page 229 refers to the $1 star note for the Series of 1928.

BLOCK LETTERS

Many collectors are now seeking certain kinds of notes by their prefix-suffix letter combinations in serial numbers, such as A–A, A–B, A–C, and so on. This is called collecting by "block letters." Some combinations are obviously more difficult to find than others because of the varying amounts that might have been made. Scarcer combinations when sold may bring much more than the catalog valuations.

MULES

In modern United States paper money, the term "mule" indicates a note with face and back plate serial numbers (sometimes called check numbers) which differ in size. Mules came about because the size of the plate numbers was increased in the 1930's from 0.6 mm to 0.8 mm. Various issues dated 1934 and 1935 contain mule notes, and some are apparently very scarce.

COLLECTING "BY THE NUMBERS..."

Many collectors are seeking notes with numbers which are special in some specific way. The most sought-after kinds of numbers include the following:

Solid Number — a number with numerals all the same, such as 22222222.

Low Number — the lower the better, with 00000001 being the ultimate. In United States issues some of these may bring considerable premiums.

Radar Number or Palindrome — a number reading the same forward or backward, such as 25388352. (All Solid Numbers are, of course, Radars too.)

Ladder — a number in unbroken order, such as 23456789 or 98765432.

Sequence — a recurring pattern in a number, such as 13243546 or 22556699.

Matched Beginning and Ending — this is a number such as 85000085.

Matching Digits and Sets — this is where the last one, two, three (or more) digits of more than one note are the same.

Even Notes — numbers in the tens (00000020), hundreds (00000500), thousands (00006000), and higher.

Poker Hand — number with three/two of a kind, four of a kind and other combinations.

At times a number contains elements of more than one peculiarity, such as 13243546 (sequence and ladder), 25526886 (sequence and radar), or 33445566 (ladder, sequence, solid). This kind of collecting is becoming more and more popular with a growing number of collectors. Star notes with unusual numbers are of added interest.

THE SERIES YEAR ON U.S. CURRENCY

The series year which appears on the face of each note signifies the year in which the design was adopted. The series year does not change each calendar year; it changes when the basic design has a major revision. Beginning in 1974, the series year also changes when a new Treasury Secretary is appointed. The capital letter often found following the series year indicates that a minor change was authorized in a particular currency.

The series year appears twice on older printings of modern U.S. currency. More recent issues carry this designation only once.

THE TREASURY SEAL

The design of the Treasury Seal now imprinted on the face of all U.S. currency is older than the Constitution. On September 25, 1778, the Continental Congress appointed a committee composed of John Witherspoon, Gouverneur Morris and Richard Henry Lee to design a seal. In the Journals of Congress of that date is a resolution providing "that the Comptroller shall keep the Treasury books and seal...shall draw bills under said seal." The resulting design was submitted and approved, and the Seal is found on official documents dating back to 1782. It was retained after the ratification of the Constitution in 1788.

Through the years, the design of the Seal has remained basically the same though minor changes were effected in 1849 when a new die was prepared. The third die made by the Bureau of Engraving in 1915 and in use until mid-1968 is described as follows: The design includes a shield on which appear a balance scale representing Justice and a key which symbolizes official authority. They are separated by a chevron bearing 13 stars for the 13 original colonies or states. The shield is surrounded by a spray of laurel in blossom. The following Latin legend surrounds the shield: THESAUR. • AMER. • SEPTENT. •SIGIL. Written out, this is "Thesauri Americae Septentrionalis Sigillum," meaning "The Seal of the Treasury of North America." There is no reverse to the Treasury Seal.

As found on currency, the Treasury Seal was originated by Spencer M. Clark, Chief Engineer of the Currency Bureau. It is imprinted on official Treasury documents and on the face side of U.S. currency beginning with the first issue of Legal Tender Notes authorized in 1862. The Demand Note Series 1861 and the first three issues of Fractional Currency constitute the only U.S. paper money which does not bear the Treasury Seal.

NEW SEAL ADOPTED

A new rendition of the Seal was adopted during 1968 after its approval by Treasury Secretary Fowler in January of that year. While generally similar in appearance to previous designs, several major changes took place. English inscription "The Department of the Treasury 1789" replaced the Latin legend, and the surrounding laurel spray was removed.

The new Seal was first used on the $100 United States Note Series 1966 (issued in 1968); it is also being used for all currency dated 1969 or later.

THE GREAT SEAL OF THE UNITED STATES

On August 15, 1935, the Treasury Department announced that production of a new $1.00 Silver Certificate had begun. The design chosen for the new back was the Great Seal of the United States. This was the first time both sides of the Great Seal were to appear on any U.S. money.

The obverse of the Great Seal is the familiar American eagle with a shield, holding an olive branch in one talon and arrows in the other. Above are thirteen stars and the Latin motto "E Pluribus Unum."

The reverse of the Great Seal shows an unfinished pyramid, surmounted by an eye in a triangular glory. The pyramid bears in Roman numerals the year of the Declaration of Independence, 1776. Above the eye is the Latin motto "Annuit Coeptis," rendered as "He (God) favored our undertakings." The motto at the bottom is "Novus Ordo Seclorum" and is translated as "A new order of the ages." The eye and triangular glory represent an all seeing Deity. The pyramid is the symbol of strength; its unfinished condition denotes the belief of the Seal's designers that there was yet work to be done. Both mottoes on the reverse are condensations of excerpts from Virgil's Aeneid.

The first committee on the Great Seal was formed on the afternoon of July 4, 1776, and consisted of Benjamin Franklin, Thomas Jefferson and John Adams. The Great Seal as finally adopted was largely the work of Charles Thomson, Secretary of Congress, and William Barton, a private citizen of Philadelphia. The design was officially adopted on June 20, 1782, by Fundamental Law. The Great Seal was again ratified after the Constitution was adopted in 1789.

According to Treasury records, the only previous use of the reverse of the Great Seal was in 1882, when a centennial medal was issued by the United States mint to celebrate the 100th anniversary of the Great Seal's adoption.

THE NATIONAL MOTTO ON U.S. CURRENCY

An Act of Congress approved by the President on July 11, 1955, authorized the appearance of the National Motto on all U.S. currency. The first notes to bear the motto were $1 Silver Certificates Series 1957, which were released to circulation on October 1 of that year.

The changeover was implemented gradually, as the Bureau installed new high-speed rotary presses using the dry-print method to produce sheets of 32 subjects. By April of 1968 the process of change was completed, and all currency now produced bears the motto.

TREASURY OFFICIALS

Modern U.S. currency is very often collected by signature combination. These facsimile signatures appear on currency made either during the respective tenures of office of the Treasury officials or until one or both new officials are appointed. National Currency and Federal Reserve Bank Notes Series of 1929 used the Register-Treasurer signatures; all the rest from the first issue series dated 1928 to the present show the Treasurer-Secretary combination.

When the Treasurer or Secretary, or both, leave office and a new official is appointed, a letter is added after the series date and of course the signatures are changed. Originally these signatures were engraved on the face plates, which then had to be replaced upon the appearance of a new official. From the late 1930s until 1968, the signatures (along with other numbers and symbols) were overprinted.

As explained on page 219, the Bureau has again resumed the practice of engraving the signatures and series dates on the face plates. All notes printed since 1969 have been made from plates bearing engraved signatures and series dates.

Important: It should be clearly understood that the printing time of a particular issue does not generally coincide with the actual term of office of the officials whose names appear on the notes. Thus, while the length of joint tenancy of any two officials might serve as a rough indication of possible scarcity of notes containing their signatures, in actual practice it means little.

CHART OF CONCURRENT TERMS OF OFFICE

Following is a chart showing the length of time the various signatories of modern U.S. currency have held concurrent office:

Treasurer-Secretary	First Day	Last Day
H.T. Tate — A.W. Mellon	Apr. 30, 1928	Jan. 17, 1929
W.O. Woods — A.W. Mellon	Jan. 18, 1929	Feb. 12, 1932
W.O. Woods — Ogden L. Mills	Feb. 13, 1932	Mar. 3, 1933
W.O. Woods — W.H. Woodin	Mar. 4, 1933	May 31, 1933
W.A. Julian — W.H. Woodin	June 1, 1933	Dec. 31, 1933
W.A. Julian — Henry Morgenthau, Jr.	Jan. 1, 1934	July 22, 1945
W.A. Julian — Fred M. Vinson	July 23, 1945	July 23, 1946
W.A. Julian — John W. Snyder	July 25, 1946	May 29, 1949

Treasurer-Secretary	First Day	Last Day
Georgia Neese Clark — John W. Snyder	June 21, 1949	Jan. 20, 1953
Ivy Baker Priest — G.M. Humphrey	Jan., 28, 1953	July 28, 1957
Ivy Baker Priest — Robert B. Anderson	July 29, 1957	Jan. 20, 1961
Elizabeth Rudel Smith — C. Douglas Dillon	Jan. 30, 1961	Apr. 13, 1962
Kathryn O'Hay Granahan — C. Douglas Dillon	Jan. 3, 1963	Mar. 31, 1965
*Kathryn O'Hay Granahan — Henry H. Fowler	Apr. 1, 1965	Oct. 13, 1966
Kathryn O'Hay Granahan — Joseph W. Barr	Dec. 21, 1968	Jan. 20, 1969
Dorothy Andrews Elston — David M. Kennedy	May 8, 1969	Sept. 16, 1970
†Dorothy Andrews Kabis — David M. Kennedy	Sept. 17, 1970	Feb. 1, 1971
Dorothy Andrews Kabis — John B. Connally	Feb. 8, 1971	July 3, 1971
Romana Acosta Bañuelos — John B. Connally	Dec. 17, 1971	June 12, 1972
Romana Acosta Bañuelos — George P. Shultz	June 12, 1972	May 8, 1974
Francine I. Neff — William E. Simon	June 21, 1974	Jan. 20, 1977
Azie Taylor Morton — W. Michael Blumenthal	Sept. 12, 1977	Aug. 4, 1979
Azie Taylor Morton — G. William Miller	Aug. 6, 1979	Jan. 4, 1981
Angela M. Buchanan — Donald T. Regan	Mar. 7, 1981	July 1, 1983
Katherine Davalos Ortega — Donald T. Regan	Sept. 23, 1983	Jan. 29, 1985
Katherine Davalos Ortega — James A. Baker II	Jan. 29, 1985	Aug. 17, 1988
Katherine Davalos Ortega — Nicholas F. Brady	Sept. 15, 1988	June 30, 1989
Catalina Vasquez Villalpando — Nicholas F. Brady	Dec. 11, 1989	Oct. 29, 1992
Mary Ellen Withrow—Lloyd Bentsen	Feb. 10, 1994	Dec. 22, 1994
Mary Ellen Withrow—Robert Rubin	Jan. 10, 1995	—
Mary Ellen Withrow—Lawrence H. Summers	July 2, 1999	Jan. 20, 2001

Register - Treasurer		
E.E. Jones — W.O. Woods	Jan. 22, 1929	May 31, 1933

*Mrs. Granahan resigned as Treasurer on October 13, 1966, but no replacement was appointed for over 2-1/2 years. During this time her signature continued in use, explaining why her name is listed with Joseph W. Barr for his brief tenure of office.

†On September 17, 1970, the former Mrs. Elston became Mrs. Kabis. This is the first time the Treasurer's name was changed during tenure of office.

Catalog Values

In compiling the average retail valuations as shown in this book, we have found that there is often a great deal of variation in pricing among the contributors. This is especially true with respect to the more popular issues, which often exhibit spurts of localized activity. We therefore wish to stress the idea that the values included here are meant only as a guide to general retail prices; the notes may be quoted at higher or lower prices depending on local supply and demand.

UNITED STATES NOTES — Red Seal

United States Notes, also known as Legal Tender Notes or Greenbacks, were first authorized by the Act of Congress of February 25, 1862. Denominations for the large-size notes ranged from $1 to $10,000. Modern-size notes were printed in denominations of $1, $2, $5 and $100. Delivery of $2 notes was terminated in July of 1965 and $5 in November of 1967.* The $1 Series of 1928 was released mainly in Puerto Rico years after the notes were printed, but it is no longer in circulation.

When finished, United States Notes were delivered to a vault under custody of the Treasurer of the United States. As required by the Act of May 31, 1878, and the Old Series Currency Adjustment Act, the amount outstanding was kept at $322,681,016. The Treasury holds a reserve in gold of $156,039,431 to back these notes. The seal and serial numbers are in red.

*$10 and $20 plates were made, as a specimen of each note (Series of 1928, Woods-Mills) was in the Treasury's currency exhibit at the Chicago World's Fair 1933-1934.

UNITED STATES NOTES

Explanatory Notations for Various Series

Series of 1928 — The legal tender clause on earlier issues of this type reads, "This Note Is A Legal Tender at its Face Value For All Debts Public and Private Except Duties on Imports and Interest on the Public Dept."

Series of 1928 B — The Act of May 12, 1933 removed legal tender restrictions from all U.S. money, and the clause on $5.00 notes of this type was changed as follows: "This Note Is A Legal Tender at its Face Value For All Debts Public and Private." For $2.00 notes, this change began with Series of 1928 C issues. All subsequent printings up to Series 1963 carry this same clause.

Series of 1928 C — For $5 notes, the Face Plate Number appears in larger-size numerals on this and succeeding issues. For $2 notes this begins with Series of 1928 D. Lathework also added to frame of $2 notes, 1928 C.

Series 1953 — Along with a general rearrangement of the face side, the following changes occurred on this and succeeding issues:

> Series designation appears only once, and the word "OF" is deleted.
> The Treasury seal and serial numbers are reduced in size.

ONE DOLLAR

Face Design 1928. Back Design on page 238.

Series 1963 — The addition of the motto to the backs of United States Notes took place in 1963, along with the changeover in printing method from wet to dry and increase in number of subjects per sheet from 18 to 32. The new legal tender clause reads, "This Note is Legal Tender For All Debts, Public and Private." The "Will Pay…" clause, near the bottom of the face side on previous issues no longer appears on the notes.

Series 1966 — The $100 denomination was introduced late in 1968, but bearing the series date 1966. Signatures and series date were engraved in the plates for this issue. A new Treasury Seal was also used for the first time. The series was discontinued in 1996, and all existing stocks destroyed.

UNITED STATES NOTES

ONE DOLLAR

Series	Treasurer-Secretary	Fine	VF	Ex. Fine	CU	Ch. CU
1928	Woods-Woodin	50.00	70.00	100.00	140.00	200.00*
★28	(highest Serial No. seen 7643)	1,200	1,800	4,500	12,000	—

24,000 star notes reportedly assigned to be printed. BEP is unable to tell how many were actually made, or even to confirm the 24,000 assigned numbers.

*Value is for a well centered note. These usually have serial numbers below 8000 (original April-May 1933 issue); those between 8001 and 1872000 were released in Puerto Rico in 1949 and most are imperfectly centered. Such notes are worth less than listed values.

TWO DOLLARS

Face Design 1928 through 1928 G

Series	Treasurer-Secretary	Fine	VF	Ex. Fine	CU	Ch. CU
1928	Tate-Mellon	8.00	10.00	12.00	25.00	50.00
★ 28		80.00	110.00	175.00	450.00	600.00
1928 A	Woods-Mellon	12.00	18.00	30.00	90.00	225.00
★ 28 A		750.00	1,000	2,000	4,500	6,000
1928 B	Woods-Mills	40.00	90.00	200.00	500.00	800.00
★ 28 B		1,600	2,500	4,000	5,000	7,000
1928 C	Julian-Morgenthau	8.00	10.00	15.00	35.00	80.00
★ 28 C		200.00	400.00	800.00	1,000	2,000
1928 D	Julian-Morgenthau	7.00	8.00	9.00	20.00	30.00
★ 28 D		45.00	100.00	200.00	300.00	600.00

Back Design 1928 through 1953 C

UNITED STATES NOTES
TWO DOLLARS

Series	Treasurer-Secretary	Fine	VF	Ex. Fine	CU	Ch. CU
1928 E	Julian-Vinson	7.00	10.00	16.00	30.00	50.00
★ 28 E		1,500	2,000	3,000	6,000	8,000
1928 F	Julian-Snyder	6.00	8.00	10.00	20.00	30.00
★ 28 F		50.00	75.00	150.00	350.00	500.00
1928 G	Clark-Snyder	6.00	7.00	9.00	20.00	30.00
★ 28 G		40.00	60.00	120.00	300.00	400.00

Total star note printing for 1928 through 1928 G is 4,152,000.

Face Design 1953 through 1953 C

Series	Treasurer-Secretary	VF	Ex. Fine	CU	Ch. CU
1953	Priest-Humphrey	5.00	6.00	10.00	12.00
★ 53		8.00	15.00	25.00	35.00
1953 A	Priest-Anderson	5.00	6.00	10.00	12.00
★ 53 A		12.00	20.00	50.00	70.00
1953 B	Smith-Dillon	5.00	6.00	10.00	12.00
★ 53 B		7.00	15.00	40.00	60.00
1953 C	Granahan-Dillon	5.00	6.00	10.00	12.00
★ 53 C		7.00	15.00	40.00	60.00

Face Design 1963 and 1963 A

UNITED STATES NOTES
TWO DOLLARS

Back Design 1963 and 1963 A

Series	Treasurer-Secretary	VF	Ex. Fine	CU	Ch. CU
1963	Granahan-Dillon	5.00	6.00	9.00	11.00
★ 63		7.00	9.00	17.00	22.00
1963 A	Granahan-Fowler	5.00	6.00	9.00	11.00
★ 63 A		9.00	12.00	30.00	45.00

FIVE DOLLARS

Face Design 1928 through 1928 F

Back Design U.S. Notes 1928-1953 C; Silver Certificates; National Currency;
Federal Reserve Bank Notes; Federal Reserve Notes 1928-1950 E

UNITED STATES NOTES
FIVE DOLLARS

Series	Treasurer-Secretary	VF	Ex. Fine	CU	Ch. CU
1928	Woods-Mellon	12.00	16.00	30.00	50.00
★ 28		90.00	250.00	700.00	900.00
1928 A	Woods-Mills	13.00	30.00	45.00	75.00
★ 28 A		650.00	1,800	3,000	4,000
1928 B	Julian-Morgenthau	10.00	15.00	30.00	40.00
★ 28 B		75.00	250.00	550.00	750.00
1928 C	Julian-Morgenthau	10.00	15.00	30.00	35.00
★ 28 C		40.00	175.00	350.00	450.00
1928 D	Julian-Vinson	40.00	50.00	175.00	275.00
★ 28 D		450.00	1,250	2,000	3,000
1928 E	Julian-Snyder	10.00	15.00	25.00	40.00
★ 28 E		45.00	150.00	300.00	375.00
1928 F	Clark-Snyder	10.00	15.00	25.00	40.00
★ 28 F		35.00	90.00	275.00	400.00

Total star note printing for 1928 through 1928 F is 9,744,000.

Face Design 1953 through 1953 C and 1963

Series	Treasurer-Secretary	VF	Ex. Fine	CU	Ch. CU
1953	Priest-Humphrey	11.00	15.00	20.00	25.00
★ 53		17.00	50.00	125.00	150.00
1953 A	Priest-Anderson	11.00	15.00	20.00	25.00
★ 53 A		15.00	30.00	75.00	100.00
1953 B	Smith-Dillon	8.00	10.00	16.00	20.00
★ 53 B		14.00	25.00	50.00	70.00
1953 C	Granahan-Dillon	8.00	10.00	16.00	20.00
★ 53 C		18.00	50.00	90.00	120.00
1963	Granahan-Dillon	8.00	10.00	16.00	20.00
★ 63		10.00	15.00	40.00	50.00

UNITED STATES NOTES
FIVE DOLLARS

Back Design U.S. Notes 1963, Federal Reserve Notes 1963-present.

ONE HUNDRED DOLLARS

Face Design 1966 and 1966 A. Back Design on page 307.
Notice the extremely desirable low number.
Courtesy Amon G. Carter, Jr.

Series	Treasurer-Secretary	Ex. Fine	AU	CU	Ch. CU
1966	Granahan-Fowler	160.00	200.00	275.00	350.00
★ 66		450.00	600.00	1,500	2,500
1966 A	Elston-Kennedy	300.00	400.00	575.00	675.00

The remaining Treasury stocks of these notes were destroyed in 1996.

SILVER CERTIFICATES, Blue Seal

Certificates backed by silver dollars were first authorized by the Bland-Allison Act of February 28, 1878. Large-size notes were made in denominations from $1 to $1000 at various intervals.

Modern-size Silver Certificates were made only in the $1, $5 and $10 denominations. Upon completion they were delivered to a vault under the custody of the Treasurer of the United States. However, Silver Certificates are no longer being printed, as they were abolished by the Act of June 4, 1963 (at which time Federal Reserve $1 and $2 notes were authorized).

The seal and serial numbers are in blue.

SILVER CERTIFICATES

Redemption and Catalog Value

Early issues of modern-size Silver Certificates were also backed by silver dollars; their wording referred to their redemption in "One Silver Dollar" as had all previous issues of Silver Certificates. All this was changed by the Silver Purchase Act of 1934, which allowed for such certificates to be issued against any standard silver dollars, silver or silver bullion held by the Treasury. Accordingly, the wording in the redemption clause was changed to read "One Dollar in Silver," allowing for the option of redemption in silver dollars or bullion.

On March 25, 1964, Secretary of the Treasury Dillon halted the outflow of silver dollars, stating that thenceforth silver bullion would be used for the redemption of Silver Certificates presented for that purpose.

On June 24, 1968, redemption in bullion was discontinued, but not before literally millions had been turned in. The initial effect on the collector market was a downward adjustment of catalog values.

$1.00 Note Varieties

Late issues of the $1 Silver Certificates present an unusual combination of significant technical and numismatic developments. The result of this is an array of different varieties created by the gradual changeover from wet to dry printing method and the addition of the motto "In God We Trust."

Notes Dated 1935

All notes with the date 1935, with or without suffix letter, were produced by the old "wet-intaglio" method. These notes were made from 1935 through 1963. The motto was added to these notes in 1962 *during* the printing of the 1935 G issue; therefore, notes dated 1935 G come both without and with the motto. All 1935 H notes have the motto.

Notes Dated 1957

All notes dated 1957, with or without suffix letter, were produced by the present "dry-intaglio" process. Three varieties are involved — 1957, 1957 A and 1957 B, made from 1957 through 1963. All such notes bear the motto on the back.

Order of Appearance

From the above, it may be seen that notes of both the wet-printed 1935 series and the dry-printed 1957 series were being produced and released concurrently from 1957 to 1963. According to delivery records, notes of both kinds were introduced in the following order: Series 1957, 1935 F, 1957 A, 1935 G (no motto), 1935 G (with motto), 1957 B and 1935 H.

Explanatory Notations for Various Series

Series of 1928 — The legal tender clause first read, "This Certificate is Receivable For All Public Dues and When So Received May Be Reissued."

Series of 1928 A and B — Experimental notes.

Series of 1928 E — See below under *Series of 1934.*

Series of 1933 — Pursuant to the Act of May 12, 1933, a new series of Silver Certificates was initiated. Issued only in the $10 denomination, this is one of the most desirable and unique notes in the modern U.S. currency series. It is in fact a "Silver Coin Note," so stated on the face side. Its legal tender clause is as follows: "This Certificate is Issued Pursuant to Section 16 of the Act of May 12, 1933, and is Legal Tender at its Face Value For All Debts Public and Private."

SILVER CERTIFICATES

Series of 1934 — The Act of June 19, 1934 necessitated further change in the legal tender clause; it was altered on the Series of 1928 E $1 notes, on all Series of 1934 notes and for the remainder of Silver Certificate issues, reading as follows: "This Certificate is Legal Tender For All Debts, Public and Private." On $1 notes of the 1934 series, the Treasury seal was moved to the right side and a large blue numeral 1 was added on the left.

Series of 1934 A — Numerals in the Face Plate Serial Number are larger on this and succeeding issues of $5 and $10 notes.

Series 1935 — The word OF was deleted from the series designation on these $1 notes and succeeding series dates. "Series 1935" appears twice on the face. Also, the large word ONE at the right is removed, and the numeral 1 at the left is gray instead of blue.

There was an issue of experimental notes of this series in 1937.

Series 1935 A — The size of the numerals in the Face Plate Serial Number was made larger, and the series designation appears only once on this and succeeding issues of $1 notes.

Aside from issues for regular circulation, notes from this series were used as part of the special HAWAII overprint and Yellow Seal emissions of World War II.

Series 1953 — The following changes took place on the face side of this and succeeding issues of $5 and $10 notes:

Series designation appears only once, and the word OF is deleted.
Signatures are overprinted instead of engraved.
The Treasury seal and serial numbers are reduced in size.
The numeral at the left is gray instead of blue.

Series 1957 — For the first time the motto appears on U.S. currency. Also, printings of 32-subject sheets begin with this series.

ONE DOLLAR

Face Design 1928 through 1928 E

SILVER CERTIFICATES
ONE DOLLAR

Back Design U.S. Note 1928; Silver Certificates 1928-1934

Series	Treasurer-Secretary	VF	Ex. Fine	CU	Ch. CU
1928	Tate-Mellon	22.00	25.00	40.00	50.00
★ 28		55.00	125.00	300.00	450.00
1928 A	Woods-Mellon	22.00	25.00	40.00	50.00
★ 28 A		40.00	60.00	200.00	300.00
1928 B	Woods-Mills	22.00	25.00	40.00	50.00
★ 28 B		95.00	250.00	600.00	750.00
1928 C	Woods-Woodin	125.00	200.00	400.00	600.00
★ 28 C		2,000	3,500	12,000	—
1928 D	Julian-Woodin	50.00	120.00	200.00	400.00
★ 28 D		2,000	3,500	10,000	—
1928 E	Julian-Morgenthau	400.00	600.00	1,000	1,500
★ 28 E		4,500	6,000	—	—

Face Design 1934

Series	Treasurer-Secretary	VF	Ex. Fine	CU	Ch. CU
1934	Julian-Morgenthau	18.00	23.00	50.00	70.00
★ 34		75.00	150.00	600.00	800.00
1935	Julian-Morgenthau	2.50	3.50	8.00	14.00
★ 35		40.00	90.00	300.00	375.00
*1935 A	Julian-Morgenthau	2.00	2.50	5.00	8.00
★ 35 A		6.00	10.00	30.00	35.00
1935 B	Julian-Vinson	2.00	2.75	12.00	14.00
★ 35 B		20.00	60.00	150.0	200.00

*For HAWAII, yellow seal, and R & S notes, see World War II Issues.

SILVER CERTIFICATES
ONE DOLLAR

Series	Treasurer-Secretary	VF	Ex. Fine	CU	Ch. CU
1935 C	Julian-Snyder	2.00	2.50	5.00	7.00
★ 35 C		6.00	12.50	40.00	50.00
†1935 D	Clark-Snyder, wide	2.00	3.00	5.50	8.00
†★ 35 D	wide	3.00	5.00	45.00	55.00
†1935 D	Clark-Snyder, narrow	2.00	3.00	5.50	8.00
† ★ 35 D	narrow	3.00	5.00	30.00	35.00
1935 E	Priest-Humphrey	2.00	3.00	5.50	8.00
★ 35 E		2.00	5.00	12.00	15.00
1935 F	Priest-Anderson	2.00	3.00	5.50	8.00
★ 35 F		2.00	5.00	12.00	15.00
1935 G	Smith-Dillon	2.00	3.00	5.50	8.00
★ 35 G	no motto	2.00	5.00	12.00	15.00

The 1935 D series was printed in sheets of 12 and 18 subjects:

4,510,024,000	in sheets of 12 notes
146,944,000	in sheets of 18 notes
4,656,968,000	Total 1935 D notes

† Wide and Narrow Designs — See explanation on following page.

Face Design 1935. General Face Design 1935–1957 B

Series	Treasurer-Secretary	VF	Ex. Fine	CU	Ch. CU
† 1935 G	Smith-Dillon	2.25	2.50	30.00	50.00
★ 35 G	with motto	10.00	40.00	90.00	125.00
† 1935 H	Granahan-Dillon	2.00	3.00	6.00	8.50
★ 35 H		2.50	6.00	25.00	28.00
1957	Priest-Anderson	2.00	3.00	5.50	8.00
★ 57		2.00	7.00	15.00	17.00
1957 A	Smith-Dillon	2.00	3.00	5.50	8.00
★ 57 A		2.00	3.00	8.00	10.00
1957 B	Granahan-Dillon	2.00	3.00	5.50	8.00
★ 57 B		2.00	3.00	8.00	10.00

† With Motto "In God We Trust." 1935 G comes with and without the Motto.

SILVER CERTIFICATES
ONE DOLLAR
THE "GREAT SEAL" BACK DESIGN

Wide Back Design 1935 through 1935 D

There are two varieties of backs for Series 1935 D notes designated as the Wide and Narrow designs. The Wide design is about 1/16 inch wider, easily recognized when compared with the Narrow design. The most obvious area for comparison is the lathe work border under ONE DOLLAR.

The Narrow design was used for subsequent issues of the 1935 series.

Back Design Silver Certificates 1935 G and H; also 1957 through 1957 B.
All Federal Reserve Notes

FIVE DOLLARS

Face Design 1934 through 1934 D. Back Design on page 231.

SILVER CERTIFICATES
FIVE DOLLARS

Series	Treasurer-Secretary	VF	Ex. Fine	CU	Ch. CU
1934	Julian-Morgenthau	8.00	9.00	20.00	28.00
★ 34		25.00	75.00	300.00	500.00
1934 A	Julian-Morgenthau	8.00	9.00	15.00	25.00
★ 34 A		20.00	65.00	115.00	200.00
1934 B	Julian-Vinson	9.00	10.00	20.00	30.00
★ 34 B		50.00	120.00	300.00	450.00
1934 C	Julian-Snyder	7.00	9.00	15.00	18.00
★ 34 C		20.00	65.00	125.00	200.00
1934 D	Clark-Snyder	7.00	8.00	15.00	18.00
★ 34 D		10.00	35.00	75.00	90.00

Face Design 1953 through 1953 C. Back Design on page 231.

Series	Treasurer-Secretary	VF	Ex. Fine	CU	Ch. CU
1953	Priest-Humphrey	6.00	8.00	13.00	18.00
★ 53		7.00	12.00	30.00	35.00
1953 A	Priest-Anderson	6.00	8.00	13.00	18.00
★ 53 A		7.00	12.00	35.00	40.00
1953 B	Smith-Dillon†	6.00	8.00	13.00	18.00
★ 53 B		900.00	2,500	4,500	6,000
1953 C	Granahan-Dillon		Not Released		

† Of the 1953 B issue only 14,196,000 notes were released because of the discontinuance of Silver Certificates. Apparently less than 400,000 star notes were released, according to O'Donnell's listings.

TEN DOLLARS

Face Design 1933 and 1933 A

SILVER CERTIFICATES
TEN DOLLARS

Back Design Silver Certificates; National Currency; Federal Reserve Bank Notes; Federal Reserve Notes 1928-1950 E; Gold Certificates.

The 1933 and 1933 A $10 Issues

The matter of just how many of the 1933 and 1933 A $10 notes were issued has never been cleared up satisfactorily. Bureau records show that 216,000 of the 1933 series and 336,000 of the 1933 A series were delivered; however, records of the Treasury Department Cash Division are at variance. Those records indicate 156,000 of the 1933 notes and 396,000 of the 1933 A notes as having been delivered. Further, their issue figures show that all 156,000 of the 1933 series and 28,000 of the 1933 A were released. The balance — 368,000 of the 1933 A notes — were destroyed.

Though records show that one uncut sheet was released, no regular issue 1933 A notes are known today in collectors' hands; perhaps the only ones yet in existence are those of the single sheet of Specimen notes retained by the Bureau of Engraving and Printing.

As a matter of interest, the following letter written by former Bureau Director A.W. Hall on April 3, 1941 is included:

"…in regard to the $10 silver certificates, series of 1933 and 1933-A, you are advised that a total of 552,000 of the two were delivered to the Treasurer of the United States in 1934. Of this number at least 300,000 were series 1933-A.

"Of the number delivered to the Treasurer, 184,000 were issued between January and August, 1934, and the remainder, 368,000, were destroyed in November, 1935. Whether any 1933-A's were among those issued apparently cannot be determined. However, as the 1933 plate was first at press, it is possible that all the certificates issued were from this plate."

This letter appeared in *The Numismatist,* June, 1941, and was addressed to Mr. Robert H. Lloyd.

Series	Treasurer-Secretary	Fine	VF	Ex. Fine	CU
1933	Julian-Woodin	**3,000**	**6,000**	**7,500**	**9,500**
★ 33			Unique		
1933 A	Julian-Morgenthau		None known in any collection.		

Face Design 1934 through 1934 D

SILVER CERTIFICATES
TEN DOLLARS

Series	Treasurer-Secretary	VF	Ex. Fine	CU	Ch. CU
1934	Julian-Morgenthau	25.00	28.00	50.0	100.00
★ 34		90.00	250.00	1,000	2,000
1934 A	Julian-Morgenthau	25.00	28.00	70.00	125.00
★ 34 A		90.00	200.00	1,500	2,500
1934 B	Julian-Vinson	125.00	225.00	900.00	1,500
★ 34 B		900.00	3,000	8,000	—
1934 C	Julian-Snyder	25.00	30.00	80.00	120.00
★ 34 C		45.00	75.00	300.00	425.00
1934 D	Clark-Snyder	25.00	28.00	50.00	100.00
★ 34 D		90.00	250.00	1,500	2,300

Face Design 1953 through 1953 B

Series	Treasurer-Secretary	VF	Ex. Fine	CU	Ch. CU
1953	Priest-Humphrey	25.00	30.00	50.00	100.00
★ 53		45.00	200.00	500.00	625.00
1953 A	Priest-Anderson	25.00	40.00	75.00	200.00
★ 53 A		45.00	200.00	1,000	1,500
1953 B	Smith-Dillon	22.00	28.00	45.00	80.00
★ 53 B			None printed		

NATIONAL CURRENCY, Brown Seal

National Currency was first authorized by the National Banking Act of 1863, superseded by the National Currency Act of June 3, 1864. This Act provided for the establishment of national banks and the issuance of circulating notes. These notes were to be secured by United States interest-bearing registered bonds deposited with the Treasurer, upon which the banks could receive 90% of current market value in notes.

Modern-size National Currency was first issued on July 15, 1929. Unusual features of this issue include the use of the Register-Treasurer signature combination (instead of Secretary-Treasurer as found on most other modern-size notes) and the series date which is 1929. The printing plates for the face side are also quite different from other modern-size types. The engraved borders are reduced in proportion and size to make room for the imprinting of bank names, locations, charter numbers and names of bank officials. All these details were printed by a logotype process onto the notes; since so many different banks issued such notes a great saving was thus made in the preparation of plates. The seal and serial numbers are in brown. The backs are uniform with other modern types. No star notes as such were made for the National Currency series.

NATIONAL CURRENCY

There are two distinct types of modern-size National Currency. Type One, issued from July, 1929, to May, 1933, has the bank's charter number in two places, in black. National Currency was printed 12 notes to a sheet, then cut, overprinted, and delivered in vertical sheets of six. For Type One, each of these six notes had the same serial numbers and suffix letter but a different prefix letter, A through F, which served to denote its position on the vertical sheet.

Type Two notes were issued from May, 1933, to May, 1935. These bore consecutive serial numbers, the suffix letters were dropped and the charter number of the bank was added twice more, in thinner brown numerals. Thus, the charter number appears four times on Type Two notes — twice in black logotype and twice in brown as described. Type Two notes are much scarcer than those of Type One.

National Currency is most often collected by states, cities or banks with odd names, places of historical interest, low charter numbers or low or unusual serial numbers. Recently there has been a surging interest in these notes, spurred by the publication of a specialized book sponsored by the Society of Paper Money Collectors.

Because of their high face value, $50 and $100 notes were not popularly collected until the last several years. None were issued from Alabama, Alaska, Arizona, Georgia, Maine, New Mexico and South Carolina.

Throughout the years National Bank Notes were in use, various amendments were made affecting their circulation and redemption. Provisions were made for the transfer of redemption liability from the separate banks to the United States, which now cancels and retires any National Bank Notes that are turned in. National Currency became obsolete on May 20, 1935, as bonds matured or were otherwise declared ineligible for security purposes.

The redemption clause on these notes reads as follows: "Redeemable in Lawful Money of the United States at United States Treasury or at the Bank of Issue."

Valuations are at best a guide to general availability. Some states are very difficult to obtain, others may have one issue commonly available but very scarce otherwise.

The following table lists the states alphabetically with their respective rarity ratings. Values follow accordingly.

TABLE OF RARITY
Valuations following the Table of Rarity are based on this list:

State	Rarity	State	Rarity	State	Rarity
Alabama	4	Kentucky	3	North Dakota	4
Alaska	9	Louisiana	5	Ohio	1
Arizona	7	Maine	4	Oklahoma	4
Arkansas	5	Maryland	3	Oregon	5
California	2	Massachusetts	3	Pennsylvania	1
Colorado	4	Michigan	3	Rhode Island	6
Connecticut	4	Minnesota	3	South Carolina	4
Delaware	6	Mississippi	6	South Dakota	5
District of Columbia	4	Missouri	3	Tennessee	4
Florida	6	Montana	7	Texas	1
Georgia	6	Nebraska	3	Utah	6
Hawaii	7	Nevada	8	Vermont	5
Idaho	7	New Hampshire	6	Virginia	3
Illinois	1	New Jersey	3	Washington	5
Indiana	1	New Mexico	6	West Virginia	3
Iowa	2	New York	1	Wisconsin	2
Kansas	3	North Carolina	5	Wyoming	7

NATIONAL CURRENCY
FIVE DOLLARS

Face Design National Currency. Type 1, Back Design on page 231.

Face Design National Currency. Type 2. Back Design on page 231.

	$5.00 TYPE ONE					$5.00 TYPE TWO			
Rarity	Fine	VF	Ex. Fine	CU	Rarity	Fine	VF	Ex. Fine	CU
1	50.00	60.00	65.00	80.00	1	50.00	60.00	65.00	85.00
2	52.00	62.00	70.00	85.00	2	52.00	62.00	70.00	90.00
3	55.00	65.00	75.00	90.00	3	58.00	67.00	80.00	100.00
4	58.00	70.00	85.00	110.00	4	60.00	72.00	90.00	120.00
5	60.00	75.00	95.00	135.00	5	65.00	78.00	100.00	150.00
6	70.00	90.00	110.00	190.00	6	75.00	95.00	120.00	200.00
7	85.00	120.00	150.00	225.00	7	90.00	130.00	160.00	265.00
8	100.00	160.00	220.00	375.00	8	125.00	220.00	340.00	475.00
9	500.00	650.00	950.00	1,500	9	550.00	700.00	1,100	1,750

NATIONAL CURRENCY
TEN DOLLARS

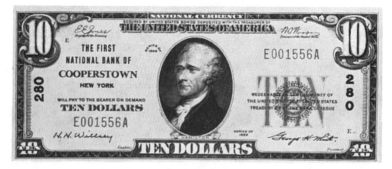

Face Design National Currency. Type 1. Back Design on page 240.

Face Design National Currency. Type 2. Back Design on page 240.

	$10.00 TYPE ONE					$10.00 TYPE TWO			
Rarity	Fine	VF	Ex. Fine	CU	Rarity	Fine	VF	Ex. Fine	CU
1	55.00	65.00	70.00	85.00	1	55.00	65.00	75.00	90.00
2	57.00	67.00	75.00	90.00	2	57.00	67.00	80.00	95.00
3	60.00	70.00	80.00	95.00	3	60.00	70.00	85.00	100.00
4	65.00	75.00	90.00	120.00	4	65.00	75.00	95.00	125.00
5	67.00	80.00	100.00	140.00	5	67.00	80.00	105.00	145.00
6	75.00	95.00	120.00	165.00	6	75.00	95.00	125.00	175.00
7	90.00	125.00	160.00	240.00	7	90.00	135.00	170.00	250.00
8	125.00	200.00	325.00	475.00	8	130.00	240.00	375.00	535.00
9	600.00	750.00	1,100	1,600	9	625.00	775.00	1,200	1,750

NATIONAL CURRENCY
TWENTY DOLLARS

Face Design National Currency. Type 1. Back Design on page 283.

Face Design National Currency. Type 2. Back Design on page 283.

$20.00 TYPE ONE					$20.00 TYPE TWO			
Rarity	Fine	VF	Ex. Fine	CU	Rarity	Fine	VF	Ex. Fine	CU
1	65.00	75.00	80.00	95.00	1	65.00	75.00	85.00	100.00
2	67.00	77.00	85.00	100.00	2	67.00	77.00	90.00	110.00
3	70.00	80.00	90.00	110.00	3	70.00	80.00	95.00	120.00
4	75.00	85.00	100.00	130.00	4	75.00	85.00	110.00	135.00
5	77.00	90.00	110.00	155.00	5	77.00	90.00	120.00	160.00
6	85.00	110.00	130.00	175.00	6	85.00	110.00	140.00	185.00
7	100.00	135.00	165.00	250.00	7	100.00	140.00	180.00	265.00
8	135.00	215.00	340.00	500.00	8	140.00	225.00	360.00	550.00
9	625.00	775.00	1,150	1,750	9	650.00	800.00	1,250	1,850

NATIONAL CURRENCY
FIFTY DOLLARS

Face Design National Currency. Type 1. Back Design on page 294.

$50.00 TYPE ONE and $50.00 TYPE TWO

Rarity	Fine	VF	Ex. Fine	CU
1	120.00	135.00	150.00	175.00
2	125.00	140.00	160.00	200.00
3	130.00	150.00	175.00	225.00
4	135.00	160.00	185.00	250.00
5	145.00	175.00	200.00	275.00
6	160.00	185.00	220.00	300.00
7	175.00	200.00	250.00	385.00
8	225.00	325.00	460.00	700.00
9	Not Issued			

Values shown above are for notes of Type One. Type Two notes are worth 25–300% more.

ONE HUNDRED DOLLARS

Face Design National Currency. Type 1. Back Design on Page 303.

NATIONAL CURRENCY
ONE HUNDRED DOLLARS
$100 TYPE ONE, and $100 TYPE TWO

Rarity	Fine	VF	Ex. Fine	CU
1	200.00	240.00	260.00	300.00
2	210.00	250.00	275.00	325.00
3	220.00	260.00	290.00	360.00
4	230.00	270.00	310.00	385.00
5	240.00	285.00	325.00	400.00
6	260.00	300.00	345.00	425.00
7	290.00	350.00	390.00	480.00
8	350.00	410.00	450.00	675.00
9	Not Issued			

Values shown above are for notes of Type One. Type Two notes are worth 25–300% more.

FEDERAL RESERVE BANK NOTES, Brown Seal

Federal Reserve Bank Notes were first authorized by the Act of December 23, 1913, which established the Federal Reserve System. Unlike Federal Reserve Notes, these Bank Notes were not obligations of the United States. Rather, they were obligations of the specific Federal Reserve Banks named on the face. The seal and serial numbers are in brown.

Modern-size Federal Reserve Bank Notes were authorized by the Act of March 9, 1933. This Act permitted Federal Reserve Banks to issue currency equal to 100% of the face value of United States bonds, or 90% of the estimated value of commercial paper used as collateral. These Bank Notes were issued to relieve the emergency brought about by heavy withdrawals of Federal Reserve Notes in January and February of 1933.

Plates originally made for the Series of 1929 National Currency discussed on page 241 were hastily adapted and the Bank Notes were quickly prepared and issued. Naturally, these notes very closely resembled the National Currency issues: alterations were made only in the overprint on the face side. Instead of the local bank's Cashier and President signatures, there appeared the signatures of the Federal Reserve Bank's Cashier and Governor, with but three exceptions. The Cashier's signature was replaced by the Deputy Governor on New York District notes, the Assistant Deputy Governor on Chicago District notes and the Controller on the St. Louis District notes. The designated letter of each Federal Reserve Bank and District was placed on the notes in four places. The brown seal was slightly larger than that used on the National Bank notes, and words OR BY LIKE DEPOSIT OF OTHER SECURITIES were logotyped near the top. The series date remained 1929 and the engraved signatures of Jones and Woods (Register and Treasurer) were also retained.

Serial numbers for each Federal Reserve Bank started with 00000001A, preceded by a District letter A to L. Star notes were made for these issues and are extremely scarce.

Federal Reserve Bank Notes were delivered in sheets of six notes, as were the National Currency issues. Denominations included $5, $10, $20, $50 and $100. Their issuance was discontinued in July, 1935. However, during World War II (1942) and a temporary shortage of currency, additional supplies of these Bank Notes were released from storage and charged out as Federal Reserve Notes. In new condition FRBN's have become very scarce.

FEDERAL RESERVE BANK NOTES
FIVE DOLLARS

Face Design Federal Reserve Bank Notes. Back Design on page 231.

District	Federal Reserve Bank	VF	Ex. Fine	CU
A	BOSTON	30.00	40.00	50.00
B	NEW YORK	25.00	30.00	40.00
C	PHILADELPHIA	28.00	32.00	45.00
D	CLEVELAND	25.00	30.00	40.00
E	RICHMOND	None Printed	—	—
F	ATLANTA	32.00	45.00	135.00
G	CHICAGO	25.00	30.00	40.00
H	ST. LOUIS	140.00	240.00	725.00
I	MINNEAPOLIS	40.00	120.00	240.00
J	KANSAS CITY	28.00	40.00	65.00
K	DALLAS	30.00	50.00	110.00
L	SAN FRANCISCO	365.00	775.00	2,250

Star note values: at least twice as much for used; five times as much, or more, for New condition.

TEN DOLLARS

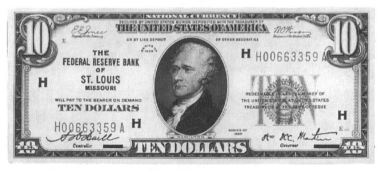

Face Design Federal Reserve Bank Notes. Back Design on page 240.

FEDERAL RESERVE BANK NOTES
TEN DOLLARS

District	Federal Reserve Bank	VF	Ex. Fine	CU
A	BOSTON	32.00	45.00	95.00
B	NEW YORK	30.00	35.00	50.00
C	PHILADELPHIA	32.00	40.00	60.00
D	CLEVELAND	32.00	40.00	60.00
E	RICHMOND	35.00	45.00	100.00
F	ATLANTA	32.00	40.00	75.00
G	CHICAGO	30.00	35.00	50.00
H	ST. LOUIS	32.00	40.00	60.00
I	MINNEAPOLIS	32.00	45.00	85.00
J	KANSAS CITY	32.00	40.00	75.00
K	DALLAS	240.00	360.00	1,250
L	SAN FRANCISCO	35.00	55.00	125.00

Star notes: see notice under $5 listing.

TWENTY DOLLARS

Face Design Federal Reserve Bank Notes. Back Design on page 283.

District	Federal Reserve Bank	VF	Ex. Fine	CU
A	BOSTON	50.00	90.00	165.00
B	NEW YORK	40.00	45.00	100.00
C	PHILADELPHIA	40.00	50.00	105.00
D	CLEVELAND	40.00	55.00	125.00
E	RICHMOND	40.00	55.00	135.00
F	ATLANTA	45.00	60.00	140.00
G	CHICAGO	40.00	50.00	115.00
H	ST. LOUIS	45.00	65.00	140.00
I	MINNEAPOLIS	45.00	65.00	140.00
J	KANSAS CITY	45.00	65.00	140.00
K	DALLAS	80.00	140.00	360.00
L	SAN FRANCISCO	65.00	115.00	240.00

FEDERAL RESERVE BANK NOTES
FIFTY DOLLARS

Face Design Federal Reserve Bank Notes. Back Design on page 294.

District	Federal Reserve Bank	VF	Ex. Fine	CU
A	BOSTON	None Issued	—	—
B	NEW YORK	90.00	100.00	180.00
C	PHILADELPHIA	None Issued	—	—
D	CLEVELAND	100.00	120.00	185.00
E	RICHMOND	None Issued	—	—
F	ATLANTA	None Issued	—	—
G	CHICAGO	90.00	100.00	150.00
H	ST. LOUIS	None Issued	—	—
I	MINNEAPOLIS	100.00	130.00	230.00
J	KANSAS CITY	90.00	100.00	160.00
K	DALLAS	100.00	145.00	260.00
L	SAN FRANCISCO	120.00	175.00	350.00

ONE HUNDRED DOLLARS

Courtesy G.A. Siegwart
Face Design Federal Reserve Bank Notes. Back Design on page 303.

FEDERAL RESERVE BANK NOTES
ONE HUNDRED DOLLARS

Federal Reserve Bank		VF	Ex. Fine	CU
A	BOSTON	None Issued	—	—
B	NEW YORK	150.00	170.00	260.00
C	PHILADELPHIA	None Issued	—	—
D	CLEVELAND	150.00	160.00	250.00
E	RICHMOND	140.00	160.00	420.00
F	ATLANTA	None Issued	—	—
G	CHICAGO	140.00	160.00	250.00
H	ST. LOUIS	None Issued	—	—
I	MINNEAPOLIS	140.00	170.00	285.00
J	KANSAS CITY	140.00	160.00	250.00
K	DALLAS	180.00	350.00	625.00
L	SAN FRANCISCO	None Issued	—	—

FEDERAL RESERVE NOTES, Green Seal

Federal Reserve Notes were first authorized by the Federal Reserve Act of December 23, 1913. Since then, the issues of these notes have increased to the point that today they comprise over 99% of the total volume of paper money in circulation. Federal Reserve Notes are obligations of the United States and until 1968 were secured by Gold Certificates or Gold Certificate credits to the amount of at least 25% of the notes in actual circulation. Government securities accounted for the other 75% of the backing for these notes.

Modern-size Federal Reserve Notes were first issued in 1929, series dated 1928. Denominations range from $1 to $10,000. Those of $500 and higher were discontinued by action of the Board of Governors of the Federal Reserve System on June 26, 1946; on July 14, 1969, they were retired from circulation, but a few are still held in banks.

The twelve Federal Reserve Banks are organized and operate for public service as authorized by Congress. They are under supervision of the Board of Governors of the Federal Reserve System, an agency of the Federal Government. Members of this Board are appointed by the President and confirmed by the Senate.

Each of the twelve Banks has nine directors. Three of these, including the Chairman, are appointed by the Board of Governors. The other six are elected by member banks.

When Federal Reserve Notes are finished, they are delivered to the Federal Reserve vault which is under supervision of the Comptroller of the Currency. They are then sent to the issuing Banks as needed, which in turn distribute them to member banks and to the public.

Federal Reserve Banks release these notes according to the needs of their regions. One can easily tell which Bank issued a particular note by examining its face side. A number and corresponding letter were assigned to each of the Federal Reserve Districts, and both have been used on the notes in various combinations. At present a Bank seal to the left of the portrait carries the letter (and the name of the Bank); this same letter serves as the prefix letter for every serial number on all notes issued by the respective Bank. The District number is imprinted in four places, also on the face of the note. The Treasury seal and serial numbers are in green.

FEDERAL RESERVE NOTES

Explanatory Notations for Various Series

Series of 1928 — The redemption clause on notes issued before 1934 reads as follows: "Redeemable in Gold on Demand at the United States Treasury, or in Gold or Lawful Money at Any Federal Reserve Bank."

Series of 1934 — In 1933, Acts of Congress removed existing legal tender restrictions from all U.S. money, and in 1934 the Gold Reserve Act halted redemption of Federal Reserve Notes with gold. The redemption clause became a legal tender clause in accordance with these Acts, appearing on notes issued from 1934 to 1963 as follows: "This Note is Legal Tender For All Debts, Public and Private, and is Redeemable in Lawful Money at the United States Treasury, or at Any Federal Reserve Bank."

Series of 1934 A — The size of the numerals in the Face Plate Serial Number was made larger on this and succeeding issues.

Series 1950 — The following changes are incorporated on the face side of the notes for this and succeeding issues until 1963 B:

> Series designation appears only once, and the word "OF" is deleted.
> The Treasury seal and serial numbers are reduced in size.
> Signatures are overprinted instead of engraved.
> The Bank seal is smaller and has a toothed edge.

Series 1950 E — Notes of this series date were released after the 1963 issue.

Series 1963 — The change in printing method and increase in number of subjects per sheet took place with this issue. Also, this series marks the first appearance of $1 Federal Reserve Notes. The new legal tender clause is the same as that on United States Notes and reads, "This Note is Legal Tender For All Debts, Public and Private." The motto appears on the backs of denominations higher than $1, and the "Will Pay..." clause near the bottom no longer appears on any of the notes. No $50 or $100 notes were printed series dated 1963.

Series 1963 A — This is the first issue of $50 and $100 notes bearing the motto. Vignettes are also slightly enlarged on the backs and show better detail.

Series 1963 B — Only $1 notes were made with this series date; these were the 'Barr Notes" which caused so much publicity a few years ago. Joseph W. Barr served as Treasury Secretary one month (December 21, 1968 to January 20, 1969) but notes with his signature were made into June of 1969. That, plus speculation that notes with Barr's signature would obviously be rarities, caused many to be saved. They remain easily available today.

This issue is also the first of the current $1 notes to have signatures and series date engraved in the plates (see page 219).

Series 1969 — A new rendition of the Treasury seal is introduced on all denominations.

Series 1969 A — This is the first time in a number of years that all notes of the same type and series do *not* bear the same signature combination. The $1 notes have the Kabis-Kennedy signatures and all higher denominations the Kabis-Connally signatures.

Printing of the Kabis-Kennedy $1 notes started October 26, 1970, and it was expected that higher denominations would follow soon afterwards. The announcement that Kennedy would resign effective February 1, 1971, caused a halt to preparations for all denominations higher than the $1. After Connally's name replaced Kennedy's, notes from $5 through $100 were made with the 1969 A designation but with the new Kabis-Connally combination.

FEDERAL RESERVE NOTES

Series 1969 B, C and D — Because of the signature changes which occurred on the previous issue, the succeeding three series also show a variance in the $1 from all the rest. Signatures appear as follows:

    1969 B — $1, Kabis-Connally; $5-$50 Bañuelos-Connally.

    1969 C — $1, Bañuelos-Connally; $5-$100 Bañuelos-Schultz.

    1969 D — $1, Bañuelos-Shultz.

Series 1974 — This is the first issue under the new policy that each time a different Treasury Secretary is appointed there will be a new series date on the notes. All denominations thus carry the same date and signatures (Neff-Simon). Only the $1 notes have serial numbers starting over again from (A) 00 000 001A. Higher values continue the serial numbering from the previous issue.

Series 1976 — This date marks the introduction of the $2 with the Bicentennial back design. Many consider this to be a commemorative issue, though the intention is to include the $2 as a regularly circulating note.

Series 1981-A and 1985 — Some of the $1 notes of these series were printed with a unique back plate, number 129, which has the identification number placed at the lower left side of the back near the Great Seal. These are all scarce and generally valued at three to four times as much as the normal notes.

Series 1988-A — Operation of the Government printing plant in Forth Worth, Texas began in 1991. $1 notes for the Dallas and San Francisco districts have been produced there. These have small letters FW preceding the face plate position number near the lower right side of the face design. Some of the notes in this series were printed on new web-fed equipment. These notes do not have the plate location or check number on the face. On the back of these notes the plate number has been moved from the bottom of E in ONE to the top.

Series 1988 and later — Incomplete information may be shown for some of the current issues where not all of the notes have been printed or released for circulation. Current notes with little or no premium value are listed as face value.

Series 1990 — The first notes with advanced counterfeit deterrents were the Series 1990 $100 bills with signatures of Villalpando and Brady. Lower denominations, starting with the $50 notes, were introduced into circulation thereafter.

Series 1996 — Notes of this and later issues are redesigned with larger numerals and portrait. Additional security devices are incorporated into the paper and printing. A watermark is used to show a duplicate of the central portrait.

Federal Reserve Banks and their Letter Designations

There are 12 Federal Reserve Banks, and each has a specific letter designation on every note currently issued under its name. In this section either the bank name or its letter designation will be used for each note. Following is the listing of banks and their respective letters:

A — Boston	E — Richmond	I — Minneapolis
B — New York	F — Atlanta	J — Kansas City, Mo.
C — Philadelphia	G — Chicago	K — Dallas
D — Cleveland	H — St. Louis	L — San Francisco

Note: There are some scarce Block Letters in various issues, which are of interest to collectors. See the Oakes/Schwartz book listed in the Bibliography on page 336 for details.

FEDERAL RESERVE NOTES
ONE DOLLAR

Face Design 1963 to present. Back Design on page 238.

$1 SERIES 1963 — Signatures: *Granahan-Dillon*

Federal Reserve Bank		CU	Ch. CU	Federal Reserve Bank		CU	Ch. CU
A	BOSTON	3.00	5.00	G	CHICAGO	3.00	5.00
A★	BOSTON	4.00	6.00	G★	CHICAGO	4.00	6.00
B	NEW YORK	3.00	5.00	H	ST. LOUIS	3.00	5.00
B★	NEW YORK	4.00	7.00	H★	ST. LOUIS	4.00	7.00
C	PHILADELPHIA	3.00	5.00	I	MINNEAPOLIS	3.00	5.00
C★	PHILADELPHIA	5.00	7.00	I★	MINNEAPOLIS	4.00	6.00
D	CLEVELAND	3.00	5.00	J	KANSAS CITY	3.00	5.00
D★	CLEVELAND	5.00	700	J★	KANSAS CITY	4.00	6.00
E	RICHMOND	3.00	5.00	K	DALLAS	3.00	5.00
E★	RICHMOND	5.00	7.00	K★	DALLAS	4.00	6.00
F	ATLANTA	3.00	5.00	L	SAN FRANCISCO	3.00	5.00
F★	ATLANTA	5.00	7.00	L★	SAN FRANCISCO	5.00	7.00

$1 SERIES 1963-A — Signatures: *Granahan-Fowler*

Federal Reserve Bank		CU	Ch. CU	Federal Reserve Bank		CU	Ch. CU
A	BOSTON	3.00	5.00	G	CHICAGO	3.00	5.00
A★	BOSTON	4.00	6.00	G★	CHICAGO	4.00	6.00
B	NEW YORK	3.00	5.00	H	ST. LOUIS	3.00	5.00
B★	NEW YORK	4.00	7.00	H★	ST. LOUIS	4.00	6.00
C	PHILADELPHIA	3.00	5.00	I	MINNEAPOLIS	3.00	5.00
C★	PHILADELPHIA	4.00	6.00	I★	MINNEAPOLIS	4.00	6.00
D	CLEVELAND	3.00	5.00	J	KANSAS CITY	3.00	5.00
D★	CLEVELAND	5.00	6.00	J★	KANSAS CITY	4.00	6.00
E	RICHMOND	3.00	5.00	K	DALLAS	3.00	5.00
E★	RICHMOND	5.00	6.00	K★	DALLAS	4.00	6.00
F	ATLANTA	3.00	5.00	L	SAN FRANCISCO	3.00	5.00
F★	ATLANTA	5.00	7.00	L★	SAN FRANCISCO	4.00	6.00

FEDERAL RESERVE NOTES
ONE DOLLAR

$1 SERIES 1963-B — Signatures: *Granahan-Barr*

Federal Reserve Bank		CU	Ch. CU	Federal Reserve Bank		CU	Ch. CU
B	NEW YORK	4.00	6.00	J	KANSAS CITY	4.00	6.00
B★	NEW YORK	5.00	7.00	J★	KANSAS CITY	not printed	
E	RICHMOND	4.00	6.00	L	SAN FRANCISCO	4.00	6.00
E★	RICHMOND	6.00	8.00	L★	SAN FRANCISCO	5.00	7.00
G	CHICAGO	4.00	6.00				
G★	CHICAGO	5.00	7.00				

$1 SERIES 1969 — Signatures: *Elston-Kennedy*

Federal Reserve Bank		CU	Ch. CU	Federal Reserve Bank		CU	Ch. CU
A	BOSTON	3.00	4.00	G	CHICAGO	3.00	4.00
A★	BOSTON	4.00	5.00	G★	CHICAGO	4.00	6.00
B	NEW YORK	3.00	4.00	H	ST. LOUIS	3.00	4.00
B★	NEW YORK	4.00	5.00	H★	ST. LOUIS	4.00	5.00
C	PHILADELPHIA	3.00	4.00	I	MINNEAPOLIS	3.00	4.00
C★	PHILADELPHIA	4.00	5.00	I★	MINNEAPOLIS	4.00	5.00
D	CLEVELAND	3.00	4.00	J	KANSAS CITY	3.00	4.00
D★	CLEVELAND	5.00	6.00	J★	KANSAS CITY	4.00	5.00
E	RICHMOND	3.00	4.00	K	DALLAS	3.00	4.00
E★	RICHMOND	5.00	6.00	K★	DALLAS	5.00	6.00
F	ATLANTA	3.00	4.00	L	SAN FRANCISCO	3.00	4.00
F★	ATLANTA	5.00	6.00	L★	SAN FRANCISCO	5.00	6.00

$1 SERIES 1969-A — Signatures: *Kabis-Kennedy*

Federal Reserve Bank		CU	Ch. CU	Federal Reserve Bank		CU	Ch. CU
A	BOSTON	3.00	4.00	G	CHICAGO	3.00	4.00
A★	BOSTON	4.00	5.00	G★	CHICAGO	4.00	5.00
B	NEW YORK	3.00	4.00	H	ST. LOUIS	3.00	4.00
B★	NEW YORK	4.00	5.00	H★	ST. LOUIS	4.00	6.00
C	PHILADELPHIA	3.00	4.00	I	MINNEAPOLIS	3.00	4.00
C★	PHILADELPHIA	4.00	5.00	I★	MINNEAPOLIS	5.00	7.00
D	CLEVELAND	3.00	4.00	J	KANSAS CITY	3.00	4.00
D★	CLEVELAND	4.00	5.00	J★	KANSAS CITY	4.00	5.00
E	RICHMOND	3.00	4.00	K	DALLAS	3.00	4.00
E★	RICHMOND	4.00	5.00	K★	DALLAS	not printed	
F	ATLANTA	3.00	4.00	L	SAN FRANCISCO	3.00	4.00
F★	ATLANTA	4.00	5.00	L★	SAN FRANCISCO	4.00	5.00

FEDERAL RESERVE NOTES
ONE DOLLAR
$1 SERIES 1969-B — Signatures: *Kabis-Connally*

Federal Reserve Bank		CU	Ch. CU	Federal Reserve Bank		CU	Ch. CU
A	BOSTON	3.00	4.00	G	CHICAGO	3.00	4.00
A★	BOSTON	4.00	5.00	G★	CHICAGO	4.00	6.00
B	NEW YORK	3.00	4.00	H	ST. LOUIS	3.00	4.00
B★	NEW YORK	5.00	7.00	H★	ST. LOUIS	4.00	5.00
C	PHILADELPHIA	3.00	4.00	I	MINNEAPOLIS	3.00	4.00
C★	PHILADELPHIA	4.00	6.00	I★	MINNEAPOLIS	4.00	5.00
D	CLEVELAND	3.00	4.00	J	KANSAS CITY	3.00	4.00
D★	CLEVELAND	4.00	5.00	J★	KANSAS CITY	4.00	6.00
E	RICHMOND	3.00	4.00	K	DALLAS	3.00	4.00
E★	RICHMOND	4.00	5.00	K★	DALLAS	4.00	6.00
F	ATLANTA	3.00	4.00	L	SAN FRANCISCO	3.00	4.00
F★	ATLANTA	4.00	5.00	L★	SAN FRANCISCO	5.00	7.00

$1 SERIES 1969-C — Signatures: *Bañuelos-Connally*

Federal Reserve Bank		CU	Ch. CU	Federal Reserve Bank		CU	Ch. CU
A	BOSTON	not printed		G	CHICAGO	3.00	4.00
A★	BOSTON	not printed		G★	CHICAGO	4.00	7.00
B	NEW YORK	3.00	4.00	H	ST. LOUIS	3.00	4.00
B★	NEW YORK	not printed		H★	ST. LOUIS	4.00	7.00
C	PHILADELPHIA	not printed		I	MINNEAPOLIS	3.00	4.00
C★	PHILADELPHIA	not printed		I★	MINNEAPOLIS	4.00	7.00
D	CLEVELAND	3.00	4.00	J	KANSAS CITY	3.00	4.00
D★	CLEVELAND	5.00	8.00	J★	KANSAS CITY	4.00	7.00
E	RICHMOND	3.00	4.00	K	DALLAS	3.00	4.00
E★	RICHMOND	5.00	8.00	K★	DALLAS	4.00	7.00
F	ATLANTA	3.00	4.00	L	SAN FRANCISCO	3.00	4.00
F★	ATLANTA	5.00	8.00	L★	SAN FRANCISCO	7.00	14.00

$1 SERIES 1969-D — Signatures: *Bañuelos-Schultz*

Federal Reserve Bank		CU	Ch. CU	Federal Reserve Bank		CU	Ch. CU
A	BOSTON	3.00	4.00	G	CHICAGO	3.00	4.00
A★	BOSTON	4.00	5.00	G★	CHICAGO	4.00	5.00
B	NEW YORK	3.00	4.00	H	ST. LOUIS	3.00	4.00
B★	NEW YORK	4.00	5.00	H★	ST. LOUIS	4.00	5.00
C	PHILADELPHIA	3.00	4.00	I	MINNEAPOLIS	3.00	4.00
C★	PHILADELPHIA	4.00	5.00	I★	MINNEAPOLIS	not printed	
D	CLEVELAND	3.00	4.00	J	KANSAS CITY	3.00	4.00
D★	CLEVELAND	4.00	5.00	J★	KANSAS CITY	4.00	5.00
E	RICHMOND	3.00	4.00	K	DALLAS	3.00	4.00
E★	RICHMOND	4.00	5.00	K★	DALLAS	4.00	5.00
F	ATLANTA	3.00	4.00	L	SAN FRANCISCO	3.00	4.00
F★	ATLANTA	4.00	5.00	L★	SAN FRANCISCO	4.00	5.00

FEDERAL RESERVE NOTES
ONE DOLLAR

$1 SERIES 1974 — Signatures: *Neff-Simon*

Federal Reserve Bank		CU	Ch. CU	Federal Reserve Bank		CU	Ch. CU
A	BOSTON	3.00	4.00	G	CHICAGO	3.00	4.00
A★	BOSTON	4.00	5.00	G★	CHICAGO	4.00	5.00
B	NEW YORK	3.00	4.00	H	ST. LOUIS	3.00	4.00
B★	NEW YORK	4.00	5.00	H★	ST. LOUIS	4.00	5.00
C	PHILADELPHIA	3.00	4.00	I	MINNEAPOLIS	3.00	4.00
C★	PHILADELPHIA	4.00	5.00	I★	MINNEAPOLIS	4.00	6.00
D	CLEVELAND	3.00	4.00	J	KANSAS CITY	3.00	4.00
D★	CLEVELAND	4.00	5.00	J★	KANSAS CITY	4.00	5.00
E	RICHMOND	3.00	4.00	K	DALLAS	3.00	4.00
E★	RICHMOND	4.00	5.00	K★	DALLAS	4.00	5.00
F	ATLANTA	3.00	4.00	L	SAN FRANCISCO	3.00	4.00
F★	ATLANTA	4.00	5.00	L★	SAN FRANCISCO	4.00	5.00

$1 SERIES 1977 — Signatures: *Morton-Blumenthal*

Federal Reserve Bank		CU	Ch. CU	Federal Reserve Bank		CU	Ch. CU
A	BOSTON	3.00	4.00	G	CHICAGO	3.00	4.00
A★	BOSTON	4.00	5.00	G★	CHICAGO	4.00	5.00
B	NEW YORK	3.00	4.00	H	ST. LOUIS	3.00	4.00
B★	NEW YORK	4.00	5.00	H★	ST. LOUIS	4.00	5.00
C	PHILADELPHIA	3.00	4.00	I	MINNEAPOLIS	3.00	4.00
C★	PHILADELPHIA	4.00	5.00	I★	MINNEAPOLIS	4.00	6.00
D	CLEVELAND	3.00	4.00	J	KANSAS CITY	3.00	4.00
D★	CLEVELAND	4.00	5.00	J★	KANSAS CITY	4.00	5.00
E	RICHMOND	3.00	4.00	K	DALLAS	3.00	4.00
E★	RICHMOND	4.00	5.00	K★	DALLAS	4.00	5.00
F	ATLANTA	3.00	4.00	L	SAN FRANCISCO	3.00	4.00
F★	ATLANTA	4.00	5.00	L★	SAN FRANCISCO	4.00	5.00

$1 SERIES 1977-A — Signatures: *Morton-Miller*

Federal Reserve Bank		CU	Ch. CU	Federal Reserve Bank		CU	Ch. CU
A	BOSTON	2.00	4.00	G	CHICAGO	2.00	4.00
A★	BOSTON	3.00	5.00	G★	CHICAGO	3.00	5.00
B	NEW YORK	2.00	4.00	H	ST. LOUIS	2.00	4.00
B★	NEW YORK	3.00	5.00	H★	ST. LOUIS	3.00	5.00
C	PHILADELPHIA	2.00	4.00	I	MINNEAPOLIS	2.00	4.00
C★	PHILADELPHIA	3.00	5.00	I★	MINNEAPOLIS	3.00	5.00
D	CLEVELAND	2.00	4.00	J	KANSAS CITY	2.00	4.00
D★	CLEVELAND	3.00	5.00	J★	KANSAS CITY	3.00	5.00
E	RICHMOND	2.00	4.00	K	DALLAS	2.00	4.00
E★	RICHMOND	3.00	5.00	K★	DALLAS	3.00	5.00
F	ATLANTA	2.00	4.00	L	SAN FRANCISCO	2.00	4.00
F★	ATLANTA	3.00	5.00	L★	SAN FRANCISCO	3.00	5.00

FEDERAL RESERVE NOTES
ONE DOLLAR

$1 SERIES 1981 — Signatures: *Buchanan-Regan*

Federal Reserve Bank		CU	Ch. CU	Federal Reserve Bank		CU	Ch. CU
A	BOSTON	2.00	3.00	G	CHICAGO	2.00	3.00
A★	BOSTON	3.00	4.00	G★	CHICAGO	3.00	4.00
B	NEW YORK	2.00	3.00	H	ST. LOUIS	3.00	4.00
B★	NEW YORK	3.00	4.00	H★	ST. LOUIS	4.00	9.00
C	PHILADELPHIA	2.00	3.00	I	MINNEAPOLIS	3.00	4.00
C★	PHILADELPHIA	6.00	6.00	I★	MINNEAPOLIS	6.00	9.00
D	CLEVELAND	2.00	4.00	J	KANSAS CITY	2.00	3.00
D★	CLEVELAND	3.00	5.00	J★	KANSAS CITY	3.00	4.00
E	RICHMOND	2.00	3.00	K	DALLAS	2.00	4.00
E★	RICHMOND	3.00	4.00	K★	DALLAS	3.00	4.00
F	ATLANTA	2.00	5.00	L	SAN FRANCISCO	2.00	3.00
F★	ATLANTA	3.00	5.00	L★	SAN FRANCISCO	3.00	4.00

$1 SERIES 1981-A — Signatures: *Ortega-Regan*

Federal Reserve Bank		CU	Ch. CU	Federal Reserve Bank		CU	Ch. CU
A	BOSTON	2.00	3.00	G	CHICAGO	2.00	3.00
B	NEW YORK	2.00	3.00	G★	CHICAGO	3.00	4.00
B★	NEW YORK	3.00	4.00	H	ST. LOUIS	2.00	3.00
C	PHILADELPHIA	2.00	3.00	I	MINNEAPOLIS	2.00	3.00
D	CLEVELAND	2.00	3.00	J	KANSAS CITY	2.00	3.00
E	RICHMOND	2.00	3.00	K	DALLAS	2.00	3.00
E★	RICHMOND	3.00	4.00	K★	DALLAS	30.00	75.00
F	ATLANTA	2.00	3.00	L	SAN FRANCISCO	3.00	3.00
				L★	SAN FRANCISCO	3.50	3.50

Notes with back plate number 129 at left are valued higher.

$1 SERIES 1985 — Signatures: *Ortega-Baker*

Federal Reserve Bank		CU	Ch. CU	Federal Reserve Bank		CU	Ch. CU
A	BOSTON	2.00	3.00	H	ST. LOUIS	2.00	3.00
B	NEW YORK	2.00	3.00	H★	ST. LOUIS	3.00	4.00
C	PHILADELPHIA	2.00	3.00	I	MINNEAPOLIS	2.00	3.00
D	CLEVELAND	2.00	3.00	I★	MINNEAPOLIS	3.00	4.00
E	RICHMOND	2.00	3.00	J	KANSAS CITY	2.00	3.00
E★	RICHMOND	3.00	4.00	K	DALLAS	2.00	3.00
F	ATLANTA	2.00	3.00	K★	DALLAS	3.00	4.00
G	CHICAGO	2.00	3.00	L	SAN FRANCISCO	2.00	3.00
G★	CHICAGO	3.00	4.00	L★	SAN FRANCISCO	2.50	3.50

Notes with back plate number 129 at left are valued higher.

FEDERAL RESERVE NOTES
ONE DOLLAR

$1 SERIES 1988 — Signatures: *Ortega-Brady*

Federal Reserve Bank		CU	Ch. CU	Federal Reserve Bank		CU	Ch. CU
A	BOSTON	2.50	4.00	G	CHICAGO	2.00	3.00
A★	BOSTON	3.00	6.00	H	ST. LOUIS	2.00	3.00
B	NEW YORK	2.00	3.00	I	MINNEAPOLIS	2.00	3.00
B★	NEW YORK	3.00	4.00	J	KANSAS CITY	2.50	4.00
C	PHILADELPHIA	3.00	5.00	J★	KANSAS CITY	3.00	5.00
D	CLEVELAND	2.50	4.00	K	DALLAS	3.00	5.00
E	RICHMOND	2.50	4.00	K★	DALLAS	4.00	7.00
E★	RICHMOND	3.00	5.00	L	SAN FRANCISCO	2.50	4.00
F	ATLANTA	2.50	4.00	L★	SAN FRANCISCO	4.00	7.00
F★	ATLANTA	175.00	275.00				

Sheet-fed, Washington facility. With normal face check letter/number.

$1 SERIES 1988-A — Signatures: *Vallalpando-Brady*   Sheet-Fed

Federal Reserve Bank		CU	Ch. CU	Federal Reserve Bank			CU	Ch. CU
A	BOSTON	2.00	3.00	G★	CHICAGO	W or FW	2.50	3.50
B	NEW YORK	2.00	3.00	H	ST. LOUIS	W or FW	2.00	3.00
B★	NEW YORK	2.50	3.50	H★	ST. LOUIS		2.50	3.50
C	PHILADELPHIA	2.00	3.00	I	MINNEAPOLIS	W/FW	2.00	3.00
D	CLEVELAND	2.00	3.00	I★	MINNEAPOLIS	W/FW	2.50	3.50
D★	CLEVELAND	2.50	3.50	J	KANSAS CITY	W/FW	2.00	3.00
E	RICHMOND	2.00	3.00	K	DALLAS	W or FW	2.00	3.00
E★	RICHMOND	3.00	4.00	K★	DALLAS	FW	2.50	3.50
F	ATLANTA W or FW	2.00	3.00	L	SAN FRANCISCO	W/FW	2.00	3.00
F★	ATLANTA	2.50	3.50	L★	SAN FRANCISCO	FW	2.50	3.50
G	CHICAGO W or FW	2.00	3.00					

All sheet-fed: Washington (W), has normal face check letter/number. Fort Worth (FW) has a check letter and number preceded by small letters FW.

$1 SERIES 1988-A — Signatures: *Vallalpando-Brady*   Web-Fed

Federal Reserve Bank		VF	Ch. CU	Federal Reserve Bank		VF	Ch. CU
A	BOSTON	5.00	20.00	F	ATLANTA	5.00	20.00
B	NEW YORK	250.00	1,200	F★	ATLANTA	450.00	900.00
C	PHILADELPHIA	5.00	20.00	G	CHICAGO	15.00	100.00
E	RICHMOND	5.00	20.00				

Web-fed notes were printed in Washington, D.C. from 1992 to 1996 on an experimental press. They have only a face check number, and no letter in the lower right corner. The back check number is to the right of TRUST.

BEP Washington

Fort Worth

Web Press

FEDERAL RESERVE NOTES
ONE DOLLAR

$1 SERIES 1993 — Signatures: *Withrow-Bentsen* Sheet-Fed

Federal Reserve Bank		CU	Ch. CU	Federal Reserve Bank		CU	Ch. CU
A	BOSTON	2.00	3.00	F★	ATLANTA	2.50	3.50
B	NEW YORK	2.00	3.00	G	CHICAGO W or FW	2.00	3.00
B★	NEW YORK	2.50	3.50	G★	CHICAGO FW	2.50	3.50
C	PHILADELPHIA	2.00	3.00	H	ST. LOUIS W/FW	2.00	3.00
C★	PHILADELPHIA	40.00	100.00	I	MINNEAPOLIS FW	30.00	50.00
D	CLEVELAND	2.00	3.00	K	DALLAS FW	2.00	3.00
E	RICHMOND	2.00	3.00	K★	DALLAS FW	2.50	3.50
F	ATLANTA	2.00	3.00	L	SAN FRANCISCO W/FW	2.00	3.00

All sheet-fed: Washington (W), has normal face check letter/number. Fort Worth (FW) has check letter and number preceded by small letters FW.

$1 SERIES 1993 — Signatures: *Withrow-Bentsen* Web-Fed

Federal Reserve Bank		CU	Ch. CU	Federal Reserve Bank		CU	Ch. CU
B	NEW YORK	8.00	12.00	C	PHILADELPHIA	8.00	12.00

Web-fed notes were printed in Washington, D.C. from 1992 to 1996 on an experimental press. They have only a face check number, and no letter in the lower right corner. The back check number is to the right of TRUST.

$1 SERIES 1995 — Signatures: *Withrow-Rubin* Sheet-Fed

Federal Reserve Bank		CU	Ch. CU	Federal Reserve Bank		CU	Ch. CU
A	BOSTON	2.00	3.00	F	ATLANTA	2.00	3.00
A★	BOSTON	2.50	3.50	F★	ATLANTA	2.50	3.50
B	NEW YORK	2.00	3.00	G	CHICAGO FW	2.00	3.00
B★	NEW YORK	2.50	3.75	H	ST. LOUIS FW	2.00	3.00
C	PHILADELPHIA	2.00	3.00	I	MINNEAPOLIS FW	2.50	3.50
C★	PHILADELPHIA	3.00	4.00	J	KANSAS CITY FW	2.00	3.00
D	CLEVELAND	2.00	3.00	K	DALLAS FW	2.00	3.00
E	RICHMOND	2.00	3.00	L	SAN FRANCISCO FW	2.00	3.00
				L★	SAN FRANCISCO FW	2.50	3.50

All sheet-fed: Washington (W), has normal face check letter/number. Fort Worth (FW) has check letter and number preceded by small letters FW.

$1 SERIES 1995 — Signatures: *Withrow-Rubin* Web-Fed

Federal Reserve Bank		CU	Ch. CU	Federal Reserve Bank		CU	Ch. CU
A	BOSTON	7.00	10.00	D	CLEVELAND	7.00	10.00
B	NEW YORK	7.00	10.00	F	ATLANTA	7.00	10.00

FEDERAL RESERVE NOTES
TWO DOLLARS

Face Design 1976

Back Design 1976

$2 SERIES 1976 — Signatures: *Neff-Simon*

	Federal Reserve Bank	CU	Ch. CU		Federal Reserve Bank	CU	Ch. CU
A	BOSTON	3.00	4.00	G	CHICAGO	3.00	4.00
A★	BOSTON	10.00	20.00	G★	CHICAGO	10.00	20.00
B	NEW YORK	3.00	4.00	H	ST. LOUIS	3.00	4.00
B★	NEW YORK	10.00	20.00	H★	ST. LOUIS	10.00	20.00
C	PHILADELPHIA	3.00	4.00	I	MINNEAPOLIS	3.00	4.00
C★	PHILADELPHIA	10.00	20.00	I★	MINNEAPOLIS	100.00	200.00
D	CLEVELAND	3.00	4.00	J	KANSAS CITY	3.00	4.00
D★	CLEVELAND	10.00	20.00	J★	KANSAS CITY	75.00	125.00
E	RICHMOND	3.00	4.00	K	DALLAS	3.00	4.00
E★	RICHMOND	10.00	20.00	K★	DALLAS	10.00	20.00
F	ATLANTA	3.00	4.00	L	SAN FRANCISCO	3.00	4.00
F★	ATLANTA	10.00	20.00	L★	SAN FRANCISCO	10.00	20.00

$2 SERIES 1995 — Signatures: *Withrow-Rubin*

	Federal Reserve Bank	CU	Ch. CU		Federal Reserve Bank	CU	Ch. CU
F	ATLANTA FW	3.50	5.00	F★	ATLANTA FW	7.00	10.00

Fort Worth (FW) printings have face check letter and number preceded by small letters FW.

FEDERAL RESERVE NOTES
FIVE DOLLARS

Face Design 1928 and 1928 A. Back Design on page 231.

$5 SERIES 1928 — Signatures: *Tate-Mellon*

Large District numeral of Bank at left.

District	Federal Reserve Bank	VF	Ex. Fine	CU	Ch. CU
1	BOSTON	20.00	60.00	100.00	150.00
2	NEW YORK	20.00	60.00	100.00	150.00
3	PHILADELPHIA	20.00	60.00	100.00	150.00
4	CLEVELAND	20.00	60.00	100.00	150.00
5	RICHMOND	20.00	60.00	100.00	150.00
6	ATLANTA	20.00	60.00	100.00	150.00
7	CHICAGO	20.00	60.00	100.00	150.00
8	ST. LOUIS	20.00	60.00	100.00	150.00
9	MINNEAPOLIS	50.00	200.00	600.00	900.00
10	KANSAS CITY	20.00	60.00	100.00	150.00
11	DALLAS	20.00	60.00	100.00	150.00
12	SAN FRANCISCO	20.00	60.00	100.00	150.00

Star notes: about two to five times more than regular issues.

$5 SERIES 1928-A — Signatures: *Woods-Mellon*

Large District numeral at left, similar to Series of 1928 issues.

District	Federal Reserve Bank	VF	Ex. Fine	CU	Ch. CU
1	BOSTON	20.00	60.00	100.00	150.00
2	NEW YORK	20.00	60.00	100.00	150.00
3	PHILADELPHIA	20.00	60.00	100.00	150.00
4	CLEVELAND	20.00	60.00	100.00	150.00
5	RICHMOND	20.00	60.00	100.00	150.00
6	ATLANTA	20.00	60.00	100.00	150.00
7	CHICAGO	20.00	60.00	100.00	150.00
8	ST. LOUIS	20.00	60.00	100.00	150.00
9	MINNEAPOLIS	60.00	180.00	300.00	700.00
10	KANSAS CITY	20.00	60.00	100.00	150.00
11	DALLAS	20.00	60.00	100.00	150.00
12	SAN FRANCISCO	20.00	60.00	100.00	150.00

FEDERAL RESERVE NOTES
FIVE DOLLARS

$5 SERIES 1928-B — Signatures: *Woods-Mellon*

Large District letter replaces numeral in seal on this and succeeding issues.

District	Federal Reserve Bank	VF	Ex. Fine	CU	Ch. CU
A	BOSTON	20.00	40.00	75.00	100.00
B	NEW YORK	20.00	40.00	75.00	100.00
C	PHILADELPHIA	20.00	40.00	75.00	100.00
D	CLEVELAND	20.00	40.00	75.00	100.00
E	RICHMOND	20.00	40.00	75.00	100.00
F	ATLANTA	20.00	40.00	75.00	100.00
G	CHICAGO	20.00	40.00	75.00	100.00
H	ST. LOUIS	20.00	40.00	75.00	100.00
I	MINNEAPOLIS	40.00	80.00	150.00	250.00
J	KANSAS CITY	20.00	40.00	75.00	100.00
K	DALLAS	20.00	40.00	75.00	100.00
L	SAN FRANCISCO	20.00	40.00	75.00	100.00

$5 SERIES 1928-C — Signatures: *Woods-Mills*

District	Federal Reserve Bank	VF	Ex. Fine	CU	Ch. CU
D	CLEVELAND	—	—	—	—
F	ATLANTA	350.00	750.00	1,500	2,500
L	SAN FRANCISCO	—	—	—	—

$5 SERIES 1928-D — Signatures: *Woods-Woodin*

District	Federal Reserve Bank	VF	Ex. Fine	CU	Ch. CU
F	ATLANTA	850.00	1,500	3,000	4,500

Bureau records do not give any indication of the serial numbers for the Series of 1928 D $5. However, a fair number of them have been confirmed with serial numbers scattered from F26 282 729A to F28 617 186A. These were well interspersed with 1928 C notes*.

General Face Design 1928 B – 1928 D. Face Design 1934 – 1934 D.
Back Design on page 231.

*Robert H. Loloyd has also pulished the fact that 9 plates are on record as having been used for the $5.00 Series of 1928D notes.

FEDERAL RESERVE NOTES
FIVE DOLLARS

$5 SERIES 1934 — Signatures: *Julian-Morgenthau*

Light or dark green seal. Star notes exist for all Districts.

District	Federal Reserve Bank	VF	Ex. Fine	CU	Ch. CU
A	BOSTON	10.00	22.00	50.00	85.00
B	NEW YORK	10.00	22.00	50.00	85.00
C	PHILADELPHIA	10.00	22.00	50.00	85.00
D	CLEVELAND	10.00	22.00	50.00	85.00
E	RICHMOND	10.00	22.00	50.00	85.00
F	ATLANTA	10.00	22.00	50.00	85.00
G	CHICAGO	10.00	22.00	50.00	85.00
H	ST. LOUIS	10.00	22.00	50.00	85.00
I	MINNEAPOLIS	12.00	27.00	60.00	100.00
J	KANSAS CITY	10.00	22.00	50.00	85.00
K	DALLAS	10.00	22.00	50.00	85.00
L	SAN FRANCISCO	10.00	22.00	50.00	85.00

$5 SERIES 1934-A — Signatures: *Julian-Morgenthau*

Star notes exist for all issuing Districts; they are scarce.†

District	Federal Reserve Bank	VF	Ex. Fine	CU	Ch. CU
A	BOSTON	8.00	20.00	45.00	75.00
B	NEW YORK	8.00	20.00	45.00	75.00
C	PHILADELPHIA	8.00	20.00	45.00	75.00
D	CLEVELAND	65.00	100.00	250.00	400.00
E	RICHMOND	8.00	20.00	45.00	75.00
F	ATLANTA	8.00	20.00	45.00	75.00
G	CHICAGO	8.00	20.00	45.00	75.00
H	ST. LOUIS	8.00	20.00	45.00	75.00
L	SAN FRANCISCO	8.00	20.00	45.00	75.00

†Bureau records do not show any printings, regular or star, for $5.00 notes Series of 1934 A for Minneapolis, Kansas City or Dallas.

$5 SERIES 1934-B — Signatures: *Julian-Vinson*

District	Federal Reserve Bank	VF	Ex. Fine	CU	Ch. CU
A	BOSTON	12.00	25.00	60.00	90.00
B	NEW YORK	12.00	25.00	60.00	90.00
C	PHILADELPHIA	12.00	25.00	60.00	90.00
D	CLEVELAND	12.00	25.00	60.00	90.00
E	RICHMOND	12.00	25.00	60.00	90.00
F	ATLANTA	12.00	25.00	60.00	90.00
G	CHICAGO	12.00	25.00	60.00	90.00
H	ST. LOUIS	12.00	25.00	60.00	90.00
I	MINNEAPOLIS	40.00	65.00	90.00	150.00
J	KANSAS CITY	500.00	1,000	2,000	3,000
L	SAN FRANCISCO	12.00	25.00	60.00	90.00

FEDERAL RESERVE NOTES
FIVE DOLLARS

$5 SERIES 1934-C — Signatures: *Julian-Snyder*

District	Federal Reserve Bank	VF	Ex. Fine	CU
A	BOSTON	12.00	25.00	60.00
B	NEW YORK	12.00	25.00	60.00
C	PHILADELPHIA	12.00	25.00	60.00
D	CLEVELAND	12.00	25.00	60.00
E	RICHMOND	12.00	25.00	60.00
F	ATLANTA	12.00	25.00	60.00
G	CHICAGO	12.00	25.00	60.00
H	ST. LOUIS	12.00	25.00	60.00
I	MINNEAPOLIS	24.00	50.00	120.00
J	KANSAS CITY	12.00	25.00	60.00
K	DALLAS	12.00	25.00	60.00
L	SAN FRANCISCO	12.00	25.00	60.00

$5 SERIES 1934-D — Signatures: *Clark-Snyder*

District	Federal Reserve Bank	VF	Ex. Fine	CU
A	BOSTON	12.00	25.00	60.00
B	NEW YORK	12.00	25.00	60.00
C	PHILADELPHIA	12.00	25.00	60.00
D	CLEVELAND	12.00	25.00	60.00
E	RICHMOND	25.00	50.00	120.00
F	ATLANTA	250.00	650.00	1,500
G	CHICAGO	12.00	25.00	60.00
H	ST. LOUIS	12.00	25.00	60.00
I	MINNEAPOLIS	25.00	50.00	120.00
J	KANSAS CITY	12.00	25.00	60.00
K	DALLAS	25.00	50.00	120.00
L	SAN FRANCISCO	12.00	25.0	60.00

FIVE DOLLARS

Face Design 1950-1950 E. General Face Design 1963-1995.
Back Design on page 231.

FEDERAL RESERVE NOTES
FIVE DOLLARS

$5 SERIES 1950 — Signatures: *Clark-Snyder*

Federal Reserve Bank		CU	Ch. CU	Federal Reserve Bank		CU	Ch. CU
A	BOSTON	30.00	40.00	G	CHICAGO	30.00	40.00
A★	BOSTON	60.00	100.00	G★	CHICAGO	50.00	80.00
B	NEW YORK	28.00	55.00	H	ST. LOUIS	30.00	40.00
B★	NEW YORK	60.00	100.00	H★	ST. LOUIS	60.00	150.00
C	PHILADELPHIA	30.00	40.00	I	MINNEAPOLIS	30.00	50.00
C★	PHILADELPHIA	60.00	150.00	I★	MINNEAPOLIS	60.00	500.00
D	CLEVELAND	30.00	40.00	J	KANSAS CITY	30.00	45.00
D★	CLEVELAND	50.00	80.00	J★	KANSAS CITY	60.00	90.00
E	RICHMOND	30.00	40.00	K	DALLAS	30.00	45.00
E★	RICHMOND	50.00	80.00	K★	DALLAS	50.00	200.00
F	ATLANTA	30.00	40.00	L	SAN FRANCISCO	30.00	40.00
F★	ATLANTA	50.00	80.00	L★	SAN FRANCISCO	50.00	80.00

$5 SERIES 1950-A — Signatures: *Priest-Humphrey*

Federal Reserve Bank		CU	Ch. CU	Federal Reserve Bank		CU	Ch. CU
A	BOSTON	20.00	30.00	G	CHICAGO	20.00	30.00
A★	BOSTON	35.00	50.00	G★	CHICAGO	35.00	50.00
B	NEW YORK	20.00	30.00	H	ST. LOUIS	20.00	30.00
B★	NEW YORK	35.00	50.00	H★	ST. LOUIS	40.00	150.00
C	PHILADELPHIA	20.00	30.00	I	MINNEAPOLIS	25.00	35.00
C★	PHILADELPHIA	35.00	50.00	I★	MINNEAPOLIS	250.00	450.00
D	CLEVELAND	20.00	30.00	J	KANSAS CITY	25.00	35.00
D★	CLEVELAND	35.00	50.00	J★	KANSAS CITY	75.00	125.00
E	RICHMOND	20.00	30.00	K	DALLAS	25.00	35.00
E★	RICHMOND	35.00	50.00	K★	DALLAS	75.00	125.00
F	ATLANTA	20.00	30.00	L	SAN FRANCISCO	20.00	30.00
F★	ATLANTA	35.00	50.00	L★	SAN FRANCISCO	35.00	50.00

$5 SERIES 1950-B — Signatures: *Priest-Anderson*

Federal Reserve Bank		CU	Ch. CU	Federal Reserve Bank		CU	Ch. CU
A	BOSTON	20.00	30.00	G	CHICAGO	20.00	30.00
A★	BOSTON	34.00	45.00	G★	CHICAGO	34.00	45.00
B	NEW YORK	20.00	30.00	H	ST. LOUIS	20.00	30.00
B★	NEW YORK	34.00	45.00	H★	ST. LOUIS	34.00	45.00
C	PHILADELPHIA	20.00	30.00	I	MINNEAPOLIS	20.00	30.00
C★	PHILADELPHIA	34.00	45.00	I★	MINNEAPOLIS	80.00	150.00
D	CLEVELAND	20.00	30.00	J	KANSAS CITY	20.00	30.00
D★	CLEVELAND	34.00	45.00	J★	KANSAS CITY	34.00	45.00
E	RICHMOND	20.00	30.00	K	DALLAS	20.00	30.00
E★	RICHMOND	34.00	45.00	K★	DALLAS	34.00	45.00
F	ATLANTA	20.00	30.00	L	SAN FRANCISCO	20.00	30.00
F★	ATLANTA	34.00	45.00	L★	SAN FRANCISCO	34.00	45.00

FEDERAL RESERVE NOTES
FIVE DOLLARS

$5 SERIES 1950-C — Signatures: *Smith-Dillon*

Federal Reserve Bank		CU	Ch. CU	Federal Reserve Bank		CU	Ch. CU
A	BOSTON	15.00	25.00	G	CHICAGO	15.00	25.00
A★	BOSTON	25.00	40.00	G★	CHICAGO	25.00	40.00
B	NEW YORK	15.00	25.00	H	ST. LOUIS	20.00	30.00
B★	NEW YORK	25.00	40.00	H★	ST. LOUIS	75.00	150.00
C	PHILADELPHIA	20.00	30.00	I	MINNEAPOLIS	20.00	30.00
C★	PHILADELPHIA	25.00	40.00	I★	MINNEAPOLIS	150.00	250.00
D	CLEVELAND	20.00	30.00	J	KANSAS CITY	15.00	25.00
D★	CLEVELAND	25.00	40.00	J★	KANSAS CITY	75.00	150.00
E	RICHMOND	20.00	30.00	K	DALLAS	20.00	30.00
E★	RICHMOND	75.00	150.00	K★	DALLAS	150.00	250.00
F	ATLANTA	15.00	25.00	L	SAN FRANCISCO	15.00	25.00
F★	ATLANTA	25.00	40.00	L★	SAN FRANCISCO	75.00	150.00

$5 SERIES 1950-D — Signatures: *Granahan-Dillon*

Federal Reserve Bank		CU	Ch. CU	Federal Reserve Bank		CU	Ch. CU
A	BOSTON	20.00	30.00	G	CHICAGO	20.00	30.00
A★	BOSTON	50.00	100.00	G★	CHICAGO	30.00	40.00
B	NEW YORK	20.00	30.00	H	ST. LOUIS	20.00	30.00
B★	NEW YORK	30.00	40.00	H★	ST. LOUIS	30.00	40.00
C	PHILADELPHIA	20.00	30.00	I	MINNEAPOLIS	20.00	30.00
C★	PHILADELPHIA	30.00	40.00	I★	MINNEAPOLIS	75.00	150.00
D	CLEVELAND	20.00	30.00	J	KANSAS CITY	20.00	30.00
D★	CLEVELAND	30.00	40.00	J★	KANSAS CITY	30.00	40.00
E	RICHMOND	20.00	30.00	K	DALLAS	20.00	30.00
E★	RICHMOND	30.00	40.00	K★	DALLAS	75.00	150.00
F	ATLANTA	20.00	30.00	L	SAN FRANCISCO	20.00	30.00
F★	ATLANTA	30.00	40.00	L★	SAN FRANCISCO	30.00	40.00

$5 SERIES 1950-E — Signatures: *Granahan-Fowler*

Federal Reserve Bank		CU	Ch. CU	Federal Reserve Bank		CU	Ch. CU
A	BOSTON	not printed		G	CHICAGO	60.00	125.00
A★	BOSTON	not printed		G★	CHICAGO	125.00	150.00
B	NEW YORK	30.00	40.00	H	ST. LOUIS	not printed	
B★	NEW YORK	60.00	75.00	H★	ST. LOUIS	not printed	
C	PHILADELPHIA	not printed		I	MINNEAPOLIS	not printed	
C★	PHILADELPHIA	not printed		I★	MINNEAPOLIS	not printed	
D	CLEVELAND	not printed		J	KANSAS CITY	not printed	
D★	CLEVELAND	not printed		J★	KANSAS CITY	not printed	
E	RICHMOND	not printed		K	DALLAS	not printed	
E★	RICHMOND	not printed		K★	DALLAS	not printed	
F	ATLANTA	not printed		L	SAN FRANCISCO	40.00	100.00
F★	ATLANTA	not printed		L★	SAN FRANCISCO	175.00	300.00

Notes of the 1950-E series do not have the motto on the back. These were released *after* the 1963 series.

FEDERAL RESERVE NOTES
FIVE DOLLARS

$5 SERIES 1963 — Signatures: *Granahan-Dillon*

Motto "In God We Trust" added on the back. Back design on page 233.

Federal Reserve Bank		CU	Ch. CU	Federal Reserve Bank		CU	Ch. CU
A	BOSTON	15.00	30.00	G	CHICAGO	15.00	20.00
A★	BOSTON	30.00	60.00	G★	CHICAGO	17.00	25.00
B	NEW YORK	15.00	20.00	H	ST. LOUIS	15.00	20.00
B★	NEW YORK	17.00	25.00	H★	ST. LOUIS	17.00	25.00
C	PHILADELPHIA	15.00	20.00	I	MINNEAPOLIS	not printed	
C★	PHILADELPHIA	17.00	25.00	I★	MINNEAPOLIS	not printed	
D	CLEVELAND	15.00	20.00	J	KANSAS CITY	15.00	20.00
D★	CLEVELAND	17.00	25.00	J★	KANSAS CITY	20.00	25.00
E	RICHMOND	not printed		K	DALLAS	15.00	20.00
E★	RICHMOND	not printed		K★	DALLAS	17.00	25.00
F	ATLANTA	15.00	17.00	L	SAN FRANCISCO	15.00	20.00
F★	ATLANTA	17.00	25.00	L★	SAN FRANCISCO	17.00	25.00

$5 SERIES 1963-A — Signatures: *Granahan-Fowler*

Federal Reserve Bank		CU	Ch. CU	Federal Reserve Bank		CU	Ch. CU
A	BOSTON	15.00	17.00	G	CHICAGO	15.00	17.00
A★	BOSTON	17.00	20.00	G★	CHICAGO	17.00	20.00
B	NEW YORK	15.00	17.00	H	ST. LOUIS	15.00	17.00
B★	NEW YORK	17.00	20.00	H★	ST. LOUIS	17.00	20.00
C	PHILADELPHIA	15.00	17.00	I	MINNEAPOLIS	15.00	17.00
C★	PHILADELPHIA	17.00	20.00	I★	MINNEAPOLIS	17.00	20.00
D	CLEVELAND	15.00	17.00	J	KANSAS CITY	15.00	17.00
D★	CLEVELAND	17.00	20.00	J★	KANSAS CITY	17.00	20.00
E	RICHMOND	15.00	17.00	K	DALLAS	15.00	17.00
E★	RICHMOND	17.00	20.00	K★	DALLAS	17.00	20.00
F	ATLANTA	15.00	17.00	L	SAN FRANCISCO	15.00	17.00
F★	ATLANTA	17.00	20.00	L★	SAN FRANCISCO	17.00	20.00

$5 SERIES 1969 — Signatures: *Elston-Kennedy*

Federal Reserve Bank		CU	Ch. CU	Federal Reserve Bank		CU	Ch. CU
A	BOSTON	7.00	10.00	G	CHICAGO	7.00	10.00
A★	BOSTON	10.00	15.00	G★	CHICAGO	10.00	15.00
B	NEW YORK	7.00	10.00	H	ST. LOUIS	7.00	10.00
B★	NEW YORK	10.00	15.00	H★	ST. LOUIS	10.00	15.00
C	PHILADELPHIA	7.00	10.00	I	MINNEAPOLIS	7.00	10.00
C★	PHILADELPHIA	10.00	15.00	I★	MINNEAPOLIS	10.00	15.00
D	CLEVELAND	7.00	10.00	J	KANSAS CITY	7.00	10.00
D★	CLEVELAND	10.00	15.00	J★	KANSAS CITY	10.00	15.00
E	RICHMOND	7.00	10.00	K	DALLAS	7.00	10.00
E★	RICHMOND	10.00	15.00	K★	DALLAS	10.00	15.00
F	ATLANTA	7.00	10.00	L	SAN FRANCISCO	7.00	10.00
F★	ATLANTA	10.00	15.00	L★	SAN FRANCISCO	10.00	15.00

FEDERAL RESERVE NOTES
FIVE DOLLARS

$5 SERIES 1969-A — Signatures: *Kabis-Connally*

Federal Reserve Bank	CU	Ch. CU	Federal Reserve Bank	CU	Ch. CU
A BOSTON	7.00	10.00	G CHICAGO	7.00	10.00
A★ BOSTON	10.00	15.00	G★ CHICAGO	10.00	15.00
B NEW YORK	7.00	10.00	H ST. LOUIS	7.00	10.00
B★ NEW YORK	10.00	15.00	H★ ST. LOUIS	10.00	15.00
C PHILADELPHIA	7.00	10.00	I MINNEAPOLIS	7.00	10.00
C★ PHILADELPHIA	10.00	15.00	I★ MINNEAPOLIS	10.00	15.00
D CLEVELAND	7.00	10.00	J KANSAS CITY	7.00	10.00
D★ CLEVELAND	10.00	15.00	J★ KANSAS CITY	10.00	15.00
E RICHMOND	7.00	10.00	K DALLAS	7.00	10.00
E★ RICHMOND	10.00	15.00	K★ DALLAS	10.00	15.00
F ATLANTA	7.00	10.00	L SAN FRANCISCO	7.00	10.00
F★ ATLANTA	10.00	15.00	L★ SAN FRANCISCO	10.00	15.00

$5 SERIES 1969-B — Signatures: *Bañuelos-Connally*

Federal Reserve Bank	CU	Ch. CU	Federal Reserve Bank	CU	Ch. CU
A BOSTON	7.00	9.00	G CHICAGO	7.00	9.00
A★ BOSTON	not printed		G★ CHICAGO	15.00	20.00
B NEW YORK	7.00	9.00	H ST. LOUIS	7.00	9.00
B★ NEW YORK	15.00	20.00	H★ ST. LOUIS	not printed	
C PHILADELPHIA	7.00	9.00	I MINNEAPOLIS	7.00	9.00
C★ PHILADELPHIA	not printed		I★ MINNEAPOLIS	not printed	
D CLEVELAND	7.00	9.00	J KANSAS CITY	7.00	9.00
D★ CLEVELAND	not printed		J★ KANSAS CITY	15.00	20.00
E RICHMOND	7.00	9.00	K DALLAS	7.00	9.00
E★ RICHMOND	15.00	20.00	K★ DALLAS	not printed	
F ATLANTA	7.00	9.00	L SAN FRANCISCO	7.00	9.00
F★ ATLANTA	15.00	20.00	L★ SAN FRANCISCO	15.00	20.00

$5 SERIES 1969-C — Signatures: *Bañuelos-Shultz*

Federal Reserve Bank	CU	Ch. CU	Federal Reserve Bank	CU	Ch. CU
A BOSTON	7.00	9.00	G CHICAGO	7.00	9.00
A★ BOSTON	10.00	15.00	G★ CHICAGO	not printed	
B NEW YORK	7.00	9.00	H ST. LOUIS	7.00	9.00
B★ NEW YORK	10.00	15.00	H★ ST. LOUIS	10.00	15.00
C PHILADELPHIA	7.00	9.00	I MINNEAPOLIS	7.00	9.00
C★ PHILADELPHIA	10.00	15.00	I★ MINNEAPOLIS	not printed	
D CLEVELAND	7.00	9.00	J KANSAS CITY	7.00	9.00
D★ CLEVELAND	10.00	15.00	J★ KANSAS CITY	10.00	15.00
E RICHMOND	7.00	9.00	K DALLAS	7.00	9.00
E★ RICHMOND	10.00	15.00	K★ DALLAS	10.00	15.00
F ATLANTA	7.00	9.00	L SAN FRANCISCO	7.00	9.00
F★ ATLANTA	10.00	15.00	L★ SAN FRANCISCO	10.00	15.00

FEDERAL RESERVE NOTES
FIVE DOLLARS

$5 SERIES 1974 — Signatures: *Neff-Simon*

Federal Reserve Bank	CU	Ch. CU	Federal Reserve Bank	CU	Ch. CU
A BOSTON	7.00	9.00	G CHICAGO	7.00	9.00
A★ BOSTON	10.00	15.00	G★ CHICAGO	10.00	15.00
B NEW YORK	7.00	9.00	H ST. LOUIS	7.00	9.00
B★ NEW YORK	10.00	15.00	H★ ST. LOUIS	10.00	15.00
C PHILADELPHIA	7.00	9.00	I MINNEAPOLIS	7.00	9.00
C★ PHILADELPHIA	10.00	15.00	I★ MINNEAPOLIS	10.00	15.00
D CLEVELAND	7.00	9.00	J KANSAS CITY	7.00	9.00
D★ CLEVELAND	10.00	15.00	J★ KANSAS CITY	10.00	15.00
E RICHMOND	7.00	9.00	K DALLAS	7.00	9.00
E★ RICHMOND	10.00	15.00	K★ DALLAS	10.00	15.00
F ATLANTA	7.00	9.00	L SAN FRANCISCO	7.00	9.00
F★ ATLANTA	10.00	15.00	L★ SAN FRANCISCO	10.00	15.00

$5 SERIES 1977 — Signatures: *Morton-Blumenthal*

Federal Reserve Bank	CU	Ch. CU	Federal Reserve Bank	CU	Ch. CU
A BOSTON	6.00	8.00	G CHICAGO	6.00	8.00
A★ BOSTON	10.00	15.00	G★ CHICAGO	10.00	15.00
B NEW YORK	6.00	8.00	H ST. LOUIS	6.00	8.00
B★ NEW YORK	10.00	15.00	H★ ST. LOUIS	20.00	30.00
C PHILADELPHIA	6.00	8.00	I MINNEAPOLIS	6.00	8.00
C★ PHILADELPHIA	10.00	15.00	I★ MINNEAPOLIS	not printed	
D CLEVELAND	6.00	8.00	J KANSAS CITY	6.00	8.00
D★ CLEVELAND	10.00	15.00	J★ KANSAS CITY	10.00	15.00
E RICHMOND	6.00	8.00	K DALLAS	6.00	8.00
E★ RICHMOND	10.00	15.00	K★ DALLAS	10.00	15.00
F ATLANTA	6.00	8.00	L SAN FRANCISCO	6.00	8.00
F★ ATLANTA	10.00	15.00	L★ SAN FRANCISCO	10.00	15.00

$5 SERIES 1977-A — Signatures: *Morton-Miller*

Federal Reserve Bank	CU	Ch. CU	Federal Reserve Bank	CU	Ch. CU
A BOSTON	6.00	8.00	G CHICAGO	6.00	8.00
A★ BOSTON	8.00	12.00	G★ CHICAGO	8.00	12.00
B NEW YORK	6.00	8.00	H ST. LOUIS	6.00	8.00
B★ NEW YORK	8.00	12.00	H★ ST. LOUIS	8.00	12.00
C PHILADELPHIA	6.00	8.00	I MINNEAPOLIS	6.00	8.00
C★ PHILADELPHIA	8.00	12.00	I★ MINNEAPOLIS	8.00	12.00
D CLEVELAND	6.00	8.00	J KANSAS CITY	6.00	8.00
D★ CLEVELAND	8.00	12.00	J★ KANSAS CITY	8.00	12.00
E RICHMOND	6.00	8.00	K DALLAS	6.00	8.00
E★ RICHMOND	8.00	12.00	K★ DALLAS	8.00	12.00
F ATLANTA	6.00	8.00	L SAN FRANCISCO	6.00	8.00
F★ ATLANTA	8.00	12.00	L★ SAN FRANCISCO	8.00	12.00

FEDERAL RESERVE NOTES
FIVE DOLLARS

$5 SERIES 1981 — Signatures: *Buchanan-Regan*

Federal Reserve Bank	CU	Ch. CU	Federal Reserve Bank	CU	Ch. CU
A BOSTON	5.00	6.00	G CHICAGO	5.00	6.00
A★ BOSTON	—	—	G★ CHICAGO	7.00	10.00
B NEW YORK	5.00	6.00	H ST. LOUIS	5.00	6.00
B★ NEW YORK	7.00	10.00	H★ ST. LOUIS	10.00	15.00
C PHILADELPHIA	5.00	6.00	I MINNEAPOLIS	5.00	6.00
C★ PHILADELPHIA	7.00	10.00	I★ MINNEAPOLIS	10.00	18.00
D CLEVELAND	5.00	6.00	J KANSAS CITY	5.00	6.00
D★ CLEVELAND	10.00	15.00	J★ KANSAS CITY	10.00	20.00
E RICHMOND	5.00	6.00	K DALLAS	5.00	6.00
E★ RICHMOND	7.00	10.00	K★ DALLAS	10.00	20.00
F ATLANTA	5.00	6.00	L SAN FRANCISCO	5.00	6.00
F★ ATLANTA	7.00	10.00	L★ SAN FRANCISCO	10.00	20.00

$5 SERIES 1981-A — Signatures: *Ortega-Regan*

Federal Reserve Bank	CU	Ch. CU	Federal Reserve Bank	CU	Ch. CU
A BOSTON	5.00	6.00	G CHICAGO	5.00	6.00
A★ BOSTON	not printed		G★ CHICAGO	not printed	
B NEW YORK	5.00	6.00	H ST. LOUIS	5.00	6.00
B★ NEW YORK	10.00	20.00	H★ ST. LOUIS	not printed	
C PHILADELPHIA	5.00	6.00	I MINNEAPOLIS	5.00	6.00
C★ PHILADELPHIA	not printed		I★ MINNEAPOLIS	not printed	
D CLEVELAND	5.00	6.00	J KANSAS CITY	5.00	6.00
D★ CLEVELAND	not printed		J★ KANSAS CITY	not printed	
E RICHMOND	5.00	6.00	K DALLAS	5.00	6.00
E★ RICHMOND	not printed		K★ DALLAS	not printed	
F ATLANTA	5.00	6.00	L SAN FRANCISCO	5.00	6.00
F★ ATLANTA	not printed		L★ SAN FRANCISCO	10.00	20.00

$5 SERIES 1985— Signatures: *Ortega-Baker*

Federal Reserve Bank	CU	Ch. CU	Federal Reserve Bank	CU	Ch. CU
A BOSTON	5.00	6.00	F★ ATLANTA	6.00	10.00
B NEW YORK	5.00	6.00	G CHICAGO	5.00	6.00
B★ NEW YORK	6.00	10.00	G★ CHICAGO	6.00	12.00
C PHILADELPHIA	5.00	6.00	H ST. LOUIS	5.00	6.00
C★ PHILADELPHIA	6.00	10.00	I MINNEAPOLIS	5.00	6.00
D CLEVELAND	5.00	6.00	J KANSAS CITY	5.00	6.00
E RICHMOND	5.00	6.00	K DALLAS	5.00	6.00
E★ RICHMOND	6.00	10.00	K★ DALLAS	6.00	10.00
F ATLANTA	5.00	6.00	L SAN FRANCISCO	5.00	6.00
			L★ SAN FRANCISCO	6.00	12.00

FEDERAL RESERVE NOTES
FIVE DOLLARS

$5 SERIES 1988 — Signatures: *Ortega-Brady*

Issues from all 12 Federal Reserve Districts have nominal values and are commonly available in high grade condition. Star replacement notes have a 25% premium.

$5 SERIES 1988-A — Signatures: *Villalpando-Brady*

Issues from all 12 Federal Reserve Districts have nominal values and are commonly available in high grade condition. Star replacement notes have a 25% premium.

$5 SERIES 1988-A — Signatures: *Villalpando-Brady*

Sheet-fed, Fort Worth facility. Face check letter/number is preceded by small letters FW.

Issues from most Federal Reserve Districts have nominal values and are commonly available in high grade condition. Star replacement notes have a 25% premium.

$5 SERIES 1993 — Signatures: *Withrow-Bentsen*

Added Security Devices. Sheet-fed, Washington facility. With normal face check letter/number.

Issues from Boston, New York, Philadelphia, Richmond, and Atlanta have nominal values and are commonly available in high grade condition. Star replacement notes have a 25% premium.

$5 SERIES 1993 — Signatures: *Withrow-Bentsen*

Added Security Devices. Sheet-fed, Forth Worth facility. Face check letter/number is preceded by small letters FW. Issues from most Federal Reserve Districts have nominal values and are commonly available in high grade condition. Star replacement notes have a 25% premium.

$5 SERIES 1995 — Signatures: *Withrow-Rubin*

Added Security Devices. Sheet-fed at both Washington and Fort Worth facilities. Issues from all Federal Reserve Districts have nominal values and are commonly available in high grade condition. Star replacement notes have a 25% premium.

$5 SERIES 1999 — Signatures: *Withrow-Summers*

Added Security devices. Sheet-fed at both Washington and Fort Worth facilities. Issues from all Federal Reserve Districts have nominal values and are commonly available in high grade condition. Star replacement notes have a 25% premium.

$5 SERIES 2001 — Signatures: *Withrow-O'Neil*

Added Security Devices. Sheet-fed at both Washington and Fort Worth facilities. Issues from all Federal Reserve Districts have nominal values and are commonly available in high grade condition. Star replacement notes have a 25% premium.

$5 SERIES 2003 — Signatures: *Marin-Snow*

Added Security Devices. Sheet-fed at both Washington and Forth Worth facilities. Issues from all Federal Reserve Districts have nominal values and are commonly available in high grade condition. Star replacement notes have a 25% premium.

FEDERAL RESERVE NOTES
TEN DOLLARS

Face Design 1928 and 1928 A. Back Design on page 240.

$10 SERIES 1928 — Signatures: *Tate-Mellon*

Large District numeral of Bank at left.

District	Federal Reserve Bank	VF	Ex. Fine	CU	Ch. CU
1	BOSTON	35.00	75.00	160.00	250.00
2	NEW YORK	35.00	75.00	160.00	250.00
3	PHILADELPHIA	35.00	75.00	160.00	250.00
4	CLEVELAND	35.00	75.00	160.00	250.00
5	RICHMOND	35.00	75.00	160.00	250.00
6	ATLANTA	35.00	75.00	160.00	250.00
7	CHICAGO	35.00	75.00	160.00	250.00
8	ST. LOUIS	35.00	75.00	160.00	250.00
9	MINNEAPOLIS	50.00	100.00	300.00	450.00
10	KANSAS CITY	35.00	75.00	160.00	250.00
11	DALLAS	50.00	100.00	300.00	450.00
12	SAN FRANCISCO	35.00	75.00	160.00	250.00

$10 SERIES 1928-A — Signatures: *Woods-Mellon*

Large District numeral at left, similar to Series of 1928 issues.

District	Federal Reserve Bank	VF	Ex. Fine	CU	Ch. CU
1	BOSTON	42.00	100.00	225.00	300.00
2	NEW YORK	40.00	90.00	200.00	275.00
3	PHILADELPHIA	40.00	90.00	200.00	275.00
4	CLEVELAND	40.00	90.00	200.00	275.00
5	RICHMOND	75.00	200.00	600.00	900.00
6	ATLANTA	40.00	90.00	200.00	275.00
7	CHICAGO	40.00	90.00	200.00	275.00
8	ST. LOUIS	40.00	90.00	200.00	275.00
9	MINNEAPOLIS	125.00	300.00	700.00	1,500
10	KANSAS CITY	40.00	90.00	200.00	275.00
11	DALLAS	40.00	90.00	200.00	275.00
12	SAN FRANCISCO	40.00	90.00	200.00	275.00

FEDERAL RESERVE NOTES
TEN DOLLARS

General Face Design 1928 B and 1928 C. Face Design 1934-1934 D.
Back Design on page 240.

$10 SERIES 1928-B — Signatures: *Woods-Mellon*

Large District letter replaces numeral in seal on this and succeeding issues

District	Federal Reserve Bank	VF	Ex. Fine	CU	Ch. CU
A	BOSTON	16.00	25.00	75.00	100.00
B	NEW YORK	16.00	25.00	75.00	100.00
C	PHILADELPHIA	16.00	25.00	75.00	100.00
D	CLEVELAND	16.00	25.00	75.00	100.00
E	RICHMOND	16.00	25.00	75.00	100.00
F	ATLANTA	16.00	25.00	75.00	100.00
G	CHICAGO	16.00	25.00	75.00	100.00
H	ST. LOUIS	16.00	25.00	75.00	100.00
I	MINNEAPOLIS	16.00	25.00	90.00	110.00
J	KANSAS CITY	16.00	25.00	75.00	100.00
K	DALLAS	16.00	25.00	75.00	100.00
L	SAN FRANCISCO	16.00	25.00	85.00	110.00

$10 SERIES 1928-C — Signatures: *Woods-Mills*

District	Federal Reserve Bank	VF	Ex. Fine	CU	Ch. CU
B	NEW YORK	35.00	60.00	300.00	450.00
D	CLEVELAND	300.00	650.00	1,500	3,000
E	RICHMOND	1,800	2,500	4,000	6,000
F	ATLANTA	—	—	—	—
G	CHICAGO	35.00	60.00	300.00	450.00

$10 SERIES 1934 — Signatures: *Julian-Morgenthau*

District	Federal Reserve Bank	VF	Ex. Fine	CU	Ch. CU
A	BOSTON	—	19.00	40.00	60.00
B	NEW YORK	—	19.00	40.00	60.00
C	PHILADELPHIA	—	19.00	40.00	60.00
D	CLEVELAND	—	19.00	40.00	60.00
E	RICHMOND	—	19.00	40.00	60.00
F	ATLANTA	—	19.00	40.00	60.00

FEDERAL RESERVE NOTES
TEN DOLLARS
$10 SERIES 1934 — Signatures: *Julian-Morgenthau*

District	Federal Reserve Bank	Ex. Fine	CU	Ch. CU
G	CHICAGO	19.00	40.00	60.00
H	ST. LOUIS	19.00	40.00	60.00
I	MINNEAPOLIS	19.00	40.00	60.00
J	KANSAS CITY	19.00	40.00	60.00
K	DALLAS	19.00	40.00	60.00
L	SAN FRANCISCO	19.00	40.00	60.00

Values are for both the light and dark seals.

$10 SERIES 1934-A — Signatures: *Julian-Morgenthau*

Federal Reserve Bank	CU	Ch. CU		Federal Reserve Bank	CU	Ch. CU
A BOSTON	30.00	40.00	G	CHICAGO	30.00	40.00
B NEW YORK	30.00	50.00	H	ST. LOUIS	30.00	50.00
C PHILADELPHIA	30.00	40.00	I	MINNEAPOLIS	30.00	50.00
D CLEVELAND	30.00	40.00	J	KANSAS CITY	30.00	40.00
E RICHMOND	30.00	40.00	K	DALLAS	30.00	40.00
F ATLANTA	30.00	40.00	L	SAN FRANCISCO	30.00	40.00

$10 SERIES 1934-B — Signatures: *Julian-Vinson*

Federal Reserve Bank	CU	Ch. CU		Federal Reserve Bank	CU	Ch. CU
A BOSTON	40.00	50.00	G	CHICAGO	40.00	50.00
B NEW YORK	40.00	50.00	H	ST. LOUIS	40.00	50.00
C PHILADELPHIA	40.00	50.00	I	MINNEAPOLIS	40.00	50.00
D CLEVELAND	40.00	50.00	J	KANSAS CITY	40.00	50.00
E RICHMOND	40.00	50.00	K	DALLAS	40.00	50.00
F ATLANTA	40.00	50.00	L	SAN FRANCISCO	40.00	50.00

$10 SERIES 1934-C — Signatures: *Julian-Snyder*

Federal Reserve Bank	CU	Ch. CU		Federal Reserve Bank	CU	Ch. CU
A BOSTON	30.00	40.00	G	CHICAGO	30.00	40.00
B NEW YORK	30.00	40.00	H	ST. LOUIS	30.00	40.00
C PHILADELPHIA	30.00	40.00	I	MINNEAPOLIS	30.00	50.00
D CLEVELAND	35.00	50.00	J	KANSAS CITY	30.00	40.00
E RICHMOND	30.00	40.00	K	DALLAS	30.00	40.00
F ATLANTA	30.00	40.00	L	SAN FRANCISCO	30.00	40.00

$10 SERIES 1934-D — Signatures: *Clark-Snyder*

Federal Reserve Bank	CU	Ch. CU		Federal Reserve Bank	CU	Ch. CU
A BOSTON	45.00	60.00	G	CHICAGO	45.00	60.00
B NEW YORK	45.00	60.00	H	ST. LOUIS	45.00	60.00
C PHILADELPHIA	45.00	60.00	I	MINNEAPOLIS	45.00	60.00
D CLEVELAND	45.00	60.00	J	KANSAS CITY	45.00	60.00
E RICHMOND	45.00	60.00	K	DALLAS	45.00	60.00
F ATLANTA	45.00	60.00	L	SAN FRANCISCO	45.00	60..00

FEDERAL RESERVE NOTES
TEN DOLLARS

Face Design 1950-1950 E. Back Design on page 240.

$10 SERIES 1950 — Signatures: *Clark-Snyder*

Federal Reserve Bank		CU	Ch. CU	Federal Reserve Bank		CU	Ch. CU
A	BOSTON	40.00	75.00	G	CHICAGO	40.00	75.00
A★	BOSTON	300.00	500.00	G★	CHICAGO	300.00	500.00
B	NEW YORK	40.00	75.00	H	ST. LOUIS	40.00	75.00
B★	NEW YORK	300.00	500.00	H★	ST. LOUIS	300.00	500.00
C	PHILADELPHIA	40.00	75.00	I	MINNEAPOLIS	40.00	75.00
C★	PHILADELPHIA	300.00	500.00	I★	MINNEAPOLIS	300.00	600.00
D	CLEVELAND	40.00	75.00	J	KANSAS CITY	40.00	75.00
D★	CLEVELAND	300.00	500.00	J★	KANSAS CITY	300.00	500.00
E	RICHMOND	40.00	75.00	K	DALLAS	40.00	75.00
E★	RICHMOND	300.00	500.00	K★	DALLAS	300.00	500.00
F	ATLANTA	40.00	75.00	L	SAN FRANCISCO	40.00	75.00
F★	ATLANTA	300.00	500.00	L★	SAN FRANCISCO	300.00	500.00

$10 SERIES 1950-A — Signatures: *Priest-Humphrey*

Federal Reserve Bank		CU	Ch. CU	Federal Reserve Bank		CU	Ch. CU
A	BOSTON	40.00	75.00	G	CHICAGO	40.00	75.00
A★	BOSTON	150.00	300.00	G★	CHICAGO	150.00	300.00
B	NEW YORK	40.00	75.00	H	ST. LOUIS	40.00	75.00
B★	NEW YORK	150.00	300.00	H★	ST. LOUIS	150.00	300.00
C	PHILADELPHIA	40.00	75.00	I	MINNEAPOLIS	40.00	75.00
C★	PHILADELPHIA	150.00	300.00	I★	MINNEAPOLIS	170.00	400.00
D	CLEVELAND	40.00	75.00	J	KANSAS CITY	40.00	75.00
D★	CLEVELAND	150.00	300.00	J★	KANSAS CITY	150.00	300.00
E	RICHMOND	40.00	75.00	K	DALLAS	40.00	75.00
E★	RICHMOND	150.00	300.00	K★	DALLAS	150.00	300.00
F	ATLANTA	40.00	75.00	L	SAN FRANCISCO	40.00	75.00
F★	ATLANTA	150.00	300.00	L★	SAN FRANCISCO	150.00	300.00

$10 SERIES 1950-B — Signatures: *Priest-Anderson*

Federal Reserve Bank		CU	Ch. CU	Federal Reserve Bank		CU	Ch. CU
A	BOSTON	40.00	75.00	C	PHILADELPHIA	40.00	75.00
A★	BOSTON	100.00	150.00	C★	PHILADELPHIA	100.00	150.00
B	NEW YORK	40.00	75.00	D	CLEVELAND	40.00	75.00
B★	NEW YORK	100.000	150.00	D★	CLEVELAND	100.00	150.00

FEDERAL RESERVE NOTES
TEN DOLLARS
$10 SERIES 1950-B — Signatures: *Priest-Anderson*

E	RICHMOND	40.00	75.00	I	MINNEAPOLIS	40.00	75.00
E★	RICHMOND	100.00	150.00	I★	MINNEAPOLIS	150.00	200.00
F	ATLANTA	40.00	75.00	J	KANSAS CITY	40.00	75.00
F★	ATLANTA	100.00	150.00	J★	KANSAS CITY	100.00	150.00
G	CHICAGO	40.00	75.00	K	DALLAS	40.00	75.00
G★	CHICAGO	100.00	150.00	K★	DALLAS	150.00	200.00
H	ST. LOUIS	40.00	75.00	L	SAN FRANCISCO	40.00	75.00
H★	ST. LOUIS	100.00	150.00	L★	SAN FRANCISCO	100.00	150.00

$10 SERIES 1950-C — Signatures: *Smith-Dillon*

Federal Reserve Bank		CU	Ch. CU	Federal Reserve Bank		CU	Ch. CU
A	BOSTON	40.00	75.00	G	CHICAGO	40.00	75.00
A★	BOSTON	100.00	150.00	G★	CHICAGO	100.00	150.00
B	NEW YORK	40.00	75.00	H	ST. LOUIS	40.00	75.00
B★	NEW YORK	100.00	150.00	H★	ST. LOUIS	100.00	150.00
C	PHILADELPHIA	40.00	75.00	I	MINNEAPOLIS	40.00	75.00
C★	PHILADELPHIA	100.00	150.00	I★	MINNEAPOLIS	100.00	150.00
D	CLEVELAND	40.00	75.00	J	KANSAS CITY	40.00	75.00
D★	CLEVELAND	100.00	150.00	J★	KANSAS CITY	100.00	150.00
E	RICHMOND	40.00	75.00	K	DALLAS	40.00	75.00
E★	RICHMOND	100.00	150.00	K★	DALLAS	100.00	150.00
F	ATLANTA	40.00	75.00	L	SAN FRANCISCO	40.00	75.00
F★	ATLANTA	100.00	150.00	L★	SAN FRANCISCO	100.00	150.00

$10 SERIES 1950-D — Signatures: *Granahan-Dillon*

Federal Reserve Bank		CU	Ch. CU	Federal Reserve Bank		CU	Ch. CU
A	BOSTON	40.00	75.00	G	CHICAGO	40.00	75.00
A★	BOSTON	100.00	150.00	G★	CHICAGO	100.00	150.00
B	NEW YORK	40.00	75.00	H	ST. LOUIS	40.00	75.00
B★	NEW YORK	100.00	150.00	H★	ST. LOUIS	100.00	150.00
C	PHILADELPHIA	40.00	75.00	I	MINNEAPOLIS	not printed	
C★	PHILADELPHIA	100.00	150.00	I★	MINNEAPOLIS	not printed	
D	CLEVELAND	40.00	75.00	J	KANSAS CITY	40.00	75.00
D★	CLEVELAND	100.00	150.00	J★	KANSAS CITY	100.00	150.00
E	RICHMOND	40.00	75.00	K	DALLAS	40.00	75.00
E★	RICHMOND	100.00	150.00	K★	DALLAS	100.00	150.00
F	ATLANTA	40.00	75.00	L	SAN FRANCISCO	40.00	75.00
F★	ATLANTA	100.00	150.00	L★	SAN FRANCISCO	100.00	150.00

$10 SERIES 1950-E — Signatures: *Granahan-Fowler*

Federal Reserve Bank		CU	Ch. CU	Federal Reserve Bank		CU	Ch. CU
A	BOSTON	not printed		G	CHICAGO	75.00	150.00
A★	BOSTON	not printed		G★	CHICAGO	200.00	300.00
B	NEW YORK	75.00	150.00	H	ST. LOUIS	not printed	
B★	NEW YORK	200.00	300.00	H★	ST. LOUIS	not printed	
C	PHILADELPHIA	not printed		I	MINNEAPOLIS	not printed	
C★	PHILADELPHIA	not printed		I★	MINNEAPOLIS	not printed	
D	CLEVELAND	not printed		J	KANSAS CITY	not printed	
D★	CLEVELAND	not printed		J★	KANSAS CITY	not printed	
E	RICHMOND	not printed		K	DALLAS	not printed	
E★	RICHMOND	not printed		K★	DALLAS	not printed	
F	ATLANTA	not printed		L	SAN FRANCISCO	100.00	200.00
F★	ATLANTA	not printed		L★	SAN FRANCISCO	250.00	400.00

Notes of the 1950-E series do not have the motto on the back. These were released *after* the 1963 series.

FEDERAL RESERVE NOTES
TEN DOLLARS

Face Design 1963 through the 1995

Back Design 1963 through the 1995

$10 SERIES 1963 — Signatures: *Granahan-Dillon*

Federal Reserve Bank		CU	Ch. CU	Federal Reserve Bank		CU	Ch. CU
A	BOSTON	30.00	40.00	G	CHICAGO	30.00	40.00
A★	BOSTON	60.00	75.00	G★	CHICAGO	60.00	75.00
B	NEW YORK	30.00	40.00	H	ST. LOUIS	30.00	40.00
B★	NEW YORK	60.00	75.00	H★	ST. LOUIS	60.00	75.00
C	PHILADELPHIA	30.00	40.00	I	MINNEAPOLIS	not printed	
C★	PHILADELPHIA	60.00	75.00	I★	MINNEAPOLIS	not printed	
D	CLEVELAND	30.00	40.00	J	KANSAS CITY	30.00	40.00
D★	CLEVELAND	60.00	75.00	J★	KANSAS CITY	60.00	75.00
E	RICHMOND	30.00	40.00	K	DALLAS	30.00	40.00
E★	RICHMOND	60.00	75.00	K★	DALLAS	60.00	75.00
F	ATLANTA	30.00	40.00	L	SAN FRANCISCO	30.00	40.00
F★	ATLANTA	60.00	75.00	L★	SAN FRANCISCO	60.00	75.00

FEDERAL RESERVE NOTES
TEN DOLLARS
$10 SERIES 1963-A — Signatures: *Granahan-Fowler*

Federal Reserve Bank		CU	Ch. CU	Federal Reserve Bank		CU	Ch. CU
A	BOSTON	30.00	40.00	G	CHICAGO	30.00	40.00
A★	BOSTON	60.00	75.00	G★	CHICAGO	60.00	75.00
B	NEW YORK	30.00	40.00	H	ST. LOUIS	30.00	40.00
B★	NEW YORK	60.00	75.00	H★	ST. LOUIS	60.00	75.00
C	PHILADELPHIA	30.00	40.00	I	MINNEAPOLIS	30.00	40.00
C★	PHILADELPHIA	60.00	75.00	I★	MINNEAPOLIS	60.00	90.00
D	CLEVELAND	30.00	40.00	J	KANSAS CITY	30.00	40.00
D★	CLEVELAND	60.00	75.00	J★	KANSAS CITY	60.00	75.00
E	RICHMOND	30.00	40.00	K	DALLAS	30.00	40.00
E★	RICHMOND	60.00	75.00	K★	DALLAS	60.00	90.00
F	ATLANTA	30.00	40.00	L	SAN FRANCISCO	30.00	40.00
F★	ATLANTA	60.00	75.00	L★	SAN FRANCISCO	60.00	75.00

$10 SERIES 1969 — Signatures: *Elston-Kennedy*

Federal Reserve Bank		CU	Ch. CU	Federal Reserve Bank		CU	Ch. CU
A	BOSTON	25.00	35.00	G	CHICAGO	25.00	35.00
A★	BOSTON	50.00	60.00	G★	CHICAGO	50.00	60.00
B	NEW YORK	25.00	35.00	H	ST. LOUIS	25.00	35.00
B★	NEW YORK	50.00	60.00	H★	ST. LOUIS	50.00	60.00
C	PHILADELPHIA	25.00	35.00	I	MINNEAPOLIS	25.00	35.00
C★	PHILADELPHIA	50.00	60.00	I★	MINNEAPOLIS	50.00	60.00
D	CLEVELAND	25.00	35.00	J	KANSAS CITY	25.00	35.00
D★	CLEVELAND	50.00	60.00	J★	KANSAS CITY	50.00	60.00
E	RICHMOND	25.00	35.00	K	DALLAS	25.00	35.00
E★	RICHMOND	50.00	60.00	K★	DALLAS	50.00	60.00
F	ATLANTA	25.00	35.00	L	SAN FRANCISCO	25.00	35.00
F★	ATLANTA	50.00	60.00	L★	SAN FRANCISCO	50.00	60.00

$10 SERIES 1969-A — Signatures: *Kabis-Connally*

Federal Reserve Bank		CU	Ch. CU	Federal Reserve Bank		CU	Ch. CU
A	BOSTON	25.00	35.00	G	CHICAGO	25.00	35.00
A★	BOSTON	50.00	60.00	G★	CHICAGO	50.00	60.00
B	NEW YORK	25.00	35.00	H	ST. LOUIS	25.00	35.00
B★	NEW YORK	50.00	60.00	H★	ST. LOUIS	55.00	65.00
C	PHILADELPHIA	25.00	35.00	I	MINNEAPOLIS	25.00	35.00
C★	PHILADELPHIA	50.00	60.00	I★	MINNEAPOLIS	not printed	
D	CLEVELAND	25.00	35.00	J	KANSAS CITY	25.00	35.00
D★	CLEVELAND	50.00	60.00	J★	KANSAS CITY	not printed	
E	RICHMOND	25.00	35.00	K	DALLAS	25.00	35.00
E★	RICHMOND	55.00	65.00	K★	DALLAS	55.00	65.00
F	ATLANTA	25.00	35.00	L	SAN FRANCISCO	25.00	35.00
F★	ATLANTA	55.00	65.00	L★	SAN FRANCISCO	50.00	60.00

FEDERAL RESERVE NOTES
TEN DOLLARS
$10 SERIES 1969-B — Signatures: *Bañuelos-Connally*

Federal Reserve Bank		CU	Ch. CU	Federal Reserve Bank		CU	Ch. CU
A	BOSTON	100.00	150.00	G	CHICAGO	100.00	150.00
A★	BOSTON	not printed		G★	CHICAGO	200.00	300.00
B	NEW YORK	100.00	150.00	H	ST. LOUIS	100.00	150.00
B★	NEW YORK	200.00	300.00	H★	ST. LOUIS	200.00	300.00
C	PHILADELPHIA	100.00	150.00	I	MINNEAPOLIS	100.00	150.00
C★	PHILADELPHIA	not printed		I★	MINNEAPOLIS	not printed	
D	CLEVELAND	100.00	150.00	J	KANSAS CITY	100.00	150.00
D★	CLEVELAND	not printed		J★	KANSAS CITY	200.00	300.00
E	RICHMOND	100.00	150.00	K	DALLAS	100.00	150.00
E★	RICHMOND	200.00	300.00	K★	DALLAS	not printed	
F	ATLANTA	100.00	150.00	L	SAN FRANCISCO	100.00	150.00
F★	ATLANTA	200.00	300.00	L★	SAN FRANCISCO	200.00	300.00

$10 SERIES 1969-C — Signatures: *Bañuelos-Shultz*

Federal Reserve Bank		CU	Ch. CU	Federal Reserve Bank		CU	Ch. CU
A	BOSTON	25.00	30.00	G	CHICAGO	25.00	30.00
A★	BOSTON	30.00	35.00	G★	CHICAGO	30.00	35.00
B	NEW YORK	25.00	30.00	H	ST. LOUIS	25.00	30.00
B★	NEW YORK	30.00	35.00	H★	ST. LOUIS	30.00	35.00
C	PHILADELPHIA	25.00	30.00	I	MINNEAPOLIS	25.00	30.00
C★	PHILADELPHIA	30.00	35.00	I★	MINNEAPOLIS	30.00	35.00
D	CLEVELAND	25.00	30.00	J	KANSAS CITY	25.00	30.00
D★	CLEVELAND	30.00	35.00	J★	KANSAS CITY	30.00	35.00
E	RICHMOND	25.00	30.00	K	DALLAS	25.00	30.00
E★	RICHMOND	30.00	35.00	K★	DALLAS	30.00	35.00
F	ATLANTA	25.00	30.00	L	SAN FRANCISCO	25.00	30.00
F★	ATLANTA	30.00	35.00	L★	SAN FRANCISCO	30.00	35.00

$10 SERIES 1974 — Signatures: *Neff-Simon*

Federal Reserve Bank		CU	Ch. CU	Federal Reserve Bank		CU	Ch. CU
A	BOSTON	25.00	30.00	G	CHICAGO	25.00	30.00
A★	BOSTON	35.00	50.00	G★	CHICAGO	35.00	50.00
B	NEW YORK	25.00	30.00	H	ST. LOUIS	25.00	30.00
B★	NEW YORK	35.00	50.00	H★	ST. LOUIS	30.00	35.00
C	PHILADELPHIA	25.00	30.00	I	MINNEAPOLIS	25.00	30.00
C★	PHILADELPHIA	30.00	35.00	I★	MINNEAPOLIS	35.00	50.00
D	CLEVELAND	25.00	30.00	J	KANSAS CITY	25.00	30.00
D★	CLEVELAND	30.00	35.00	J★	KANSAS CITY	30.00	35.00
E	RICHMOND	25.00	30.00	K	DALLAS	25.00	30.00
E★	RICHMOND	30.00	35.00	K★	DALLAS	30.00	35.00
F	ATLANTA	25.00	30.00	L	SAN FRANCISCO	25.00	30.00
F★	ATLANTA	30.00	35.00	L★	SAN FRANCISCO	30.00	35.00

FEDERAL RESERVE NOTES
TEN DOLLARS
$10 SERIES 1977 — Signatures: *Morton-Blumenthal*

Federal Reserve Bank		CU	Ch. CU	Federal Reserve Bank		CU	Ch. CU
A	BOSTON	25.00	30.00	G	CHICAGO	25.00	30.00
A★	BOSTON	35.00	50.00	G★	CHICAGO	35.00	50.00
B	NEW YORK	25.00	30.00	H	ST. LOUIS	25.00	30.00
B★	NEW YORK	35.00	50.00	H★	ST. LOUIS	35.00	50.00
C	PHILADELPHIA	25.00	30.00	I	MINNEAPOLIS	25.00	30.00
C★	PHILADELPHIA	35.00	50.00	I★	MINNEAPOLIS	35.00	50.00
D	CLEVELAND	25.00	30.00	J	KANSAS CITY	25.00	30.00
D★	CLEVELAND	35.00	50.00	J★	KANSAS CITY	35.00	50.00
E	RICHMOND	25.00	30.00	K	DALLAS	25.00	30.00
E★	RICHMOND	35.00	50.00	K★	DALLAS	35.00	50.00
F	ATLANTA	25.00	30.00	L	SAN FRANCISCO	25.00	30.00
F★	ATLANTA	35.00	50.00	L★	SAN FRANCISCO	35.00	50.00

$10 SERIES 1977-A — Signatures: *Morton-Miller*

Federal Reserve Bank		CU	Ch. CU	Federal Reserve Bank		CU	Ch. CU
A	BOSTON	25.00	30.00	G	CHICAGO	25.00	30.00
A★	BOSTON	30.00	45.00	G★	CHICAGO	30.00	45.00
B	NEW YORK	25.00	30.00	H	ST. LOUIS	25.00	30.00
B★	NEW YORK	30.00	45.00	H★	ST. LOUIS	30.00	45.00
C	PHILADELPHIA	25.00	30.00	I	MINNEAPOLIS	25.00	30.00
C★	PHILADELPHIA	30.00	45.00	I★	MINNEAPOLIS	30.00	45.00
D	CLEVELAND	25.00	30.00	J	KANSAS CITY	25.00	30.00
D★	CLEVELAND	30.00	45.00	J★	KANSAS CITY	30.00	45.00
E	RICHMOND	25.00	30.00	K	DALLAS	25.00	30.00
E★	RICHMOND	30.00	45.00	K★	DALLAS	30.00	45.00
F	ATLANTA	25.00	30.00	L	SAN FRANCISCO	25.00	30.00
F★	ATLANTA	30.00	45.00	L★	SAN FRANCISCO	30.00	45.00

$10 SERIES 1981 — Signatures: *Buchanan-Regan*

Federal Reserve Bank		CU	Ch. CU	Federal Reserve Bank		CU	Ch. CU
A	BOSTON	25.00	30.00	G	CHICAGO	25.00	30.00
A★	BOSTON	30.00	40.00	G★	CHICAGO	30.00	40.00
B	NEW YORK	25.00	30.00	H	ST. LOUIS	25.00	30.00
B★	NEW YORK	30.00	40.00	H★	ST. LOUIS	not printed	
C	PHILADELPHIA	25.00	30.00	I	MINNEAPOLIS	25.00	30.00
C★	PHILADELPHIA	30.00	40.00	I★	MINNEAPOLIS	30.00	40.00
D	CLEVELAND	25.00	30.00	J	KANSAS CITY	25.00	30.00
D★	CLEVELAND	30.00	40.00	J★	KANSAS CITY	not printed	
E	RICHMOND	25.00	30.00	K	DALLAS	25.00	30.00
E★	RICHMOND	30.00	40.00	K★	DALLAS	not printed	
F	ATLANTA	25.00	30.00	L	SAN FRANCISCO	25.00	30.00
F★	ATLANTA	30.00	40.00	L★	SAN FRANCISCO	30.00	40.00

FEDERAL RESERVE NOTES
TEN DOLLARS

$10 1981-A — Signatures: *Ortega-Regan*

Federal Reserve Bank		CU	Ch. CU	Federal Reserve Bank		CU	Ch. CU
A	BOSTON	20.00	25.00	F	ATLANTA	20.00	25.00
B	NEW YORK	20.00	25.00	G	CHICAGO	20.00	25.00
B★	NEW YORK	75.00	100.00	H	ST. LOUIS	20.00	25.00
C	PHILADELPHIA	20.00	25.00	I	MINNEAPOLIS	20.00	25.00
D	CLEVELAND	20.00	25.00	J	KANSAS CITY	20.00	25.00
E	RICHMOND	20.00	25.00	K	DALLAS	20.00	25.00
E★	RICHMOND	50.00	80.00	L	SAN FRANCISCO	20.00	25.00

$10 SERIES 1985 — Signatures: *Ortega-Baker*

Federal Reserve Bank		CU	Ch. CU	Federal Reserve Bank		CU	Ch. CU
A	BOSTON	20.00	25.00	G	CHICAGO	20.00	25.00
A★	BOSTON	45.00	60.00	H	ST. LOUIS	20.00	25.00
B	NEW YORK	20.00	25.00	H★	ST. LOUIS	45.00	60.00
B★	NEW YORK	45.00	60.00	I	MINNEAPOLIS	20.00	25.00
C	PHILADELPHIA	20.00	25.00	J	KANSAS CITY	20.00	25.00
D	CLEVELAND	20.00	25.00	K	DALLAS	20.00	25.00
D★	CLEVELAND	45.00	60.00	K★	DALLAS	45.00	60.00
E	RICHMOND	20.00	25.00	L	SAN FRANCISCO	20.00	25.00
F	ATLANTA	20.00	25.00	L★	SAN FRANCISCO	45.00	60.00
F★	ATLANTA	45.00	60.00				

$10 SERIES 1988-A — Signatures: *Villalpando-Brady*

Issues from all 12 Federal Reserve Districts have nominal values and are commonly available in high grade condition. Star replacement notes have a 25% premium.

$10 SERIES 1990 — Signatures: *Villalpando-Brady*

Added Security Devices. Issues from all 12 Federal Reserve Districts have nominal values and are commonly available in high grade condition. Star replacement notes have a 25% premium.

$10 SERIES 1993 — Signatures: *Withrow-Bentsen*

Added Security Devices. Issued from most Federal Reserve Districts. All have nominal values and are commonly available in high grade condition. Star replacement notes from New York, Philadelphia and Chicago have a 25% premium.

$10 SERIES 1995 — Signatures: *Withrow-Rubin*

Added Security Devices. Sheet-fed at both Washington and Fort Worth facilities. Issues from all Federal Reserve Districts have nominal values and are commonly available in high grade condition. Star replacement notes have a 25% premium.

$10 SERIES 1999 — Signatures: *Withrow-Summers*

Added Security Devices Sheet-fed at both Washington and Fort Worth facilities. Issues from all Federal Reserve Districts have nominal values and are commonly available in high grade condition. Star replacement notes have a 25% premium.

$10 SERIES 2001 — Signatures: *Withrow-O'Neil*

Added Security Devices. Sheet-fed at both Washington and Fort Worth facilities. Issues from all Federal Reserve Districts have nominal values and are commonly available in high grade condition. Star replacement notes have a 25% premium.

$10 SERIES 2003 — Signatures: *Marin-Snow*

Added Security Devices. Sheet-fed at both Washington and Fort Worth facilities. Issues from all Federal Reserve Districts have nominal values and are commonly available in high grade condition. Star replacement notes have a 25% premium.

FEDERAL RESERVE NOTES
TWENTY DOLLARS

Face Design 1928 and 1928 A

Back Design Federal Reserve Notes 1928 through 1934 C; National Currency;
Federal Reserve Bank Notes; Gold Certificates

$20 SERIES 1928 — Signatures: *Tate-Mellon*

Large District numeral of Bank at left.

District	Federal Reserve Bank	Ex. Fine	CU	Ch. CU
1	BOSTON	65.00	150.00	200.00
2	NEW YORK	65.00	150.00	200.00
3	PHILADELPHIA	65.00	150.00	200.00
4	CLEVELAND	65.00	150.00	200.00
5	RICHMOND	70.00	165.00	225.00
6	ATLANTA	70.00	165.00	225.00
7	CHICAGO	70.00	165.00	225.00
8	ST. LOUIS	70.00	165.00	225.00
9	MINNEAPOLIS	70.00	165.00	225.00
10	KANSAS CITY	65.00	150.00	200.00
11	DALLAS	65.00	150.00	200.00
12	SAN FRANCISCO	65.00	150.00	200.00

FEDERAL RESERVE NOTES
TWENTY DOLLARS
$20 SERIES 1928-A — Signatures: *Woods-Mellon*

Large District numeral at left, similar to Series of 1928 issues.

District	Federal Reserve Bank	Ex. Fine	CU	Ch. CU
1	BOSTON	75.00	200.00	350.00
2	NEW YORK	75.00	200.00	350.00
3	PHILADELPHIA	75.00	200.00	350.00
4	CLEVELAND	80.00	225.00	360.00
5	RICHMOND	75.00	225.00	350.00
6	ATLANTA	75.00	225.00	350.00
7	CHICAGO	80.00	225.00	375.00
8	ST. LOUIS	80.00	225.00	360.00
9	MINNEAPOLIS	—	—	—
10	KANSAS CITY	200.00	400.00	650.00
11	DALLAS	80.00	225.00	360.00
12	SAN FRANCISCO	80.00	200.00	350.00

Face Design 1928 B and 1928 C. General Face Design 1934-1934 D.

$20 SERIES 1928-B — Signatures: *Woods-Mellon*

Large District letter replaces numeral in seal on this and succeeding issues.

District	Federal Reserve Bank	Ex. Fine	CU	Ch. CU
A	BOSTON	60.00	100.00	200.00
B	NEW YORK	60.00	100.00	200.00
C	PHILADELPHIA	60.00	100.00	200.00
D	CLEVELAND	60.00	100.00	200.00
E	RICHMOND	60.00	100.00	200.00
F	ATLANTA	70.00	120.00	250.00
G	CHICAGO	60.00	100.00	200.00
H	ST. LOUIS	60.00	100.00	200.00
I	MINNEAPOLIS	60.00	100.00	200.00
J	KANSAS CITY	60.00	100.00	200.00
K	DALLAS	70.00	120.00	250.00
L	SAN FRANCISCO	60.00	100.00	200.00

FEDERAL RESERVE NOTES
TWENTY DOLLARS
$20 SERIES 1928-C — Signatures: *Woods-Mills*

District	Federal Reserve Bank	VF	Ex. Fine	CU	Ch. CU
G	CHICAGO	400.00	750.00	1,500	2,500
L	SAN FRANCISCO	800.00	1,500	3,000	4,500

$20 SERIES 1934 — Signatures: *Julian-Morgenthau*

Light or dark green seal.

District	Federal Reserve Bank	Ex. Fine	CU	Ch. CU
A	BOSTON	30.00	40.00	60.00
B	NEW YORK	30.00	40.00	60.00
C	PHILADELPHIA	30.00	40.00	60.00
D	CLEVELAND	30.00	40.00	60.00
E	RICHMOND	30.00	40.00	60.00
F	ATLANTA	30.00	40.00	60.00
G	CHICAGO	30.00	40.00	60.00
H	ST. LOUIS	30.00	45.00	65.00
I	MINNEAPOLIS	30.00	45.00	65.00
J	KANSAS CITY	30.00	45.00	65.00
K	DALLAS	30.00	45.00	65.00
L	SAN FRANCISCO	30.00	45.00	65.00

$20 SERIES 1934-A — Signatures: *Julian-Morgenthau*

District	Federal Reserve Bank	Ex. Fine	CU	Ch. CU
A	BOSTON	30.00	40.00	60.00
B	NEW YORK	30.00	40.00	60.00
C	PHILADELPHIA	30.00	40.00	60.00
D	CLEVELAND	30.00	40.00	60.00
E	RICHMOND	30.00	40.00	60.00
F	ATLANTA	30.00	40.00	60.00
G	CHICAGO	30.00	40.00	60.00
H	ST. LOUIS	30.00	40.00	60.00
I	MINNEAPOLIS	30.00	40.00	60.00
J	KANSAS CITY	30.00	40.00	60.00
K	DALLAS	30.00	40.00	60.00
L	SAN FRANCISCO	30.00	40.00	60.00

FEDERAL RESERVE NOTES
TWENTY DOLLARS
$20 SERIES 1934-B — Signatures: *Julian-Vinson*

District	Federal Reserve Bank	Ex. Fine	CU	Ch. CU
A	BOSTON	30.00	40.00	60.00
B	NEW YORK	30.00	40.00	60.00
C	PHILADELPHIA	30.00	40.00	70.00
D	CLEVELAND	30.00	40.00	70.00
E	RICHMOND	30.00	40.00	60.00
F	ATLANTA	30.00	40.00	60.00
G	CHICAGO	30.00	40.00	60.00
H	ST. LOUIS	30.00	40.00	60.00
I	MINNEAPOLIS	30.00	50.00	70.00
J	KANSAS CITY	30.00	50.00	70.00
K	DALLAS	30.00	50.00	70.00
L	SAN FRANCISCO	30.00	40.00	60.00

New White House Vignette — Series 1934 C

On November 10, 1948, Treasury Secretary Snyder announced that the $20.00 note was to bear a new engraving of the White House on the back side. The "new look" was made from a photograph of the south front and grounds after the building was renovated. The design used until this time showed the south front as it appeared in 1929. The modified design was actually put to press for the first time on July 20, 1948.

Back Design 1934 C through 1950 E (see old back on page 283)

Various structural modifications can be seen when the two designs are compared. These include a balcony at the second floor level and four chimneys instead of two. Other differences are also visible. Lettering beneath the building is changed from "White House" to "The White House."

The new White House vignette was first used during the issue of notes Series of 1934 C. Both the old and new back designs can be found with this same series date. Subsequent issues through 1950 E use the new design.

FEDERAL RESERVE NOTES
TWENTY DOLLARS
$20 SERIES 1934-C — Signatures: *Julian-Snyder*

District	Federal Reserve Bank	Ex. Fine	CU	Ch. CU
A	BOSTON	25.00	50.00	75.00
B	NEW YORK	25.00	50.00	75.00
C	PHILADELPHIA	25.00	50.00	75.00
D	CLEVELAND	25.00	50.00	75.00
E	RICHMOND	25.00	50.00	75.00
F	ATLANTA	25.00	50.00	75.00
G	CHICAGO	25.00	50.00	75.00
H	ST. LOUIS	25.00	55.00	80.00
I	MINNEAPOLIS	25.00	55.00	80.00
J	KANSAS CITY	25.00	55.00	80.00
K	DALLAS	25.00	55.00	80.00
L	SAN FRANCISCO	25.00	50.00	75.00

Above listing includes both the old or new back designs. At present there is no difference in value between them.

$20 SERIES 1934-D — Signatures: *Clark-Snyder*

District	Federal Reserve Bank	Ex. Fine	CU	Ch. CU
A	BOSTON	25.00	50.00	65.00
B	NEW YORK	25.00	50.00	65.00
C	PHILADELPHIA	25.00	50.00	65.00
D	CLEVELAND	25.00	50.00	65.00
E	RICHMOND	25.00	50.00	65.00
F	ATLANTA	25.00	50.00	65.00
G	CHICAGO	25.00	50.00	65.00
H	ST. LOUIS	25.00	50.00	65.00
I	MINNEAPOLIS	25.00	50.00	65.00
J	KANSAS CITY	25.00	50.00	65.00
K	DALLAS	25.00	50.00	65.00
L	SAN FRANCISCO	25.00	50.00	65.00

Face Design 1950-1950 E. General Face Design 1963-1995

FEDERAL RESERVE NOTES
TWENTY DOLLARS
$20 SERIES 1950 — Signatures: *Clark-Snyder*

District	Federal Reserve Bank	Ex. Fine	CU	Ch. CU
A	BOSTON	25.00	60.00	80.00
B	NEW YORK	25.00	60.00	80.00
C	PHILADELPHIA	25.00	60.00	80.00
D	CLEVELAND	25.00	60.00	80.00
E	RICHMOND	25.00	60.00	80.00
F	ATLANTA	25.00	60.00	80.00
G	CHICAGO	25.00	60.00	80.00
H	ST. LOUIS	25.00	60.00	80.00
I	MINNEAPOLIS	25.00	60.00	80.00
J	KANSAS CITY	25.00	60.00	80.00
K	DALLAS	25.00	60.00	80.00
L	SAN FRANCISCO	25.00	60.00	80.00

$20 SERIES 1950-A — Signatures: *Priest-Humphrey*

District	Federal Reserve Bank	Ex. Fine	CU	Ch. CU
A	BOSTON	25.00	50.00	60.00
B	NEW YORK	25.00	50.00	60.00
C	PHILADELPHIA	25.00	50.00	60.00
D	CLEVELAND	25.00	50.00	60.00
E	RICHMOND	25.00	50.00	60.00
F	ATLANTA	25.00	50.00	60.00
G	CHICAGO	25.00	50.00	60.00
H	ST. LOUIS	25.00	50.00	60.00
I	MINNEAPOLIS	25.00	50.00	60.00
J	KANSAS CITY	25.00	50.00	60.00
K	DALLAS	25.00	50.00	60.00
L	SAN FRANCISCO	25.00	50.00	60.00

$20 SERIES 1950-B — Signatures: *Priest-Anderson*

District	Federal Reserve Bank	Ex. Fine	CU	Ch. CU
A	BOSTON	25.00	45.00	55.00
B	NEW YORK	25.00	45.00	55.00
C	PHILADELPHIA	25.00	45.00	55.00
D	CLEVELAND	25.00	45.00	55.00
E	RICHMOND	25.00	45.00	55.00
F	ATLANTA	25.00	45.00	55.00
G	CHICAGO	25.00	45.00	55.00
H	ST. LOUIS	25.00	45.00	55.00
I	MINNEAPOLIS	25.00	45.00	55.00
J	KANSAS CITY	25.00	45.00	55.00
K	DALLAS	25.00	45.00	55.00
L	SAN FRANCISCO	25.00	45.00	55.00

FEDERAL RESERVE NOTES
TWENTY DOLLARS
$20 SERIES 1950-C — Signatures: *Smith-Dillon*

District	Federal Reserve Bank	Ex. Fine	CU	Ch. CU
A	BOSTON	24.00	40.00	50.00
B	NEW YORK	24.00	40.00	50.00
C	PHILADELPHIA	24.00	40.00	50.00
D	CLEVELAND	24.00	40.00	50.00
E	RICHMOND	24.00	40.00	50.00
F	ATLANTA	24.00	40.00	50.00
G	CHICAGO	24.00	40.00	50.00
H	ST. LOUIS	24.00	40.00	50.00
I	MINNEAPOLIS	24.00	40.00	50.00
J	KANSAS CITY	24.00	· 40.00	50.00
K	DALLAS	24.00	40.00	50.00
L	SAN FRANCISCO	24.00	40.00	50.00

$20 SERIES 1950-D — Signatures: *Granahan-Dillon*

	Federal Reserve Bank	CU	Ch. CU		Federal Reserve Bank	CU	Ch. CU
A	BOSTON	35.00	40.00	G	CHICAGO	35.00	40.00
B	NEW YORK	35.00	40.00	H	ST. LOUIS	35.00	40.00
C	PHILADELPHIA	35.00	40.00	I	MINNEAPOLIS	35.00	40.00
D	CLEVELAND	35.00	40.00	J	KANSAS CITY	35.00	40.00
E	RICHMOND	35.00	40.00	L	SAN FRANCISCO	35.00	40.00

$20 SERIES 1950-E — Signatures: *Granahan-Fowler*

	Federal Reserve Bank	CU	Ch. CU		Federal Reserve Bank	CU	Ch. CU
B	NEW YORK	100.00	125.00	L	SAN FRANCISCO	100.00	125.00
G	CHICAGO	100.00	125.00				

Back Design 1963 through 1995

FEDERAL RESERVE NOTES
TWENTY DOLLARS
$20 SERIES 1963 — Signatures: *Granahan-Dillon*

Motto "In God We Trust" added.

Federal Reserve Bank		CU	Ch. CU	Federal Reserve Bank		CU	Ch. CU
A	BOSTON	30.00	50.00	G	CHICAGO	30.00	50.00
B	NEW YORK	30.00	50.00	H	ST. LOUIS	30.00	50.00
C	PHILADELPHIA	not printed		I	MINNEAPOLIS	not printed	
D	CLEVELAND	30.00	50.00	J	KANSAS CITY	30.00	50.00
E	RICHMOND	30.00	50.00	K	DALLAS	30.00	50.00
F	ATLANTA	30.00	50.00	L	SAN FRANCISCO	30.00	50.00

$20 SERIES 1963-A — Signatures: *Granahan-Fowler*

Federal Reserve Bank		CU	Ch. CU	Federal Reserve Bank		CU	Ch. CU
A	BOSTON	30.00	40.00	G	CHICAGO	30.00	40.00
A★	BOSTON	75.00	100.00	G★	CHICAGO	75.00	100.00
B	NEW YORK	30.00	40.00	H	ST. LOUIS	30.00	40.00
B★	NEW YORK	75.00	100.00	H★	ST. LOUIS	75.00	100.00
C	PHILADELPHIA	30.00	40.00	I	MINNEAPOLIS	30.00	40.00
C★	PHILADELPHIA	75.00	100.00	I★	MINNEAPOLIS	75.00	100.00
D	CLEVELAND	30.00	40.00	J	KANSAS CITY	30.00	40.00
D★	CLEVELAND	75.00	100.00	J★	KANSAS CITY	75.00	100.00
E	RICHMOND	30.00	40.00	K	DALLAS	30.00	40.00
E★	RICHMOND	75.00	100.00	K★	DALLAS	75.00	100.00
F	ATLANTA	30.00	40.00	L	SAN FRANCISCO	30.00	40.00
F★	ATLANTA	75.00	100.00	L★	SAN FRANCISCO	75.00	100.00

$20 SERIES 1969 — Signatures: *Elston-Kennedy*

Federal Reserve Bank		CU	Ch. CU	Federal Reserve Bank		CU	Ch. CU
A	BOSTON	30.00	40.00	G	CHICAGO	30.00	40.00
A★	BOSTON	50.00	75.00	G★	CHICAGO	50.00	75.00
B	NEW YORK	30.00	40.00	H	ST. LOUIS	30.00	40.00
B★	NEW YORK	50.00	75.00	H★	ST. LOUIS	50.00	75.00
C	PHILADELPHIA	30.00	40.00	I	MINNEAPOLIS	30.00	40.00
C★	PHILADELPHIA	50.00	75.00	I★	MINNEAPOLIS	50.00	75.00
D	CLEVELAND	30.00	40.00	J	KANSAS CITY	30.00	40.00
D★	CLEVELAND	50.00	75.00	J★	KANSAS CITY	50.00	75.00
E	RICHMOND	30.00	40.00	K	DALLAS	30.00	40.00
E★	RICHMOND	50.00	75.00	K★	DALLAS	50.00	75.00
F	ATLANTA	30.00	40.00	L	SAN FRANCISCO	30.00	40.00
F★	ATLANTA	50.00	75.00	L★	SAN FRANCISCO	50.00	75.00

FEDERAL RESERVE NOTES
TWENTY DOLLARS
$20 1969-A — Signatures: *Kabis-Connally*

Federal Reserve Bank		CU	Ch. CU	Federal Reserve Bank		CU	Ch. CU
A	BOSTON	25.00	35.00	G	CHICAGO	25.00	35.00
A★	BOSTON	not printed		G★	CHICAGO	50.00	75.00
B	NEW YORK	25.00	35.00	H	ST. LOUIS	25.00	35.00
B★	NEW YORK	50.00	75.00	H★	ST. LOUIS	50.00	75.00
C	PHILADELPHIA	25.00	35.00	I	MINNEAPOLIS	25.00	35.00
C★	PHILADELPHIA	not printed		I★	MINNEAPOLIS	not printed	
D	CLEVELAND	25.00	35.00	J	KANSAS CITY	25.00	35.00
D★	CLEVELAND	50.00	75.00	J★	KANSAS CITY	not printed	
E	RICHMOND	25.00	35.00	K	DALLAS	25.00	35.00
E★	RICHMOND	50.00	75.00	K★	DALLAS	50.00	75.00
F	ATLANTA	25.00	35.00	L	SAN FRANCISCO	25.00	35.00
F★	ATLANTA	not printed		L★	SAN FRANCISCO	50.00	75.00

$20 SERIES 1969-B — Signatures: *Bañuelos-Connally*

Federal Reserve Bank		CU	Ch. CU	Federal Reserve Bank		CU	Ch. CU
A	BOSTON	not printed		G	CHICAGO	100.00	200.00
A★	BOSTON	not printed		G★	CHICAGO	300.00	500.00
B	NEW YORK	100.00	200.00	H	ST. LOUIS	100.00	200.00
B★	NEW YORK	300.00	500.00	H★	ST. LOUIS	not printed	
C	PHILADELPHIA	not printed		I	MINNEAPOLIS	100.00	200.00
C★	PHILADELPHIA	not printed		I★	MINNEAPOLIS	not printed	
D	CLEVELAND	100.00	200.00	J	KANSAS CITY	100.00	200.00
D★	CLEVELAND	not printed		J★	KANSAS CITY	300.00	500.00
E	RICHMOND	100.00	200.00	K	DALLAS	100.00	200.00
E★	RICHMOND	not printed		K★	DALLAS	not printed	
F	ATLANTA	100.00	200.00	L	SAN FRANCISCO	100.00	200.00
F★	ATLANTA	300.00	500.00	L★	SAN FRANCISCO	300.00	500.00

$20 SERIES 1969-C — Signatures: *Bañuelos-Shultz*

Federal Reserve Bank		CU	Ch. CU	Federal Reserve Bank		CU	Ch. CU
A	BOSTON	25.00	35.00	G	CHICAGO	25.00	35.00
A★	BOSTON	50.00	75.00	G★	CHICAGO	50.00	75.00
B	NEW YORK	25.00	35.00	H	ST. LOUIS	25.00	35.00
B★	NEW YORK	50.00	75.00	H★	ST. LOUIS	50.00	75.00
C	PHILADELPHIA	25.00	35.00	I	MINNEAPOLIS	25.00	35.00
C★	PHILADELPHIA	50.00	75.00	I★	MINNEAPOLIS	50.00	75.00
D	CLEVELAND	25.00	35.00	J	KANSAS CITY	25.00	35.00
D★	CLEVELAND	50.00	75.00	J★	KANSAS CITY	50.00	75.00
E	RICHMOND	25.00	35.00	K	DALLAS	25.00	35.00
E★	RICHMOND	50.00	75.00	K★	DALLAS	50.00	75.00
F	ATLANTA	25.00	35.00	L	SAN FRANCISCO	25.00	35.00
F★	ATLANTA	50.00	75.00	L★	SAN FRANCISCO	50.00	75.00

FEDERAL RESERVE NOTES
TWENTY DOLLARS
$20 SERIES 1974 — Signatures: *Neff-Simon*

Federal Reserve Bank		CU	Ch. CU	Federal Reserve Bank		CU	Ch. CU
A	BOSTON	25.00	35.00	G	CHICAGO	25.00	35.00
A★	BOSTON	40.00	65.00	G★	CHICAGO	40.00	65.00
B	NEW YORK	25.00	35.00	H	ST. LOUIS	25.00	35.00
B★	NEW YORK	40.00	65.00	H★	ST. LOUIS	40.00	65.00
C	PHILADELPHIA	25.00	35.00	I	MINNEAPOLIS	25.00	35.00
C★	PHILADELPHIA	40.00	65.00	I★	MINNEAPOLIS	40.00	65.00
D	CLEVELAND	25.00	35.00	J	KANSAS CITY	25.00	35.00
D★	CLEVELAND	40.00	65.00	J★	KANSAS CITY	40.00	70.00
E	RICHMOND	25.00	30.00	K	DALLAS	25.00	35.00
E★	RICHMOND	40.00	65.00	K★	DALLAS	40.00	70.00
F	ATLANTA	25.00	30.00	L	SAN FRANCISCO	25.00	35.00
F★	ATLANTA	40.00	65.00	L★	SAN FRANCISCO	40.00	70.00

$20 SERIES 1977 — Signatures: *Morton-Blumenthal*

Federal Reserve Bank		CU	Ch. CU	Federal Reserve Bank		CU	Ch. CU
A	BOSTON	25.00	35.00	G	CHICAGO	25.00	35.00
A★	BOSTON	40.00	65.00	G★	CHICAGO	40.00	65.00
B	NEW YORK	25.00	35.00	H	ST. LOUIS	25.00	35.00
B★	NEW YORK	40.00	65.00	H★	ST. LOUIS	40.00	65.00
C	PHILADELPHIA	25.00	35.00	I	MINNEAPOLIS	25.00	35.00
C★	PHILADELPHIA	40.00	65.00	I★	MINNEAPOLIS	40.00	65.00
D	CLEVELAND	25.00	35.00	J	KANSAS CITY	25.00	35.00
D★	CLEVELAND	40.00	65.00	J★	KANSAS CITY	40.00	65.00
E	RICHMOND	25.00	35.00	K	DALLAS	25.00	35.00
E★	RICHMOND	40.00	65.00	K★	DALLAS	40.00	65.00
F	ATLANTA	25.00	35.00	L	SAN FRANCISCO	25.00	35.00
F★	ATLANTA	40.00	65.00	L★	SAN FRANCISCO	40.00	65.00

$20 SERIES 1981 — Signatures: *Buchanan-Regan*

Federal Reserve Bank		CU	Ch. CU	Federal Reserve Bank		CU	Ch. CU
A	BOSTON	25.00	30.00	G	CHICAGO	25.00	30.00
A★	BOSTON	35.00	50.00	G★	CHICAGO	35.00	50.00
B	NEW YORK	25.00	30.00	H	ST. LOUIS	25.00	30.00
B★	NEW YORK	35.00	50.00	H★	ST. LOUIS	35.00	50.00
C	PHILADELPHIA	25.00	30.00	I	MINNEAPOLIS	25.00	30.00
C★	PHILADELPHIA	35.00	50.00	I★	MINNEAPOLIS	35.00	50.00
D	CLEVELAND	25.00	30.00	J	KANSAS CITY	25.00	30.00
D★	CLEVELAND	35.00	50.00	J★	KANSAS CITY	35.00	50.00
E	RICHMOND	25.00	30.00	K	DALLAS	25.00	30.00
E★	RICHMOND	35.00	50.00	K★	DALLAS	35.00	50.00
F	ATLANTA	25.00	30.00	L	SAN FRANCISCO	25.00	30.00
F★	ATLANTA	35.00	50.00	L★	SAN FRANCISCO	35.00	50.00

FEDERAL RESERVE NOTES
TWENTY DOLLARS

$20 SERIES 1981-A — Signatures: *Ortega-Regan*

Federal Reserve Bank		CU	Ch. CU	Federal Reserve Bank		CU	Ch. CU
A	BOSTON	25.00	30.00	F★	ATLANTA	35.00	50.00
B	NEW YORK	25.00	30.00	G	CHICAGO	25.00	30.00
C	PHILADELPHIA	25.00	30.00	H	ST. LOUIS	25.00	30.00
C★	PHILADELPHIA	not printed		J	KANSAS CITY	25.00	30.00
D	CLEVELAND	25.00	30.00	K	DALLAS	25.00	30.00
D★	CLEVELAND	35.00	50.00	L	SAN FRANCISCO	25.00	30.00
E	RICHMOND	25.00	30.00	L★	SAN FRANCISCO	35.00	50.00
F	ATLANTA	25.00	30.00				

$20 SERIES 1985 — Signatures: *Ortega-Baker*

Federal Reserve Bank		CU	Ch. CU	Federal Reserve Bank		CU	Ch. CU
A	BOSTON	23.00	28.00	G	CHICAGO	23.00	28.00
A★	BOSTON	30.00	40.00	G★	CHICAGO	30.00	40.00
B	NEW YORK	23.00	28.00	H	ST. LOUIS	23.00	28.00
B★	NEW YORK	30.00	40.00	I	MINNEAPOLIS	23.00	28.00
C	PHILADELPHIA	23.00	28.00	J	KANSAS CITY	23.00	28.00
C★	PHILADELPHIA	30.00	40.00	J★	KANSAS CITY	30.00	40.00
D	CLEVELAND	23.00	28.00	K	DALLAS	23.00	28.00
D★	CLEVELAND	30.00	40.00	K★	DALLAS	30.00	40.00
E	RICHMOND	23.00	28.00	L	SAN FRANCISCO	23.00	28.00
E★	RICHMOND	30.00	40.00	L★	SAN FRANCISCO	30.00	40.00
F	ATLANTA	23.00	28.00				

$20 SERIES 1988-A — Signatures: *Villalpando-Brady*

Issues from all 12 Federal Reserve Districts have nominal values and are commonly available in high grade condition. Star replacement notes have a 25% premium.

$20 SERIES 1990 — Signatures: *Villalpando-Brady*

Added Security Devices. Sheet-fed at both Washington and Fort Worth facilities. Fort Worth notes have a face check letter/number that is preceded by small letters FW. All of these notes have nominal values and are commonly available in high grade condition. Star replacement notes have a 25% premium.

$20 SERIES 1993 — Signatures: *Withrow-Bentsen*

Added Security Devices. Sheet-fed at both Washington and Fort Worth facilities. Fort Worth notes have a face check letter/number that is preceded by small letters FW. All of these notes have nominal values and are commonly available in high grade condition. None were issued from Minneapolis. Star replacement notes have a 25% premium.

$20 SERIES 1995 — Signatures: *Withrow-Rubin*

Added Security Devices. Sheet-fed at both Washington and Fort Worth facilities. All have nominal values and are commonly available in high grade condition. Star replacement notes have a 25% premium.

$20 SERIES 1996 — Signatures: *Withrow-Rubin*

New design with larger portrait.

$20 SERIES 1996-2001 — Signatures: *Withrow-Rubin*

Added Security Devices. Sheet-fed at both Washington and Fort Worth facilities. Issues from all Federal Reserve Districts have nominal values and are commonly available in high grade condition. Star replacement notes have a 25% premium.

$20 SERIES 2004 — Signatures: *Marin-Snow*

Added Security Devices. Sheet-fed at both Washington and Fort Worth facilities. Issues from all Federal Reserve Districts have nominal values are commonly available in high grade condition. Star replacement notes have a 25% premium.

FEDERAL RESERVE NOTES
FIFTY DOLLARS

Face Design 1928

Back Design Federal Reserve Notes 1928-1950 E; National Currency;
Federal Reserve Bank Notes; Gold Certificates

$50 SERIES 1928 — Signatures: *Woods-Mellon*

Large District numeral of Bank at left.

District	Federal Reserve Bank	Ex. Fine	CU	Ch. CU
1	BOSTON	125.00	500.00	750.00
2	NEW YORK	125.00	500.00	750.00
3	PHILADELPHIA	125.00	550.00	850.00
4	CLEVELAND	125.00	500.00	750.00
5	RICHMOND	125.00	500.00	750.00
6	ATLANTA	125.00	500.00	750.00
7	CHICAGO	125.00	550.00	850.00
8	ST. LOUIS	125.00	500.00	750.00
9	MINNEAPOLIS	125.00	500.00	750.00
10	KANSAS CITY	125.00	550.00	850.00
11	DALLAS	125.00	500.00	750.00
12	SAN FRANCISCO	125.00	500.00	750.00

FEDERAL RESERVE NOTES
FIFTY DOLLARS
$50 SERIES 1928-A — Signatures: *Woods-Mellon*

Large District letter replaces numeral in Bank seal on this and succeeding issues.

District	Federal Reserve Bank	Ex. Fine	CU	Ch. CU
A	BOSTON	100.00	400.00	600.00
B	NEW YORK	100.00	400.00	600.00
C	PHILADELPHIA	100.00	400.00	600.00
D	CLEVELAND	100.00	400.00	600.00
E	RICHMOND	100.00	400.00	600.00
F	ATLANTA	150.00	500.00	700.00
G	CHICAGO	100.00	400.00	600.00
H	ST. LOUIS	100.00	400.00	600.00
I	MINNEAPOLIS	100.00	400.00	600.00
J	KANSAS CITY	100.00	400.00	600.00
K	DALLAS	100.00	400.00	600.00
L	SAN FRANCISCO	100.00	400.00	600.00

$50 SERIES 1934 — Signatures: *Julian-Morgenthau*

Light or dark green seal.

District	Federal Reserve Bank	Ex. Fine	CU	Ch. CU
A	BOSTON	75.00	225.00	375.00
B	NEW YORK	75.00	200.00	350.00
C	PHILADELPHIA	75.00	200.00	350.00
D	CLEVELAND	75.00	200.00	350.00
E	RICHMOND	75.00	200.00	350.00
F	ATLANTA	75.00	200.00	350.00
G	CHICAGO	75.00	200.00	350.00
H	ST. LOUIS	75.00	200.00	350.00
I	MINNEAPOLIS	110.00	225.00	400.00
J	KANSAS CITY	100.00	200.00	350.00
K	DALLAS	100.00	200.00	350.00
L	SAN FRANCISCO	100.00	200.00	350.00

$50 SERIES 1934-A — Signatures: *Julian-Morgenthau*

District	Federal Reserve Bank	Ex. Fine	CU	Ch. CU
A	BOSTON	100.00	275.00	375.00
B	NEW YORK	100.00	275.00	375.00
C	PHILADELPHIA		not printed	
D	CLEVELAND	100.00	275.00	375.00
E	RICHMOND	100.00	275.00	375.00
F	ATLANTA	100.00	275.00	375.00
G	CHICAGO	100.00	275.00	375.00
H	ST. LOUIS	100.00	275.00	375.00
I	MINNEAPOLIS	100.00	275.00	375.00
J	KANSAS CITY	100.00	275.00	375.00
K	DALLAS	100.00	275.00	375.00
L	SAN FRANCISCO	100.00	275.00	375.00

FEDERAL RESERVE NOTES
FIFTY DOLLARS

$50 SERIES 1934-B — Signatures: *Julian-Vinson*

District	Federal Reserve Bank	Ex. Fine	CU	Ch. CU
A	BOSTON		not printed	
B	NEW YORK		not printed	
C	PHILADELPHIA	90.00	200.00	300.00
D	CLEVELAND	90.00	200.00	300.00
E	RICHMOND	90.00	200.00	300.00
F	ATLANTA	90.00	200.00	300.00
G	CHICAGO	90.00	200.00	300.00
H	ST. LOUIS	90.00	200.00	300.00
I	MINNEAPOLIS	90.00	200.00	300.00
J	KANSAS CITY	90.00	200.00	300.00
K	DALLAS	90.00	200.00	300.00
L	SAN FRANCISCO	90.00	200.00	300.00

$50 SERIES 1934-C — Signatures: *Julian-Snyder*

District	Federal Reserve Bank	Ex. Fine	CU	Ch. CU
A	BOSTON	75.00	175.00	275.00
B	NEW YORK	75.00	175.00	275.00
C	PHILADELPHIA	75.00	175.00	275.00
D	CLEVELAND	75.00	175.00	275.00
E	RICHMOND	75.00	175.00	275.00
F	ATLANTA	75.00	175.00	275.00
G	CHICAGO	75.00	175.00	275.00
H	ST. LOUIS	75.00	175.00	275.00
I	MINNEAPOLIS	75.00	175.00	275.00
J	KANSAS CITY	75.00	175.00	275.00
K	DALLAS	75.00	175.00	275.00
L	SAN FRANCISCO		not printed	

$50 SERIES 1934-D — Signatures: *Clark-Snyder*

District	Federal Reserve Bank	Ex. Fine	CU	Ch. CU
A	BOSTON	65.00	150.00	250.00
B	NEW YORK	65.00	150.00	250.00
C	PHILADELPHIA	65.00	150.00	250.00
D	CLEVELAND		not printed	
E	RICHMOND	65.00	150.00	250.00
F	ATLANTA	65.00	150.00	250.00
G	CHICAGO	65.00	150.00	250.00
H	ST. LOUIS		not printed	
I	MINNEAPOLIS		reported	
J	KANSAS CITY		not printed	
K	DALLAS	65.00	150.00	250.00
L	SAN FRANCISCO		not printed	

FEDERAL RESERVE NOTES
FIFTY DOLLARS

Face Design 1950-1950 E. General Face Design 1963 A-1993

$50 SERIES 1950 — Signatures: *Clark-Snyder*

Federal Reserve Bank		CU	Ch. CU	Federal Reserve Bank		CU	Ch. CU
A	BOSTON	100.00	150.00	G	CHICAGO	100.00	150.00
B	NEW YORK	100.00	150.00	H	ST. LOUIS	100.00	150.00
C	PHILADELPHIA	100.00	150.00	I	MINNEAPOLIS	100.00	150.00
D	CLEVELAND	100.00	150.00	J	KANSAS CITY	100.00	150.00
E	RICHMOND	100.00	150.00	K	DALLAS	100.00	150.00
F	ATLANTA	100.00	150.00	L	SAN FRANCISCO	100.00	150.00

$50 SERIES 1950-A — Signatures: *Priest-Humphrey*

Federal Reserve Bank		CU	Ch. CU	Federal Reserve Bank		CU	Ch. CU
A	BOSTON	100.00	150.00	G	CHICAGO	100.00	150.00
B	NEW YORK	100.00	150.00	H	ST. LOUIS	100.00	150.00
C	PHILADELPHIA	100.00	150.00	I	MINNEAPOLIS	not printed	
D	CLEVELAND	100.00	150.00	J	KANSAS CITY	100.00	150.00
E	RICHMOND	100.00	150.00	K	DALLAS	100.00	150.00
F	ATLANTA	100.00	150.00	L	SAN FRANCISCO	100.00	150.00

$50 SERIES 1950-B — Signatures: *Priest-Anderson*

Federal Reserve Bank		CU	Ch. CU	Federal Reserve Bank		CU	Ch. CU
A	BOSTON	100.00	150.00	G	CHICAGO	100.00	150.00
B	NEW YORK	100.00	150.00	H	ST. LOUIS	100.00	150.00
C	PHILADELPHIA	100.00	150.00	I	MINNEAPOLIS	not printed	
D	CLEVELAND	100.00	150.00	J	KANSAS CITY	100.00	150.00
E	RICHMOND	100.00	150.00	K	DALLAS	100.00	150.00
F	ATLANTA	not printed		L	SAN FRANCISCO	100.00	150.00

FEDERAL RESERVE NOTES
FIFTY DOLLARS
$50 SERIES 1950-C — Signatures: *Smith-Dillon*

Federal Reserve Bank		CU	Ch. CU	Federal Reserve Bank		CU	Ch. CU
A	BOSTON	100.00	150.00	G	CHICAGO	100.00	150.00
B	NEW YORK	100.00	150.00	H	ST. LOUIS	100.00	150.00
C	PHILADELPHIA	100.00	150.00	I	MINNEAPOLIS	100.00	150.00
D	CLEVELAND	100.00	150.00	J	KANSAS CITY	100.00	150.00
E	RICHMOND	100.00	150.00	K	DALLAS	100.00	150.00
F	ATLANTA	not printed		L	SAN FRANCISCO	100.00	150.00

$50 SERIES 1950-D — Signatures: *Granahan-Dillon*

Federal Reserve Bank		CU	Ch. CU	Federal Reserve Bank		CU	Ch. CU
A	BOSTON	100.00	150.00	G	CHICAGO	100.00	150.00
B	NEW YORK	100.00	150.00	H	ST. LOUIS	100.00	150.00
C	PHILADELPHIA	100.00	150.00	I	MINNEAPOLIS	100.00	150.00
D	CLEVELAND	100.00	150.00	J	KANSAS CITY	100.00	150.00
E	RICHMOND	100.00	150.00	K	DALLAS	100.00	150.00
F	ATLANTA	100.00	150.00	L	SAN FRANCISCO	100.00	150.00

$50 SERIES 1950-E — Signatures: *Granahan-Fowler*

Federal Reserve Bank		CU	Ch. CU	Federal Reserve Bank		CU	Ch. CU
B	NEW YORK	500.00	700.00	L	SAN FRANCISCO	500.00	750.00
G	CHICAGO	750.00	1,000				

Back Design 1963 A-through the 1993. Motto on back.

FEDERAL RESERVE NOTES
FIFTY DOLLARS
$50 SERIES 1963-A — Signatures: *Granahan-Fowler*

Federal Reserve Bank		CU	Ch. CU	Federal Reserve Bank		CU	Ch. CU
A	BOSTON	100.00	150.00	G	CHICAGO	100.00	150.00
A★	BOSTON	300.00	500.00	G★	CHICAGO	300.00	500.00
B	NEW YORK	100.00	150.00	H	ST. LOUIS	100.00	150.00
B★	NEW YORK	300.00	500.00	H★	ST. LOUIS	300.00	500.00
C	PHILADELPHIA	100.00	150.00	I	MINNEAPOLIS	100.00	150.00
C★	PHILADELPHIA	300.00	500.00	I★	MINNEAPOLIS	300.00	500.00
D	CLEVELAND	100.00	150.00	J	KANSAS CITY	100.00	150.00
D★	CLEVELAND	300.00	500.00	J★	KANSAS CITY	700.00	950.00
E	RICHMOND	100.00	150.00	K	DALLAS	100.00	150.00
E★	RICHMOND	300.00	500.00	K★	DALLAS	500.00	750.00
F	ATLANTA	100.00	150.00	L	SAN FRANCISCO	100.00	150.00
F★	ATLANTA	100.00	500.00	L★	SAN FRANCISCO	300.00	500.00

$50 SERIES 1969 — Signatures: *Elston-Kennedy*

Federal Reserve Bank		CU	Ch. CU	Federal Reserve Bank		CU	Ch. CU
A	BOSTON	75.00	100.00	G	CHICAGO	75.00	100.00
A★	BOSTON	not printed		G★	CHICAGO	200.00	300.00
B	NEW YORK	75.00	100.00	H	ST. LOUIS	75.00	100.00
B★	NEW YORK	200.00	300.00	H★	ST. LOUIS	not printed	
C	PHILADELPHIA	75.00	100.00	I	MINNEAPOLIS	75.00	100.00
C★	PHILADELPHIA	225.00	325.00	I★	MINNEAPOLIS	not printed	
D	CLEVELAND	75.00	100.00	J	KANSAS CITY	75.00	100.00
D★	CLEVELAND	200.00	300.00	J★	KANSAS CITY	350.00	600.00
E	RICHMOND	75.00	100.00	K	DALLAS	75.00	100.00
E★	RICHMOND	300.00	500.00	K★	DALLAS	200.00	350.00
F	ATLANTA	75.00	100.00	L	SAN FRANCISCO	75.00	100.00
F★	ATLANTA	not printed		L★	SAN FRANCISCO	200.00	350.00

$50 SERIES 1969-A — Signatures: *Kabis-Connally*

Federal Reserve Bank		CU	Ch. CU	Federal Reserve Bank		CU	Ch. CU
A	BOSTON	75.00	100.00	G	CHICAGO	75.00	100.00
A★	BOSTON	200.00	300.00	G★	CHICAGO	200.00	300.00
B	NEW YORK	75.00	100.00	H	ST. LOUIS	75.00	100.00
B★	NEW YORK	200.00	300.00	H★	ST. LOUIS	not printed	
C	PHILADELPHIA	75.00	100.00	I	MINNEAPOLIS	75.00	100.00
C★	PHILADELPHIA	not printed		I★	MINNEAPOLIS	not printed	
D	CLEVELAND	75.00	100.00	J	KANSAS CITY	75.00	100.00
D★	CLEVELAND	not printed		J★	KANSAS CITY	not printed	
E	RICHMOND	75.00	100.00	K	DALLAS	75.00	100.00
E★	RICHMOND	300.00	500.00	K★	DALLAS	300.00	500.00
F	ATLANTA	75.00	100.00	L	SAN FRANCISCO	75.00	100.00
F★	ATLANTA	200.00	300.00	L★	SAN FRANCISCO	200.00	300.00

FEDERAL RESERVE NOTES
FIFTY DOLLARS
$50 SERIES 1969-B— Signatures: *Bañuelos-Connally*

Federal Reserve Bank		CU	Ch. CU	Federal Reserve Bank		CU	Ch. CU
A	BOSTON	60.00	75.00	G	CHICAGO	60.00	75.00
A★	BOSTON	not printed		G★	CHICAGO	not printed	
B	NEW YORK	60.00	75.00	H	ST. LOUIS	not printed	
B★	NEW YORK	not printed		H★	ST. LOUIS	not printed	
C	PHILADELPHIA	not printed		I	MINNEAPOLIS	not printed	
C★	PHILADELPHIA	not printed		I★	MINNEAPOLIS	not printed	
D	CLEVELAND	not printed		J	KANSAS CITY	not printed	
D★	CLEVELAND	not printed		J★	KANSAS CITY	not printed	
E	RICHMOND	60.00	75.00	K	DALLAS	60.00	75.00
E★	RICHMOND	not printed		K★	DALLAS	75.00	100.00
F	ATLANTA	60.00	75.00	L	SAN FRANCISCO	not printed	
F★	ATLANTA	not printed		L★	SAN FRANCISCO	not printed	

$50 SERIES 1969-C— Signatures: *Bañuelos-Shultz*

Federal Reserve Bank		CU	Ch. CU	Federal Reserve Bank		CU	Ch. CU
A	BOSTON	60.00	75.00	G	CHICAGO	60.00	75.00
A★	BOSTON	75.00	100.00	G★	CHICAGO	75.00	100.00
B	NEW YORK	60.00	75.00	H	ST. LOUIS	60.00	75.00
B★	NEW YORK	75.00	100.00	H★	ST. LOUIS	75.00	100.00
C	PHILADELPHIA	60.00	75.00	I	MINNEAPOLIS	60.00	75.00
C★	PHILADELPHIA	75.00	100.00	I★	MINNEAPOLIS	75.00	100.00
D	CLEVELAND	60.00	75.00	J	KANSAS CITY	60.00	75.00
D★	CLEVELAND	75.00	100.00	J★	KANSAS CITY	75.00	100.00
E	RICHMOND	60.00	75.00	K	DALLAS	60.00	75.00
E★	RICHMOND	75.00	100.00	K★	DALLAS	75.00	100.00
F	ATLANTA	60.00	75.00	L	SAN FRANCISCO	60.00	75.00
F★	ATLANTA	75.00	100.00	L★	SAN FRANCISCO	75.00	100.00

$50 SERIES 1974— Signatures: *Neff-Simon*

Federal Reserve Bank		CU	Ch. CU	Federal Reserve Bank		CU	Ch. CU
A	BOSTON	60.00	75.00	G	CHICAGO	60.00	75.00
A★	BOSTON	75.00	100.00	G★	CHICAGO	75.00	100.00
B	NEW YORK	60.00	75.00	H	ST. LOUIS	60.00	75.00
B★	NEW YORK	75.00	100.00	H★	ST. LOUIS	75.00	100.00
C	PHILADELPHIA	60.00	75.00	I	MINNEAPOLIS	60.00	75.00
C★	PHILADELPHIA	75.00	100.00	I★	MINNEAPOLIS	75.00	100.00
D	CLEVELAND	60.00	75.00	J	KANSAS CITY	60.00	75.00
D★	CLEVELAND	75.00	100.00	J★	KANSAS CITY	75.00	100.00
E	RICHMOND	60.00	75.00	K	DALLAS	60.00	75.00
E★	RICHMOND	75.00	100.00	K★	DALLAS	75.00	100.00
F	ATLANTA	60.00	75.00	L	SAN FRANCISCO	60.00	75.00
F★	ATLANTA	75.00	100.00	L★	SAN FRANCISCO	75.00	100.00

FEDERAL RESERVE NOTES
FIFTY DOLLARS
$50 SERIES 1977— Signatures: *Morton-Blumenthal*

Federal Reserve Bank		*CU*	*Ch. CU*	*Federal Reserve Bank*		*CU*	*Ch. CU*
A	BOSTON	60.00	75.00	G	CHICAGO	60.00	75.00
A★	BOSTON	75.00	100.00	G★	CHICAGO	75.00	100.00
B	NEW YORK	60.00	75.00	H	ST. LOUIS	60.00	75.00
B★	NEW YORK	75.00	100.00	H★	ST. LOUIS	75.00	100.00
C	PHILADELPHIA	60.00	75.00	I	MINNEAPOLIS	60.00	75.00
C★	PHILADELPHIA	75.00	100.00	I★	MINNEAPOLIS	75.00	100.00
D	CLEVELAND	60.00	75.00	J	KANSAS CITY	60.00	75.00
D★	CLEVELAND	75.00	100.00	J★	KANSAS CITY	75.00	100.00
E	RICHMOND	60.00	75.00	K	DALLAS	60.00	75.00
E★	RICHMOND	75.00	100.00	K★	DALLAS	75.00	100.00
F	ATLANTA	60.00	75.00	L	SAN FRANCISCO	60.00	75.00
F★	ATLANTA	75.00	100.00	L★	SAN FRANCISCO	75.00	100.00

$50 SERIES 1981— Signatures: *Buchanan-Regan*

Federal Reserve Bank		*CU*	*Ch. CU*	*Federal Reserve Bank*		*CU*	*Ch. CU*
A	BOSTON	60.00	75.00	G★	CHICAGO	75.00	100.00
B	NEW YORK	60.00	75.00	H	ST. LOUIS	60.00	75.00
B★	NEW YORK	75.00	100.00	I	MINNEAPOLIS	60.00	75.00
C	PHILADELPHIA	60.00	75.00	I★	MINNEAPOLIS	75.00	100.00
D	CLEVELAND	60.00	75.00	J	KANSAS CITY	60.00	75.00
D★	CLEVELAND	75.00	100.00	J★	KANSAS CITY	75.00	100.00
E	RICHMOND	60.00	75.00	K	DALLAS	60.00	75.00
F	ATLANTA	60.00	75.00	L	SAN FRANCISCO	60.00	75.00
F★	ATLANTA	75.00	100.00	L★	SAN FRANCISCO	75.00	100.00
G	CHICAGO	60.00	75.00				

$50 SERIES 1981-A— Signatures: *Ortega-Regan*

Federal Reserve Bank		*CU*	*Ch. CU*	*Federal Reserve Bank*		*CU*	*Ch. CU*
A	BOSTON	60.00	75.00	H	ST. LOUIS	60.00	75.00
B	NEW YORK	60.00	75.00	I	MINNEAPOLIS	60.00	75.00
B★	NEW YORK	75.00	100.00	J	KANSAS CITY	60.00	75.00
D	CLEVELAND	60.00	75.00	J★	KANSAS CITY	not printed	
E	RICHMOND	60.00	75.00	K	DALLAS	60.00	75.00
E★	RICHMOND	75.00	100.00	L	SAN FRANCISCO	60.00	75.00
F	ATLANTA	60.00	75.00	L★	SAN FRANCISCO	75.00	100.00
G	CHICAGO	60.00	75.00				

FEDERAL RESERVE NOTES
FIFTY DOLLARS

$50 SERIES 1985 — Signatures: *Ortega-Baker*

Issues from all 12 Federal Reserve Districts have nominal values and are commonly available in high grade condition. Star replacement notes have a 20% premium.

$50 SERIES 1988 — Signatures: *Ortega-Brady*

Issued from only seven districts. All are commonly available in high grade condition. Star notes were issued only from New York and have a 20% premium.

$50 SERIES 1990 — Signatures: *Villalpando-Brady*

Added Security Devices. Washington facility printings for all twelve Federal Reserve Districts. All are commonly available. Star notes have a 20% premium.

$50 SERIES 1993 — Signatures: *Withrow-Bentsen*

Added Security Devices. Produced only at Washington facility and not for all of the 12 Federal Reserve Districts. All of these have nominal values and are commonly available in high grade condition. Star replacement notes have a 20% premium.

FIFTY DOLLARS

Face Design 1996

Back Design 1996 Federal Reserve Note

$50 SERIES 1996-2001 — Signatures: *Withrow-Rubin*

Redesigned issue with larger portrait and new devices. In circulation. All have nominal values and are commonly available in high grade condition. Star replacement notes have a 20% premium.

FEDERAL RESERVE NOTES
ONE HUNDRED DOLLARS

Face Design 1928

Back Design Federal Reserve Notes 1928-1950 E; National Currency;
Federal Reserve Bank Notes; Gold Certificates

$100 SERIES 1928 — Signatures: *Woods-Mellon*

Large District numeral of Bank at left.

District	Federal Reserve Bank	Ex. Fine	CU	Ch. CU
1	BOSTON	200.00	600.00	800.00
2	NEW YORK	200.00	600.00	800.00
3	PHILADELPHIA	200.00	600.00	800.00
4	CLEVELAND	200.00	600.00	800.00
5	RICHMOND	200.00	625.00	825.00
6	ATLANTA	200.00	625.00	825.00
7	CHICAGO	200.00	625.00	825.00
8	ST. LOUIS	200.00	650.00	850.00
9	MINNEAPOLIS	300.00	850.00	1,000
10	KANSAS CITY	200.00	600.00	825.00
11	DALLAS	350.00	1,000	1,500
12	SAN FRANCISCO	200.00	600.00	825.00

FEDERAL RESERVE NOTES
ONE HUNDRED DOLLARS

Face Design 1928 A. General Face Design 1934-1934 D.

$100 SERIES 1928-A — Signatures: *Woods-Mellon*

Large District letter replaces numeral in Bank seal on this and succeeding issues.

District	Federal Reserve Bank	Ex. Fine	CU	Ch. CU
A	BOSTON	250.00	500.00	800.00
B	NEW YORK	250.00	500.00	800.00
C	PHILADELPHIA	250.00	500.00	800.00
D	CLEVELAND	250.00	500.00	800.00
E	RICHMOND	250.00	500.00	800.00
F	ATLANTA	250.00	500.00	800.00
G	CHICAGO	250.00	500.00	800.00
H	ST. LOUIS	250.00	500.00	800.00
I	MINNEAPOLIS	275.00	650.00	1,000
J	KANSAS CITY	250.00	500.00	800.00
K	DALLAS	275.00	650.00	1,000
L	SAN FRANCISCO	250.00	500.00	800.00

$100 SERIES 1934 — Signatures: *Julian-Morgenthau*

Light or dark green Treasury Seal.

District	Federal Reserve Bank	Ex. Fine	CU	Ch. CU
A	BOSTON	250.00	500.00	800.00
B	NEW YORK	250.00	500.00	800.00
C	PHILADELPHIA	250.00	500.00	800.00
D	CLEVELAND	250.00	500.00	800.00
E	RICHMOND	250.00	500.00	800.00
F	ATLANTA	250.00	500.00	800.00
G	CHICAGO	250.00	500.00	800.00
H	ST. LOUIS	250.00	500.00	800.00
I	MINNEAPOLIS	250.00	500.00	800.00
J	KANSAS CITY	250.00	500.00	800.00
K	DALLAS	250.00	500.00	800.00
L	SAN FRANCISCO	250.00	500.00	800.00

FEDERAL RESERVE NOTES
ONE HUNDRED DOLLARS

$100 SERIES 1934-A — Signatures: *Julian-Morgenthau*

District	Federal Reserve Bank	Ex. Fine	CU	Ch. CU
A	BOSTON	175.00	300.00	500.00
B	NEW YORK	175.00	300.00	500.00
C	PHILADELPHIA	175.00	300.00	500.00
D	CLEVELAND	175.00	300.00	500.00
E	RICHMOND	175.00	300.00	500.00
F	ATLANTA	175.00	300.00	500.00
G	CHICAGO	175.00	300.00	500.00
H	ST. LOUIS	175.00	300.00	500.00
I	MINNEAPOLIS	175.00	300.00	500.00
J	KANSAS CITY	175.00	300.00	500.00
K	DALLAS	175.00	300.00	500.00
L	SAN FRANCISCO	175.00	300.00	500.00

$100 SERIES 1934-B — Signatures: *Julian-Vinson*

District	Federal Reserve Bank	Ex. Fine	CU	Ch. CU
A	BOSTON	200.00	350.00	600.00
B	NEW YORK		not printed	
C	PHILADELPHIA	200.00	350.00	600.00
D	CLEVELAND	200.00	350.00	600.00
E	RICHMOND	200.00	350.00	600.00
F	ATLANTA	200.00	350.00	600.00
G	CHICAGO	200.00	350.00	600.00
H	ST. LOUIS	200.00	350.00	600.00
I	MINNEAPOLIS	200.00	350.00	600.00
J	KANSAS CITY	200.00	350.00	600.00
K	DALLAS	200.00	350.00	600.00
L	SAN FRANCISCO		not printed	

$100 SERIES 1934-C — Signatures: *Julian-Snyder*

District	Federal Reserve Bank	Ex. Fine	CU	Ch. CU
A	BOSTON	185.00	325.00	525.00
B	NEW YORK	185.00	325.00	500.00
C	PHILADELPHIA	185.00	325.00	525.00
D	CLEVELAND	185.00	325.00	500.00
E	RICHMOND	185.00	325.00	500.00
F	ATLANTA	185.00	325.00	500.00
G	CHICAGO	185.00	325.00	500.00
H	ST. LOUIS	185.00	325.00	500.00
I	MINNEAPOLIS	185.00	325.00	500.00
J	KANSAS CITY	185.00	325.00	500.00
K	DALLAS	185.00	325.00	500.00
L	SAN FRANCISCO	185.00	325.00	500.00

FEDERAL RESERVE NOTES
ONE HUNDRED DOLLARS

$100 SERIES 1934-D — Signatures: *Clark-Snyder*

District	Federal Reserve Bank	Ex. Fine	CU	Ch. CU
A	BOSTON		not printed	
B	NEW YORK	170.00	325.00	550.00
C	PHILADELPHIA	150.00	300.00	500.00
D	CLEVELAND		not printed	
E	RICHMOND	150.00	not printed	
F	ATLANTA	150.00	300.00	500.00
G	CHICAGO	150.00	300.00	500.00
H	ST. LOUIS	150.00	300.00	500.00
I	MINNEAPOLIS	—	—	—
J	KANSAS CITY	—	—	—
K	DALLAS	150.00	300.00	500.00
L	SAN FRANCISCO		not printed	

Face Design 1950-1950 E. General Face Design 1963 A-1993

$100 SERIES 1950 — Signatures: *Clark-Snyder*

Federal Reserve Bank		CU	Ch. CU	Federal Reserve Bank		CU	Ch. CU
A	BOSTON	350.00	600.00	G	CHICAGO	350.00	600.00
B	NEW YORK	350.00	600.00	H	ST. LOUIS	350.00	600.00
C	PHILADELPHIA	350.00	600.00	I	MINNEAPOLIS	350.00	600.00
D	CLEVELAND	350.00	600.00	J	KANSAS CITY	350.00	600.00
E	RICHMOND	350.00	600.00	K	DALLAS	350.00	600.00
F	ATLANTA	350.00	600.00	L	SAN FRANCISCO	350.00	600.00

$100 SERIES 1950-A — Signatures: *Priest-Humphrey*

Federal Reserve Bank		CU	Ch. CU	Federal Reserve Bank		CU	Ch. CU
A	BOSTON	250.00	500.00	G	CHICAGO	250.00	500.00
B	NEW YORK	250.00	500.00	H	ST. LOUIS	250.00	500.00
C	PHILADELPHIA	250.00	500.00	I	MINNEAPOLIS	250.00	500.00
D	CLEVELAND	250.00	500.00	J	KANSAS CITY	250.00	500.00
E	RICHMOND	250.00	500.00	K	DALLAS	250.00	500.00
F	ATLANTA	250.00	500.00	L	SAN FRANCISCO	250.00	500.00

$100 SERIES 1950-B — Signatures: *Priest-Anderson*

Federal Reserve Bank		CU	Ch. CU	Federal Reserve Bank		CU	Ch. CU
A	BOSTON	350.00	600.00	G	CHICAGO	350.00	600.00
B	NEW YORK	350.00	600.00	H	ST. LOUIS	350.00	600.00
C	PHILADELPHIA	350.00	600.00	I	MINNEAPOLIS	350.00	600.00
D	CLEVELAND	350.00	600.00	J	KANSAS CITY	350.00	600.00
E	RICHMOND	350.00	600.00	K	DALLAS	350.00	600.00
F	ATLANTA	250.00	300.00	L	SAN FRANCISCO	350.00	600.00

FEDERAL RESERVE NOTES
ONE HUNDRED DOLLARS

$100 SERIES 1950-C — Signatures: *Smith-Dillon*

Federal Reserve Bank	CU	Ch. CU	Federal Reserve Bank	CU	Ch. CU
A BOSTON	300.00	350.00	G CHICAGO	300.00	350.00
B NEW YORK	300.00	350.00	H ST. LOUIS	300.00	350.00
C PHILADELPHIA	300.00	350.00	I MINNEAPOLIS	300.00	350.00
D CLEVELAND	300.00	350.00	J KANSAS CITY	300.00	350.00
E RICHMOND	300.00	350.00	K DALLAS	300.00	350.00
F ATLANTA	300.00	350.00	L SAN FRANCISCO	300.00	350.00

$100 SERIES 1950-D — Signatures: *Granahan-Dillon*

Federal Reserve Bank	CU	Ch. CU	Federal Reserve Bank	CU	Ch. CU
A BOSTON	350.00	400.00	G CHICAGO	350.00	400.00
B NEW YORK	350.00	400.00	H ST. LOUIS	350.00	400.00
C PHILADELPHIA	350.00	400.00	I MINNEAPOLIS	350.00	400.00
D CLEVELAND	350.00	400.00	J KANSAS CITY	350.00	400.00
E RICHMOND	350.00	400.00	K DALLAS	350.00	400.00
F ATLANTA	350.00	400.00	L SAN FRANCISCO	350.00	400.00

$100 SERIES of 1950-E — Signatures: *Granahan-Fowler*

Federal Reserve Bank	CU	Ch. CU	Federal Reserve Bank	CU	Ch. CU
B NEW YORK	600.00	800.00	L SAN FRANCISCO	600.00	800.00
G CHICAGO	800.00	1,000			

Back Design Federal Reserve Notes 1963 A-through 1993
(motto on back); also United States Notes

$100 SERIES 1963-A — Signatures: *Granahan-Fowler*

Federal Reserve Bank	CU	Ch. CU	Federal Reserve Bank	CU	Ch. CU
A BOSTON	150.00	225.00	G CHICAGO	150.00	225.00
A★ BOSTON	200.00	300.00	G★ CHICAGO	200.00	300.00
B NEW YORK	150.00	225.00	H ST. LOUIS	150.00	225.00
B★ NEW YORK	200.00	300.00	H★ ST. LOUIS	200.00	300.00
C PHILADELPHIA	150.00	225.00	I MINNEAPOLIS	150.00	225.00
C★ PHILADELPHIA	200.00	300.00	I★ MINNEAPOLIS	200.00	300.00
D CLEVELAND	150.00	225.00	J KANSAS CITY	150.00	225.00
D★ CLEVELAND	200.00	300.00	J★ KANSAS CITY	200.00	300.00
E RICHMOND	150.00	225.00	K DALLAS	150.00	225.00
E★ RICHMOND	200.00	300.00	K★ DALLAS	200.00	300.00
F ATLANTA	150.00	225.00	L SAN FRANCISCO	150.00	225.00
F★ ATLANTA	200.00	300.00	L★ SAN FRANCISCO	200.00	300.00

FEDERAL RESERVE NOTES
ONE HUNDRED DOLLARS

$100 SERIES 1969 — Signatures: *Elston-Kennedy*

Federal Reserve Bank		CU	Ch. CU	Federal Reserve Bank		CU	Ch. CU
A	BOSTON	140.00	175.00	G	CHICAGO	140.00	175.00
A★	BOSTON	175.00	275.00	G★	CHICAGO	175.00	275.00
B	NEW YORK	140.00	175.00	H	ST. LOUIS	140.00	175.00
B★	NEW YORK	175.00	275.00	H★	ST. LOUIS	175.00	275.00
C	PHILADELPHIA	140.00	175.00	I	MINNEAPOLIS	140.00	175.00
C★	PHILADELPHIA	175.00	275.00	I★	MINNEAPOLIS	175.00	275.00
D	CLEVELAND	140.00	175.00	J	KANSAS CITY	140.00	175.00
D★	CLEVELAND	175.00	280.00	J★	KANSAS CITY	175.00	275.00
E	RICHMOND	140.00	175.00	K	DALLAS	140.00	175.00
E★	RICHMOND	175.00	275.00	K★	DALLAS	175.00	275.00
F	ATLANTA	140.00	175.00	L	SAN FRANCISCO	140.00	175.00
F★	ATLANTA	175.00	275.00	L★	SAN FRANCISCO	175.00	275.00

$100 SERIES 1969-A — Signatures: *Kabis-Connally*

Federal Reserve Bank		CU	Ch. CU	Federal Reserve Bank		CU	Ch. CU
A	BOSTON	140.00	175.00	G	CHICAGO	140.00	175.00
A★	BOSTON	175.00	275.00	G★	CHICAGO	175.00	275.00
B	NEW YORK	140.00	175.00	H	ST. LOUIS	140.00	175.00
B★	NEW YORK	175.00	275.00	H★	ST. LOUIS	175.00	275.00
C	PHILADELPHIA	140.00	175.00	I	MINNEAPOLIS	140.00	175.00
C★	PHILADELPHIA	175.00	275.00	I★	MINNEAPOLIS		not printed
D	CLEVELAND	140.00	175.00	J	KANSAS CITY	140.00	175.00
D★	CLEVELAND	175.00	275.00	J★	KANSAS CITY		not printed
E	RICHMOND	140.00	175.00	K	DALLAS	140.00	175.00
E★	RICHMOND	175.00	275.00	K★	DALLAS	175.00	275.00
F	ATLANTA	140.00	175.00	L	SAN FRANCISCO	140.00	175.00
F★	ATLANTA	175.00	275.00	L★	SAN FRANCISCO	175.00	275.00

$100 SERIES 1969-C — Signatures: *Bañuelos-Shultz*

Federal Reserve Bank		CU	Ch. CU	Federal Reserve Bank		CU	Ch. CU
A	BOSTON	140.00	175.00	G	CHICAGO	140.00	175.00
A★	BOSTON	175.00	275.00	G★	CHICAGO	175.00	275.00
B	NEW YORK	140.00	175.00	H	ST. LOUIS	140.00	175.00
B★	NEW YORK	175.00	275.00	H★	ST. LOUIS	175.00	275.00
C	PHILADELPHIA	140.00	175.00	I	MINNEAPOLIS	140.00	175.00
C★	PHILADELPHIA	175.00	275.00	I★	MINNEAPOLIS	175.00	275.00
D	CLEVELAND	140.00	175.00	J	KANSAS CITY	140.00	175.00
D★	CLEVELAND	175.00	275.00	J★	KANSAS CITY	175.00	275.00
E	RICHMOND	140.00	175.00	K	DALLAS	140.00	175.00
E★	RICHMOND	175.00	275.00	K★	DALLAS	175.00	275.00
F	ATLANTA	140.00	175.00	L	SAN FRANCISCO	140.00	175.00
F★	ATLANTA	175.00	275.00	L★	SAN FRANCISCO	175.00	275.00

FEDERAL RESERVE NOTES
ONE HUNDRED DOLLARS

$100 SERIES 1974 — Signatures: *Neff-Simon*

Federal Reserve Bank		CU	Ch. CU	Federal Reserve Bank		CU	Ch. CU
A	BOSTON	125.00	150.00	G	CHICAGO	125.00	150.00
A★	BOSTON	150.00	250.00	G★	CHICAGO	150.00	250.00
B	NEW YORK	125.00	150.00	H	ST. LOUIS	125.00	150.00
B★	NEW YORK	150.00	250.00	H★	ST. LOUIS	150.00	250.00
C	PHILADELPHIA	125.00	150.00	I	MINNEAPOLIS	125.00	150.00
C★	PHILADELPHIA	150.00	250.00	I★	MINNEAPOLIS	150.00	250.00
D	CLEVELAND	125.00	150.00	J	KANSAS CITY	125.00	150.00
D★	CLEVELAND	150.00	250.00	J★	KANSAS CITY	150.00	250.00
E	RICHMOND	125.00	150.00	K	DALLAS	125.00	150.00
E★	RICHMOND	150.00	250.00	K★	DALLAS	150.00	250.00
F	ATLANTA	125.00	150.00	L	SAN FRANCISCO	125.00	150.00
F★	ATLANTA	150.00	250.00	L★	SAN FRANCISCO	150.00	250.00

$100 SERIES 1977 — Signatures: *Morton-Blumenthal*

Federal Reserve Bank		CU	Ch. CU	Federal Reserve Bank		CU	Ch. CU
A	BOSTON	125.00	150.00	G	CHICAGO	125.00	150.00
A★	BOSTON	150.00	250.00	G★	CHICAGO	150.00	250.00
B	NEW YORK	125.00	150.00	H	ST. LOUIS	125.00	150.00
B★	NEW YORK	150.00	250.00	H★	ST. LOUIS	150.00	250.00
C	PHILADELPHIA	125.00	150.00	I	MINNEAPOLIS	125.00	150.00
C★	PHILADELPHIA	150.00	250.00	I★	MINNEAPOLIS	150.00	250.00
D	CLEVELAND	125.00	150.00	J	KANSAS CITY	125.00	150.00
D★	CLEVELAND	150.00	250.00	J★	KANSAS CITY	150.00	250.00
E	RICHMOND	125.00	150.00	K	DALLAS	125.00	150.00
E★	RICHMOND	150.00	250.00	K★	DALLAS	150.00	250.00
F	ATLANTA	125.00	150.00	L	SAN FRANCISCO	125.00	150.00
F★	ATLANTA	150.00	250.00	L★	SAN FRANCISCO	150.00	250.00

$100 SERIES 1981 — Signatures: *Buchanan-Regan*

Federal Reserve Bank		CU	Ch. CU	Federal Reserve Bank		CU	Ch. CU
A	BOSTON	125.00	150.00	G	CHICAGO	125.00	150.00
B	NEW YORK	125.00	150.00	H	ST. LOUIS	125.00	150.00
C	PHILADELPHIA	125.00	150.00	I	MINNEAPOLIS	125.00	150.00
D	CLEVELAND	125.00	150.00	J	KANSAS CITY	125.00	150.00
E	RICHMOND	125.00	150.00	K	DALLAS	125.00	150.00
E★	RICHMOND	500.00	1,000	L	SAN FRANCISCO	125.00	150.00
F	ATLANTA	125.00	150.00				

$100 SERIES 1981-A — Signatures: *Ortega-Regan*

Federal Reserve Bank		CU	Ch. CU	Federal Reserve Bank		CU	Ch. CU
A	BOSTON	125.00	150.00	G	CHICAGO	125.00	150.00
B	NEW YORK	125.00	150.00	H	ST. LOUIS	125.00	150.00
C	PHILADELPHIA	125.00	150.00	I	MINNEAPOLIS	125.00	150.00
D	CLEVELAND	125.00	150.00	K	DALLAS	125.00	150.00
E	RICHMOND	125.00	150.00	L	SAN FRANCISCO	125.00	150.00
F	ATLANTA	125.00	150.00	L★	SAN FRANCISCO	500.00	1,000

FEDERAL RESERVE NOTES
ONE HUNDRED DOLLARS

$100 SERIES 1985 — Signatures: *Ortega-Baker*

Issues from all 12 Federal Reserve Districts have nominal values and are commonly available in high grade condition. Star replacement notes have a 20% premium.

$100 SERIES 1988 — Signatures: *Ortega-Brady*

Issued from only nine districts. All are commonly available in high grade condition. Star notes were issued only from New York and have a 50% premium.

$100 SERIES 1990 — Signatures: *Villalpando-Brady*

Added Security Devices. Washington facility printings for each of the 12 Federal Reserve Districts. All are commonly available. Star notes have a 20% premium.

$100 SERIES 1993 — Signatures: *Withrow-Bentsen*

Added Security Devices. Produced for each of the 12 Federal Reserve Districts at the Washington facility. All are commonly available in high grade condition. Star replacement notes have a 10% premium.

REVISED LARGER PORTRAIT DESIGN

Face Design 1996

Back Design 1996 Federal Reserve Note

$100 SERIES 1996-2001 — Signatures: *Withrow-Rubin*

Redesigned issue with larger portrait and new security devices. In circulation. All have nominal values and are commonly available in high grade condition. Star replacement notes have a 10% premium.

FEDERAL RESERVE NOTES
FIVE HUNDRED DOLLARS

Illustrations for the following high denomination Federal Reserve Notes were obtained through courtesy of the U.S. Bureau of Engraving. Notes shown are Specimen printings.

No notes higher than $100 are now in general circulation but they may on occasion be located in some banks. Circulated examples of these high denominations have a collector premium of about 15-25% above face value. Star notes are very rare.

General Face Design Federal Reserve Notes. Resembling Face Design Gold Certificates.

Back Design Federal Reserve Notes and Gold Certificates

Series 1928	$500 notes	AU	$1,200
Series 1934	$500 notes	AU	1,100

Issues of $500 Federal Reserve Notes have been recorded for the following series: *Series of 1928* (Woods-Mellon); *1934* (Julian-Morgenthau); *1934 A* (Julian-Morgenthau); 1934 B (Julian-Vinson); *1934 C* (Julian-Snyder).

FEDERAL RESERVE NOTES
ONE THOUSAND DOLLARS

General Face Design Federal Reserve Notes. Resembling Face Design Gold Certificates.

Back Design Federal Reserve Notes and Gold Certificates

Series 1928	$1,000 notes	..........................AU	$2,400
Series 1934	$1,000 notes	..........................AU	2,200

Issues of $1,000 Federal Reserve Notes have been recorded for the following series: *Series of 1928* (Woods-Mellon); *1934* (Julian-Morgenthau); *1934 A* (Julian-Morgenthau); *1934 C* (Julian-Snyder).

FIVE THOUSAND DOLLARS

General Face Design Federal Reserve Notes. Resembling Face Design Gold Certificates.

Series 1928	$5,000 notes	..........................AU	$40,000
Series 1934	$5,000 notes	..........................AU	35,000

FEDERAL RESERVE NOTES
FIVE THOUSAND DOLLARS

Back Design Federal Reserve Notes and Gold Certificates

TEN THOUSAND DOLLARS

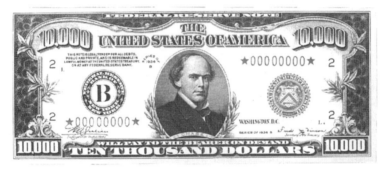

General Face Design FRN's. Resembling Face Design Gold Certificates.

Back Design Federal Reserve Notes and Gold Certificates

Series 1928	$10,000 notes	. . . . AU	$70,000
Series 1934	$10,000 notes	. . . . AU	42,000

Issues of both the $5,000 and $10,000 Federal Reserve Notes have been recorded for the following series: *1928* (Woods-Mellon); *1934* (Julian-Morgenthau); *1934 A* (Julian-Morgenthau); *1934 B* (Julian-Vinson).

GOLD CERTIFICATES, Gold Seal

Gold Certificates were not made for general circulation until 1882, though they first appeared in 1865. The first three issues were used for larger commercial transactions and were held mainly by banks and clearing houses. Denominations of large-size notes ranged from $10 to $10,000. These notes were often referred to as "gold backs" because of their orange or gold color backs.

Modern-size Gold Certificates were issued for general circulation from 1929 to 1933. Most were dated 1928 only, but it is possible that some 1928 A $10 notes were also released. There could not have been many, as the Emergency Bank Act of 1933 prevented further use of any Gold Certificates and required that they be turned in and exchanged for other currency. On December 28 of that year, Treasury Secretary Morgenthau issued an order prohibiting the holding of these notes by any private individual for any reason. Relatively few modern-size Gold notes were thus saved, especially in new condition; if any could have been hidden, they would more likely have been the large-size pieces which were naturally included in Morgenthau's order.

The Gold Reserve Act of January 31, 1934 immediately followed; this Act raised the value of gold from $20.67 to $35 per troy ounce, prohibited the circulation of gold coins and allowed Gold Certificates to be issued only to Federal Reserve Banks. A new series of Gold Certificates, Series of 1934, was made and released to the Federal Reserve Banks in exchange for gold coin or bullion. No specimen of any notes of this series was released outside the Federal Reserve System. The $100,000 note, the highest denomination printed, is included in the Series of 1934 issue.

On April 24, 1964, Treasury Secretary Dillon signed an order removing all restrictions from the holding or acquiring of Gold Certificates issued before passage of the Gold Reserve Act of 1934. This action made possible the entry of these notes into the numismatic market, and they are now openly collected and exhibited.

Modern-size Gold Certificates Series of 1928 and 1928 A are "Gold Coin" notes, so stated on the face. No heading is found in the usual place at the top; instead, it is to the left of the portrait near the Treasury seal. The color of the seal and serial numbers is gold.

Explanatory Notations for Various Series

Series of 1928 — Notes of this series and Series of 1928 A carry the following legal tender clause: "This Certificate Is A Legal Tender in the Amount Thereof in Payment of All Debts and Dues Public and Private."

The backs of these notes are all uniform with other modern types of similar denominations, and are printed in green.

Series of 1928 A — Apparently a small quantity of $10 Gold Certificates of this series was in fact released. The following excerpts from a sworn and notarized statement dated Feb. 5, 1971 by Robert H. Lloyd are revealing:

Robert H. Lloyd, of Silver Lake, Wyoming County, State of New York, being duly sworn, deposes, and says —

1. That during the year 1933, he was employed as a cashier in…Buffalo, New York, and

2. That on at least two occasions between April, 1933 and July, 1933 he received and paid out Gold Certificates, $10 denomination, Series of 1928 A (Woods-Mills) in circulated condition, and

3. That because the Certificates were soiled and wrinkled, he did not retain them for collection purposes, and

4. That he believes that the information supplied that none of these Certificates were issued is an oversight, and

GOLD CERTIFICATES

5. That he believes that the early printings of the Series of 1928 A were shipped in packages bearing the label "Series of 1928" and

6. That it is known that other types of notes were shipped in packages bearing 1928 designations, while the contents were Series of 1928 A or 1928 B, and

7. That it is unlikely that the Bureau had printed a supply of labels designating the Gold Certificates, Series of 1928 A.

Series of 1934 — No notes of this series were released to circulation; therefore, they are not included in the catalog listings. The $100,000 note is illustrated, however, on page 318.

The backs of notes in this series are printed in gold, a radical departure from the green backs of all other types and series of modern notes. The "Gold Coin" clause is not used for this series, but the legal tender clause is the same as on earlier issues except for the deletion of the word "A."

TEN DOLLARS

Face Design 1928 and 1928 A. Back Design on page 240.

Series	Treasurer-Secretary	Fine	VF	Ex. Fine	CU	Ch. CU
1928	Woods-Mellon	80.00	110.00	140.00	320.00	450.00
★28		210.00	500.00	650.00	1,750	2,200
1928 A	Woods-Mills			Unconfirmed in any collection		

GOLD CERTIFICATES
TWENTY DOLLARS

Face Design 1928 and 1928 A. Back Design on page 283.

Series	Treasurer-Secretary	Fine	VF	Ex. Fine	CU	Ch. CU
1928	Woods-Mellon	95.00	125.00	160.00	360.00	500.00
★ 28		200.00	550.00	750.00	1,750	2,500
1928 A	Woods-Mills			Not Issued		

FIFTY DOLLARS

Face Design 1928. Back Design on page 294.

Series	Treasurer-Secretary	Fine	VF	Ex. Fine	CU	Ch. CU
1928	Woods-Mellon	225.00	375.00	525.00	1,400	2,200
★28		900.00	2,000	5,000	12,000	—

GOLD CERTIFICATES
ONE HUNDRED DOLLARS

Face Design 1928. Back Design on page 303.

Series	Treasurer-Secretary	Fine	VF	Ex. Fine	CU	Ch. CU
1928	Woods-Mellon	400.00	525.00	950.00	2,500	3,000
★28		1,000	2,000	3,000	9,000	12,000

FIVE HUNDRED DOLLARS
PORTRAIT OF McKINLEY
See pages 311 for Resembling Face and Back Designs.

Series	Treasurer-Secretary	Fine	VF	Ex. Fine	CU	Ch. CU
1928	Woods-Mellon	2,500	4,750	7,250	13,500	15,000

ONE THOUSAND DOLLARS
PORTRAIT OF CLEVELAND
See pages 312 for Resembling Face and Back Designs.

Series	Treasurer-Secretary	Fine	VF	Ex. Fine	CU	Ch. CU
1928	Woods-Mellon	2,750	5,500	8,750	17,500	22,500

FIVE THOUSAND DOLLARS
PORTRAIT OF MADISON
See pages 312-313 for Resembling Face and Back Designs.

Series	Treasurer-Secretary	Fine	VF	Ex. Fine	CU	Ch. CU
1928	Woods-Mellon			40,000		

GOLD CERTIFICATES
TEN THOUSAND DOLLARS

PORTRAIT OF CHASE
See pages 313 for Resembling Face and Back Designs.

Series	Treasurer-Secretary	Fine	VF	Ex. Fine	CU	Ch. CU
1928	Woods-Mellon			50,000		

Gold Certificates were made in the Series of 1934 for use within the Federal Reserve System, and were not allowed into outside circulation. Denominations were $100, $1000, $10,000 and $100,000. This last is the highest denomination of modern-size currency ever printed by the United States, and is shown below. The portrait is of Woodrow Wilson.

Face Deisgn $100,000 Gold Certificate, Series of 1934.

Back Deisgn $100,000 Gold Certificate, Series of 1934.

The order of April 24, 1964 legalizing the holding of Gold Certificates covered all such Certificates released to general circulation through January 30, 1934. Thus, no Gold Certificates Series of 1934 may be legally held, since they were all made and delivered after the January 30 cutoff date. For this reason, no Series of 1934 Gold Certificates are included in the listings.

WORLD WAR II ISSUES

The Yellow Seal Silver Certificates

These were issued in North Africa during operations there in 1942. Later they were issued briefly at the beginning of the Sicilian campaign.

All bear the Julian-Morgenthau signature combination. Though the Treasury seals were printed in yellow, the serial numbers retained their usual blue color.

Denomination	Series	VF	Ex. Fine	CU	Ch. CU
$1.00	1935 A	30.00	38.00	100.00	125.00
	★ 35 A	350.00	500.00	2,000	2,750
5.00	1934 A	45.00	60.00	170.00	215.00
	★ 34 A	150.00	250.00	750.00	1,000
10.00	1934	3,800	7,200	12,500	18,500
	★ 34	Very Rare—only 1 known			
10.00	1934 A	45.00	65.00	190.00	260.00
	★ 34 A	150.00	300.00	900.00	1,200

The $5.00 1934 series was reported some years ago but has never been confirmed. Verification is welcomed.

The HAWAII Overprints — Brown Seal

In July of 1942, specially marked U.S. currency was introduced in Hawaii as an economic defense measure against a possible Japanese invasion. If these notes had fallen into enemy hands, they could have been isolated easily and declared valueless. After August 15, 1942, no currency other than the "Hawaiian Series" was allowable without a license from the Territorial Governor. It was not until October 21, 1944, that all restrictions were revoked and normal monetary conditions returned to the area.

The notes are overprinted HAWAII face and back as illustrated. They also contain brown seals and serial numbers. All bear the Julian-Morgenthau signature combination. $1 notes are Silver Certificates; all the rest are San Francisco Federal Reserve notes.

It is significant that the HAWAII dollars were also used to redeem Japanese Military Yen on the liberated Central Pacific islands.

Face Design $1 HAWAII

WORLD WAR II ISSUES

Back Design $10 HAWAII

Face Design $20 HAWAII

Denomination	Series	VF	Ex. Fine	CU	Ch. CU
$1.00	1935 A	38.00	42.00	90.00	125.00
	★ 35 A	300.00	500.00	2,000	2,750
5.00	1934	72.00	95.00	350.00	420.00
	★ 34	1,000	2,000	5,000	7,500
5.00	1934 A	72.00	95.00	360.00	420.00
	★ 34 A	3,000	4,000	11,000	20,000
10.00	1934 A	75.00	100.00	400.00	500.00
	★ 34 A	1,500	2,500	5,500	8,000
20.00	1934	95.00	140.00	725.00	1,000
	★ 34	1,200	2,000	6,000	8,500
20.00	1934 A	75.00	100.00	460.00	750.00
	★ 34 A	1,100	1,800	5,000	7,500

Experimental "R" and "S" $1.00 Silver Certificates

These notes were made during World War II to test the wearing qualities of regular and special paper. Equal quantities were overprinted on the face with a red R or S, in the position shown. All bear signatures of Julian-Morgenthau and are dated Series 1935 A.

WORLD WAR II ISSUES

Face Design "R" Note

Face Design "S" Note

Denomination	Fine	VF	Ex. Fine	CU	Ch. CU
$1.00 with Red R	35.00	40.00	60.00	125.00	190.00
R Star note	700.00	1,500	2,500	3,750	4,000
$1 with Red S	35.00	40.00	60.00	110.00	180.00
S Star note	600.00	1,600	2,100	3,500	3,950

The "R" and "S" overprints were made to determine whether a special kind of paper might wear better in circulation than the regular paper normally used. The "R" represented those notes made of regular paper and the "S" was for those notes made of the special paper. Results of the experiment were inconclusive and no change was made in the kind of paper used for U.S. currency. 12,000 star notes of each were printed, though the surviving number is very small.

UNCUT SHEETS OF CURRENCY

Subjects Per Sheet and Check Letters

Modern U.S. currency has been printed in sheets of 12, 18 and 32 notes. All issues up to April of 1953 were made in 12-subject sheets, with Check Letters from A to L (12 letters for 12 notes). Each note carries two identical Check Letters, which serve to indicate its particular position on the sheet when it was printed. These small capital letters are found in the upper left and lower right areas on the face side. The little number accompanying the lower right Check Letter is the Face Plate Number; it has nothing to do with the sheet position of the note.

On April 2, 1953, the Treasury issued the first notes printed in 18-subject sheets. These carry Check Letters from A through R but are otherwise similar to earlier issues.

On July 25, 1957, the Bureau of Engraving began production of notes printed in sheets of 32 subjects. Each sheet consists of four quadrants of eight notes, as shown in the diagram on page 327. The upper left quadrant contains Check Letters and numbers A_1 through H_1, the lower left A_2 through H_2, the upper right A_3 through H_3 and the lower right A_4 through H_4. The letter indicates position and the number indicates the quadrant. As with earlier issues, each note bears two identical Check Letters, but there is an important difference. The quadrant number (1 to 4) appears only with the *upper left* Check Letter. The number found with the lower right Check Letter is the Face Plate Serial Number; while it may correspond at times with the quadrant number, it has no relationship to the position or quadrant of the note. (Backs also carry a Back Plate Serial Number; its position varies with the design or denomination.)

Serial Numbering for Different Sizes of Sheets

As the number of subjects per sheet was changed, so also was the system used for placing serial numbers on the notes. The following table shows which system was used for each size of sheet, and applies to all issues except National Currency Series of 1929 and Federal Reserve Bank Notes:

Size of Sheet	Check Letters	System of Numbering
12 Subjects	A through L	Consecutive numbering by half sheet, six down on the left and six down on the right.*
18 Subjects	A through R	Numbering advances by 8,000, six down on the left, six following in the middle and six down on the right.
32 Subjects	A_1–H_1 A_2-H_2 A_3-H_3 A_4-H_4	Numbering advances by 20,000 proceeding by quadrant from the upper left to the lower right.

*See next page for numbering of sheets released in uncut form.

Sheet Sizes for Currency Issues 1929 to Date

Type	Denomination	12 Subjects	18 Subjects	32 Subjects
		SHEET SIZE AND SERIES		
United States Notes	$1	1928		
	$2	1928-1928G	1953-1953C	1963-1963A
	$5	1928-1928F	1953-1953C	1963
	$100			1966-1966A
Silver Certificates	$1	1928-1935D	1935D-1935H	1957-1957B
	$5	1934-1934D	1953-1953C	
	$10	1933-1934D	1953-1953B	
Federal Reserve Notes	$1			1963
	$2			1976
	$5, $10, $20	1928-1950	1950A-1950E	1963
	$50, $100	1928-1950	1950A-1950E	1963A
	All above $100	12 subjects		

In addition, all modern-size National Currency, Federal Reserve Bank Notes and Gold Certificates were printed in 12-subject sheets, with the overprinting and serial numbering applied to 6-subject sheets.

Clarification of 12-Subject Numbering

12-subject sheets exist both with consecutive serial numbers by half sheet as described above and with all *twelve notes* in full consecutive order. An example of this is illustrated on page 324. As explained by the Bureau, the general rule was that sheets intended for processing as regular issues for circulation were numbered by the half sheet according to the following example: Suppose that the total of a particular run was to be 1,200 notes, or 100 sheets. The first sheet would contain serial numbers from 1 to 6 on the left side and 601 to 606 on the right side, the second sheet would have numbers 7 to 12 and 607 to 612, and so on until the end of the run.

Sheets delivered to the Treasurer in uncut form, presumably for release upon request to collectors and others, often but not always bore consecutive numbers for all the notes on the sheet. In 1950, it was officially ordered that all uncut 12-subject sheets scheduled for delivery to the Treasurer should thenceforth bear serial numbers in fully consecutive order for the entire sheet.

Reconstructed Sheets and Consecutive Numbers

If a collector is able to locate all of the single notes originally printed as one unit or sheet, he will then be able to show them in the positions they formerly occupied before being cut apart. This group of notes comprises what is termed a "reconstructed sheet" of currency.

Reconstructed half-sheets of 12-subject printings could easily be assembled by obtaining six consecutively numbered notes from a new pack, making sure that Check Letters ran from A to F, or G to L. It would be extremely difficult to assemble all notes for a full 12-subject sheet as evidenced by the explanation of the numbering system (see above). Reconstruction of larger sheets is practically impossible, since the changes in the numbering system make a difference of 136,000 numbers on each 18-subject sheet and 640,000 numbers on each 32-subject sheet.

Consecutively numbered notes from the 18 or 32-subject sheets are readily available, but are of little consequence since *each note* comes from a *different* sheet. Easy proof of this fact can be seen on the notes themselves; they will all have the same Check Letters indicating identical positions on their respective sheets.

12-subject sheet of currency with all notes consecutively numbered.

Sheets with this kind of numbering were the ones generally made available to collectors during the early years when uncut sheets could be obtained.

National Currency and Federal Reserve Bank Notes

National Currency and Federal Reserve Bank Notes were printed in sheets of 12 subjects, then cut, overprinted, and delivered to the banks in vertical sheets of six subjects.

Type One National Currency used the same serial number and suffix letter for all six notes; however, each note had a different prefix letter (A through F) which also served to denote its position on that particular six-subject sheet.

Type Two National Currency notes were consecutively numbered and bore the same prefix letter, but the suffix letter was dropped. The only way to tell the sheet position of a Type Two note or a Federal Reserve Bank Note is by its Check Letters.

Since National Currency and Federal Reserve Bank Notes were all printed in 12-subject sheets (even though delivered in six-subject sheets), Check Letters proceeded from A to L as on all other 12-subject printings. Thus, it is always possible to pinpoint the exact position of any note on the original 12-subject sheet. Check Letters A through F indicate the left strip of six notes, and G through L indicate the right strip of six notes.

Each note also carries a Face Plate Serial Number in its normal position alongside the lower right Check Letter.

Numbering for Federal Reserve Bank Notes was also consecutive. Every serial number was preceded by the District letter as a prefix, and "A" as a suffix. No single issue was large enough to require the change of suffix letter to "B".

VALUATIONS OF UNCUT SHEETS

The most readily available uncut sheets of any U.S. currency are the six-subject sheets of National Currency which were delivered to issuing banks intact. It is easy to see why quantities of these sheets exist; the banks released the notes as they were needed, and many never used all that they had ordered. Also, quantities of sheets with low serial numbers were preserved for various reasons.

The following valuations apply to any sheet of these notes after the particular rarity rating of the issue as single notes has been ascertained from the listing on page 242.

National Currency Series of 1929
Six-subject Sheets

Denomination	Rarity 1&2	Rarity 3&4	Rarity 5	Rarity 6	Rarity 7	Rarity 8
$5.00	$750.00	$900.00	$1,000	$1,200	$1,700	$3,200
10.00	800.00	950.00	1,100	1,300	1,850	4,250
20.00	950.00	1,200	1,350	1,500	2,100	5,000
50.00	3,000	3,500	4,200	6,000	7,500	12,500
100.00	4,000	4,750	5,550	6,750	9,500	15,000

Until about 1954, limited quantities of certain uncut sheets of currency were available from the Bureau of Engraving for numismatic and educational purposes. Most sheets released in this manner were of 12 subjects, since the Bureau had only begun the printing of 18-subject sheets during 1953. Shortly thereafter, no more uncut sheets were made available to anyone until the new Series 1981 (and later) sheets were produced.

Apparently the two types generally released in sheets were United States Notes and Silver Certificates. Other types are known but are extremely rare.*

All uncut sheets are considered to be in new condition, even though the edges, corners or margins may have minor flaws. The following listing represents all sheets which may occasionally be available. Number of sheets issued is given where known. NR = Not Reported.

*One six-subject sheet of $10 New York Federal Reserve Bank Notes is recorded in the Grinnell Collection. Another, a 12-subject sheet of the same issue, was uncovered in the estate of a Federal Reserve Bank official in 1966. Both are possibly unique.

A few sheets of Federal Reserve Notes from $5 to $50, mostly dated Series 1928, were released probably for official use. They are rarely seen on the numismatic market.

UNCUT SHEETS OF CURRENCY
UNITED STATES NOTES
ONE DOLLAR

Series	Issued	Sheet Size	Valuation
1928	11 (8 traced)	12 Subjects	$20,000

TWO DOLLARS

1928	5 (3 traced)	12 Subjects	Rare
1928C	25 (18 traced)	12 Subjects	2,000
1928D	50	12 Subjects	—*
1928E	50 (21 traced)	12 Subjects	1,600
1928F	100	12 Subjects	1,200
1928G	100	12 Subjects	1,100
1953	100	18 Subjects	1,800

FIVE DOLLARS

1928	5	12 Subjects	—
1928D	NR (15 traced)	12 Subjects	3,200
1928E	100	12 Subjects	1,600
1953	100	18 Subjects	2,300

*At present there is no verification of any 1928D $2 sheet. Confirmation is invited.

SILVER CERTIFICATES
ONE DOLLAR

1928	80	12 Subjects	3,000
1928B	6 (None verified)		—
1928C	11 (6 traced)	12 Subjects	Rare
1928D	60 (20 traced)	12 Subjects	Rare
1928E	25† (7 traced)	12 Subjects	Very Rare
1934	25 (9 traced)	12 Subjects	2,750
1935	100	12 Subjects	2,000
1935A	100	12 Subjects	1,800
1935B	100 (28 traced)	12 Subjects	2,000
1935C	100	12 Subjects	1,500
1935D	300	12 Subjects	1,200
1935D	102	18 Subjects	1,900
1935E	400?	18 Subjects	1,200

†Most were cut into single notes.

FIVE DOLLARS

1934	25 (12 traced)	12 Subjects	2,400
1934B	20? (10 traced)	12 Subjects	3,750
1934C	100	12 Subjects	2,000
1934D	100	12 Subjects	1,800
1953	100?	18 Subjects	2,200

TEN DOLLARS

1933	1	12 Subjects	—
1933A	1	12 Subjects	Not Located
1934	10 (7 traced)	12 Subjects	Rare
1953	100	18 Subjects	4,250

UNCUT SHEETS OF CURRENCY

A_1 A	E_1 E	A_3 A	E_3 E
B_1 B	F_1 F	B_3 B	F_3 F
C_1 C	G_1 G	C_3 C	G_3 G
D_1 D	H_1 H	D_3 D	H_3 H
A_2 A	E_2 E	A_4 A	E_4 E
B_2 B	F_2 F	B_4 B	F_4 F
C_2 C	G_2 G	C_4 C	G_4 G
D_2 D	H_2 H	D_4 D	H_4 H

Layout of 32 Subject Currency Sheet showing check letters and quadrant numbers.

WORLD WAR II ISSUES
ONE DOLLAR
HAWAII OVERPRINT

Series	Issued	Sheet Size	Valuation
1935A	25	12 Subjects	$4,500

Serial numbers indicate a probable release of 60 sheets.

ONE DOLLAR
YELLOW SEAL

Series	Issued	Sheet Size	Valuation
1935A	25	12 Subjects	4,750

RECENT ISSUES OF UNCUT SHEETS OF U.S. CURRENCY

The Bureau of Engraving and Printing began openly offering collectors uncut sheets of currency in October 1981. Series 1981 Buchannan-Regan notes were the first in the new series which has continued to be offered ever since, and includes issues of 1981-A, 1985, 1988, 1993, 1995, 1996,1999 and 2001. Uncut sheets of Series 1976 $2 star notes were sold before the Bureau's current offering of 1995 $2 notes. Prior to that, in the 1950s, sheets had been available in only very limited quantities.

Current production consists of sheets of 32, 16, 8 and 4-subject $1 notes notes (series 2001) ; $2 and $5 notes (series 1995; and sheets of 16, 8 and 4-subject $10 and $20 star notes (series 1995). 16- subject sheets of $1 star notes (series 1999) have also been printed.

Uncut sheets,which are price at a premium over their face value, may be ordered directly from the Bureau of Engraving and Printing at www.moneyfactory.gov Telephone: 1-800-456-3408, or Fax: 1-888-891-7585.

ERROR NOTES

Though every effort is made to prevent error notes from slipping into circulation, some have occasionally been found by alert collectors. Error notes are those which show some irregularity from having gone incorrectly through one or more of the printing and cutting processes. Much collector interest has been focused on such notes, especially in recent years as a parallel to the spiraling demand for error coins.

There are many ways an error can occur on currency. Consider that the sheets must undergo separate processes for printing the faces, backs, and the overprint which for years consisted of seals, serial numbers, series, signatures (and District numbers where applicable). In addition, there are the trimming and cutting operations — and it is not difficult to imagine all sorts of errors or error combinations appearing on some notes.

VALUATIONS OF ERROR NOTES

As a general rule, the prominence of the error directly affects its numismatic desirability. Valuations included here are thus to be considered as approximate premiums only, *in addition to the face value of any note*. Rare notes with a high catalog value may have an additional premium.

Caution: collectors should be aware of contrived error notes which have recently been reported on the market.

On rare occasions a piece of paper will adhere to a currency sheet, take some of the imprint, go through the various processes and fall off at a later time. The above note carries a large blank space formerly occupied by just such a piece of paper, perhaps a marker or some sort of tab. On rarer occasions, such a note *with the stray piece of paper still adhering to it* has been found.

VF	Ex. Fine	New
100.00	250.00	350.00

ERROR NOTES

This note carries a double impression because the sheet on which it was printed went twice through the same overprinting process for its seals, signatures and serial numbers.

VF	Ex. Fine	New
1,500	2,500	4,000

The above note has an extra flap of paper on one corner, the result of an accidental folding of the sheet before it was face printed and cut. The flap is unfolded to show a corner of the face printing.

VF	Ex. Fine	New
150.00	300.00	450.00

ERROR NOTES

This note has long white streaks of unprinted paper through it, the result of inner folds in the sheet before the face side was printed. This kind of note usually has one single white streak. Multiple streaking is rare. Values below are for the usually found single streak error.

VF	Ex. Fine	New
20.00	35.00	50.00

The following note has the top of the next note showing, and a slice of its own top missing — resulting from the face of this note having been printed off-register.

Since notes are trimmed with faces showing, the faulty alignment went undetected.

VF	Ex. Fine	New
30.00	40.00	75.00

ERROR NOTES

A double denomination note, showing $5 on the face and $10 on the back. This is the result of a sheet printed on one side being inadvertently placed with sheets of another denomination which were also printed only on one side. Such notes are among the rarest and most desirable of all errors.

VF	Ex. Fine	New
8,500	12,000	16,000

A wet ink transfer, front printing on back. This was caused by the impression roller making contact with the plate, the plate transferring ink to the roller, then the roller placing the image in retrograde on the next sheet fed into the press.

	VF	Ex. Fine	New
High denominations	65.00	95.00	150.00
One Dollar bill	35.00	50.00	100.00

ERROR NOTES

Note with part of the overprinting on a corner of the face and some of the back is pictured with fold intact. Later the sheet became unfolded for cutting into individual notes.

VF	Ex. Fine	New
100.00	140.00	250.00

This note has its serial numbers mis-matched on the second digit.

VF	Ex. Fine	New
50.00	75.00	125.00

This United States Note never received any of the usual overprinting features. Missing are the seal and serial numbers.

VF	Ex. Fine	New
170.00	220.00	450.00

ERROR NOTES

This note was overprinted too low and too far to the right. It was caused by faulty alignment of sheets for the overprinting operation.

VF	Ex. Fine	New
100.00	150.00	250.00

This extraordinary item is a fragment that went through the normal printing process as of a finished note. As such it is an obvious rarity.

This misprint was caused by a large fold in the sheet prior to the overprint only, the back and face being normal. The fold remained intact through the cutting operation.

VF	Ex. Fine	New
125.00	200.00	350.00

ERROR NOTES

This note had a large portion of the sheet covered during the overprinting operation, thus deleting some features of the overprint.

VF	Ex. Fine	New
75.00	100.00	175.00

The above note received its overprint; however, the sheet was turned upside down as it was overprinted with seals, District numbers, series date, signatures and serial numbers.

VF	Ex. Fine	New
100.00	200.00	300.00

The above note came from a sheet grossly out of alignment during the cutting process. Beware of such notes cut from Series 1981 or later sheets.

VF	Ex. Fine	New
300.00	400.00	600.00

ERROR NOTES

The note above received the overprinting of seals and serial numbers (third process) on the back instead of the face.

VF	Ex. Fine	New
110.00	160.00	225.00

Aside from those illustrated, some other errors are as follows:

a.Mis-matched type designation vs. overprint, such as a Silver Certificate frame with green seal, serial numbers and a Federal Reserve Bank seal. This is truly an amazing error and obviously of extreme rarity.

VF	Ex. Fine	New
2,000	3,000	5,000

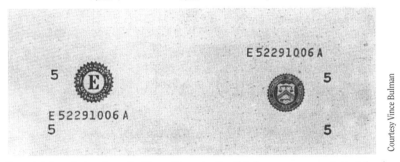

Courtesy Vince Bulman

b.Completely missing face design, with only the third process overprinting (seal and serial numbers) on the blank face side.

VF	Ex. Fine	New
200.00	250.00	500.00

c.So-called inverted backs; in reality, inverted faces. This is because the backs are printed first and the sheet becomes rotated for the printing of its face side, the second operation.

VF	Ex. Fine	New
400.00	800.00	1,200

d.Uneven printing, where a section of the note may be lightly printed or practically missing.

VF	Ex. Fine	New
25.00	50.00	75.00

e. The "Red Dye Strip" note — this piece has a bright red strip diagonally across both the face and the back. The red strip on the paper meant the end of the roll was near. One example verified.

THE NEW U. S. PAPER CURRENCY WILL BE THIS SIZE

According to latest information the new bills will bear a portrait of a famous American on the front:

Washington	$ 1
Jefferson	$ 2
Lincoln	$ 5
Hamilton	$10
Jackson	$20
Grant	$50

The $1 bills and denominations over $100 will have ornamental backs. All the others will have engravings of buildings on the backs.

Franklin	$ 100
McKinley	$ 500
Cleveland	$ 1,000
Madison	$ 5,000
Chase	$10,000

It is estimated that the reduced size of the new paper currency will save the government several million dollars in printing cost.

IT WILL NOT BE IN CIRCULATION UNTIL JULY 1, 1929

This is an example of a privately made circular describing the coming "reduced size" currency. Such circulars were distributed by various businessmen shortly before the new currency was placed into circulation in 1929. The back of the one shown contains an advertisement.

BIBLIOGRAPHY

Along with various smaller articles from a wide variety of sources, the following books and periodicals were consulted:

Bart, Dr. Frederich J., *United States Paper Money Errors*, Krause Publications, Iola, WI, 2003.

DeLorey, Tom, and Reed, Fred, *Price Guide For the Collector of Modern United States Paper Money Errors*, Amos Press, Inc., Sidney, Ohio, Fourth Edition, 1978.

Donlon, William P., *Donlon Price Catalog of United States Small Size Paper Money*, Hewitt Bros., Chicago, Illinois, various editions 1964-1979.

Friedberg, Robert, *Paper Money of the United States*, Coin and Currency Institute, Inc., New York. Various editions.

Gengerke, Martin, *United States Paper Money Records*, New York, 9th edition, 1998.

Hessler, Gene, *The Comprehensive Catalog of U.S. Paper Money*, BNR Press, 1997.

History of the Bureau of Engraving and Printing 1862-1962, Treasury Department, Washington, D.C., 1964.

Huntoon, P., and Van Belkum, L., *The National Bank Note Issues of 1929-1935*, ed. by M.O. Warns. Published by the Society of Paper Money Collectors, Hewitt Bros., Chicago, Illinois, 1970.

Kemm, Theodore, *Official Guide of United States Paper Money*, New York, various editions 1968-.

Lloyd, Robert, H., *National Bank Notes, Federal Reserve Bank Notes, Federal Reserve Notes 1928-1950*, Coin Collector's Journal, January-February 1953, Wayte Raymond, Inc., 1953. Also other articles from this magazine.

Oakes, Dean and Schwartz, John, *Standard Guide to Small-Size U.S. Paper Money 1928 to Date*, Krause Publications, Iola, WI, Fourth Edition, 2002.

O'Donnell et al., *Standard Handbook of Modern U.S. Paper Money*. Sixth Edition 1977.

Petrov, Vladimir, *Money and Conquest – Allied Occupational Currencies in World War II*, The John Hopkins Press, Baltimore, Maryland, 1967.

Rundell, Walter, Jr., *Black Market Money*, Louisiana State University Press, 1964.

Shafer, Neil, *A Guide Book of Philippine Paper Money*, Whitman Publishing Co., Racine, Wisconsin, 1964.

Schwan, C.F., and Boling, J.E. *World War II Military Currency*, BNR Press, Portage, Ohio, 1978.

The Numismatist

Banknote Reporter

Numismatic News Weekly

Coin World weekly newspaper

Numismatic Scrapbook

Paper Money, published by the Society of Paper Money Collectors